1992

Programming Languages

Concepts and Constructs

Programming Languages

Concepts and Constructs

RAVI SETHI

AT&T Bell Laboratories
Murray Hill, New Jersey

▲▼ **ADDISON-WESLEY PUBLISHING COMPANY**
Reading, Massachusetts • Menlo Park, California • New York
Don Mills, Ontario • Wokingham, England • Amsterdam • Bonn
Madrid • Sydney • Singapore • Tokyo • San Juan

This book is in the **Addison-Wesley Series in Computer Science**
Michael A. Harrison, Consulting Editor

James T. DeWolf/Sponsoring Editor
Bette J. Aaronson/Production Supervisor
Stephanie Kaylin/Copy Editor
Beth Anderson/Cover Illustration
Hugh Crawford/Manufacturing Supervisor

Library of Congress Cataloging-in-Publication Data

```
Sethi, Ravi.
   Programming languages.

   Bibliography: p.
   Includes index.
   1. Programming languages (Electronic computers)
I. Title.
QA76.7.S48  1989          005.13          88-7477
ISBN 0-201-10365-6
```

AT&T

6 7 8 9 10 DO 9594939291

For Dianne

who taught me yet another language

Preface

This book is designed for a junior- or senior-level course on programming languages. When supplemented by readings from the literature, it could also be used for a graduate course. It presumes that the reader is familiar enough with any one programming language to have run some programs.

Organization of the Book

Two observations have guided the selection and organization of material in this book:

1. A small number of concepts underlie most of the hundreds of programming languages that have been designed and implemented.

2. The best way to learn programming is by doing—by using a language to solve problems. Programming experience with a few carefully selected languages is preferable to passing acquaintance with lots of languages.

Part I, Chapters 1 and 2, provides background information and introduces basic concepts.

The main part of this book is Part II, consisting of Chapters 3 through 9. Its organization is illustrated by the following diagram:

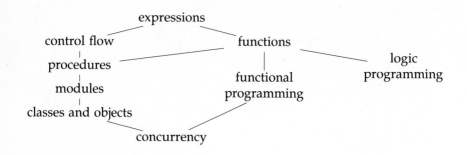

With this organization in mind, representative languages were chosen to illustrate the concepts. The use of real languages allows students to explore the concepts by writing and running some programs. The organization allows related concepts to be introduced together, so meaningful examples can accompany the features.

The path from expressions, through control flow, procedures, modules, and classes, to concurrency leads us through the features of an imperative language. Modules and classes are of course relevant to other styles of languages as well—they are discussed with respect to imperative languages for continuity. Thus the concepts of control flow through classes can be illustrated using extensions of the popular languages Pascal and C.

For perspective, the chapters in Part II each use two working languages, where possible. The use of two languages allows language design choices to be studied. Thus, control flow and procedures are illustrated using Modula-2 and C. Modula-2 is essentially a superset of Pascal, formed by adding modules. Classes, objects, and inheritance are illustrated using Smalltalk and C++, an extension of C.

Functional programming is illustrated by Scheme, a dialect of Lisp, and Standard ML. Logic programming and Prolog go hand in hand. Finally, concurrency is treated using Ada.

Part III, Chapters 10 through 12, deals with language description. Syntactic structure is the starting point for language descriptions and implementations. Chapter 10, on syntactic structure, is brief because parsing is covered adequately in courses and textbooks on compilers. Syntax-directed approaches to language definition are illustrated in Chapter 11 by writing an interpreter in Scheme for a small subset of Scheme. The final chapter studies types, using the lambda calculus.

Use of the Book

The three-part organization allows students with varying backgrounds to use this book. Expressions provide a simple setting for the introduction of names, functions, recursion, and types in Chapter 2. Material from Part II can then be selected as desired. The following table shows the sections that are essential to the various programming styles:

imperative programming
    core   3.1-3.3
    procedures   4.1-4.6

object-oriented programming
    core   5.1-5.3, 5.6-5.7, 6.1
    inheritance   5.9, 6.2-6.4, 6.6

functional programming
    core   7.1-7.3, 7.5-7.6
    interpreters   11.1-11.5

logic programming
    core   8.1-8.3, 11.1
    advanced   8.4-8.6

concurrent programming
    core   9.1-9.7

The treatment of language description in Part III, particularly Chapter 12, is intended for advanced students.

Exercises

Exercises with stars are intended for advanced students.

Acknowledgments

A graduate seminar at Rutgers University gave me both the opportunity and the incentive to collect material on programming languages. I'd like to thank Alex Borgida, Martin Carroll, Fritz Henglein, Naftaly Minsky, Bob Paige, and Barbara Ryder for keeping the seminar lively.

An undergraduate course at Harvard University used an early draft of this book. Written comments by the students in the course were very helpful.

The organization of this book has benefited greatly from the comments and especially the criticism of the then anonymous reviewers contacted by Addison-Wesley. They are Tom Cheatham, Harvard University, John Crenshaw, Western Kentucky University, Paul Hilfinger, University of California, Berkeley, Barry Kurtz, New Mexico State University, Robert Noonan, College of William and Mary, Ron Olsson, University of California, Davis, William Pervin, University of Texas at Dallas, Paul Reynolds, University of Virginia, David Schmidt, Kansas State University, and Laurie Werth, University of Texas at Austin.

For all their technical help, I am grateful to Al Aho, Jon Bentley, Gerard Berry, Eric Cooper, Bruce Duba, Tom Duncan, Rich Drechsler, Peggy Ellis, Charlie Fischer, Dan Friedman, Georges Gonthier, Bob Harper, Mike Harrison, Bruce Hillyer, Brian Kernighan, Kim King, Chandra Kintala, Dave MacQueen, Dianne Maki, Doug McIlroy, John Mitchell, Mike O'Donnell, Dennis Ritchie, Bjarne Stroustrup, Chris Van Wyk, and Carl Woolf.

This book on programming languages was produced with the help of a number of little languages. The diagrams were drawn using Brian Kernighan's Pic language; the grey-tones in the diagrams rely on the work of Rich Drechsler. The tables were laid out using Mike Lesk's Tbl program. Eqn, Lorinda Cherry and Brian Kernighan's language for typesetting mathematics, handled the pseudo-code as well. The Troff program was originally written by the late Joe Ossanna and is kept vital by Brian Kernighan. Page layout would have suffered without a new Troff macro package and post-processor by Brian Kernighan and Chris Van Wyk. The indexing programs were supplied by Jon Bentley and Brian Kernighan. Cross references were managed using scripts written with the help of Al Aho for managing the text of the "dragon" book.

Finally, I'd like to thank AT&T Bell Laboratories for its support. I have learnt more from my colleagues here than they might suspect. Whenever a question occurred, someone in the building always seemed to have the answer.

RS

Contents

PART II: CONCEPTS AND CONSTRUCTS 63

Part I

Introduction

A *program* is a specification of a computation. A *programming language* is a notation for writing programs.

Chapter 1 provides background information on programming languages— their origins in machines, the emergence of higher-level languages, and grammars, which are a notation for describing the syntax of programming languages. Language development has been guided by the realization that complexity can be managed by imposing structure on data, operations, programs, even language descriptions.

Chapter 2 uses expressions, which are found in almost all programming languages, to introduce names, functions, recursion, and types.

Part I

Introduction

One

The Role of Structure in Programming

A rocket carrying Mariner I, an unmanned Venus probe, had to be destroyed 290 seconds after launch on July 22, 1962. The loss was estimated at between $18 and $20 million.

The program in the ground computer should have contained the fragment

> **if not** in radar contact with the rocket **then**
>   do not correct its flight path

The **not** was inadvertently left out, so the ground computer continued to blindly guide the rocket after radar contact was lost. The rocket wobbled astray and was destroyed before it could endanger human lives. The program had previously been used without fault in four lunar launches.

"Who is responsible for leaving this out?" demanded the chairman of a Congressional hearing into the loss. It was explained that the program had been tested in three hundred separate runs and that it did not seem reasonable to have an outside inspector check the work of every programmer. Nevertheless, the chairman concluded uneasily:

> "I can understand the intricacies of this, or I feel that I have a vague knowledge of what you are talking about, but we certainly should be able to devise some system for checks that will not allow this type of error to creep in."

It is hopeless to establish the correctness of a program by testing, unless the internal structure of the program is taken into account, argues Dijkstra [1972]. Our only hope is to carefully design a program so that its correctness can be understood in terms of its structure. In his words,

- "the art of programming is the art of organising complexity," and

- "we must organise the computations in such a way that our limited powers are sufficient to guarantee that the computation will establish the desired effect."

Programming languages provide constructs for organizing computations. Based on experience, the following are minimal requirements for a language:

> The language must help us write good programs, where a program is good if it is easy to read, easy to understand, and easy to modify.

Before we examine languages, let us briefly address what programming is. There is more to programming than *development*, which consists of the initial creation and testing of a program. *Maintenance* refers to corrections and changes to a program after it is developed. Maintenance occurs because the life of a useful program is just beginning when it is first written and checked. After the initial development, its users may find errors that have to be fixed, or they may have needs that can be met by changing the program.

Techniques for dealing with small programs do not necessarily scale up. Any one change to a program is easy to make. Any isolated program fragment can be understood and improved easily. Difficulties arise when the effect of a change can ripple through a large program, perhaps introducing bugs or errors into some forgotten corner. Such bugs can lie undetected, perhaps for years.

Structure and organization are the key to managing large programs. The readability of a program can be improved by organizing it so that each part can be understood relatively independently of the rest.

Structure helps us to cope with limited human attention spans. Miller [1967] observes that people can keep track of about seven things, be they bits (binary digits), words, colors, tones, or tastes. Is this why there are seven wonders of the world, seven ages of man, seven deadly sins, and so on? More seriously, he continues, "Tentatively, therefore, we are justified in assuming that our memories are limited by the number of units or symbols we must master, and not by the amount of information that these symbols represent. Thus it is helpful to organize material intelligently before we try to memorize it. The process of organization enables us to package the same amount of information into far fewer symbols, and so eases the task of remembering."

1.1 THE VON NEUMANN MACHINE

The origins of programming languages lie in machines. The original so-called von Neumann machine was designed in the late 1940s at the Institute for Advanced Study in Princeton. Modern computers have enough in common with the original that they are said to have a von Neumann architecture.

The native language of a computer, its *machine language*, is the notation to which the computer responds directly. Machine language was originally referred to as *code*, although now code is used more broadly to refer to any program text.

Elements of a Machine Language

Burks, Goldstine, and von Neumann [1947] describe a computer outlined in Fig. 1.1. Together, the control, arithmetic, and input/output units constituted what would now be called the CPU or central processing unit. The remaining "organ" was the memory. The role of the instructions and the interactions between the memory and other units are summarized in the following paragraphs.

The minuscule memory held both instructions and data. Plans called for a memory consisting of 4096 words or locations, each holding 40 bits; the completed machine had only 1024 words. When viewed as data, the bits in a location held a single number in binary notation. When viewed as instructions, the 40 bits in a location held two 20-bit instructions. A program in machine language consisted of a sequence of instructions.

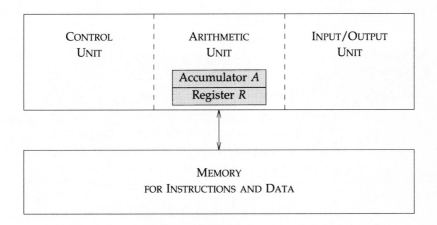

Fig. 1.1. Organization of the von Neumann machine.

The features of the machine can be summarized as follows:

- *Data*. Integers were the only form of data. Floating point numbers were considered, but not included.
- *Arithmetic operations*. The machine could add, subtract, multiply, divide, and take the absolute value of a number. The result of an add or subtract operation was placed in a register called the *accumulator*, shown within the arithmetic unit in Fig. 1.1.
- *Assignments to memory locations*. A memory location could be *assigned* the value in the accumulator; that is, the contents of the accumulator replaced the previous contents of the location.
- *Control flow*. The normal flow of control from one instruction to the next could be interrupted by a "go to" instruction; the next instruction executed was taken from the memory word mentioned in the goto instruction. The design document includes the following motivation for gotos: "The utility of an automatic computer lies in the possibility of using a given sequence of instructions repeatedly, the number of times it is iterated being either preassigned or dependent upon the results of computation."

For history buffs, a terse description of the instruction set is included in Fig. 1.2; it will not be needed in the sequel.

In the figure, A refers to the accumulator, R to another register within the arithmetic unit, $M[i]$ to memory location i, and $M[i].left$ and

ARITHMETIC	$A := A+M[i]$; $\ A := A-M[i]$; $A := A+ \mid M[i] \mid$; $\ A := A- \mid M[i] \mid$ $A := -M[i]$; $\ A := \mid M[i] \mid$; $\ A := - \mid M[i] \mid$ $A := A * 2$; $\ A := A$ **div** 2 $A, \ R := (M[i]*R)$ **div** 2^{39}, $\ (M[i]*R)$ **mod** 2^{39} $A, \ R := A$ **mod** $M[i]$, $\ A$ **div** $M[i]$
MOVE	$A := M[i]$; $M[i] := A$; $R := M[i]$; $A := R$
CONTROL FLOW	**goto** $M[i].left$; $\ $ **goto** $M[i].right$ **if** $A \geq 0$ **goto** $M[i].left$; $\ $ **if** $A \geq 0$ **goto** $M[i].right$
OTHER	Modify the address in $M[i].left$ from A. Modify the address in $M[i].right$ from A.

Fig. 1.2. Instructions supported by the von Neumann machine.

$M[i].right$ to the two instructions in word i. The symbol := stands for assignment, so the instruction

$$A := A + M[i]$$

adds the value in memory location i to the value in the accumulator. $|M[i]|$ represents the absolute value of the number in location i. The **div** operator returns the quotient after integer division and the **mod** operator returns the remainder.

The multiplication and division operations affected both the accumulator A and the register R. The remainder after division was left in A and the quotient was left in R. This effect is expressed in Fig. 1.2 by a parallel assignment instruction of the form

$$A, R := y, z$$

which simultaneously assigns y to A and z to R. For example, $u, v := v, u$ exchanges the values of u and v. Thus,

$$A, R := A \textbf{ mod } M[i], A \textbf{ div } M[i]$$

divides the old value in A by $M[i]$ and then assigns the remainder to A and the quotient to R.[1]

Machine Language Is Unintelligible

Unfortunately, programs in machine language are unintelligible. Neither the machine language fragment

```
00000010101111001010
00000010111111001000
00000011001110101000
```

nor its symbolic variant

```
LOAD   I
ADD    J
STORE  K
```

is as clear as $k = i + j$.

An *assembly language* is a variant of a machine language in which names take the place of the actual codes for machine operations, values, and storage locations. Machine and assembly languages are referred to as *low-level languages*. By contrast, we reserve the term "programming language"

---

[1] A *machine address* is the number of a location in memory. Two key instructions modified the address part of an instruction in memory. They were used, for example, to step through an array. Newer machines achieve a similar effect without modifying instructions in memory; they allow an address to be computed by adding in a value held in a register. Address modification interferes with multiple activations of a piece of code (see Chapter 4).

for higher-level languages, where *higher-level* connotes greater distance from machines.

1.2   EARLY EXPERIENCE

In the 1950s, it was widely believed that efficient programs could be crafted only by hand, using some variant of machine language. This belief was challenged by Fortran, one of the earliest programming languages.

Preoccupation with Run-Time Efficiency

The high cost of creating machine or assembly code was a prime motivation for the development of Fortran, which takes its name from *For*mula *Tran*slation. Backus et al. [1957] had as their goal: "to enable the programmer to specify a numerical procedure using a concise language like that of mathematics and obtain automatically from this specification an efficient [machine language] program to carry out the procedure." *Debugging*, the finding and fixing of errors, was thought to account for between 25 and 50 percent of a computer's time. Its developers hoped that Fortran would reduce program development "to less than one-fifth of the job it had been."

The Fortran expression

```
B*B - 4*A*C
```

is close to the formula $b^2 - 4ac$.

Any notation other than machine language cannot be run directly on a machine; it must be translated into a form the machine can understand. A translator from a programming language into machine or assembly code is called a *compiler*. The distinction between the input and output languages of a compiler is made by saying that a compiler starts with a program in a *source* language and produces an equivalent program in a *target* language. The target language of the compiler in Fig. 1.3 is assumed to be machine language. When the target program is run, it takes some input and produces some output.

Performance penalties due to translation take two forms:

1. *Translation time.* Machine time is needed to compile a source program into target code.

2. *Added run time and space.* The target code created by a compiler typically takes longer to run and occupies more space than carefully tailored code written by hand.

The problem of translating Fortran into efficient machine code dominated the Fortran project. The developers believed that if any reasonable

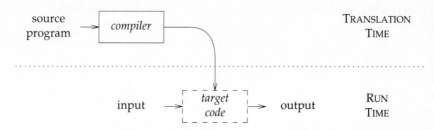

Fig. 1.3. A source program is translated into a target program, which is run.

Fortran program ran "only half as fast as its hand coded counterpart, then acceptance of our system would be in serious danger (Backus [1981])."

Benefits of Higher-Level Languages

Fortran quickly became the language of choice for scientific programming. It provided readable notations like arithmetic expressions, so a program could be written in a notation closer to that in which the original problem was described, making the program easier to develop. New users took to the machine.

Fortran programs were *portable*; that is, they could be run on different machines with little or no change. Users could therefore exchange software, leading to the creation of program libraries and a loyal user community.

Gradually, higher-level languages displaced assembly language in virtually all areas of programming. The reasons are echoed in case histories like the following.

Example 1.1. Originally written in assembly language, the kernel of the UNIX operating system was rewritten in the programming language C in 1973. Ritchie [1978] recounts the resulting benefits:

- *New users and programs.* The use of a higher-level language led to software packages "that would never have been written at all if their authors had had to write assembly code; many of our most inventive contributors do not know, and do not wish to learn, the instruction set of the machine."

- *Portability.* "An extremely valuable, though originally unplanned, benefit of writing in C is the portability of the system.... It appears to be possible to produce an operating system and set of software that runs on several machines and whose expression in source code is, except for a few modules, identical on each machine."

- *Readability.* "The C versions of programs that were rewritten after C became available are much more easily understood, repaired, and extended than the assembler versions. This applies especially to the operating system itself. The original system was very difficult to modify, especially to add new devices, but also to make even minor changes."

Ritchie concludes, "Although [a comprehensive study of the space and time inflation due to the use of C] might be interesting, it would be somewhat irrelevant, in that no matter what the results turned out to be, they would not cause us to start writing assembly language."   □

Efficiency Revisited

Does an emphasis on structure and readability of programs mean that efficiency is no longer important? No, quite the contrary. Readability and modifiability of programs can contribute to efficiency as well.

The efficiency of a program depends on decisions made at all design levels, from conception to the choice of data structures and algorithms to the final coding. Not only does a programming language affect the decisions made at the various design levels, it affects the ease with which the decisions can be modified. Code tuning (see below) is also affected by the language.

Where a program will spend its time is far from obvious at the outset. Knuth [1971] notes, "There has been a long history of optimizing the wrong things, using elaborate mechanisms to produce beautiful code in cases that hardly ever arise in practice, while doing nothing about certain frequently occurring situations." The development of an efficient program is therefore likely to consist of a sequence of evolutionary changes, guided by performance analysis.

Code tuning is done by improving hot spots, which are the small heavily used portions where a program spends most of the running time. In an empirical study of Fortran programs, Knuth [1971] "found that less than 4 per cent of a program generally accounts for more than half of its running time." Variants of compilers, called *profilers*, can be used to find hot spots by monitoring the execution of the compiled target program at run time. Careful coding of just the hot spots can significantly improve the running time.

1.3   REBUILDING THE MACHINE

Machine language programs have no structure to speak of. Fortran provided local structure in the form of expressions like

```
B*B - 4*A*C
```

This section develops the view that a programming language is an extension of the underlying machine and that a program is an extension of the programming language (see Fig. 1.4). In this view, a language rebuilds the machine to provide more convenient facilities, and a program further rebuilds the language to provide facilities closer to the problem to be solved. Figuratively, the tiny general building blocks provided by a machine are rebuilt into larger, more specialized building blocks.

Example 1.2. Most machines provide an operation < to test whether one character appears earlier in the alphabet than another. Character 'a' appears earlier than 'b', and so on.

A language might then use operation < on characters to build operation *stringlt* to test whether one string appears earlier in dictionary order than another. String **dragon** appears earlier than **dry** in dictionary order.

A program might use string comparison operations to build an operation *find* to search for a string in a collection of strings. Every compiler needs an operation like *find* to keep track of the names in the source code.   □

What Languages Provide

What languages provide will be examined in some detail in Chapters 3-9; the following is just a brief preview.

Programming languages improve on machines in several ways:

- *Computation model.* A language can choose to let the underlying machine show through, or it can choose to support a substantially different approach to computation. For example, concurrent languages make it appear as if a program is executing simultaneously on several machines, even if there is actually just one machine underneath.

- *Data types and operations.* It is up to a language to provide constructs for structuring the basic values supported by a machine. A machine may support characters, integers, and real numbers, but it is up to the language to provide structured values such as arrays, records, and lists. With each type of structured data, operations are needed to manipulate the components of the structured data.

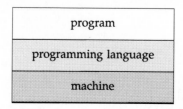

Fig. 1.4. Each layer extends the facilities of the layer below.

- *Abstraction facilities.* Functions are abstractions of built-in operations like addition, and procedures are abstractions of built-in actions like assignment. A program might define a function *sqrt* to compute square roots, and then use *sqrt* as freely as the built-in addition operation +. Or it might define an operation *sort* to rearrange the data in an array. Another use of abstraction facilities is to define new data types that can be used as freely as the ones built into the language. Thus, a program might define a data type *queue* and then use queues as freely as arrays or lists.

- *Checking and enforcement.* Compile-time checking of a program can detect errors before the program is run. If at compile time we can determine that a variable *x* must represent an integer, then we can predict that an attempt to use *x* as an array will result in an error at run time. Another equally important use of checking is to enforce data encapsulation, studied in Chapter 5.

The Structure of a Program

Structure in programs will be illustrated by considering a specific example, dealing with line drawings because drawings are easy to visualize. The neutral term *object* refers to something a program manipulates. The objects supported by a language depend on its intended application. Just as languages for numerical applications provide integers and floating point numbers, languages for line drawings provide geometric shapes and curves.

Example 1.3. The flower in Fig. 1.5 can be built up out of nine simpler objects: a circle at the center with eight petals around it. One such petal appears in Fig. 1.5(b). The petals look alike, in that a petal can be rotated to match any other.

Consider two operations: *petal* for drawing each of the eight petals, and *circle* for drawing a circle. Operation *petal* takes a parameter specifying the angle at which a petal is to be drawn. This description of *petal* and *circle* hints at how the following program draws the flower in Fig. 1.5(a):

```
for i = 0 to 7 do 'petal(i*pi/4)'
circle at Here
```

The petals are drawn at the angles $0, \pi/4, \ldots, 7\pi/4$. This program is written in Pic, a language for drawing pictures (Kernighan [1982]).

The *circle* operation is provided directly by Pic, but *petal* is not. Although Pic was used to draw the figures, it is not one of the languages to be discussed in this book, so feel free to skip the following outline of how *petal* can be implemented using the facilities provided by Pic.

(a)   (b)

Fig. 1.5. A flower made up from a circle and petals.

A *spline* is a special curve that is drawn to fit a sequence of points. The spline in Fig. 1.6(a) is specified by points $P_1, P_2, \ldots, P_5$. The dashed lines are not part of the spline; they simply show how the spline fits between the points.

Operation *petal* takes an angle θ as a parameter and computes the positions of the points $P_1, P_2, \ldots, P_5$, with respect to point *Here*, as in Fig. 1.6(b). It then asks Pic to draw a spline between these points.

In summary, the language provides the operations *circle* and *spline*, which are rebuilt by the program into the operations *circle* and *petal*, more suited to drawing flowers.   □

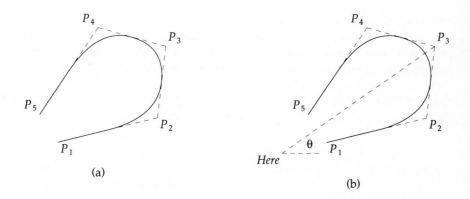

(a)   (b)

Fig. 1.6. The use of splines to implement petals.

1.4   HOW SHALL I STRUCTURE THEE?

There's more than one way to solve a problem. Hence, there's more than one way to structure a program. Structure is therefore not something unique, waiting to be discovered, but something we impose on a program.

This section illustrates a top-down approach to programming: Decompose a problem into simpler subproblems that can be solved relatively independently of each other. The design of an appropriate decomposition is the hardest part of reducing this approach to practice, because a clean decomposition need not be obvious at the outset.

The problem in this section is to find duplicates in a list of elements and to produce them as output. The operation of finding duplicates will be decomposed into simpler operations. Two alternative decompositions of this problem follow.

A First Decomposition

The decomposition in Fig. 1.7 partitions the operation of finding duplicates into two independent subproblems. When a list is sorted, duplicates move next to each other, so they can be found by comparing each element on the sorted list with the previous element. When the list

    617 201 415 201

is sorted, the two elements **201** move next to each other

    201 201 415 617

and can be found by comparing adjacent elements.

A virtue of this solution is that sorting and finding adjacent duplicates are self-contained subproblems that can be solved independently. If a sorting program is already available, then the solution in Fig. 1.7 can be implemented by writing a program to find adjacent duplicates. Note, however, that the entire list is examined before any duplicates are detected; the last element on the original list may well be the first on the sorted list.

Fig. 1.7. Finding duplicates in a list of strings.

A Second Decomposition

A decomposition different from that in Fig. 1.7 is convenient if duplicates must be found incrementally. In this case, as an element of a list is presented, the solution must determine whether the element has been seen before. The new solution is based on the following:

> **for** each element in the list **do**
> > **if** the element appears anywhere earlier in the list **then**
> > > write out the element

Words like **for** and **if**, written in boldface, can be read as English for the moment. When used to delimit program fragments, they are called *keywords*.

The test "**if** the element appears anywhere earlier in the list" requires information about the earlier elements to be saved, say in a table. The table is empty when the program starts, and elements are inserted into it as they arrive. The solution can therefore be restated as

> **for** each element in the list **do**
> > **if** the element is in the table **then**
> > > write out the element
> > **else**
> > > insert the element into the table

This solution uses the table, but is independent of how the table is implemented. It does not need to know whether the table is managed by the simple strategy of searching through the entire table to find elements, or a faster more complex strategy. It simply enters and looks up elements in the table using the operations *insert* and *find* described in Fig. 1.8. The solution becomes:

> **for** each element x in the list **do**
> > **if** *find* (x) **then**
> > > write x
> > **else**
> > > *insert* (x)

OPERATION	ARGUMENT	RESULT
insert	element x	none
find	element x	**true** if x was previously inserted **false** if not

Fig. 1.8. Operations on a table of elements.

Discussion

In the first solution, in Fig. 1.7, the output of the sorting subprogram becomes the input to the subprogram for finding adjacent duplicates. The subprograms are otherwise independent; they need not even be implemented in the same language.

The second solution uses two interacting objects: a table and its client, which concentrates on reading elements and writing duplicates. The client uses the operations in Fig. 1.8, but it neither knows nor cares about the implementation of the operations.

1.5   SYNTACTIC STRUCTURE

The *syntax* of a language specifies how programs in the language are built up. Syntactic structure, the structure imposed by syntax on a language, is the primary tool for working with a language. It has been used to organize language descriptions and translators, as well as rules for reasoning about programs in a language.

The syntax of a programming language is almost always specified using some variant of a notation called context-free grammars, or simply grammars. The variants introduced in this section are BNF (from Backus-Naur Form), EBNF (Extended BNF), and syntax charts. Subsequent chapters rely primarily on BNF.

Introduction to BNF

The following is an example of a grammar in BNF. It describes the syntax of real numbers like **3.142** with an integer part, a decimal point, and a fractional part:

$\langle real\text{-}number \rangle$ ::= $\langle digit\text{-}sequence \rangle$. $\langle digit\text{-}sequence \rangle$

$\langle digit\text{-}sequence \rangle$ ::= $\langle digit \rangle$ | $\langle digit \rangle$ $\langle digit\text{-}sequence \rangle$

$\langle digit \rangle$ ::=   **0** | **1** | **2** | **3** | **4** | **5** | **6** | **7** | **8** | **9**

The special symbols $\langle$ and $\rangle$ enclose variables representing constructs. Let us begin with $\langle digit \rangle$, representing digits. The symbol ::= is read as "is" and | is read as "or," so the notation

$$\langle digit \rangle \ ::= \ \mathbf{0} \mid \mathbf{1} \mid \mathbf{2} \mid \mathbf{3} \mid \mathbf{4} \mid \mathbf{5} \mid \mathbf{6} \mid \mathbf{7} \mid \mathbf{8} \mid \mathbf{9} \tag{1.1}$$

is read as

A *digit* is **0** or **1** or **2** or **3** or **4** or **5** or **6** or **7** or **8** or **9**.
Nothing else is a *digit*.

Thus, **3** is a digit, but **%** is not, because **%** is not one of the alternatives to the right of ::= in (1.1).

The notation

$$\langle digit\text{-}sequence \rangle ::= \langle digit \rangle \mid \langle digit \rangle \langle digit\text{-}sequence \rangle \tag{1.2}$$

says that a digit sequence can be a single digit as in **3**, or it can be a digit followed by another digit sequence, as in **142**.

Finally, the notation

$$\langle real\text{-}number \rangle ::= \langle digit\text{-}sequence \rangle \ . \ \langle digit\text{-}sequence \rangle \tag{1.3}$$

says that a real number consists of a digit sequence, a dot, and another digit sequence. It is sometimes convenient to use subscripts, as in

$$\langle real\text{-}number \rangle ::= \langle digit\text{-}sequence \rangle_1 \ . \ \langle digit\text{-}sequence \rangle_2$$

to talk about occurrences of a construct. If $\langle real\text{-}number \rangle$ represents **3.142**, then $\langle digit\text{-}sequence \rangle_1$ represents the integer part **3** and $\langle digit\text{-}sequence \rangle_2$ represents the fractional part **142**.

Each alternative separated by $\mid$ is a distinct rule, so

$$\langle digit\text{-}sequence \rangle ::= \langle digit \rangle \mid \langle digit \rangle \langle digit\text{-}sequence \rangle$$

can be rewritten equivalently as

$$\langle digit\text{-}sequence \rangle ::= \langle digit \rangle$$
$$\langle digit\text{-}sequence \rangle ::= \langle digit \rangle \langle digit\text{-}sequence \rangle$$

Definition of Context-Free Grammars

Given a set of symbols, a *string* over the set is a finite sequence of zero or more symbols from the set. The number of symbols in the sequence is said to be the *length* of the string. The length of the string **dragon** is 6. An *empty* string is a string of length zero.

The atomic symbols of a language are called *tokens* or *terminals*. Constructs in a language are represented by variables called *nonterminals*. The nonterminal that represents the main construct of a language is called the *starting nonterminal*. The starting nonterminal may represent a portion of a complete program when fragments of a programming language are studied.

The components of a construct are identified by rules called *productions*. A production has a *left side* consisting of a nonterminal and a *right side* consisting of a sequence of zero or more terminals or nonterminals. Productions will be written with the symbol ::= between their left and right sides.

Definition. A *context-free grammar*, or simply *grammar*, has four parts:

1. A set of terminals.
2. A set of nonterminals.
3. A set of productions, where each production has a nonterminal as its left side, the symbol ::=, and a string over the sets of terminals and nonterminals as its right side.
4. A nonterminal chosen as the starting nonterminal.   □

Unless otherwise stated, the productions for the starting nonterminal appear first.

BNF

The concept of a context-free grammar, consisting of terminals, nonterminals, productions, and a starting nonterminal, is independent of the notation used to write grammars. In BNF, nonterminals are enclosed between the symbols ⟨ and ⟩ and the empty string is written as ⟨*empty*⟩.

Grammars for arithmetic expressions are based on rules like the following:

- An expression is a sequence of terms separated by + or −.
- A term is a sequence of factors separated by * or **div**.
- A factor is a parenthesized expression, a variable, or a constant.

The following is a partial grammar for expressions, without the rules for variables and constants:

$$⟨expression⟩ \quad ::= \quad ⟨expression⟩ + ⟨term⟩ \quad | \quad ⟨expression⟩ - ⟨term⟩ \quad | \quad ⟨term⟩$$

$$⟨term⟩ \quad ::= \quad ⟨term⟩ * ⟨factor⟩ \quad | \quad ⟨term⟩ \textbf{ div } ⟨factor⟩ \quad | \quad ⟨factor⟩ \quad (1.4)$$

$$⟨factor⟩ \quad ::= \quad (⟨expression⟩) \quad | \quad ⟨variable⟩ \quad | \quad ⟨constant⟩$$

Instead of the symbol ::=, Backus [1960] originally used ≡ to separate the left and right sides of productions.

Extended BNF

In *EBNF* (Extended BNF), nonterminals begin with uppercase letters, terminals consisting of symbols like + and − are quoted, and terminals in boldface like **div** appear as is. Furthermore:

- a vertical bar, | , represents a choice,
- parentheses, (and), are used for grouping,
- braces, { and }, represent zero or more repetitions, and
- brackets, [and], represent an optional construct.

An EBNF version of the grammar (1.4) is

$$Expression \quad ::= \quad Term \; \{ \; ('+' \mid '-') \; Term \; \}$$
$$Term \quad ::= \quad Factor \; \{ \; ('*' \mid \mathbf{div}) \; Factor \; \} \qquad (1.5)$$
$$Factor \quad ::= \quad '(' \; Expression \; ')' \mid Variable \mid Constant$$

Here *Term* { ('+' | '−') *Term* } represents a sequence of one or more terms separated by either + or − signs.

The quotes around + and −, which are known from the context to be terminals, will often be dropped. The quotes around the parentheses in '(' *Expression* ')' will be retained, however, to say that the parentheses are terminals in the language of expressions.

Syntax Charts

A *syntax chart*, syntax graph, or syntax diagram, is another way of writing a grammar. It is constructed as follows. There is a subchart for each non-terminal, similar to the chart in Fig. 1.9 for *Factor*. Each production for the nonterminal results in a path through the chart. Along the path for a production are the terminals and nonterminals on its right side; the terminals are enclosed in rounded boxes and the nonterminals in rectangular boxes.

Braces denoting zero or more repetitions, lead to syntax charts containing cycles. A systematic way of constructing a chart for

{ (* | **div**) *Factor* }

is to draw a loop around a chart for the enclosed string. An exit from the loop allows a path to leave after passing zero or more times through the chart for the enclosed string. This approach leads to the chart in Fig. 1.10. The shortest path through the chart goes through the leftmost box for *Factor* and out to the right end of the page. Other paths go through the leftmost box for *Factor* and then one or more times through the body of the loop.

The layout of a chart can be varied at will. The chart in Fig. 1.10 can even be redrawn so it has a single box for *Factor*, without changing the paths through the chart. Do you see how?

Factor

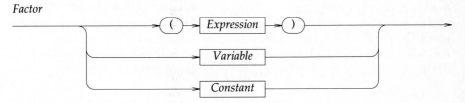

Fig. 1.9. Syntax chart for *Factor* ::= '(' *Expression* ')' | *Variable* | *Constant*

Term

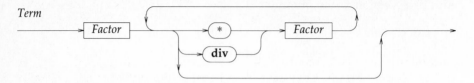

Fig. 1.10. Syntax chart for *Term* ::= *Factor* { (∗ | **div**) *Factor* }.

So far, we have described the construction of a syntax chart from a grammar. The converse is also possible; that is, given a chart for a nonterminal, with single entry and exit points, an equivalent subgrammar can be constructed.

1.6   ORGANIZATION OF LANGUAGE DESCRIPTIONS

The *semantics* of the language specifies what programs mean. Suppose that dates have the syntax

⟨*date*⟩   ::=   *D D* **/** *D D* **/** *D D D D*

where *D* is an abbreviation for ⟨*digit*⟩. Thus,

01/02/2001

is a date. The day this date refers to is not identified by the syntax. In the United States, this date refers to January 2, 2001, but elsewhere **01** is interpreted as the day and **02** as the month, so the date refers to February 1, 2001. The same syntax therefore has different semantics in different parts of the world.

Clear and complete descriptions of syntax and semantics are needed to ensure that all implementations of a language accept the same programs, nothing more, nothing less. Otherwise, it will not be possible to move a running program from one implementation to another.

Example 1.4. The IBM 1401 responded to a number of supposedly invalid operations that were not part of its machine language description. The machine therefore accepted more than the language definition allowed. Later, when the 1401 machine language was implemented on a new machine, the IBM System/360, 30 different supposedly invalid operations had come into such widespread use that they had to be considered as part of the definition of the 1401 machine language (Brooks [1975]).   □

Seldom is a single language description both readable enough to be suitable for a beginner and precise enough to specify a language fully. Tutorials, reference manuals, and formal definitions are some of the distinct styles of language descriptions that have arisen to meet these needs.

Tutorials.   A tutorial introduction is a guided tour of a language. It gives us impressions of what the main constructs of the language are and how they are meant to be used. Examples typically drive the organization of a tutorial. The syntax and semantics are introduced gradually, as needed. Complete, working, and useful examples allow a reader to learn by imitating and adapting.

Reference manuals.   A reference manual describing the syntax and semantics of a language is traditionally organized around the syntax of the language. This tradition began with the Algol 60 report, which attached English explanations and examples to the syntactic rules of the language; the report was remarkably free of ambiguities.

Formal definitions.   A formal definition is a precise description of the syntax and semantics of a language; it is aimed at specialists. English descriptions leave room for conflicting interpretations, so notations that can be checked mechanically have been developed. The training and effort needed to learn such notations are balanced by their promise for clarifying particularly subtle points. An early example of a formal definition is the description of Lisp in the language Lisp itself; see Chapter 11 for details.

EXERCISES

1.1 Give context-free grammars describing the syntax of each of the following:
  a) Strings of length one or more over the set of terminals {**blank**, **tab**, **newline**}.
  b) Sequences of letters or digits, starting with a letter.
  c) Real numbers in which either the integer part or the fractional part can be empty, but not both. Thus, the grammar must allow **31.**, **3.1**, and **.13**, but not a decimal point by itself.

1.2 Complete the syntax chart for the EBNF grammar (1.5) for expressions on page 19.

1.3 The following EBNF grammar is based on the syntax of statements in the Modula-2 programming language:

$S ::= [\,]$
  | **id** := **expr**
  | **if expr then** *SL* { **elsif expr then** *SL* } [**else** *SL*] **end**
  | **loop** *SL* **end**
  | **while expr do** *SL* **end**

$SL ::= S \{ \; ; S \,\}$

Token **id** represents a variable and token **expr** represents an expression. Note that [ ] stands for the empty string.

a) Write a BNF version of this grammar.

b) Write a syntax chart for this grammar.

1.4 Describe how you would construct an EBNF grammar from a syntax chart.

BIBLIOGRAPHIC NOTES

Programming predates computers. The so-called Jacquard loom, invented around 1801, was controlled by a program held on punched cards. The cards determined the pattern woven into the fabric produced by a loom. A different pattern could be woven by changing the cards. Morrison and Morrison [1961] mention "a remarkable woven silk portrait ... showing the inventor Jacquard surrounded by machines of his trade. This work was woven with about 1,000 threads to the inch and resembled a line engraving in fineness of detail. A total of 24,000 cards, each one capable of receiving 1,050 punch-holes, was used to weave its five square feet."

Glimmerings of modern computers appear in the 1864 description by Babbage of a proposed "Analytical Engine" consisting of two parts:

"1. The store in which all the variables to be operated upon, as well as all those quantities which have arisen from the results of other operations, are placed.

"2. The mill into which the quantities about to be operated upon are always brought (Morrison and Morrison [1961])."

For the early history of computers, see Goldstine [1972] and the collection Metropolis, Howlett, and Rota [1980].

The early history of programming languages, up to the arrival of Fortran, is traced by Knuth and Trabb Pardo [1977]. Reflections on thirteen major languages, including Fortran, appear in a collection of papers (Wexelblat [1981]) by participants in the creation of the languages. Wegner [1976] traces milestones along the development of languages.

Dijkstra's [1972] "Notes on structured programming" stressed the role of structure in programming and gave rise to the term "structured programming," explored in Section 3.3. In the same collection, Hoare [1972] considers standard structuring methods for building something out of a collection of primitives.

Context-free grammars illustrate the following structuring methods: composition, choice, repetition, and recursion. In the simplified expression grammar

$$Expression \quad ::= \quad Term \ \{ \ + Term \ \}$$

$$Term \quad ::= \quad Factor \ \{ * Factor \ \}$$

$$Factor \quad ::= \quad '(' \ Expression \ ')' \ | \ Variable \ | \ Constant$$

the string '(' *Expression* ')' is composed of the terminal '(', the nonterminal *Expression*, and the terminal ')'. A vertical bar | represents a choice between alternative strings, and braces { and } represent the repetition of the enclosed string. Recursion is also present, but it will discussed later.

BNF was introduced by Backus [1960] and initially stood for Backus Normal Form. The revised version Backus-Naur Form acknowledges Naur's contributions in using BNF to organize the report on the language Algol 60 (Naur [1963a]).

Speaking on language design, Hoare [1973] observes, "there are so many important but conflicting criteria, that their reconciliation and satisfaction is a major engineering task, demanding of the language designer a deep understanding of all aspects of the art of programming, a familiarity with a wide range of computer architecture on which his language may be implemented, and a knowledge of the wide range of applications to which his language will be put." Hoare's criteria for good language design are: "simplicity, security, fast translation, efficient [target] code, and readability."

TWO

Elements of a Programming Language

Issues common to all programming languages are raised by expressions like $a+b$, where the values of a and b are added. What types of values does a language support? What operations does it provide? What do the names a and b denote? Is it legal to add a and b?

Such questions are addressed in this chapter using expressions and functions as a vehicle. We begin with a little language of expressions, designed from scratch in Section 2.1, and end with an introduction to the Standard ML programming language.

Assignments are deferred until Chapter 3 because they raise additional issues that can be dealt with separately. Specifically, an assignment changes a value in an underlying machine, so we need to be aware of machines when discussing assignments.

2.1 A LITTLE LANGUAGE OF EXPRESSIONS

The little language in this section is small enough to permit a short description, different enough to require description, yet representative enough of programming languages to make description worthwhile. The constructs in the language are expressions denoting geometric objects called quilts, as in Fig. 2.1. The language itself is called *Little Quilt*.

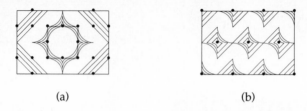

(a)   (b)

Fig. 2.1. Quilts made up of simpler pieces.

What Does Little Quilt Manipulate?

Little Quilt manipulates geometric objects with a height, a width, and a pattern. These objects can be visualized and discussed quite independently of the constructs in the language; with suitable display hardware, they can be manipulated interactively by pointing, without using a language at all. The earliest programming languages began with integers, reals, and arrays of integers and reals; these too can be visualized and discussed independently of a particular language.

The two primitive objects in the language are square pieces with the patterns:

Quilts can be turned and can be sewn together, as in Fig. 2.2. Each quilt has a fixed orientation, with a height, a width, and a pattern; turning therefore yields a different quilt. A lot of turning and sewing goes into making either quilt in Fig. 2.1 from copies of the primitive pieces; the dot in the north-east corner of each piece makes it a little easier to see how the quilts in Fig. 2.1 were put together.

Quilts and the operations on them in Fig. 2.2 are specified by the following rules:

1. A quilt is one of the primitive pieces, or

2. it is formed by turning a quilt clockwise 90°, or

3. it is formed by sewing a quilt to the right of another quilt of equal height.

4. Nothing else is a quilt.

Fig. 2.2. Operations on quilts.

Syntax of Expressions Denoting Quilts

The first step in constructing a language to specify quilts is to give names to the primitive pieces and to the operations on quilts. Let the pieces

be called *a* and *b*, respectively (for the arcs and bands in their patterns). Let the operations in Fig. 2.2 be called *turn* and *sew*.

Having chosen names for the built-in objects and operations, *expressions* are formed as follows. For the moment, the syntax of expressions mirrors the definition of quilts; complex expressions are built up from simpler ones, with the simplest ones being the names *a* and *b*.

> *E* is an *expression* if
>   1a. *E* is *a*, or
>   1b. *E* is *b*, or
>   2.   *E* is *turn* (E_1) and E_1 is an expression, or
>   3.   *E* is *sew* (E_1, E_2) and E_1 and E_2 are expressions.
>   4.   Nothing else is an expression.

A BNF version of this syntax is

> ⟨*expression*⟩ ::= *a*
> | *b*
> | *turn* (⟨*expression*⟩)
> | *sew* (⟨*expression*⟩ , ⟨*expression*⟩)

Semantics of Expressions

The semantics of expressions specifies the quilt denoted by an expression. What quilt does

   sew (turn (turn (b)), a)

denote? The answer is built up in Fig. 2.3(a) from the quilts denoted by its subexpressions. The quilts denoted by the names *a* and *b* are the basic square pieces with arcs and bands on them, respectively. The quilts denoted by expressions of the form *turn* (E_1) and *sew* (E_1, E_2) are built up by applying the operations in Fig. 2.2 to the quilts denoted by E_1 and E_2.

   The information in the table in Fig. 2.3(a) about expressions and the quilts they denote can be organized hierarchically, using a representation called a tree, as in Fig. 2.3(b). The numbers 1, 2, 3, 4, 5 in the figure relate entries in the table to corresponding nodes in the tree. Such trees are examined in Section 2.2.

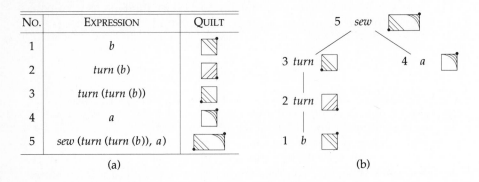

(a)   (b)

Fig. 2.3. Subexpressions and the quilts they denote.

User-Defined Functions

Expressions will now be extended by allowing functions from quilts to quilts. Functions allow quilts to be specified more conveniently.

   Frequent operations, like "unturning" a quilt counterclockwise, or attaching one quilt above another of the same width (see Fig. 2.4), are not provided directly by Little Quilt. These operations can be programmed— three turns make an "unturn," and a quilt can be "piled" above another using a combination of turning and sewing—but it would be convenient to give names to the operations. The operations can then be used without having to think about how, say, piling is implemented in terms of turning and sewing. It does not take too much turning and sewing to get an expression that is hard to understand.

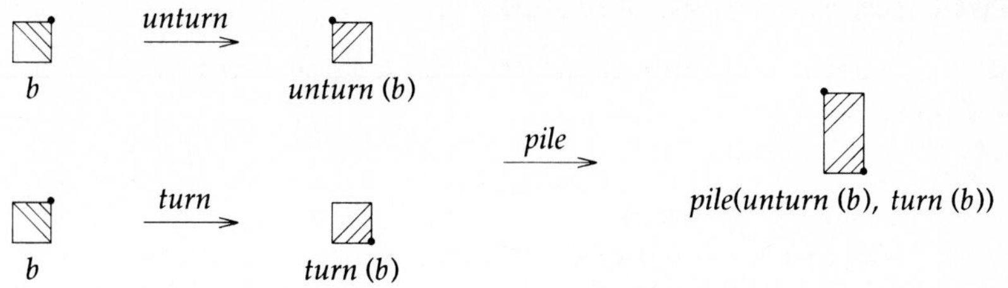

Fig. 2.4. Construction of a quilt using the derived operations *unturn* and *pile*.

The functions *unturn* and *pile* in Fig. 2.4 can be declared as follows:

fun   *unturn* (*x*) = *turn* (*turn* (*turn* (*x*)))

fun   *pile*(*x*, *y*) = *unturn* (*sew* (*turn* (*y*), *turn* (*x*)))

After these declarations, *unturn* (*E*), for any expression *E*, is equivalent to

    turn (*turn* (*turn* (*E*)))

Once declared, a function can be used to declare others; *pile* uses the previously declared function *unturn*.

Local Declarations

Let-expressions or *let-bindings* allow declarations to appear within expressions. They have the form

    let ⟨*declarations*⟩ **in** ⟨*expression*⟩ **end**

Let-expressions illustrate the use of names in programming languages and are found in functional languages, including dialects of Lisp.

For example, the following **let**-expression denotes the quilt built in Fig. 2.4:

    let **fun**   *unturn* (*x*) = *turn* (*turn* (*turn* (*x*)))
        fun   *pile*(*x*, *y*) = *unturn* (*sew* (*turn* (*y*), *turn* (*x*)))
    in
        pile(*unturn* (*b*), *turn* (*b*))
    end

User-Defined Names for Values

The final extension is convenient for writing large expressions in terms of simpler ones.

A *value* declaration

> **val** ⟨*name*⟩ = ⟨*expression*⟩

gives a name to an expression. Value declarations are used together with **let**-bindings. An expression of the form

> **let val** $x = E_1$ **in** E_2 **end**

means: Occurrences of name x in E_2 represent the value of E_1. Any other name can be used instead of x without changing the meaning of the expression.

Let us rewrite the subexpression

> *pile(unturn (b), turn (b))*

in Fig. 2.4 using suggestive names. Use name *nw* for *unturn (b)* because the dot moves to the northwest corner when *b* is "unturned." Similarly use *se* for *turn (b)*. Then the quilt is formed by piling *nw* above *se*; that is, the subexpression can be rewritten as

> **let val** *nw* = *unturn (b)* **in** *pile(nw, turn (b))* **end**

or as

> **let**   **val** *nw* = *unturn (b)*
>   **val**   *se* = *turn (b)*
> **in**
>   *pile(nw, se)*
> **end**

The larger example in Fig. 2.5 shows how a slice of the quilt in Fig. 2.1(b) can be put together. Name *bb* refers to the subquilt studied in Fig. 2.4, formed by piling *unturn (b)* above *turn (b)*. Name *aa* refers to a subquilt formed by piling a basic piece *a* above the result of turning *a* twice. The specification consists of a let-expression based on the schematic construction in the top half of the figure.

A summary of Little Quilt appears in Fig. 2.6.

Discussion

The informal treatment of expressions in this section sidesteps a number of issues that are taken up in subsequent sections:

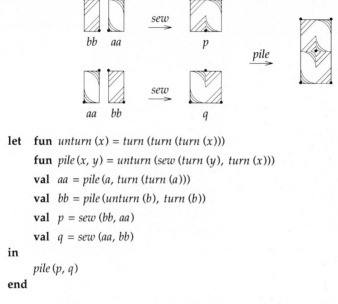

let   **fun** *unturn* (*x*) = *turn* (*turn* (*turn* (*x*)))

　　　fun *pile* (*x, y*) = *unturn* (*sew* (*turn* (*y*), *turn* (*x*)))

　　　val   *aa* = *pile* (*a, turn* (*turn* (*a*)))

　　　val   *bb* = *pile* (*unturn* (*b*), *turn* (*b*))

　　　val   *p* = *sew* (*bb, aa*)

　　　val   *q* = *sew* (*aa, bb*)

in

　　　pile (*p, q*)

end

Fig. 2.5. Specification of a quilt.

- *Notation.* The built-in function *sew* is written before its arguments in an expression *sew* (*a, b*). Section 2.2 considers alternative notations in which operators are written before, between, or after their operands.

- *Evaluation.* The value of an arithmetic expression $E_1 + E_2$ is obtained by first evaluating E_1 and E_2 and then adding their values. This approach is discussed in Section 2.3 and extended in Section 2.4 to handle user-defined functions.

- *Functions.* What happens if a function is declared in terms of itself? Section 2.5 explores such recursive declarations.

- *Scope of names.* The description of **let val** $x = E_1$ **in** E_2 **end** says that any name could be used instead of x without changing the meaning of the expression. Section 2.6 examines uses of the same name x in different contexts.

- *Checking.* What happens if the function *pile* is mistakenly applied to one argument instead of the two it expects? An error occurs. More generally, programming languages deal with several different types of objects, so we need to check that a function is applied to the right number and types of arguments. Section 2.7 deals with types. Languages perform additional checks that will not be considered in this chapter. For example, Little Quilt must check that the expressions E_1 and E_2 in *sew* (E_1, E_2) have the same height.

⟨*expression*⟩ ::= *a* | *b*

    Constant *a* = ◻ and *b* = ◻.

⟨*expression*⟩ ::= *turn* (⟨*expression*⟩) | *sew* (⟨*expression*⟩ , ⟨*expression*⟩)

    The built-in functions *turn* and *sew* are illustrated in Fig. 2.2.

⟨*expression*⟩ ::= **let** ⟨*declarations*⟩ **in** ⟨*expression*⟩ **end**
⟨*declarations*⟩ ::= ⟨*declaration*⟩ | ⟨*declaration*⟩ ⟨*declarations*⟩

    A **let**-expression localizes the effect of ⟨*declarations*⟩ to ⟨*expression*⟩. That is, the functions and variable names declared within ⟨*declarations*⟩ are available for use only within ⟨*expression*⟩. Optional semicolons are allowed after declarations.

⟨*declaration*⟩ ::= **fun** ⟨*name*⟩ (⟨*formals*⟩) = ⟨*expression*⟩
  ⟨*formals*⟩ ::= ⟨*name*⟩ | ⟨*name*⟩ , ⟨*formals*⟩

    This construct is a function declaration. When the function is applied (see below) the body ⟨*expression*⟩ is evaluated after argument values are substituted for the formals.

⟨*expression*⟩ ::= ⟨*name*⟩ (⟨*actuals*⟩)
  ⟨*actuals*⟩ ::= ⟨*expression*⟩ | ⟨*expression*⟩ , ⟨*actuals*⟩

    Here, ⟨*name*⟩ denotes a function to be applied to the actual argument expressions in parentheses. The evaluation order is: Evaluate the arguments, substitute their values for the corresponding formals in the function body, and return the value of the body.

⟨*declaration*⟩ ::= **val** ⟨*name*⟩ = ⟨*expression*⟩

    This construct is a value declaration. It associates the value of ⟨*expression*⟩ with ⟨*name*⟩.

⟨*expression*⟩ ::= ⟨*name*⟩

    A value declaration in an enclosing let-binding determines the value of ⟨*name*⟩.

Fig. 2.6. A summary of Little Quilt.

2.2 EXPRESSION NOTATIONS

A *binary* operator is applied to two operands. In *infix* notation, a binary operator is written between its operands, as in the expression $a+b$. Other alternatives are *prefix* notation, in which the operator is written first, as in $+a\ b$, and *postfix* notation, in which the operator is written last, as in $a\ b+$.

In more detail, an expression in prefix notation is written as follows (the rules for postfix notation are similar):

- The prefix notation for a constant or variable is the constant or variable itself.

- The application of an operator **op** to subexpressions E_1 and E_2 is written in prefix notation as **op** $E_1\ E_2$.

In infix notation, an expression E can be enclosed within parentheses for clarity, as in (E), without affecting its value. Parentheses are not needed in prefix notation because the operands of each operator can be found unambiguously. If a prefix expression begins with operator +, we know that the next expression after + is the first operand of + and the expression after that is the second operand of +.[1]

Example 2.1. The sum of x and y is written in prefix notation as $+\ x\ y$. The product of $+\ x\ y$ and z is written as $*\ +\ x\ y\ z$. Thus, $+\ 20\ 30$ equals 50 and

$$*\ +\ 20\ 30\ 60\ =\ *\ 50\ 60\ =\ 3000$$

Similarly,

$$*\ 20\ +\ 30\ 60\ =\ *\ 20\ 90\ =\ 1800 \qquad\qquad \square$$

Associativity and Precedence

In infix notation, operators appear between their operands; + appears between a and b in the sum $a+b$. How, then, is the expression $a+b*c$ to be decoded? Is it the sum of a and $b*c$, or is it the product of $a+b$ and c?

---

[1] This decoding of prefix notation extends to operators with a fixed number $k\geq 0$ of operands. The number of operands of an operator is called its *arity*. The application of an operator $\mathbf{op}^k$ of arity $k\geq 0$ to $E_1, E_2, \ldots, E_k$, is written in prefix notation as $op^k\ E_1\ E_2\ \cdots\ E_k$. During a left-to-right scan, the ith expression to the right of $\mathbf{op}^k$ is the ith operand of $\mathbf{op}^k$, for $1\leq i\leq k$. Parentheses are needed if the arity of an operator is not known in advance, as happens in Lisp. See Section 7.1 for a discussion of expressions in Lisp.

A traditional convention for grouping infix arithmetic expressions is that multiplication and division take *precedence* over addition and subtraction; that is, multiplications and divisions take their operands before additions and subtractions. We say that multiplication and division have *higher* precedence than addition and subtraction. The convention in programming is to put the operators ∗ and / together at the same precedence level, and to put the operators + and − together at a lower precedence level.[2]

Using parentheses to show the structure of infix expressions, $a * b + c$ is equivalent to $(a * b) + c$ and $d + e * f$ is equivalent to $d + (e * f)$. Similarly, $b * b - 4 * a * c$ is equivalent to

$$(b * b) - ((4 * a) * c)$$

Without rules for specifying the relative precedence of operators, parentheses would be needed in expressions to make explicit the operands of an operator.

Operators with the same precedence are typically grouped from left to right. The expression $4 - 2 - 1$ is grouped as $(4 - 2) - 1$, which evaluates to 1:

$$4 - 2 - 1 \; = \; (4 - 2) - 1 \; = \; 2 - 1 \; = \; 1$$

An incorrect result 3 is obtained if $4 - 2 - 1$ is evaluated as if it were written $4 - (2 - 1)$.

An operator is said to be *left associative* if subexpressions containing multiple occurrences of the operator are grouped from left to right. The subtraction operator is left associative because the subtraction to the left is done first in $4 - 2 - 1$. The arithmetic operators +, −, ∗, and / are all left associative.

An operator is said to be *right associative* if subexpressions containing multiple occurrences of the operator are grouped from right to left. For example, exponentiation is right associative:

$$2^{3^4} = 2^{(3^4)} = 2^{81}$$

Tree Representation of Expressions

The operator/operand structure of an expression can be displayed by a tree with the operator at the root and with trees for the operands as the children of the root. Constants and variables are represented by leaves in the tree. That is, if an expression is formed by applying an operator **op** to operands $E_1, E_2, \ldots, E_k$, for $k \geq 0$, then the tree for the expression has the following form:

---

[2] The Smalltalk-80 programming language in Chapter 6 is an exception to this rule. All arithmetic operators in Smalltalk have the same precedence, and expressions are read from left to right, so $a + b * c$ is equivalent to $(a + b) * c$, the product of $a + b$ and c.

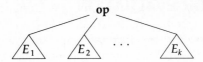

A tree for the expression $b*b-4*a*c$ appears in Fig. 2.7. This expression has the form E_1-E_2, where E_1 is $b*b$ and E_2 is $4*a*c$. The $-$ operator therefore appears at the root of the tree in Fig. 2.7. The children of the root are the subtrees for $b*b$ and $4*a*c$.

The subexpression $4*a*c$ has the form E_1*E_2, where E_1 is $4*a$ and E_2 is c. The corresponding subtree

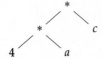

has $*$ at the root. The children of the root are subtrees for $4*a$ and c.

Trees showing the operator/operand structure of an expression are sometimes called *abstract syntax trees*, because they show the syntactic structure of an expression independent of the notation in which the expression was originally written. The tree in Fig. 2.7 is the abstract syntax for each of the following:

PREFIX: $- * b \, b * * 4 \, a \, c$
INFIX: $b * b - 4 * a * c$
POSTFIX: $b \, b * 4 \, a * c * -$

The notion of abstract syntax trees can be extended to other constructs besides expressions by making up suitable operators for the constructs.

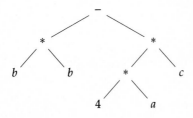

Fig. 2.7. Tree representation of $b*b-4*a*c$.

2.3   EXPRESSION EVALUATION

An expression E_1 **op** E_2 is evaluated as follows: Evaluate the sub-expressions E_1 and E_2 in some order and then apply the operator **op** to the resulting values of E_1 and E_2. Note that the subexpressions E_1 and E_2 can be evaluated in any order.

Expression Evaluation as Tree Rewriting

Expression evaluation corresponds to tree rewriting. When 7∗7 is evaluated to yield 49, the subtree for 7∗7 is replaced by a subtree for 49. The sequence of trees in Fig. 2.8 shows an evaluation of the expression

$$7 * 7 - 4 * 2 * 3$$
$$= 49 - 4 * 2 * 3$$
$$= 49 - 8 * 3$$
$$= 49 - 24$$
$$= 25$$

The left-to-right progress of evaluation in Fig. 2.8 is more explicit in postfix notation. In the following restatement of the preceding expressions, successive lines are obtained by applying the leftmost operator to its operands:

$$7\,7 * 4\,2 * 3 * -$$
$$= 49\,4\,2 * 3 * -$$
$$= 49\,8\,3 * -$$
$$= 49\,24\,-$$
$$= 25$$

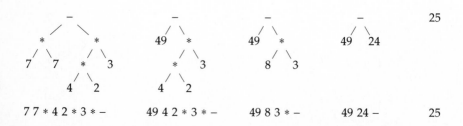

Fig. 2.8. A sequence of trees and corresponding postfix expressions.

Stack Implementation of Expression Evaluation

Although tree rewriting is convenient for explanations, expression evaluation does not usually involve rewriting. The following algorithm for evaluation using an auxiliary stack comes close to actual implementations:

1. Translate the expression to be evaluated into postfix notation.

2. Scan the postfix notation from left to right (see Fig. 2.9).
   a. On seeing a constant, push it onto the stack.
   b. On seeing a binary operator, pop two values from the top of the stack, apply the operator to the values, and push the result back onto the stack.

3. After the entire postfix notation is scanned, the value of the expression is on top of the stack.

In the example in Fig. 2.9, the current constant or operator being scanned in Step 2 of the evaluation algorithm is underlined. The top of the stack is to the right.

EXPRESSION	STACK	REMARK
7 7 * 4 2 * 3 * −	7	Push 7
7 7 * 4 2 * 3 * −	7 7	Push 7
7 7 * 4 2 * 3 * −	49	Multiply
7 7 * 4 2 * 3 * −	49 4	Push 4
7 7 * 4 2 * 3 * −	49 4 2	Push 2
7 7 * 4 2 * 3 * −	49 8	Multiply
7 7 * 4 2 * 3 * −	49 8 3	Push 3
7 7 * 4 2 * 3 * −	49 24	Multiply
7 7 * 4 2 * 3 * −	25	Subtract

Fig. 2.9. Evaluation of an postfix expression using an auxiliary stack.

2.4   FUNCTION DECLARATIONS AND APPLICATIONS

Once a function is declared, it can be applied as an operator within expressions. This section looks at function declarations and the computations that are set up when a function is applied. Computations do not always terminate, and the result of a nonterminating computation is undefined.

Functions as Maps

In mathematics, a *total function* f associates an element of a set B with each element of a set A. A is the *domain* of f and B is the *range*. A function is said to *map* elements of its domain to elements of its range.

The domain A and the range B of f are both shown in the notation $A \rightarrow B$ for the set of all functions from A to B. If f maps a to b, we write $f(a) = b$ and call b the *value* of f at a.

A function f is *partial* if, for each a in its domain A, either $f(a) = b$ for some b in B, or $f(a)$ is undefined because there is no b such that $b = f(a)$.

This view of a function as a map or mapping from a domain to a range does not specify how the value of f at a is computed. One way of defining a function is by explicitly enumerating its value at each element of its domain, as in

> *successor* (0) = 1
> *successor* (1) = 2
> *successor* (2) = 3
> *successor* (3) = 4
> $\cdots$

The following rule illustrates another way of specifying a function:

> $g(x)$ is the largest integer $n \geq 0$ such that $n^2 \leq x$

This rule does not tell us explicitly how the value of g at x is computed.

Functions as Algorithms

A function in a programming language comes together with an algorithm for computing the value of the function at each element of its domain. A function declaration has three parts:

1. the name of the declared function,
2. the parameters of the function, and
3. a rule for computing a result from the parameters.

The syntax of function declarations in this chapter is

> **fun** ⟨*name*⟩ (⟨*formal-parameters*⟩) = ⟨*body*⟩ ;

An example is

fun *successor* $(n) = n + 1$;

The keyword **fun** marks the beginning of a function declaration, ⟨*name*⟩ is the function name, ⟨*formal-parameters*⟩ is a sequence of one or more parameter names, and ⟨*body*⟩ is an expression to be evaluated. The term "formal parameter" is sometimes abbreviated to *formal*.

The use of a function within an expression is called an *application* of the function. Prefix notation is the rule for the application of declared functions:

⟨*name*⟩ (⟨*actual-parameters*⟩)

Again, ⟨*name*⟩ is the function name, and ⟨*actual-parameters*⟩ is a sequence of expressions, corresponding to the sequence of parameter names in the declaration of the function. Thus,

successor (2+3)

is the application of function *successor* to the actual parameter 2+3. The term "actual parameter" is sometimes abbreviated to *actual*. In informal usage, we use "parameter" for formal parameter and "argument" for actual parameter.

Innermost Evaluation

Under the *innermost-evaluation* rule, a function application

⟨*name*⟩ (⟨*actual-parameters*⟩)

is computed as follows:

evaluate the expressions in ⟨*actual-parameters*⟩,
substitute the results for the formals in the function body,
evaluate the body, and
return its value as the answer.[3]

After the declaration

fun *successor* $(n) = n + 1$;

innermost evaluation of the application *successor* (2+3) proceeds as follows:

evaluate the argument 2+3,
substitute its value 5 for formal n in the body $n + 1$,
evaluate the resulting expression 5+1, and
return the answer 6.

---

[3] These evaluation steps show what result a language implementation must compute, not how the result must be computed. Argument values are usually kept in machine registers and not actually substituted into the function body.

Each evaluation of a function body is called an *activation* of the function. If we rewrite *successor* (2+3) as *successor* (*plus* (2, 3)), then its computation can be described as:

activate *plus* to evaluate *plus* (2, 3),
return the result 5 from *plus*,
activate *successor* (5), and
return the answer 6.

The approach of evaluating arguments before the function body is also referred to as *call-by-value* evaluation. The term "innermost" describes the inside-out activation of nested functions in expressions like *successor* (*plus* (2, 3)).

Selective Evaluation

The ability to evaluate selectively some parts of an expression and ignore others is provided by the construct

if ⟨*condition*⟩ **then** ⟨*expression*⟩₁ **else** ⟨*expression*⟩₂

Here, ⟨*condition*⟩ is an expression that evaluates to either **true** or **false**; such expressions are called *boolean* expressions. If ⟨*condition*⟩ evaluates to **true**, then the value of ⟨*expression*⟩₁ becomes the value of the entire construct; otherwise, the value of ⟨*expression*⟩₂ becomes the value of the entire construct. Only one of ⟨*expression*⟩₁ and ⟨*expression*⟩₂ is ever evaluated.

A function that computes the absolute value of a number is defined by

fun   *abs* (*n*) = **if** $n \geq 0$ **then** *n* **else** $0 - n$

Another example is a function *or* that returns **true** if either of its arguments is **true**:

fun   *or*(*x*, *y*) =
    if *x* = **true then true**
    else if *y* = **true then true**
    else false

Provided the value of *y* is either **true** or **false**, function *or* can be declared more succinctly as

fun   *or*(*x*, *y*) =
    if *x* = **true then true else** *y*

Similarly, we can define a function *and* that returns **true** if both its arguments are **true** and returns **false** otherwise.

Under the innermost-evaluation rule, both subexpressions *E* and *F* in *or*(*E*, *F*) are evaluated before they are substituted into the function body.

The operators **andalso** and **orelse** perform *short-circuit* evaluation of boolean expressions, in which the right operand is evaluated only if it has to be. Expression E **andalso** F is false if E is false; it is true if both E and F are true. Evaluation of E **andalso** F proceeds from left to right, with F being evaluated only if E is true. Similarly, E **orelse** F is true if E is true; it is false if both E and F are false. F is evaluated only if E is false.

The operator names "andalso" and "orelse" are borrowed from the Standard ML programming language, along with the rest of the syntax of expressions in this chapter.

2.5   RECURSIVE FUNCTIONS

A function f is *recursive* if its body contains an application of f. More generally, a function f is recursive if f can activate itself, possibly indirectly through other functions. Realistic examples of recursive functions will be considered in later chapters. Meanwhile, this section uses toy examples to explore recursion.

Elements of the Fibonacci sequence 1, 1, 2, 3, 5, 8, $\cdots$ are computed by the function

> **fun** *fib* (n) =
>   **if** $n = 0$ **orelse** $n = 1$ **then** 1 **else** *fib* $(n-1) + fib$ $(n-2)$

This function is recursive because the body

> **if** $n = 0$ **orelse** $n = 1$ **then** 1 **else** *fib* $(n-1) + fib$ $(n-2)$

contains two applications of *fib*; they are *fib* $(n-1)$ and *fib* $(n-2)$. Function *fib* satisfies the following equalities:

> *fib* $(0) = 1$, *fib* $(1) = 1$, *fib* $(2) = 2$, *fib* $(3) = 3$, *fib* $(4) = 5$, *fib* $(5) = 8$, $\cdots$

No new ideas are needed to evaluate applications of recursive functions. As usual, the actual parameters are evaluated and substituted into the function body. Thus, the application *fib* (4) is evaluated by substituting 4 for n in the body of *fib*, yielding

> **if** $4 = 0$ **orelse** $4 = 1$ **then** 1 **else** *fib* $(4-1) + fib$ $(4-2)$

Since $4 = 0$ and $4 = 1$ are both false, this expression simplifies to

> *fib* $(4-1) + fib$ $(4-2)$

These two applications are evaluated separately by substituting $4-1 = 3$ and $4-2 = 2$, respectively, for n in the body of *fib*. Eventually, *fib* (3) returns 3 and *fib* (2) returns 2, so their sum 5 is the value of *fib* (4).

As an aside, function *fib* is based on a poor algorithm for computing elements of the Fibonacci sequence because it recomputes the same elements again and again. We just saw that

$$fib\,(4) \;=\; fib\,(3) + fib\,(2)$$

Similarly, $fib\,(3) = fib\,(2) + fib\,(1)$, so

$$fib\,(4) \;=\; fib\,(2) + fib\,(1) + fib\,(2)$$

As this equation implies, an evaluation of *fib* (4) recomputes *fib* (2). As *n* increases, the amount of recomputation during the evaluation of *fib* (*n*) increases rapidly.

For negative values of *n*, evaluation of *fib* (*n*) does not terminate:

$$fib\,(-1) \;=\; fib\,(-2) + fib\,(-3) \;=\; (fib\,(-3) + fib\,(-4)) + fib\,(-3) \;=\; \cdots$$

Linear Recursion

The definition of a function *f* is said to be *linear recursive* if an activation *f* (*a*) of *f* can initiate at most one new activation of *f*.

The following function *factorial* for computing factorials is linear recursive:

> **fun** *factorial* (*n*) =
>   **if** *n* = 0 **then** 1 **else** *n* * *factorial* (*n* −1);

An activation of *factorial* with argument *a* returns 1 if *a* is 0; otherwise it initiates a new activation of *factorial* with argument *a* − 1. Thus, each activation of *factorial* can initiate at most one new activation of *factorial*.

Evaluation of a linear-recursive function has two phases:

1. a *winding phase* in which new activations are initiated, and

2. a subsequent *unwinding phase* in which control returns from the activations in a last-in-first-out manner.

Example 2.2. For brevity, we write *f* instead of *factorial*; that is, function *f* is defined by

> **fun** *f* (*n*) =
>   **if** *n* = 0 **then** 1 **else** *n* * *f* (*n* −1);

For *n* ≥ 1, this function computes the factorial, so we expect

$$f\,(n) \;=\; n * (n-1) * \cdots * 1$$

The evaluation of *f* (3) begins with

> **if** 3 = 0 **then** 1 **else** 3 * *f* (3−1)

This expression is obtained by substituting the value 3 for the formal n in the body of f. Since $3 = 0$ is false, control reaches the expression $3 * f$ (3–1). 3–1 simplifies to 2, but the multiplication in

$3 * f$ (2)

cannot be performed until the value of f (2) is available.

The activations that occur during the evaluation of f (3) are shown in Fig. 2.10. While computing f (3) we discover that f (2) must be computed, and then, while computing f (2) we discover that f (1) must be computed:

$$f\ (3)\ =\ 3 * f\ (2)$$
$$f\ (2)\ =\ 2 * f\ (1) \tag{2.1}$$
$$f\ (1)\ =\ 1 * f\ (0)$$

The winding phase terminates with f (0) because no new activation is initiated. When 0 is substituted for the formal n, we get

if $0 = 0$ **then** 1 **else** $0 * f$ (0–1);

The test $0=0$ in the function body succeeds, yielding the result 1 for f (0).

In the unwinding phase, the suspended activations are resumed in a last-in-first-out order, and the expressions on the right side of (2.1) are all evaluated. A summary of the computation of f (3) is as follows:

$$
\begin{aligned}
f\ (3)\ &=\ 3 * f\ (2)\\
&=\ 3 * (2 * f\ (1))\\
&=\ 3 * (2 * (1 * f\ (0)))\\
&=\ 3 * (2 * (1 * 1)) \quad\quad\quad\quad\quad (2.2)\\
&=\ 3 * (2 * 1)\\
&=\ 3 * 2\\
&=\ 6 \quad\quad\quad\quad\quad\quad\quad\quad\quad\quad\quad\quad \square
\end{aligned}
$$

Tail Recursion

Recursive functions can be implemented efficiently if they are *tail recursive*; a function f is tail recursive if it either returns a value without needing recursion, or it simply returns the result of a recursive activation.

The following function g is tail recursive because an activation $g\ (n, a)$ either returns a, or it returns the result of a recursive activation $g\ (n-1, n*a)$:

    fun $g\ (n,\ a)\ =$
        if $n = 0$ **then** a **else** $g\ (n-1,\ n*a)$

The tail-recursive nature of g is more evident from the following restatement of its declaration:

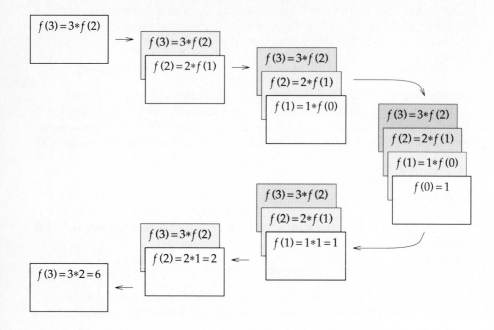

Fig. 2.10. Recursive evaluation of a factorial function.

$$g\,(n,\,a) \; = \; \begin{cases} a & \text{if } n = 0 \\ g\,(n-1,\,n*a) & \text{otherwise} \end{cases}$$

Example 2.3. The activations that occur during the evaluation of $g\,(3,1)$ are shown in Fig. 2.11. The evaluation begins with

if $3 = 0$ **then** 1 **else** $g\,(3{-}1,\,3*1)$

which simplifies to $g\,(2,\,3)$. A summary of the computation of $g\,(3,1)$ is

$$g\,(3,\,1) = g\,(2,\,3) = g\,(1,\,6) = g\,(0,\,6) = 6$$

For all values of n, the expression $g\,(n,\,1)$ evaluates to $n\,!$ and $g\,(n,\,a)$ evaluates to $n\,!*a$, where $n\,!$ is the notation for the factorial of n. ☐

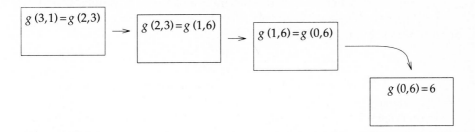

Fig. 2.11. Evaluation of a tail-recursive factorial function.

All the work of a linear tail-recursive function is done in the winding phase, as new activations are initiated. The unwinding phase is trivial because the value computed by the final activation becomes the result of the entire evaluation.[4]

By contrast, the function f in Fig. 2.10 is not tail recursive because

$$f(3) = 3 * f(2)$$

The multiplication is done after control unwinds from the activation $f(2)$.

2.6   LEXICAL SCOPE

It seems reasonable to suppose that consistent renaming of variables has no effect on the value of an expression. Renaming is made precise by introducing a notion of local or "bound" variables; bound occurrences of variables can be renamed without changing the meaning of a program. This renaming principle is the basis for the "lexical scope" rule for determining the meanings of names in programs.

Changing the formal parameter from x to n in the declaration of the successor function

    fun *successor* $(x) = x + 1$;
    fun *successor* $(n) = n + 1$;

should have no effect on the meaning of a program. The value of the expression *successor* (5) is 6 with either declaration.

---

[4] Looking ahead to Chapter 4, a linear tail-recursive function can be turned into a loop. The loop for computing $g(n,a)$ treats n and a as variables that can be assigned to

```
loop
      if  n = 0  then  return a ;
      else  a := n * a ;  n := n − 1;
      end;
end
```

Subtleties arise when a function declaration can refer to nonlocal names; that is, names that are not formal parameters. For example, the result returned by the function *addy* depends on the value of y:

fun *addy* $(x) = x + y$;

Since y is nonlocal, some context determines its value. The question is, which context?

Lexical scope rules use the program text surrounding a function declaration to determine the context in which nonlocal names are evaluated. The program text is static by contrast with run-time execution, so such rules are also called *static scope rules*.

This section uses **let**-expressions to study lexical scope rules. First, consider a single **let**-expression like

let val $x = 2$ **in** $x + x$ **end**

The occurrence of x to the right of keyword **val** in

let val $x = E_1$ **in** E_2 **end**

is called a *binding occurrence* or simply *binding* of x. All occurrences of x in E_2 are said to be within the *scope* of this binding; the scope of a binding includes itself. The occurrences of x within the scope of a binding are said to be *bound*. A binding of a name is said to be *visible* to all occurrences of the name in the scope of the binding.

The lines in the following diagram go from a binding to bound occurrences of x:

let val x = 2 **in** x + x **end**

A precise counterpart of "Variables can be renamed" is: The value of an expression is left undisturbed if we replace all occurrences of a variable x within the scope of a binding of x by a fresh variable. The following two expressions therefore have the same value:

let val $x = 2$ **in** $x + x$ **end**
let val $z = 2$ **in** $z + z$ **end**

The preceding definitions carry over directly to bindings of distinct variables. The scope of the binding of x in

let val $x = 3$ **in** **let val** $y = 4$ **in** $x * x + y * y$ **end end**

includes the two occurrences of x in $x*x + y*y$. The scope of the binding of y includes the two occurrences of y in the sum.

When faced with nested bindings of the same variable, as in

let val x = 2 **in** **let val** x = x + 1 **in** x * x **end** **end**

first apply renaming to the inner binding. Replacing x by y in the inner binding yields

let val x = 2 **in** **let val** y = x + 1 **in** y * y **end** **end**

Here, the scope of the outer binding of x includes the x in $x+1$, and the scope of the inner binding of y includes the two occurrences of y in $y*y$. Again, lines go from binding occurrences to bound occurrences within their scope.

2.7 TYPES

The *type* of an expression tells us the values it can denote and the operations that can be applied to it. Integers can be added; the boolean values **true** and **false** cannot. Thus, + can be applied to two expressions of type integer, but not to two expressions of type boolean.

A widely followed principle of language design is that every expression must have a unique type. This principle makes types a mechanism for classifying expressions.

The only structure on raw data inside a machine is its physical layout in memory. Furthermore, the same sequence of bits can be viewed as an integer by one program, as a sequence of characters by another, and as a machine instruction by a third program; for example, the bit pattern for the character @ may be the same as the bit pattern for the integer 64. Such flexibility is a characteristic of general-purpose machines. Unfortunately for the programmer, it is also an invitation to errors, since machines do not check that the data is used as intended.

Types in programming languages can be motivated at several levels:

- *Machine level.* The values supported directly by a machine can be classified into *basic types*, such as integers, characters, reals, and booleans. Since the machine instruction for adding integers is typically different from the instruction for adding reals, compilers need type information to generate machine code for expressions.

- *Language level.* In addition to the basic types, languages support *structured types*, such as arrays, records, and lists that are built up from simpler types. Structured types are used to set up the data structures manipulated by a program. A *type constructor* is a language construct for building a structured type.

- *User level.* User-defined types are groupings of named data and functions. Classes, discussed in Chapters 5 and 6, allow a user to extend a language by defining types that are suited to the problem on hand.

Structured Types

Informally, a type consists of a set of values together with some operations on the values. Since facilities for defining and using types vary widely from language to language, we examine structured types by considering ways of building up sets of values.

Set theory is a convenient setting for studying structured types, for several reasons. First, methods for constructing sets have close counterparts in programming languages, in the form of type constructors. Second, set theory provides concise notations for describing the structure of a set. Finally, the absence of restrictions on set constructors simplifies the discussion. Languages raise additional issues, such as user convenience, ease of translation, and efficient implementation, that will be addressed separately.

We assume the existence of some basic sets, including

bool	{ **true, false** }
color	{ *red, white, blue* }
int	the integers
char	a set of characters
real	a set of real numbers

Next, we consider three set constructors that have close counterparts in programming languages. They are the product, function, and sequence constructors. The description of each constructor has three parts:

1. its syntax,
2. the elements in the constructed set, and
3. some operations for examining the structure of the elements in the constructed set.

Product. The *product* $A \times B$ of two sets A and B consists of *ordered pairs* written as (a, b), where a is an element of set A and b is an element of set B.

The set **bool** × **color** has six elements:

{ (**true**, *red*), (**true**, *white*), (**true**, *blue*),
　(**false**, *red*), (**false**, *white*), (**false**, *blue*) }

The set **int** × **int** consists of pairs of integers.

Associated with the product constructor × are the operations **first** and **second**, which extract the first and second elements from a pair, respectively. Thus, **first** applied to the pair (**true**, *blue*) yields **true** and **second** applied to this pair yields *blue*. These operations are called *projection* functions.

A product of n sets $A_1 \times A_2 \times \cdots \times A_n$ consists of *tuples* written as $(a_1, a_2, \ldots, a_n)$, where a_i is an element of set A_i, for $1 \le i \le n$. The associated operations extract the ith element of a tuple.

Function. The set of all *functions* from set A to set B is written as $A \to B$. The only operation associated with the set $A \to B$ is *application*, which takes a function f in $A \to B$ and an element a in A, and yields an element b of B. The usual notation for the application of f to a is $f(a)$.

The set **color → bool** consists of all functions from set **color** to set **bool**. Since **color** has three elements and **bool** has two elements, there are are $2^3 = 8$ such functions. One of these is a function f satisfying the following equalities:

$$f\,(red) = \textbf{false}$$
$$f\,(white) = \textbf{false}$$
$$f\,(blue) = \textbf{true}$$

By convention, the product constructor × has higher precedence than the function constructor →, so

    int × int → int

is the set of all functions from pairs of integers to integers. Included in these functions are + for adding integers and ∗ for multiplying integers. Recall that the infix notation $2+3$ represents the application of + to 2 and 3. Thus, + can be treated as a function that maps the pair of integers $(2, 3)$ to the integer 5. Similarly, ∗ is a function that maps the pair of integers $(2, 3)$ to the integer 6.

The set

    int × int → bool

is the set of all functions from pairs of integers to booleans. Among these functions are <, ≤, =, ≠, ≥, > for comparing integers.

Sequences. The *Kleene closure* or *star* of set A, written A^* consists of all tuples that can be formed from elements of A. Thus, **color*** is the set

    { (), (*red*), (*white*), (*blue*), (*red, red*), (*red, white*), (*red, blue*), $\cdots$ }

Here () represents the empty tuple with no elements.

Kleene closure is related to list constructors in functional programming languages, where a list is a finite-length sequence of elements. Among the operations on lists are *null* to test whether a list has no elements, *head* to extract the first element of a list, and *tail* to extract all elements except the head.

Type Systems

A *type system* for a language is a set of rules for associating a type with expressions in the language. A type system *rejects* an expression if it does not associate a type with the expression.

Example 2.4. This example illustrates a simple type system for arithmetic expressions, based on the original Fortran manual. An expression is either a variable or a constant, or is formed by applying one of the operators +, −, *, or / to two subexpressions. The type of an expression is either **int** or **real**.

An expression gets a type if and only if one of the following rules applies to the expression:

- Variable names starting with the letters **I** through **N** have type **int**. All other names have type **real**. By this implicit rule, **COUNT** has type **real**.

- A number has type **real** if it contains a decimal point; otherwise it has type **int**. Thus, **0.5** and **.5** have type **real**, as do **1.** and **1.0**.

- The classification of variables and constants into **int** and **real** carries over to expressions.

    If expressions E and F have the same type, then

    $$E + F$$
    $$E - F$$
    $$E * F$$
    $$E / F$$

    are expressions of that same type.

Thus, **I+J** has type **int** and **X+Y** has type **real**. But what about **X+I**? The type system in this example rejects **X+I** because **X** and **I** have different types. Since none of the rules applies to **X+I**, it does not have a type and is rejected.   □

The main difference between the type system in Example 2.4 and those of Modula-2, C, and the other languages in this book lies in the rule for associating a type with a variable. Most languages require explicit declarations, which specify a type for a variable.

At the heart of all type systems is the following rule for function applications. The symbol $\rightarrow$ is a function constructor, so $S \rightarrow T$ is the type of a function from type S to type T:

> If f is a function of type $S \rightarrow T$, and a has type S, then   (2.3)
> $f(a)$ has type T.

Some variations on this rule appear below.

Arithmetic Operators. Associated with each operator **op** is a rule that specifies the type of an expression E **op** F in terms of the types of E and F. An example is:

> If E and F have type **int**, then
> E **mod** F also has type **int**.

This rule can be made to look more like (2.3) by using prefix rather than infix notation, and rewriting the expression as **mod**(E, F), with **mod** applied to the pair (E, F):

> If **mod** is a function of type **int**$\times$**int** $\rightarrow$ **int**, and
> the pair (E, F) has type **int**$\times$**int**, then
> **mod**(E, F) has type **int**.

Overloading. Familiar operator symbols like + and * are *overloaded*; that is, these symbols have different meanings in different contexts. In Example 2.4, + is used for both integer and real addition, so it has two possible types:

> + : **int**$\times$**int** $\rightarrow$ **int**
> + : **real**$\times$**real** $\rightarrow$ **real**

The treatment of + in Example 2.4 can therefore be restated using the following pair of rules:

> If E has type **int** and F has type **int**, then
> $E + F$ has type **int**

> If E has type **real** and F has type **real**, then
> $E + F$ has type **real**

These rules can also be made to look like (2.3) by using prefix notation, as with the **mod** operator above.

Coercion. The original Fortran type system (see Example 2.4) rejected expressions like **X+I** and **2*3.142**, but this restriction was lifted in later versions of Fortran. Most programming languages treat the expression **2*3.142** as if it were **2.0*3.142**. A *coercion* is a conversion from one type to another, inserted automatically by a programming language. In

2*3.142, the integer **2** is coerced to a real before the multiplication is done.

Polymorphism. A *polymorphic* function has a parameterized type, also called a *generic* type. Further discussion of polymorphic functions is deferred until Chapter 7, where such functions are used to manipulate lists.

Types Are Used for Error Checking

The rules of a type system specify the proper usage of each operator in the language. *Type checking* ensures that the operations in a program are applied properly.

The purpose of type checking is to prevent errors. During execution, an error occurs if an operation is applied incorrectly; for example, if an integer is mistakenly treated as something else. More precisely, a *type error* occurs if a function f of type $S \rightarrow T$ is applied to some a that does not have type S. A program that executes without type errors is said to be *type safe*.

As far as possible, programs are checked *statically*, once and for all, during translation of the source text. Using the rules in Example 2.4, a Fortran compiler can see from the source text that **+** will be applied to a pair of integers each time the expression **I+J** is evaluated.

Dynamic checking is done during program execution. In effect, dynamic checking is done by inserting extra code into the program to watch for impending errors. Extra code for dynamic checking takes up both time and space, so it is less efficient at run time than static checking. A more serious failing of dynamic checking is that errors can lurk in a program until they are reached during execution. Large programs tend to have portions that are rarely executed, so a program may be in use for a long time before dynamic checking detects a type error.

Static checking is effective enough and dynamic checking is expensive enough that language implementations often check only those properties that can be checked statically from the source text. Properties that depend on values computed at run time, such as division by zero or array indices being within bounds, are rarely checked.

The terms strong and weak refer to the effectiveness with which a type system prevents errors. A type system is *strong* if it accepts only safe expressions. In other words, expressions that are accepted by a strong type system are guaranteed to evaluate without a type error. A type system is *weak* if it is not strong.

By themselves, the terms strong and weak convey little information. As in Fig. 2.12, a strong type system accepts some subset of safe programs; however, we have no information about the size of this subset. If a type system carries a "better safe than sorry" philosophy too far, it will reject

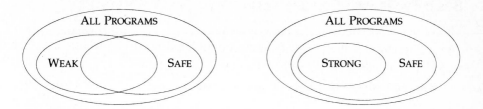

Fig. 2.12. Weak type checking allows some unsafe programs to slip through.

too many programs. A pathological example is a type system that rejects all programs. Such a system is strong but useless.

To summarize this discussion, the following are some questions to be asked about type checking in a language:

- Is the checking done statically or dynamically?

- How powerful is the type system; that is, among safe programs, how many does it accept?

- Is the type system strong or weak?

It is desirable for a language to be statically checked using a powerful and strong type system.

2.8 INTRODUCTION TO ML

From Section 2.7, the type of an expression tells us the values it can denote and the operations that can be applied to it. Structured types are illustrated in this section by considering datatype declarations in the Standard ML programming language. Datatype declarations in ML allow us to define new types of our own and then freely use the new types. All aspects of a new type must be declared explicitly, so new types are a good vehicle for illustrating types.

We have already used the syntax of ML in this chapter for expressions, functions, and let bindings. ML was not singled out for attention earlier because the concepts in this chapter apply to any language with expressions and functions. Indeed, the discussion of infix expressions, function declarations, recursion, lexical scope, and types carries over to languages like Pascal and C, with minor syntactic adjustments.

ML is statically checked and has one of the most powerful strong type systems of any language. The language is explored further in Chapter 7.

Basic Types with Equality Tests

The values associated with a basic type are atomic; they are constants with no components. A new basic type can be declared in ML by writing down its elements. The declaration

>   **datatype** *direction* = *north* | *south* | *east* | *west* ;

specifies a type *direction*. The set of values associated with this type is

>   { *north, south, east, west* }

The names *north, south, east, west* are constants that cannot be reused for other purposes, so they can belong only to the set of values associated with type *direction*.

  Now that we have a type, *direction*, and an associated set of values, we need some operations on these values. ML provides operations that test whether two values of type *direction* are equal. Equality tests of the form $x = d$, where d is a direction, are used in the following definition of function *clockwise*:

>   **fun** *clockwise* $(x) =$
>   **if** x = *north* **then** *east*
>   **else if** x = *east* **then** *south*   (2.4)
>   **else if** x = *south* **then** *west*
>   **else** *north* ;

Thus, *clockwise* (*north*) = *east*, *clockwise* (*east*) = *south*, and so on. ML allows the declaration (2.4) to be rewritten as the following declaration by cases:

>   **fun**   *clockwise* (*north*) = *east*
> | *clockwise* (*east*) = *south*
> | *clockwise* (*south*) = *west*   (2.5)
> | *clockwise* (_) = *north* ;

As usual, keyword **fun** marks the beginning of a function declaration. Cases in the declaration are separated by a vertical bar | and are tested in order. An underscore _ is a "don't-care" pattern, so the final case for *clockwise* (_) corresponds to the **else** part of (2.4).

Value Constructors with Extractor Operations

The general form of an ML datatype declaration builds values with a hierarchical structure. The operations associated with such a declaration are used to extract the components of a structured value. We illustrate the general form by building a set of values corresponding to binary trees like the following:

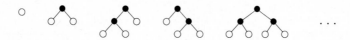

Open circles denote leaves, and filled circles denote nonleaf nodes with two subtrees.

In words, a binary tree is either a leaf or a nonleaf with two binary trees below it. Values with this structure are built up by

> **datatype**   *bitree* = *leaf* | *nonleaf* **of** *bitree* ∗ *bitree* ;

The definition of type *bitree*, for binary tree, is recursive. A *bitree* is either a *leaf*, or it is constructed by *nonleaf* from the pair *bitree* ∗ *bitree*. The notation $A*B$ is a counterpart of $A×B$ in set theory, so *bitree* ∗ *bitree* represents pairs of binary trees.

The general form of an ML datatype declaration is, for $k \geq 1$

> **datatype** ⟨*type-name*⟩ = ⟨*value-constructor*⟩$_1$ ⟨*optional-parameters*⟩$_1$
> | ⟨*value-constructor*⟩$_2$ ⟨*optional-parameters*⟩$_2$
> | . . .
> | ⟨*value-constructor*⟩$_k$ ⟨*optional-parameters*⟩$_k$;

In the declaration of *bitree*, the value constructors are *leaf* and *nonleaf*. Value constructors without parameters are also called constants. The keyword **of** marks the parameters of a value constructor.

Once the type *bitree* is declared, how do we refer to an element of its set of values? Some trees and their corresponding expressions appear in Fig. 2.13.

If variables *s* and *t* have type *bitree*, then *nonleaf* (*s*, *t*) denotes a *bitree* with subtrees *s* and *t*. The following function *leafcount* counts the number of leaves in a *bitree*:

> **fun**   *leafcount* (*leaf*) = 1
> | *leafcount* (*nonleaf* (*s*, *t*)) = *leafcount* (*s*) + *leafcount* (*t*);

The result of applying *leafcount* to *leaf* is 1. If *leafcount* is applied to a value constructed by *nonleaf* from trees represented by *s* and *t*, then the result is the sum of *leafcount* (*s*) and *leafcount* (*t*).

Implicit in the declaration of *leafcount* are operations for examining the structure of a constructed value. We therefore redefine *leafcount* to make these operations explicit.

The following function *isleaf* returns **true** if a tree *t* is a leaf; otherwise, if *t* is a nonleaf, it returns **false**.

> **fun**   *isleaf* (*leaf*) = **true**
> | *isleaf* (*nonleaf* (_)) = **false**;

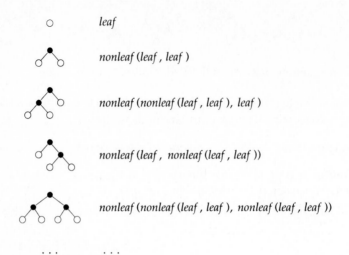

Fig. 2.13. Some binary trees and their corresponding expressions.

Now, consider a nonleaf with two subtrees. Functions *left* and *right* extract the left and right subtrees of the tree:[5]

    fun *left(nonleaf (s, t)) = s ;*
    fun *right(nonleaf (s, t)) = t ;*

Operations *isleaf, left,* and *right* on binary trees are used to redeclare *leafcount*:

    fun *leafcount (x) =*
        if *isleaf (x)* **then** 1
        else *leafcount (left(x)) + leafcount (right(x));*

Whenever structured values are constructed, operations similar to *isleaf* are needed to classify values and operations similar to *left* and *right* are needed to extract components from the constructed values.

User-Defined Operations on Data

Now that we have seen how structured values can be constructed and manipulated, let us consider an application. Problems typically deal with structured values, and datatype declarations in ML allow us to define value constructors that are appropriate to the problem on hand.

The next example implements sets of integers by trees, as in Fig. 2.14.

---

[5] The functions *left* and *right* are defined only for nonleaves. Evaluation of the expressions *left(leaf)* and *right(leaf)* raises an exception at run time. See Section 7.6 for exception handling in ML.

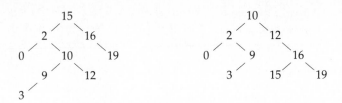

Fig. 2.14. Two binary search trees.

Example 2.5. Consider two operations on sets of integers: operation *member* determines if an integer k belongs to a set and operation *insert* constructs a new set by adding an element k to an old set. Sets of integers with these operations can be implemented using a data structure called a *binary search tree*. A binary search tree is either empty, or it consists of a node with two binary search trees as subtrees. Each node holds an integer (see Fig. 2.14). The elements in a binary search tree are arranged so that smaller elements appear in the left subtree of a node and larger elements appear in the right subtree.

Binary search trees can be implemented in ML by declaring a datatype *inttree*, for integer tree:

datatype *inttree* = *empty* | *node* **of int** * *inttree* * *inttree* ;

A value of type *inttree* is either the constant *empty*, or is formed by applying constructor *node* to a triple (n, s, t), where n represents the integer at the node and s and t represent the left and right subtrees at the node.

Binary search trees will be constructed by starting with the constant *empty* and successively inserting integers, as in Fig. 2.15 (the figure does not show subtrees that are *empty*).

Function *insert*, below, takes two arguments, an element k and a tree into which k is inserted. The function returns the resulting tree after insertion.

```
fun    insert (k, empty) =
           node (k, empty, empty)
   |   insert (k, node (n, s, t)) =
           if k < n then node (n, insert (k, s), t)
           else if k > n then node (n, s, insert (k, t))
           else node (n, s, t);
```

```
15      15          15          15          15          15          15
          \         / \        / \         / \         / \         / \
           16     2   16     2   16      2   16      2   16      2   16
                         \         \          / \         / \       / \ \
                         10        10       0   10      0   10    0  10  19
                                   /         /           /          /
                                  9         9           9          9
```

Fig. 2.15. Insertion of 15, 16, 2, 10, 9, 0, 19 into a binary search tree.

In words, the result of inserting k into *empty* is a tree *node* $(k, empty, empty)$. The result of inserting k into a tree *node* (n, s, t) is determined by comparing k with the integer n. If k is less than n, then the resulting tree is

> *node* $(n, insert \ (k, s), t)$

with k inserted into the left subtree. Otherwise, if k is greater than n, then the resulting tree is

> *node* $(n, s, insert \ (k, t))$

with k inserted into the right subtree. If neither of the above cases applies, then k must equal n and the result is the original tree.

Function *member* determines if k appears at some node in a binary search tree. An empty tree has no elements, so *member* (*empty*) returns **false**. Otherwise, suppose the tree is *node* (n, s, t), with n at the root, left subtree s, and right subtree t.

> **fun**   *member* $(k, empty)$ =
> > **false**
>
> | *member* $(k, node \ (n, s, t))$ =
> > **if** $k < n$ **then** *member* (k, s)
> > **else if** $k > n$ **then** *member* (k, t)
> > **else true**;

If $k < n$, then k can occur only in s, and the result is *member* (k, s). Otherwise, if $k > n$, then k can occur only in t. Otherwise, k must equal n, so the result is **true**.   □

A Final Look at Quilts

A datatype corresponding to the quilts of Section 2.1 is declared by

> **datatype** *quilt* = a | b | *turn* **of** *quilt* | *sew* **of** *quilt* * *quilt* ;

The syntax of Little Quilt was borrowed from ML, so this declaration converts the Little Quilt expressions in Section 2.1 into legal ML expressions. The function declaration

> **fun**   *unturn* (x) = *turn* (*turn* (*turn* (x)))

is legal in ML.

The expressions in Section 2.1 were tested using the above datatype declaration. The following approximations to the quilts at the beginning of this chapter were constructed by using list-manipulation functions that will be discussed in Chapter 7.

EXERCISES

2.1 Specify each of the quilts in Fig. 2.16 in Little Quilt.

2.2 Rewrite the following expressions in prefix notation. Treat *sqrt* as an operator with one argument.
  a) $a * b + c$
  b) $a * (b + c)$
  c) $a * b + c * d$
  d) $a * (b + c) * d$
  e) $(b/2 + sqrt((b/2)*(b/2) - a*c))/a$

2.3 Rewrite the expressions of Exercise 2.2 in postfix notation.

2.4 Draw syntax trees for the expressions of Exercise 2.2.

2.5 An integer is a prime if it is not a multiple of any smaller integer. More precisely, n is a *prime* if for all i, $2 \le i \le n - 1$, the expression $n \bmod i \neq 0$. The **mod** operator returns the remainder after integer division.
  a) Declare a function $f(n, m)$ that returns **true** if for all i, $2 \le i \le m$, the expression $n \bmod i \neq 0$.
  b) Use function f from (a) to declare a function *prime*(n) that returns **true** if n is a prime and returns **false** otherwise.

2.6 An alternative to the Fibonacci function *fib*(n) on page 41 is *fast*(n), declared as follows:

```
fun  g (i, j, k, n) =
       if  k = n  then  j
       else  g (j, i + j, k + 1, n);
fun  fast (n)  =  g (0, 1, 0, n);
```

  (a)   (b)   (c)   (d)   (e)

Fig. 2.16. Quilts for Exercise 2.1.

a) Explain why $fib(n) = fast(n)$ for all $n \geq 0$.

*b) Explain why the computation of $fast(n)$ is much more efficient than the computation of $fib(n)$.

2.7 Declare a function f satisfying the following specification. Use additional functions as needed.

For $x \geq 0$, $f(x)$ is the largest integer $n \geq 0$ such that $n^2 \leq x$.

What does your function do for negative values of x?

2.8 Evaluate the following expressions:
a) **let val** $x = 2$ **in** $x + x$ **end**
b) **let val** $x = 3$ **in let val** $y = 4$ **in** $x * x + y * y$ **end end**
c) **let val** $x = 3$ **val** $y = 4$ **in** $x * x + y * y$ **end**
d) **let val** $x = 3$ **in let val** $x = x + 1$ **in** $x * x$ **end end**

2.9 Consider a datatype *intlist* declared by

datatype *intlist* = *nil* | *cons* **of int** * *intlist* ;

A list of type *intlist* is either *nil* or it is formed by applying the constructor *cons* to an integer and an intlist. A list $1, 2, 3$ is represented by

cons (1, *cons* (2, *cons* (3, *nil*)))

a) Define a function *member* (k, x) that determines if k is in the intlist x.
b) Define a function *adjacent* (x) that determines if there are two adjacent occurrences of an integer in intlist x.
c) Define a function *min* (x) that returns the smallest integer in intlist x.
d) Define a function *less* (k, x) that creates a list consisting of all integers in x that are less than k.

2.10 Extend Example 2.5 on page 57 by defining a function that returns a binary search tree formed by deleting an integer element from a binary search tree t, as follows. In each case, return t itself if t is empty.
a) *deletemin* (t) deletes the smallest element.
b) *deletemax* (t) deletes the largest element.
c) *delete* (k, t) deletes k if k is in t.

2.11 Write a function to determine if two binary search trees contain the same elements.

2.12 Call a leaf in a binary tree a *left leaf* if it is the left child of its parent. Write a function in ML to compute the number of left leaves of a value of datatype *bitree* declared by

datatype   *bitree* = *leaf* | *nonleaf* **of** *bitree* ∗ *bitree* ;

BIBLIOGRAPHIC NOTES

The rest of this book contains further discussion and bibliographic notes for most of the concepts in this chapter.

ML is a functional language in the tradition of Landin's [1966] ISWIM, an acronym for "If You See What I Mean." ISWIM itself was based on Lisp, considered in Chapter 7, and the λ-calculus, considered in Chapter 12. Since ML was first created by Robin Milner in the 1970s a number of dialects have emerged. A standardization effort begun in 1983 has resulted in Standard ML, the dialect used in this book. See Chapter 7 for more information on ML.

Part II

Concepts and Constructs

Chapters 3 through 9 are the main part of this book. Each chapter presents a related set of concepts, illustrated by examples written in the one or two working languages of the chapter. The use of two contrasting working languages allows design choices to be explored.

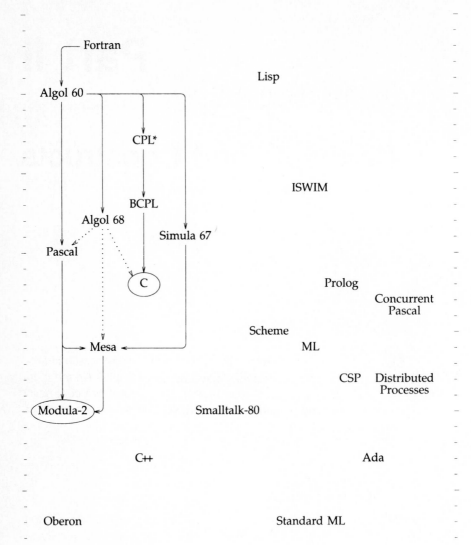

Chapters 3-9 in Part II open with a diagram like the one above, showing the primary influences on the working languages of the chapter. The "tick" marks along the margins mark the passage of time. Dates have deliberately been omitted because the date at which a language appeared could be any time between initial design and actual use.

    Modula-2 and C are the working languages of this chapter. The * next to CPL indicates that it was never fully implemented.

Three

Programming with Assignments

The program fragment

> **while** $x \neq A[i]$ **do**
> $\quad i := i - 1$
> **end**

touches on the three main concepts in this chapter. They are:

1. *Assignments.* Variables like i and x denote locations in an underlying machine. The assignment $i := i - 1$ decrements by one the value in the location for i.

2. *Assignable data structures.* A data structure is *assignable* if it has components whose values can be changed by assignments. An *array* is an assignable data structure, consisting of a sequence of elements or components of the same type. $A[i]$ is the syntax for the ith element of an array A.

3. *Control flow statements.* The flow of control through a program is specified by constructs called *statements.* The keywords **while, do,** and **end** build a while-statement out of the expression $x \neq A[i]$ and the assignment $i := i - 1$. The meaning of statements is examined in this chapter.

The early parts of this chapter use Modula-2 as a vehicle for introducing basic concepts. The subsequent introduction of C allows language design choices to be illustrated.

Modula-2 and C are examples of *imperative* programming languages, which "rebuild" an underlying machine to make it more convenient for programming. The two key words in this sentence are machine and convenience. Machines dictate what imperative languages deal with, and convenience, or ease of programming, motivates the programming style that imperative languages support.

Machines dictate the following principle for language design:

> *Machine model.* A language must allow an underlying assignment-oriented machine to be used directly and efficiently.

The accepted programming style is summed up informally as follows:

> *Structured programming.* The structure of the program text should help us understand what the program does.

3.1   EVOLUTION OF IMPERATIVE LANGUAGES

The development of imperative languages is marked by the occasional appearance of an evolutionary successor under a new name. This section traces how Modula-2 and C developed. The bibliographic notes at the end of this chapter point to the sources of some of the ideas incorporated into these languages.

From Algol 60 to Pascal to Modula-2

Language design in the 1960s was dominated by attempts to improve upon Algol 60. "Here is a language so far ahead of its time, that it was not only an improvement on its predecessors, but also on nearly all its successors," writes Hoare [1973]. Algol started a number of traditions, including the use of BNF notation to specify syntax and the additional use of BNF to organize the reference manual for a language. Yet Algol had limitations. Arrays were its only data structure, and its statement constructs were overly complex.

The sequence of languages designed by Niklaus Wirth, including Pascal and Modula-2, provides a glimpse of the evolution of imperative languages since Algol 60.

- *Algol W.* Wirth and Hoare [1966] note, "A large part of the language is, of course, taken directly from Algol 60." Data-structuring facilities are improved. "The only changes to facilities associated with control of sequencing have been made in the direction of simplification and clarification, rather than extension."

- *Pascal.* Algol W "is a direct predecessor of Pascal, and was the source of many features such as $\cdots$ the while and case statements and of record structures," according to Wirth [1971]. Although there were some syntactic differences, Algol 60 remained enough of a subset that "conversion of Algol 60 programs to Pascal can be considered as a negligible effort of transcription."

- *Modula-2.* Wirth [1983] notes that Modula-2 "includes all aspects of Pascal and extends them with the important module concept. [Modula-2 has] a more systematic syntax which facilitates the learning process. In particular, every structure starting with a keyword also ends with a keyword, i.e. is properly bracketed."

- *Oberon.* Wirth [1988] introduces a new language called Oberon. "However, the adjective 'new' has to be understood in proper context: Oberon evolved from Modula by very few additions and several subtractions. In relying on evolution rather than revolution we remain in the tradition of a long development that led from Algol to Pascal, then to Modula-2, and eventually to Oberon."

This chapter deals with a core shared by Pascal, Modula-2, and Oberon. Modula-2 is one of the two working languages in Chapters 3-5. Until modules are examined in Chapter 5, we stay within the Pascal-like subset of Modula-2. The use of Modula-2 rather than Pascal eases the transition to a discussion of modules, data encapsulation, and overall program structure.

From Algol 60 to BCPL to C

The languages in the family tree of C were the work of many people.

- *CPL.* Strachey [1966] is a collection of working papers on CPL (Combined Programming Language). The language remained a laboratory for studying concepts; it was never fully implemented. "One of the principal aims in designing CPL was to make it a practical application of a logically coherent theory of programming languages." Strachey was later to play a pivotal role in the development of the denotational approach to describing the semantics of programming languages.

- *BCPL.* Richards [1969] developed BCPL (Basic CPL) as a compiler-writing tool. "BCPL adopted much of the syntactic richness of CPL and strived for the same high standard of linguistic elegance; however, in order to achieve the efficiency necessary for system programming its scale and complexity is far less than that of CPL."

- C. C was created in 1972 by Dennis Ritchie as an implementation language for software associated with the UNIX operating system. In 1973, the UNIX system itself was rewritten in C. C provides a rich set of operators, a terse syntax, and efficient access to the machine. It is a general-purpose programming language that is available on a wide range of machines.

- C++. Stroustrup [1986] notes, "In addition to the facilities provided by C, C++ provides flexible and efficient facilities for defining new types." C programs are accepted with little change by C++. The new types in C++ are defined using classes, borrowed from the programming language Simula 67. Classes in C++ are examined in Chapters 5-6.

The major difference between C today and C in 1972 is in the stricter attitude today toward type checking. The type system was extended in 1977 to improve the portability of C programs. A project to move UNIX from one machine to another revealed widespread type-checking violations in programs that worked on one machine, but not on the other. BCPL is typeless and although C added types, it had previously been "rather permissive in allowing dubious mixtures of various types; the most flagrant violations of good practice involved the confusion between pointers and integers" (Johnson and Ritchie [1978]). Type checking now prevents pointers of one type from masquerading as integers or even as pointers of another type.

C++ has a strong type system.

Publication Format for Programs

In a tradition going back to Algol 60, the publication format for programs in this book has keywords in boldface, as in the following Pascal version:

while $x \neq A\,[i\,]$ **do**
　　$i := i-1$ 　　　　　　　　　　　　　　(Pascal, publication format)

Except where complete Modula-2 programs are shown, we use this traditional format. Modula-2 adds a trailing **end** to the Pascal fragment:

while $x \neq A\,[i\,]$ **do**
　　$i := i-1$ 　　　　　　　　　　　　　　(Modula-2, publication format)
end

Boldface keywords transliterate into uppercase letters when Modula-2 programs are written in a typewriter-like font, as in:

```
WHILE x <> A[i] DO
    i := i-1                                        (Modula-2)
END
```

C programs, on the other hand, are usually published in a typewriter-like font. Keywords appear in lowercase letters. A C version of the preceding program fragment is:

```
while( x != A[i] )
    i = i-1;                                            (C)
```

3.2   THE EFFECT OF AN ASSIGNMENT

A characteristic property of an assignment is that it changes a value held inside a machine. This section explores the effect of assignments on a theoretical model of a computer, which responds to a bare but recognizable programming language, consisting primarily of assignments. An assignment changes the state of the machine, where state corresponds roughly to a snapshot of the machine's memory.

The concepts of state, location, and value carry over directly from the model computer to imperative languages. This section also examines the relationship between the static text of a program and the dynamic computations set up by the program.

Random-Access Machines

A *random-access machine* (RAM) has

- a memory,
- a program,
- an input file, and
- an output file.

As in Fig. 3.1, a memory consists of a sequence of locations 0, 1, $\cdots$, each capable of holding a single integer value at a time. A *machine address* is the number of a location in memory. The integer held in a location will be referred to as the *contents* of the location.

A *program* consists of a sequence of *instructions*. The instruction set in Fig. 3.2 has instructions for assignment, input/output, and control flow. Assignments, examined individually in this section, have the form

$$\langle expression \rangle_1 \ := \ \langle expression \rangle_2$$

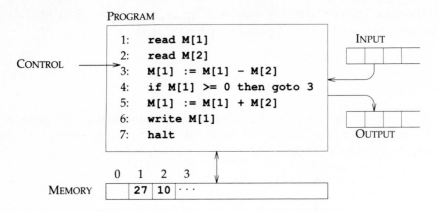

Fig. 3.1. A random-access machine (RAM).

where ⟨*expression*⟩₁ denotes a memory location and ⟨*expression*⟩₂ denotes a value. We call ⟨*expression*⟩₁ the *left side* and ⟨*expression*⟩₂ the *right side* of the assignment.

An *input file* consists of a sequence of values consumed one at a time by instructions of the form

```
read M[l]
```

which gets the next value from the input file and places it in location l.

An *output file* consists of the sequence of values produced one at a time by instructions of the form

```
write M[j]
```

which puts the value from location j into the output file.

Execution of a program begins with the first instruction. Control normally flows from one instruction to the next, except that an instruction

```
if M[j] >= 0 then goto i
```

sends control to instruction i if the value in location j is greater than or equal to 0. The program stops upon executing a

```
halt
```

L-values and *R*-values

The distinction between a location and its contents will be clarified by using the neutral terms *l-value* for a location and *r-value* for a value that can be held in a location. Thus, the *l*-value of **M[j]** is location j and its *r*-value is the value held in location j.

ASSIGNMENTS	`M[`l`]  :=` n
	 `M[`l`]  := M[`j`] + M[`k`]`
	 `M[`l`]  := M[`j`] - M[`k`]`
	 `M[`l`]  := M[M[`j`]]`
	 `M[M[`j`]]  := M[`k`]`

INPUT/OUTPUT	`read M[`l`]` `write M[`j`]`
CONTROL FLOW	`if M[`j`] >= 0 then goto` i `halt`

Fig. 3.2. Instruction set for a random-access machine.

The prefixes *l*- and *r*- are motivated by the two sides of an assignment; an *l*-value is appropriate on the left side and an *r*-value is appropriate on the right side. The effect of an assignment

$$\langle expression \rangle_1 \; := \; \langle expression \rangle_2$$

is therefore to place the *r*-value of $\langle expression \rangle_2$ in the *l*-value of $\langle expression \rangle_1$.

On the left side of an assignment, `M[`l`]` denotes an *l*-value. The instruction

$$\text{M[}l\text{]} \; := \; n$$

places the integer n into location l. In

$$\text{M[}l\text{]} \; := \; \text{M[}j\text{]} + \text{M[}k\text{]}$$

`M[`l`]` on the left side denotes an *l*-value and `M[`j`]` and `M[`k`]` on the right side denote *r*-values. This instruction places the sum of the *r*-values of `M[`j`]` and `M[`k`]` into location l, and

$$\text{M[}l\text{]} \; := \; \text{M[}j\text{]} - \text{M[}k\text{]}$$

places their difference into location l.

Expressions of the form `M[M[`j`]]` are called *indirect* addresses because the *l*-value of `M[M[`j`]]` is found indirectly through location j. Specifically, the *r*-value of `M[`j`]` serves as the *l*-value of `M[M[`j`]]`.

As in Fig. 3.3(a), suppose that location j contains k and that location k contains n. Then the *l*-value of `M[M[`j`]]` is location k and the *r*-value of `M[M[`j`]]` is n. Thus, an instruction

$$\text{M[}l\text{]} \; := \; \text{M[M[}j\text{]]}$$

places into l the contents n of the location k, where k is the *r*-value of `M[`j`]`.

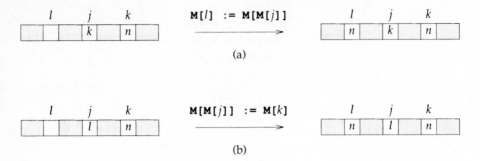

Fig. 3.3. Assignments through indirect addresses.

As in Fig. 3.3(b), an instruction

   M[M[j**]] := M[**k**]**

places the contents n of k into the location l, where l is the r-value of
M[j**]**.[1]

The Dynamic Thread of Control through a Program

A dynamic computation can be visualized as a thread laid down by the
flow of control through the static program text. Imagine program *points*
appearing before the first instruction, between any two adjacent instructions, and after the last instruction. The *thread* of a computation consists of
the sequence of program points that are reached as control flows through
the program text.

   The effect of a computation thread on a RAM will be described by taking snapshots, called *states*. Control-flow information is already included
in the thread, so a state has three parts:

1. a mapping from locations to their contents,
2. the remaining input sequence, and
3. the output sequence produced so far.

Assignment and input/output instructions change the state without
interfering with the normal flow of control from one instruction to the
next. Control-flow instructions direct the thread without changing the
state of the RAM.

---

[1] Although imperative languages are sometimes called von Neumann languages after the
machine described in Section 1.1, a RAM is a more suitable machine model. RAM programs
are static, as are imperative programs. The von Neumann machine, on the other hand,
modifies its program during execution to overcome its lack of indirect addressing.

Example 3.1. The thread of a computation may pass several times through some program points and not at all through others, as we see by examining the program inside the RAM in Fig. 3.1, page 70. (The program has no special significance beyond being short.) Its thread is shown in Fig. 3.4 by writing down instructions in the order they are executed.

When execution begins, the input file contains

    27, 10

the memory locations are all uninitialized, and the output file is empty. The state after execution of an instruction appears on the same line to the right of the instruction in Fig. 3.4.

The first instruction reads **27** from the input file and places it into location 1. Then **10** is read into location 2. Control flows three times through

    3: M[1] := M[1] - M[2]
    4: if M[1] >= 0 goto 3

before reaching instruction 5, and proceeding through the output instruction 6 to a halt.   □

THREAD	STATE			
Instruction	Remaining Input	Location 1	2	Output Produced
	27, 10			
1: `read M[1]`	10	27		
2: `read M[2]`		27	10	
3: `M[1]  := M[1] - M[2]`		17	10	
4: `if M[1] >= 0 goto 3`		17	10	
3: `M[1]  := M[1] - M[2]`		7	10	
4: `if M[1] >= 0 goto 3`		7	10	
3: `M[1]  := M[1] - M[2]`		-3	10	
4: `if M[1] >= 0 goto 3`		-3	10	
5: `M[1]  := M[1] + M[2]`		7	10	
6: `write M[1]`		7	10	7
7: `halt`		7	10	7

Fig. 3.4. A thread through the program in Fig. 3.1.

3.3   STRUCTURED PROGRAMMING

A systematic approach to program design is motivated by examples like the following.

Example 3.2. Bentley [1986] asked more than a hundred professional programmers to convert the following brief description of binary search "into a program in the language of their choice; a high-level pseudocode was fine." He reports, "I was amazed: given ample time, only about ten percent of professional programmers were able to get this small program right."

> We are to determine whether the sorted array $X[1..N]$ contains the element T. Binary search solves the problem by keeping track of the range within the array in which T must be if it is anywhere in the array. Initially, the range is the entire array. The range is shrunk by comparing its middle element to T and discarding half the range. The process continues until T is discovered in the array or until the range in which it must lie is known to be empty.

"Most programmers think that with the above description in hand, writing the code is easy; they're wrong. The only way you'll believe this is by putting down this column right now, and writing the code yourself. Try it."

Column 4 of Bentley [1986] uses binary search to illustrate the development of correct programs.   □

This section explores structured programming, an approach to developing correct and understandable programs. Structured programming grew out of a spirited debate on the merits of control-flow constructs, sparked by a letter by Dijkstra [1968a], entitled "Go to statement considered harmful." A goto statement explicitly sends control to a named program point, as in the machine model of Section 3.2. Dijkstra observed, "The **go to** statement as it stands is just too primitive; it is too much an invitation to make a mess of one's program." Instead, he advocated structured programming, which combines two ideas:

1. *Structured control flow.* A program is said to be *structured* if the flow of control is evident from the syntactic structure of the program text.

2. *Invariants.* An *invariant assertion*, or simply *invariant*, at a point p in a program is an assertion that holds every time control reaches point p. An assertion is a true/false condition about the state of a computation. An example is the condition $x \geq y$, which relates the values of x and y.

After considering statements for writing structured programs, we shall use invariants to guide program development.

Atomic Statements

The simplest statement is the *empty* statement, which does nothing and is represented by the empty string.

Assignment statements have the following form:

$\langle expression \rangle := \langle expression \rangle$

Assignments presume the existence of an underlying machine that is capable of holding several types of basic values, including booleans, characters, integers, and reals. As in Section 3.2, an *l*-value is an area of storage in the machine for holding *r*-values. The *l* in *l*-value comes from the left side of an assignment, and the *r* in *r*-value comes from the right side.

For the moment, arrays are the only data structure. An array supports random access to a sequence of elements of the same type. By random access we mean that elements can be selected by their position in the sequence. An assignment

$x := A[i]$

assigns to x the *r*-value of $A[i]$, the ith element of array A. The assignment

$A[i] := x$

changes the *r*-value of $A[i]$ to that of x.

In addition to assignments, the atomic statements in this chapter can be procedure calls of the form:

$\langle procedure\text{-}name \rangle \; (\; \langle actual\text{-}parameters \rangle \;)$

We treat a procedure call as an instruction or action that could change the state of the underlying machine. The implementation of procedures is studied in Chapter 4.

Structured Control Flow

The following structuring methods for statements are widely supported by imperative languages:

- *Composition.* If $S_1, S_2, \ldots, S_k$ are statements, $k \geq 0$, then their composition is a statement list, written here as

  $S_1; S_2; \cdots ; S_k$

  Control flows sequentially through the list. First S_1 is executed, then S_2, and so on. When k is 0, the statement list is empty.

- *Conditional.* If E is an expression and SL_1 and SL_2 are statement lists, then a conditional statement formed from them is

  if E **then** SL_1 **else** SL_2 **end**

If E evaluates to true, then control flows to SL_1; otherwise control flows to SL_2. Control flows through only one of SL_1 and SL_2. A variant of this statement is

> **if** E **then** SL **end**

with no **else** part. Here SL is executed only if E is true.

- *Loop forever.* If SL is a statement list, then an iteration or loop is

> **loop** SL **end**

The *body* of the loop, SL, is executed repeatedly, forever. Execution of an **exit** statement sends control out of an enclosing **loop** to the statement immediately after the loop.

- *While-loops.* If E is an expression and SL is a statement list, then a while-loop formed from them can be written as

> **while** E **do** SL **end**

The expression E and the statement list SL are evaluated alternately as long as E is true. As soon as E evaluates to false, control flows to the statement immediately after the while-loop.

The flow of control through conditionals and while-loops is shown by arrows in Fig. 3.5. There is an imaginary entry point just before, and an imaginary exit point just after, each statement. The entry and exit points are marked by • in Fig. 3.5; the entry point is at the top.

The above constructs are said to be *single-entry/single-exit* because each construct has a single entry point and a single exit point.

For the moment, think of a statement

> **return** ⟨*expression*⟩

as an atomic statement that brings a program to a halt with the value of ⟨*expression*⟩ as a result.

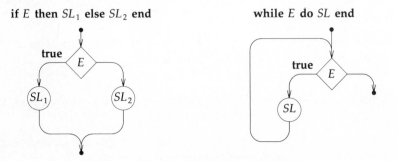

Fig. 3.5. Conditionals and while-loops.

Invariants Bridge Programs and Computations

Some of the difficulty in writing correct code is that correctness is a property not of the static source text we write, but of its dynamic computations—when the program is run it must do such and such. Invariants can help us relate the two. Invariants are attached to a program point and tell us about a property of its computations, so they are a bridge between the static program text and the dynamic thread of a computation.

Consider the single-entry/single-exit statement

$$\textbf{while } x \geq y \textbf{ do}$$
$$\qquad x := x - y; \qquad\qquad\qquad\qquad\qquad\qquad\qquad (3.1)$$
$$\textbf{end}$$

Every time control reaches the assignment $x := x - y$, it must be true that $x \geq y$. Not just the first time, not just the fifth time, but every time control reaches $x := x - y$, no matter what the rest of the program looks like, no matter what state the machine is in, it must be true that $x \geq y$.

We follow the convention of enclosing invariants between braces, { and }. Thus, the invariant $x \geq y$ can be written within the program fragment (3.1) as

$$\textbf{while } x \geq y \textbf{ do}$$
$$\qquad \{ \ x \geq y \ \ \textit{if we get here} \ \}$$
$$\qquad x := x - y; \qquad\qquad\qquad\qquad\qquad\qquad\qquad (3.2)$$
$$\textbf{end}$$

A favorite place for attaching invariants within a while-loop is at the point just before the test E, as in

$$\textbf{while } \ \{ \ \textit{loop invariant} \ \} \ E \textbf{ do } SL \textbf{ end}$$

An invariant attached at the very beginning inside a loop is called a *loop invariant*. A *precondition* for a statement is an invariant attached to a point just before the statement, and a *postcondition* is an invariant attached to a point just after the statement. The fragment (3.2) shows $x \geq y$ as a precondition for the assignment $x := x - y$.

The space between the keyword **while** and the test is an awkward place for a comment or a loop invariant, so we take the syntactic liberty of attaching a redundant word **loop**, as in[2]

$$\textbf{loop while } E \textbf{ do } SL \textbf{ end}$$

Now a loop invariant can be written between **loop** and **while**:

---

[2] This section takes two syntactic liberties with Modula-2. First, comments in Modula-2 are enclosed between (* and *), unlike Pascal, which also allows comments to be enclosed between braces, { and }. Second, Modula-2 expects just **while** instead of **loop while**.

loop
> { $x \geq 0$ **and** $y > 0$ }
> **while** $x \geq y$ **do**   (3.3)
> > $x := x - y$

end

The first time control reaches the loop, suppose that the invariant

> { $x \geq 0$ **and** $y > 0$ }

is true. The test expression $x \geq y$ between **while** and **do** further ensures that $x \geq y$ just before the assignment $x := x - y$. After the assignment, the changed value of x must satisfy $x \geq 0$, so again, the invariant will hold for the next iteration.

Example: Linear Search

Invariants will be used now to develop a small program fragment for linear or sequential search through a table of elements.

A table, organized as in Fig. 3.6, supports two operations, *insert* (x) and *find* (x). Elements are inserted from left to right, starting at position 1, so the inserted elements are $A[1], A[2], \ldots, A[n]$, for $n \geq 0$. (There will soon be a role for position 0.) Operation *find* (x) returns 0 if x is not in the table; otherwise, it returns the position in the table at which x was inserted most recently. The problem is to implement *find* (x).

The notation $A[m..n]$, where $m \leq n$, refers to the subarray consisting of the elements $A[m], A[m+1], \ldots, A[n]$.

Linear search is not a difficult problem, and perhaps the following approach has already come to mind:

> start with the last inserted element
> **while** elements remain to be examined **do**
> > **if** this element is x **then**
> > > **return** its position
> > **else**
> > > consider the element to its left
> > **end**
> **end**
> not found, so **return** 0

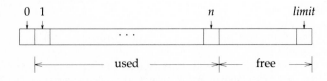

Fig. 3.6. Table organization for linear search with a sentinel.

Filling in the details, the last inserted element is $A[n]$. An element $A[i]$ remains to be examined if it is in the table; that is, if $i \geq 1$. A possible program fragment is

```
i := n ;
while i ≥ 1  do
    if x = A [i] then
        return i ;
    else
        i := i−1;
    end;
end;
return 0;
```

We can do better. Each iteration of this while-loop performs two tests. The first test, $i \geq 1$, stops the search if all elements have been examined. The second, $x = A[i]$, checks whether x is found at position i.

Linear search with a *sentinel* uses a single test to look for x and stop the search. It avoids the test $i \geq 1$ by using an initial assignment $A[0] := x$ to put x in the otherwise-unused position 0 of the array. A search for x will therefore end successfully with x found at some position i within the table, or it will end unsuccessfully with x found at position 0. Let us see how invariants can help to develop the code.

Example 3.3. The postcondition for the search is given by:

do the search;
{ (*x is not in the table*) **or** (*the most recent x is A[i] and* $0 < i \leq n$) }

For ease of comparison, Fig. 3.7 collects the code fragments with which this example deals. The initial code sketch in Fig. 3.7(a) is in three parts: initialization, the search, and a conditional to return a result. A diagram for the postcondition after the search is:

Case: *x is not in the table*   **Case**: *most recent x is A[i]*, $0 < i \leq n$

In both cases, we have

$$x = A[i] \quad \textbf{and} \quad x \text{ is not in } A[i+1..n] \tag{3.4}$$

The key difference between the two cases is in the value of i. If x is not in the table, then the search ends with $i = 0$; otherwise, it ends with $0 < i \leq n$.

Initial Code Sketch

```
initialization;
do the search;
{ (x is not in the table) or (the most recent x is A [i] and 0 < i ≤ n) }
if  x is not in the table  then                                          (a)
     return 0;
else
     return i ;
end
```

Simplify the Computation of the Result

```
initialization;
do the search;                                                           (b)
{ (x is not in the table) or (the most recent x is A [i] and 0 < i ≤ n) }
return i ;
```

Make the Sentinel Explicit

```
A [0] := x ;
further initialization;
loop
     {  x = A [0]  and  x is not in A [i +1..n ]  and  0 ≤ i ≤ n  }
     while  not yet time to stop and x not found at i  do               (c)
          i := i − 1;
end;
{  x = A [i ]  and  x is not in A [i +1..n ]  and  0 ≤ i ≤ n  }
return i ;
```

Final Developed Program Fragment

```
A [0] := x ;
i := n ;
while x ≠ A [i ] do                                                      (d)
     i := i − 1;
end;
return i ;
```

Fig. 3.7. Development of a program for linear search with a sentinel.

Thus, after doing a search, a single return statement suffices, as in the following (repeated in Fig. 3.7(b)):

> initialization;
> do the search;
> { (*x is not in the table*) **or** (*the most recent x is A* [*i*] **and** $0 < i \leq n$) }
> **return** *i* ;

The next program fragment in 3.7(c) incorporates three changes:

1. The sentinel is made explicit by the assignment $A[0] := x$ during initialization.

2. Based on the above diagram and (3.4), the postcondition

   { (*x is not in the table*) **or** (*the most recent x is A* [*i*] **and** $0 < i \leq n$) }

   is written more precisely as

   { $x = A[i]$ **and** *x is not in A* [*i* +1..*n*] **and** $0 \leq i \leq n$ }

3. The backward search from the last element to the first is written as a while-loop.

The search stops if x is found or if we run out of elements; that is, if $x = A[i]$ or if $i = 0$. From the postcondition, these both boil down to $x = A[i]$. Thus, the condition for staying within the while-loop is $x \neq A[i]$, and the completed program fragment is as in Fig. 3.7(d).   □

3.4   DATA TYPES IN MODULA-2

Types in an imperative language are used for

1. error checking and
2. laying out data in the underlying machine.

The emphasis in this section is on checking. For each type, we consider the values and operations associated with the type. Figure 3.8 is a preview of the type constructors in this section. The figure also sketches the data layouts for arrays, records, pointers, and sets.

The type constructors of Modula-2 are typical of those provided by imperative languages.[3] We therefore introduce them together even though the examples in this chapter deal primarily with basic types and arrays.

---

[3] Remarks about data types in Modula-2 apply almost without change to Pascal as well.

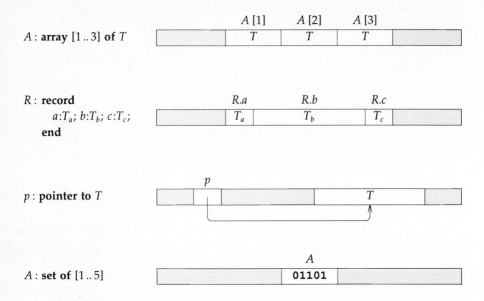

Fig. 3.8. Arrays, records, pointers, and sets in Modula-2.

Type Expressions in Modula-2

A type expression describes the structure of a data type. The simplest expressions are type names like **integer** for integer values. A type expression

   array [1 .. 99] **of integer**

describes an array of 99 integer elements.

   Modula-2 allows type constructors to be applied in any order to build up hierarchically structured data structures. For example, we can build arrays of arrays or arrays of pointers to records, as desired. A type expression describing a pointer to a record is

   pointer to record *re, im* : **real; end**

   A subset of the Modula-2 syntax for type expressions appears in Fig. 3.9, written in EBNF (Extended BNF). Since the details of the Modula-2 syntax appear in Fig. 3.9, the rest of this section can follow the spirit rather than the letter of the syntax. We use BNF notation, writing ⟨*type-expression*⟩ for *TypeExpression,* ⟨*simple-type*⟩ for *SimpleType,* and so on.

> *TypeExpression* ::= *SimpleType*
> | *TypeName*
> | **array** *SimpleType* **of** *TypeExpression*
> | **record** { *Name* { ',' *Name* } ':' *TypeExpression* ';' } **end**
> | **pointer to** *TypeExpression*
> | **set of** *SimpleType*
>
> *SimpleType* ::= *BasicType* | *Enumeration* | *Subrange*
>
> *BasicType* ::= **boolean** | **char** | **cardinal** | **integer** | **real**
>
> *Enumeration* ::= '(' *Name* { ',' *Name* } ')'
>
> *Subrange* ::= [*TypeName*] '[' *ConstantExpression* '..' *ConstantExpression* ']'

Fig. 3.9. Subset of the Modula-2 syntax for type expressions.

Structure of a Modula-2 Program

Some of the examples in this section are drawn from a Modula-2 program outlined in Fig. 3.10.

Execution of a Modula-2 program starts in a so-called program module, which begins with the keyword **module**. The program in Fig. 3.10 consists of a single program module named *calc*. Each module contains optional declarations and a statement list enclosed between **begin** and **end**. Type, constant, variable, and procedure declarations begin with the keywords **type**, **const**, **var**, and **procedure**, respectively.

The outline in Fig. 3.10 uses type expressions in type and variable declarations. The syntax of a type declaration is

type ⟨*name*⟩ = ⟨*type-expression*⟩

The only type declared in Fig. 3.10 is *Token*.

The syntax of a variable declaration is

var ⟨*name*⟩ = ⟨*type-expression*⟩

The variables declared in Fig. 3.10 are *ch*, *tok*, *lookahead*, and *lookvalue*.

As an aside, the excerpt in Fig. 3.10 is from a desk-calculator program to evaluate expressions like

```
(512 − 487) * 2
```

The calculator has three parts:

1. Procedure *scan* to read the input and group it into "tokens."

2. Procedure *expr* to analyze expressions and compute their value.

3. The program module *calc* to collect all the pieces together and to read a sequence of expressions, one per line.

```
module calc ;
    . . .
    type    Token = (eot, eol, lparen, rparen,
                          plus, minus, times, divide, number);

    var     ch  : char;
            tok : array char of Token ;
            lookahead : Token ;
            lookvalue : integer;

    const eotch = 4C ;       (* end-of-transaction, in octal *)
          eolch = 36C ;      (* end-of-line, in octal *)

    procedure scan ();
        . . .
    end scan ;

    procedure expr () : integer;
        . . .
    end expr ;
begin (* calc *)
    tok ['('] := lparen ;  tok [')'] := rparen ;
    tok ['+'] := plus ;    tok ['–'] := minus ;
        . . .
    WriteString ("goodbye"); WriteLn ;
end calc.
```

Fig. 3.10. Outline of an expression evaluator.

Enumerations

An *enumeration* is a finite sequence of names written between parentheses.
The declaration

   type *Token* = (*eot, eol, lparen, rparen, plus, minus, times, divide, number*);

makes *Token* an enumeration with nine elements. Names like *eot* are
treated as constants; a name can appear in at most one enumeration, so on
seeing the constant *eot* in a program, we know that it belongs to type
Token.

   The elements of an enumeration are ordered; that is,
$eot < eol < \cdots < number$. As for other operations, Wirth [1983] simply says,
"Operations on values of such type must be defined by programmer
declared procedures."

Basic Types

Values associated with basic types can typically be manipulated directly by machine instructions.

The basic type **boolean** is treated as the predeclared enumeration

> **type boolean** = (**false, true**);

Similarly, **char** is treated as an enumeration determined by the instruction set of the machine. The widely used ASCII (American Standard Code for Information Interchange) character set has 128 elements. A character constant can be enclosed within either single or double quotes, as in '+' and "*", or it can be specified by its octal position number followed by the letter C. In Fig. 3.10, the constant *eotch* is character 4C (ASCII control-D), and the constant *eolch* is character 36C (the ASCII record-separator character). The standard function **ord** maps a character to its position or ordinal number in a character set.

The values associated with the type **cardinal** in Modula-2 are nonnegative integers 0, 1, 2, . . . , *MaxCard*, and are intended for use in applications where negative values should not occur. Cardinals are implemented as unsigned numbers in the machine.

The values associated with the basic types **integer** and **real** are also determined by the underlying machine, with the largest and smallest numbers determined primarily by the number of bits in a machine word. Predefined constants *MinInt* and *MaxInt* delimit the range of integers supported by an implementation.

The operators of Modula-2 are

> $< \leq = \neq \geq >$ **in**
> $+ -$ **or**
> $*$ / **div mod and**
> **not**

The inequality relation $\neq$ can be typed either as **#** or as **<>**.

All binary operators associate to the left, operators on the same line have equal precedence, and operators on a line have lower precedence than those on successive lines. Thus, + has higher precedence than <, but + also has lower precedence than **and**. The parentheses in

> $(i \geq 0)$ **and** $(x \neq A[i])$

are therefore necessary.

Modula-2 uses short-circuit evaluation for the boolean operators **and** and **or**; that is, the second operand is evaluated only if necessary. In E_1 **and** E_2, if E_1 is false, then the value **false** is returned without evaluating E_2. Similarly, in E_1 **or** E_2, if E_1 is true, then the value **true** is returned without evaluating E_2.

$$<, \leq, =, \neq, \geq, > \; : \quad S \times S \; \rightarrow \; \textbf{boolean}$$

$$+, -, *, / \; : \quad \textbf{real} \times \textbf{real} \; \rightarrow \; \textbf{real}$$

$$+, -, *, \textbf{div}, \textbf{mod} \; : \quad \textbf{integer} \times \textbf{integer} \; \rightarrow \; \textbf{integer}$$

$$+, -, *, \textbf{div}, \textbf{mod} \; : \quad \textbf{cardinal} \times \textbf{cardinal} \; \rightarrow \; \textbf{cardinal}$$

$$\textbf{and, or} \; : \quad \textbf{boolean} \times \textbf{boolean} \; \rightarrow \; \textbf{boolean}$$

$$\textbf{not} \; : \quad \textbf{boolean} \; \rightarrow \; \textbf{boolean}$$

Fig. 3.11. Arguments and results of some operations on basic types.

The operator / is used only for division of reals. The division operator for integers and cardinals is **div**, and **mod** returns the remainder.

Most of the operators in Modula-2 are overloaded; that is, they have more than one type. A little notation from Section 2.7 allows the types of the operators to be stated succinctly. The following notation says that +, −, and * map pairs of integers to an integer:

$$+, -, * \; : \quad \textbf{integer} \times \textbf{integer} \rightarrow \textbf{integer}$$

The corresponding notation

$$+, -, * \; : \quad \textbf{real} \times \textbf{real} \rightarrow \textbf{real}$$

says that +, −, and * also map pairs of reals to a real.

The summary in Fig. 3.11 contains the argument and result types for some of the operations on basic types in Modula-2. Relational operators like < can be applied to any pair of simple types, noted in Fig. 3.11 by writing

$$<, \leq, =, \neq, \geq, > \; : \quad S \times S \rightarrow \textbf{boolean}$$

where S stands for simple type.

Not included in the figure are standard functions that a Modula-2 implementation is expected to supply, such as **ord**, which maps a character to its position in a character set:

$$\textbf{ord} \; : \quad \textbf{character} \rightarrow \textbf{integer}$$

Subranges

The expected range of values for a variable can be shown explicitly by using subrange types. Subranges are also used to declare arrays. The basic syntax of a *subrange* in Modula-2 is

[$\langle constant \rangle_1$ .. $\langle constant \rangle_2$]

where $\langle constant \rangle_1$ and $\langle constant \rangle_2$ are of the same type, and $\langle constant \rangle_1$ is less than $\langle constant \rangle_2$. The values in a subrange denoted by

[*low .. high*]

are *low, low* +1, . . . , *high,* if *low* and *high* are integers.

The operations on subranges are the same as those on the underlying type; that is, on the type from which the subrange is drawn. A leading type name, as in

integer [0 .. 9]

explicitly specifies the underlying type; the default underlying type for a subrange of positive integers is **cardinal**.

Arrays

The declaration of an array specifies the index of the first and last elements of the array and the type of all the elements. A type expression for an array has the form

array $\langle simple\text{-}type \rangle$ **of** $\langle type\text{-}expression \rangle$

where $\langle type\text{-}expression \rangle$ gives the type of the array elements and $\langle simple\text{-}type \rangle$ is typically a subrange of the form [*low .. high*]. Here *low* is called the *lower bound* of the array and *high* is called the *upper bound.* Index values in a subrange [*low .. high*] correspond directly to a consecutive sequence of *l*-values for the array elements.

After the declaration

var *tok* : **array char of** *Token* ;

we can use characters to index into array *tok,* as in the assignment

tok ['+'] := *plus*

Records

The components of a record are called *fields.* Field names are referred to variously as *field identifiers,* selectors, or member names. In C, records are called *structures* and fields are called *members.*

A type expression for a record with k fields can have the following form:

record
    $\langle name \rangle_1 : \langle type\text{-}expression \rangle_1;$
    $\langle name \rangle_2 : \langle type\text{-}expression \rangle_2;$
       . . .
    $\langle name \rangle_k : \langle type\text{-}expression \rangle_k;$
end

Here $\langle name \rangle_i$ is the name of field i and $\langle type\text{-}expression \rangle_i$ is the type of field i. Each field within a record has its own distinct name. Declarations of fields with the same type can be combined—see the declarations of fields *re* and *im* in

> **type** *complex* = **record** *re, im* : **real; end**

A change in the order of the fields of a record should have no effect on the meaning of a program.

A type declaration does not allocate any storage; allocation occurs only in connection with variable declarations. The record type *complex* is therefore simply a template with two fields called *re* and *im*. The type can later be used in a variable declaration, as in

> **var** *x, y, z* : *complex*

If expression E denotes a record with a field named f, then the field itself is denoted by $E.f$. As usual, $E.f$ has both an *l*-value and an *r*-value. In

> $z.re := x.re + y.re$

the sum of the *r*-values of fields *x.re* and *y.re* is placed in the *l*-value of *z.re*.

Comparison of Arrays and Records

An array is a homogeneous collection of elements; that is, all elements have the same type. So the type of $A[i]$ is known at compile time, even though the actual element denoted by $A[i]$ depends on the value of i at run time.

A record is a heterogeneous collection of elements; that is, each element can have a different type. Record components are selected by names that are known at compile time, so the type of the selected component is also known at compile time. The name f in an expression $E.f$ uniquely determines a field, so the type of $E.f$ is the type of the field named f. Component selection in arrays and records is compared in Fig. 3.12.

COMPONENT	TYPE CONSTRUCTOR	
	array	**record**
Types	homogeneous	heterogeneous
Selectors	expressions evaluated at run time	names known at compile time

Fig. 3.12. Comparison between arrays and records.

Pointers

A pointer provides indirect access to elements of a known type. If p is a pointer to an object of type T, then $p\uparrow$ denotes the object itself. The operator $\uparrow$ is called the pointer *dereferencing* operator.

Pointers are implemented as indirect machine addresses, similar to the indirect addresses in the instruction set of the random-access machine in Section 3.2.

Sets

If a variable A has type **set of** S, where S is a simple type, then A represents subsets of S. For example, consider

> **var** A : **set of** $[1 .. 3]$

A can denote one of the following sets:

> $\{\,\}, \{1\}, \{2\}, \{3\}, \{1, 2\}, \{1, 3\}, \{2, 3\}, \{1, 2, 3\}$

Since these are all the subsets of $\{1, 2, 3\}$, the type **set of** S in Modula-2 and Pascal should perhaps be called "subset of S."

The basic operation on sets is a membership test. Operation **in** tests if an element x belongs to a set A.

A set of n elements is implemented as a bit vector of length n. For this reason, the **set of** type constructor is applied only to subranges of consecutive elements. Since the bit vector must typically fit in a word, an implementation is allowed to impose a limit, say 16 or 32, on the maximum number of elements in a set, thereby restricting the usefulness of sets.

Bit vectors allow the following operations on sets to be implemented efficiently, by using bit-wise operations in the underlying machine:

> $A + B$ set union $A \cup B$
> $-$ set difference $A - B = \{ x \mid x \in A \textbf{ and } x \notin B \}$
> $*$ set intersection $A \cap B$
> $/$ symmetric difference $(A - B) \cup (B - A)$

Sets can be compared using the relational operators $\leq, =, \neq, \geq$, where $\leq$ is interpreted as subset and $\geq$ is interpreted as superset. Note, however, that the operations $<$ and $>$ are not allowed.

3.5   CONTROL FLOW IN MODULA-2

This section extends the description of the statement constructs in Section 3.3 to cover statements in Modula-2. The syntax of statements in Modula-2 is shown in Fig. 3.13 using EBNF notation because several of the constructs have optional elements that seem geared to EBNF. Note that [ ] represents the empty string. The following abbreviations allow the syntax of each construct to fit on one line:

S	for	Statement
SL	for	StatementList
E	for	Expression

Again, the rest of this section follows the spirit rather than the letter of the Modula-2 syntax.

Conditionals: Sequential Choice

The general form of a conditional in Modula-2 is

> **if** $\langle expression \rangle_1$ **then** $\langle statement\text{-}list \rangle_1$
> **elsif** $\langle expression \rangle_2$ **then** $\langle statement\text{-}list \rangle_2$
> $\qquad\qquad\quad \cdots$
> **elsif** $\langle expression \rangle_n$ **then** $\langle statement\text{-}list \rangle_n$
> **else** $\langle statement\text{-}list \rangle_{n+1}$
> **end**

The keyword **elsif** is made up from **else** and **if**. The **elsif** and **else** parts are optional; that is,

$$
\begin{aligned}
S ::= &\ [\,] \\
 | &\ Lvalue \ ':=' \ E \\
 | &\ ProcedureCall \\
 | &\ \textbf{if} \ E \ \textbf{then} \ SL \ \{ \ \textbf{elsif} \ E \ \textbf{then} \ SL \ \} \ [\ \textbf{else} \ SL \ ] \ \textbf{end} \\
 | &\ \textbf{case} \ E \ \textbf{of} \ Case \ \{ \ ' \ | \ ' \ Case \ \} \ [\ \textbf{else} \ SL \ ] \ \textbf{end} \\
 | &\ \textbf{loop} \ SL \ \textbf{end} \\
 | &\ \textbf{while} \ E \ \textbf{do} \ SL \ \textbf{end} \\
 | &\ \textbf{repeat} \ SL \ \textbf{until} \ E \\
 | &\ \textbf{for} \ Name \ ':=' \ E \ \textbf{to} \ E \ [\ \textbf{by} \ E \ ] \ \textbf{do} \ SL \ \textbf{end} \\
 | &\ \textbf{exit} \\
 | &\ \textbf{return} \ [\ E \ ]
\end{aligned}
$$

$$SL ::= S \ \{ \ ';' \ S \ \}$$

$$Case ::= [\ CaseLabel \ \{ \ ',' \ CaseLabel \ \} \ ':' \ SL \ ]$$
$$CaseLabel ::= ConstantExpression \ [\ '..' \ ConstantExpression \ ]$$

Fig. 3.13. EBNF syntax of statements in Modula-2.

> **if** ⟨*expression*⟩₁ **then** ⟨*statement-list*⟩₁
> **end**

is the simplest form of a conditional.

Looping Constructs

Looping constructs can be divided roughly into two groups, depending on whether or not we can predict the number of times the loop will be executed. A *definite* iteration is executed a predetermined number of times. By contrast, the number of executions of an *indefinite* iteration is not known when control reaches the loop; the number is determined by the course of the computation.

The following constructs set up indefinite iterations:

> **while** ⟨*expression*⟩ **do** ⟨*statement-list*⟩ **end**
> **repeat** ⟨*statement-list*⟩ **until** ⟨*expression*⟩

In each of these loops, the statements in ⟨*statement-list*⟩ will be referred to as the *body* of the loop.

Suppose that procedure *getch* () reads the next input character into variable *ch*. The postcondition for the following while-loop is that *ch* must be a nonblank character:

> **while** *ch* = ' ' **do** *getch* (); **end**;

The effect of **repeat** *SL* **until** *E* is: Do *SL*, test *E*, do *SL*, test *E*, and so on, until *E* evaluates to true, whereupon control leaves the statement. The meaning of the statement **repeat** *SL* **until** *E* is therefore given by

> *SL* ; **while not** *E* **do** *SL* **end**

Similarly, the meaning of **while** *E* **do** *SL* **end** can be given using a conditional and a repeat-until statement, as follows:

> **if** *E* **then repeat** *SL* **until not** *E* **end**

Example 3.4. In the ASCII character set, '0' is the 48th character, '1' is the 49th character, and so on. Suppose that procedure *digitval* returns the value represented by a digit character; that is, zero for '0', one for '1', through nine for '9'. The following program fragment reads a sequence of digit characters and collects their value in variable *lookvalue*:

(* *ch holds a digit character at this point* *)

lookvalue := 0;
repeat
    lookvalue := *lookvalue*∗10 + *digitval* (*ch*);
    getch ();
until not (*isdigit* (*ch*));

Control leaves the loop when *isdigit* (*ch*) evaluates to false.

Suppose that *ch* holds '5' when control reaches the program fragment and that successive calls of *getch* () read '1', '2', and ' ' into *ch*. Then, *lookvalue* takes on the values 0, 5, 51, and 512. Control leaves the loop with *lookvalue* holding 512 and *ch* holding a blank ' '.   □

Definite Iteration: For Each Element Do

The simple form of the **for** statement in Modula-2 is

    for ⟨*name*⟩ := ⟨*expression*⟩ **to** ⟨*expression*⟩ **do** ⟨*statement-list*⟩ **end**

For example,

    for *i* := 1 **to** *limit* **do** *A* [*i*] := 0; **end**

The assignment *A* [*i*] := *x* is executed with *i* taking on the values 1, 2, . . . , *limit* on successive executions; that is, *i* is incremented by 1 for the next execution.

The general form of the **for** statement in Modula-2 is:

    for ⟨*name*⟩ := ⟨*expression*⟩ **to** ⟨*expression*⟩ **by** ⟨*constant-expression*⟩ **do**
        ⟨*statement-list*⟩
    end

The constant expression specifies the amount by which the variable is incremented for the next execution of the statement list.

Linear search without a sentinel can be implemented by using a for-statement to step backwards through an array, coupled with a **return** statement that is executed if the desired element *x* is found:

    for *i* := *n* **to** 1 **by** −1 **do**
        if *x* = *A* [*i*] **then return** *i* ;
        end;
    end

Case Statements

A case statement uses the value of an expression to select one of several substatements for execution. The elements of a case statement can be seen from the following. Note that the vertical bars are part of the syntax.

> **case** ⟨*expression*⟩ **of**
> ⟨*constant*⟩$_1$: ⟨*statement-list*⟩$_1$ ' | '
> ⟨*constant*⟩$_2$: ⟨*statement-list*⟩$_2$ ' | '
>   . . .
>
> ⟨*constant*⟩$_n$: ⟨*statement-list*⟩$_n$
> **else**
>   ⟨*statement-list*⟩$_{n+1}$
> **end**

Execution begins with the evaluation of ⟨*expression*⟩. If its value equals that of one of the constants, say ⟨*constant*⟩$_i$, then control flows to the corresponding ⟨*statement-list*⟩$_i$; otherwise, ⟨*statement-list*⟩$_{n+1}$ is executed. An **else** part is optional in a case statement. After execution of the selected substatement, control leaves the case statement.

Case statements vary from language to language, but they tend to agree on the following points:

- Case constants can appear in any order.

- Case constants need not be consecutive. It is legal to have cases for 1 and 3 without a case for 2.

- Several case constants can select the same substatement.

- Case constants must be distinct. Otherwise, if ⟨*constant*⟩$_i$ and ⟨*constant*⟩$_j$ above are equal, should control go to ⟨*statement*⟩$_i$ or to ⟨*statement*⟩$_j$? This ambiguity is avoided if no two constants are equal.

Differences between case statements in various languages lie mainly in the facilities for specifying cases. The facilities provided by Modula-2 can be seen from the statement in Fig. 3.14.

Several case constants may select the same statement list, as in the cases for the characters *eotch, eolch*, . . . , '/'. Modula-2 is one of the few languages to allow ranges like '0'..'9' to appear as case constants. The alternative of writing out '0'..'9' in full,

> '0', '1', '2', '3', '4', '5', '5', '7', '8', '9' : *lookvalue* := 0;

is error-prone (look at the list again, carefully). Fifty-two constants, for the lowercase and uppercase letters, would be needed if '*a*'..'*z*', '*A*'..'*Z*' were written out in full.

```
case ch of
eotch, eolch, '(', ')',
'+', '−', '*', '/':
            lookahead := tok [ch ]; ch := ' '; return;  |
'0'..'9' :
            lookvalue := 0;
            repeat
                  lookvalue := lookvalue*10 + digitval (ch);
                  getch ();
            until (ch < '0') or (ch > '9');
            lookahead := number ; return;
else
            WriteString (" lexical error, saw "); Write (ch);
            WriteLn ; getch ();
end;
```

Fig. 3.14. A case statement from a lexical analyzer.

Exits from Loops

From Section 3.3, the body of

> **loop** ⟨*statement-list*⟩ **end**

is executed repeatedly. Execution of an **exit** statement within the loop, however, sends control out of the immediately enclosing loop.

Execution of a statement

> **return** ⟨*expression*⟩

sends control back from a procedure to a caller, carrying the value of ⟨*expression*⟩. If the **return** statement is not in a procedure, then the program halts.

Extracts from a Modula-2 Program

The extracts in Fig. 3.15 and 3.16 are from a desk-calculator program. The case statement, in darker type, on lines 25-39, is from Fig. 3.14.

Procedure *scan* is a lexical analyzer, which reads a sequence of characters and groups them into tokens. Examples of tokens are numbers, operators, keywords, and identifiers. Each time *scan* is called, the loop on lines 22-40 is executed. The while-loop on lines 23-24 skips over blanks in the input.

The case statement on lines 25-39 isolates the next token in the input and holds it in variable *lookahead* of enumerated type *Token*. Type *Token* is declared on lines 4-5 of Fig. 3.16; *lookahead* is declared on line 8.

If the next input character *ch* is '+' then the case statement assigns constant *plus* to *lookahead*. More precisely, the assignment

```
(12)    PROCEDURE scan();
(13)      PROCEDURE getch();
(14)      BEGIN
(15)        Read(ch); Write(ch);
(16)      END getch;
(17)      PROCEDURE digitval(c : CHAR) : INTEGER;
(18)      BEGIN
(19)        RETURN ORD(c) - ORD('0');
(20)      END digitval;
(21)    BEGIN (* scan *)
(22)      LOOP
(23)        WHILE ch = ' ' DO getch();
(24)        END;
(25)        CASE ch OF
(26)        eotch, eolch, '(', ')',
(27)        '+', '-', '*', '/':
(28)          lookahead := tok[ch]; ch := ' '; RETURN; |
(29)        '0'..'9' :
(30)          lookvalue := 0;
(31)          REPEAT
(32)            lookvalue := lookvalue*10 + digitval(ch);
(33)            getch();
(34)          UNTIL (ch < '0') OR (ch > '9');
(35)          lookahead := number; RETURN;
(36)        ELSE
(37)          WriteString("lexical error, saw "); Write(ch);
(38)          WriteLn; getch();
(39)        END;
(40)      END;
(41)    END scan;
```

Fig. 3.15. A lexical analyzer from an expression evaluator.

$lookahead := tok[ch]$

is executed. Elsewhere, *tok* ['+'] is initialized to *plus*.

If the next input character is a digit, then lines 30-34 accumulate its value in variable *lookvalue*.

If the next input character is neither an operator, *eotch*, *eolch*, nor a digit, then the **else** part on lines 36-38 writes an error message, skips the character, and leaves the case statement. Control then flows back to **loop** on line 22.

Program module *calc* appears in Fig. 3.16. Lines 2-3 "import" procedures *Read* and *Write* for characters, *WriteLn* to write a "newline" charac-

```
(1)  MODULE calc;
(2)    FROM InOut IMPORT Read, Write, WriteLn, WriteString;
(3)                           WriteInt;
(4)    TYPE Token = (eot, eol, lparen, rparen,
(5)                    plus, minus, times, divide, number);
(6)    VAR  ch  : CHAR;
(7)         tok : ARRAY CHAR OF Token;
(8)         lookahead : Token;
(9)         lookvalue : INTEGER;
(10)   CONST eotch =  4C;
(11)         eolch = 36C;

     ...

(88) BEGIN (* calc *)
(89)   tok['('] := lparen;  tok[')'] := rparen;
(90)   tok['+'] := plus;    tok['-'] := minus;
(91)   tok['*'] := times;   tok['/'] := divide;
(92)   tok[eolch] := eol;
(93)   tok[eotch] := eot;
(94)   WriteString("Expression evaluator:"); WriteLn;
(95)   ch := ' ';
(96)   scan();
(97)   LOOP
(98)     IF lookahead = eol THEN
(99)       scan();
(100)    ELSIF lookahead = eot THEN
(101)      EXIT;
(102)    ELSE
(103)      WriteInt(expr(), 1); WriteLn;
(104)      IF lookahead <> eol THEN
(105)        WriteString("expected new line"); WriteLn; scan();
(106)      END;
(107)    END;
(108)  END;
(109)  WriteString("goodbye"); WriteLn;
(110) END calc.
```

Fig. 3.16. Program module **calc**.

ter, and *WriteString* and *WriteInt* to write strings and integers, respectively. Unfortunately, Modula-2 implementations support different "standard" input/output procedures, so we pass over these procedures without comment.

The program as it appears in Fig. 3.16 presumes the use of the ASCII character set. Before such a program can be run, the constants *eotch* and *eolch* will probably need to be changed to conform to the conventions of the local input/output procedures. Alternative possibilities for the value of *eolch* are 12C, the ASCII line-feed character, and 15C, the ASCII carriage-return character. Another assumption built into procedure *scan* is that the characters for the digits are in consecutive positions in the character set, with $'0' < '1' < \cdots < '9'$.

3.6 CONTROL FLOW IN C

The statement constructs of C generalize those seen so far in this chapter, with one exception: Subranges are not allowed as case labels in case-statements, called **switch** statements in C. This section uses a sequence of small examples to illustrate statements in C (see Fig. 3.17 for their syntax). As in Section 3.5, examples are drawn from programs for lexical analysis and string matching, which often have complex control flow.

Introduction to C

The basic types of C include

char	characters
int	integers
unsigned int	integers, with arithmetic modulo 2^n
float	real
double	double-precision real

but they do not include booleans. In tests, a nonzero value is treated as **true** and 0 is treated as **false**.

The assignment operator is **=**, the equality-test operator is **==**, and the inequality test operator is **!=**. The following statement, taken from the program developed in Example 3.3, page 79, is a linear search for **x** in array **A**:

```
while( x != A[i] )
    i = i-1;
```

Test expressions in while-loops and conditionals must be enclosed within parentheses. C dispenses with keywords such as **begin**, **do**, **then**, and **end**; a sequence of statements is grouped by enclosing it within braces, **{** and **}**.

C provides a special increment operator, **++**, and a special decrement operator, **−−**. When applied to integer variables, these operators change the value of the variable by 1. Thus, the above while-loop could be written as

⟨*statement*⟩ ::= ;
        | ⟨*expression*⟩ ;
        | { ⟨*stmt-list*⟩ }
        | **if** (⟨*expression*⟩) ⟨*statement*⟩
        | **if** (⟨*expression*⟩) ⟨*statement*⟩ **else** ⟨*statement*⟩
        | **while** (⟨*expression*⟩) ⟨*statement*⟩
        | **do** ⟨*statement*⟩ **while** (⟨*expression*⟩) ;
        | **for** (⟨*opt-expr*⟩ ; ⟨*opt-expr*⟩ ; ⟨*opt-expr*⟩ ;) ⟨*statement*⟩
        | **switch** (⟨*expression*⟩) ⟨*statement*⟩
        | **case** ⟨*constant-expression*⟩ : ⟨*statement*⟩
        | **default** : ⟨*statement*⟩
        | **break** ;
        | **continue** ;
        | **return** ;
        | **return** ⟨*expression*⟩ ;
        | **goto** ⟨*label-name*⟩ ;
        | ⟨*label-name*⟩ : ⟨*statement*⟩

⟨*stmt-list*⟩ ::= ⟨*empty*⟩
      | ⟨*stmt-list*⟩ ⟨*statement*⟩

⟨*opt-expr*⟩ ::= ⟨*empty*⟩
      | ⟨*expression*⟩

Fig. 3.17. Syntax of statements in C.

```
while( x != A[i] )
    --i;
```

The test expression in a do-while-loop is evaluated after the statement is executed. The statement

```
do ++i; while( A[i] > v );
```

increments **i** and then tests whether **A[i] > v**. If so, control returns for another iteration of the do-while-loop.

C uses short-circuit evaluation for the boolean operators **&&** and **||**, corresponding to **and** and **or**, respectively. Both operands are evaluated by **&** and **|**, the bit-wise "and" and "or" operators. In the following while-loop, control reaches the test **c=='\n'** only if **c==' '** is false and **c=='\t'** is also false:

```
while( c==' ' || c=='\t' || c=='\n' ) {
    if( c == '\n' )
        ++lineno;                                           (3.5)
    c = getchar();
}
```

Here `'\t'` represents a tab character and `'\n'` represents a newline character. The standard procedure **getchar()** returns the next character in the input. This program skips over consecutive blank, tab, and newline characters, and keeps track of line numbers by incrementing variable **lineno** every time a newline character is seen.

Assignment Operators

C allows assignments to appear within expressions. An expression $E_1 = E_2$ is evaluated by placing the r-value of E_2 into the l-value of E_1. The value of $E_1 = E_2$ is the value assigned to the left side E_1. Thus, the expression

```
c = getchar()                                               (3.6)
```

assigns to **c** the input character read by **getchar()**. The value assigned to **c** also becomes the value of (3.6), so (3.6) can appear as a subexpression within a larger expression:

```
(c = getchar()) != EOF                                      (3.7)
```

Constant **EOF**, from "end of file," signifies the end of the input, so this expression reads a value using **getchar**, saves the value by assigning it to **c**, and then tests if the value equals the constant **EOF**. Such expressions are sometimes used as tests in while loops. The following statement reads and writes characters until the end of file is reached.

```
while( (c = getchar()) != EOF )
    putchar(c);                                             (3.8)
```

The standard procedure **putchar** writes a character. Alternatively, the effect of this statement can be achieved by:

```
while( 1 ) {
    c = getchar();
    if( c == EOF ) break;
    putchar(c);
}
```

A nonzero expression is treated as true, so this while-loop is an infinite loop that control leaves through the **break** statement.

Assignments within expressions are also needed to set up for-loops in C. The **for** statement has the form

```
for( E₁; E₂; E₃ ) S
```

E_1 is evaluated just before loop entry, E_2 is the condition for staying within the loop, and E_3 is evaluated just before every next iteration of the loop. Both E_1 and E_3 can have assignments within them, so E_1 can be used for initialization and E_3 can be used to prepare for the next iteration.

A sequence of assignments can be combined into one expression, using the comma operator in C. A sequence of expressions separated by commas

```
E , F
```

is evaluated from left to right; the value of the sequence is the value of the last expression.

The following program fragment is a linear search with a sentinel:

```
for( A[0]=x, i=n; x != A[i]; --i )
    ;
return i;
```

The body of this for-loop is an empty statement. An equivalent program fragment is

```
A[0] = x;
i = n;
while( x != A[i] )
    --i;
return i;
```

The expressions E_1, E_2, and E_3 are optional in

```
for( E₁; E₂; E₃ ) S
```

A missing E_2 is taken to be true, so **for(;;)** can be read as "forever"; it sets up an infinite loop.

Break and Continue Statements in Loops

Break and continue statements in C facilitate the handling of special cases in loops:

- A **break** statement sends control out of the enclosing loop to the statement following the loop.

- A **continue** statement repeats the enclosing loop by sending control to its beginning.

The name "break" descends from CPL into C; Modula-2 uses the name "exit," although **exit** statements can be used only within a **loop-end** in Modula-2.

As noted in Section 3.3, a loop invariant is an assertion that is true every time control reaches the beginning of a loop; a postcondition is an assertion that is true when control leaves a statement. A break statement can be used to jump out of a loop after establishing the postcondition for the loop, and a continue statement can be used to restart the loop after reestablishing the loop invariant.

One use of break statements is to break out of a loop after handling a special case, as in

```
while( E ) {
    if( special case ) {
        take care of the special case;
        break;
    }
    handle the normal cases;
}
```

This organization is convenient if the code for the special case is short. Attention can then be focused on the code for the normal case with the assurance that the special case cannot occur.

A corresponding fragment for continue statements is

```
while( E ) {
    if( normal case ) {
        handle the normal case;
        continue;
    }
    take care of the special cases;
}
```

The continue statement in this outline ensures that control flows back to the beginning of the loop immediately after taking care of the normal case.

A more mundane reason for using break and continue statements is to reduce indentation of the source text; that is, to reduce blank space at the beginning of a line. The preceding fragment can be rewritten without a continue statement as

```
while( E ) {
    if( normal case ) {
        handle the normal case;
    }
    else {
        take care of the special cases;
    }
}
```

The code for taking care of the special case now appears indented within an else clause. Nested conditionals in this code can lead to further indentation to the point where the code crowds the right margin of a page.

Execution of a continue statement within the loop body S in

$$\text{for(}\ E_1\ ;\ E_2\ ;\ E_3\ )\ S$$

is equivalent to reaching the end of the statement S. In either case, expression E_3 is executed to set up the next iteration.

The following program fragment illustrates the use of continue statements within for-loops:

```
for( ; ; c = getchar() ) {
    if( c==' ' || c=='\t' )
        continue;
    if( c != '\n' )                                    (3.9)
        break;
    ++lineno;
}
```

If **c** equals a blank or a tab, the **continue** statement restarts the loop after executing **c=getchar()**. If **c** does not equal a newline character, then control leaves the loop through the **break** statement. Otherwise, **lineno** is incremented and the loop restarts after the call **c=getchar()**. Program fragment (3.9) compares **c** with ' **\n**' just once, unlike (3.5), which compares **c** with ' **\n**' twice per execution of the loop body.

Goto Statements

A statement **goto** L interrupts the normal flow of control from one statement to the next in sequence; control flows instead to the statement labeled L somewhere in the program. Label L is typically attached to a statement by writing

$L:$ ⟨statement⟩

By itself, **goto** L gives no indication of where label L is to be found. Similarly, by itself, the labeled statement $L : \langle statement \rangle$ does not indicate from where control might come to it.

Although **goto** statements can be misused to write unreadable programs, there is still a need for them. An algorithm for generating subprograms may introduce goto statements that a person might not. Programs are not always written by people.

Implementation of Case Statements

Except for case statements, the implementation of statement constructs can be ignored because imperative languages translate them directly and efficiently into machine code. The translation of while-loops in Fig. 3.18 evaluates the expression E, and if it is false, jumps out of the loop; otherwise, the statements in the body are executed, and a jump takes control back to reevaluate the expression.

Wirth [1983] recommends that a case-statement in Modula-2 "should only be used in situations where the values occurring as case labels are essentially adjacent." He recommends that case statements should not be used with the case constants in Fig. 3.19(a); instead, the conditional in Fig. 3.19(b) should be used.

C compilers, on the other hand, encourage the use of the corresponding switch-statements. The code generated for a switch-statement depends on the distribution of case constants. One compiler considers three possibilities:

1. A small number of cases (say less than seven) is implemented using conditionals. The code therefore looks like the following: If the first condition is true then do the first substatement, else if the second condition is true then do the second substatement, and so on.

2. For a larger number of cases, the range in which the constants appear is checked to see if an array constituting a "jump table" can be used.

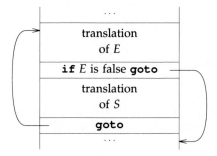

Fig. 3.18. Translation of **while(** E **)** S into target code.

case E of	$n := E$;
1 : SL_1 |	if $n = 1$ then SL_1
11 : SL_2 |	elsif $n = 11$ then SL_2
121 : SL_3	elsif $n = 121$ then SL_3
else SL_4	else SL_4
end	end
(a)	(b)

Fig. 3.19. In Modula-2, fragment (b) is recommended over fragment (a).

Entry i in the jump table is a machine instruction that sends control to the code for case i. The value of the expression becomes an index into the jump table, so selection of each case occurs efficiently by indexing into the table and then jumping to the code for the case. If the smallest constant is *min* and the largest is *max*, then the jump table has *max–min*+1 entries. Of course, only the entries for the case constants that actually appear are used. The compiler in question uses a jump table if at least half the entries will be used.

3. Finally, if the number of cases is large enough, and if too many entries in a jump table would remain unused, the compiler uses a hash table to find the code for the selected substatement.

3.7 DATA TYPES IN C

Rather than review all the data types and operations of C, this section examines two differences between C and Modula-2: coercions between characters and integers, and operations on pointers.

Syntax for Declarations

Declarations in C begin with a type name and declare a sequence of names. For example,

```
int i, j;
```

declares **i** and **j** to be integer variables. An array is declared by writing its size after the name, as in

```
int A[3], B[5][7];
```

A is an array of three integers and **B** is an array of five arrays of seven integers. Zero is the lower bound of all arrays, so the three elements of **A** are **A[0]**, **A[1]**, and **A[2]**.

A pointer to an integer is declared by writing ***** before the variable name, as in the following declaration of **p**, a pointer to an integer:

```
int *p;
```

The relationship between arrays and pointers is explored later in this section.

Characters and Integers in C

The following is a complete program from Chapter 1 of Kernighan and Ritchie [1988], a definitive book on C. Although the program reads characters from its input, and writes them to its output, the only declaration says that **c** denotes integers, not characters. Why?

```
#include <stdio.h>
main() {
    int c;
    while( (c = getchar()) != EOF )
        putchar(c);
}
```

The first line allows the program to use the standard input/output library, which defines the integer constant **EOF**. The value of **EOF** is different from the value of any character. Function **getchar** returns **EOF** if there are no more characters to be read; that is, when the end of the input file is reached. Declaring **c** to be an integer allows it to take on the integer value of **EOF**.

As noted in Section 2.7, a coercion is an automatic conversion from one type to another. C coerces characters into integers, as in Fig. 3.20. The standard Modula-2 procedure **ord** can be used to specify a similar explicit conversion.

The programming style that develops around a language is influenced by details like coercions between characters and integers and the efficiency with which case statements are implemented. Compare, for example, the corresponding Modula-2 and C program fragments in Fig. 3.21. The case constants *number* and *plus* in the Modula-2 fragment are elements of an enumerated type *Token* (as in the outline of module *calc* in Fig. 3.10, page 84). On the other hand, the case constants **NUMBER** and **'+'** in the C frag-

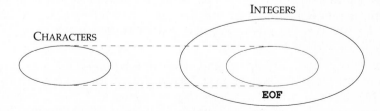

Fig. 3.20. Coercion of characters into integers in C.

```
case lookahead of              switch(lookahead) {
number :                       case NUMBER:
    temp := lookvalue ; scan ();     temp = lookvalue; scan();
    return temp ;  |                 return temp;
plus :                         case '+' :
    scan ();                         scan();
    temp := expr ();                 temp = expr();
    return temp + expr ();  |        return temp + expr();
    . . .                            . . .

end                            }
```

Fig. 3.21. Corresponding statements from Modula-2 and C, respectively.

ment are integers (the character '+' is coerced to an integer). The direct use of characters like '+' in the C fragment simplifies the lexical analyzer, which does not need to convert characters into a different type.[4]

Arrays and Pointers in C

The rest of this section considers a stylized use of pointers to maintain a table of variable-length strings—lexical analyzers use such tables to hold keywords and names. Note that the following discussion concentrates on the positive aspects of pointers, rather than on problems associated with them. For balance, see also the more complete discussion of pointers in Section 4.8.

The example we now consider is motivated by the TEX typesetting program, which uses two arrays, *pool* and *start*, to hold character strings like

```
TeX
troff
Scribe
```

The individual characters in a string are kept in array *pool*, as in Fig. 3.22. Elements of the other array, *start*, point to the first character of each string.

Element *start* [s] is the index of the first character of string s. In Fig. 3.22, *start* [0]=0 is the index of **T**, the first character of **TeX**, *start* [1]=3 is the index of **t**, the first character of **troff**, and so on. That is,

[4] The use of an enumerated type for tokens in the Modula-2 fragment is motivated by the parser in Wirth [1976], and the direct use of characters in the C fragment follows the conventions of the Yacc parser generator (Johnson [1975]). Although the Modula-2 **ord** procedure, which maps characters to integers, can be used to simulate the C approach, case labels would then be widely separated; the use of an enumerated type ensures that case labels stay within a narrow range.

	0	1	2	3	
start	0	3	8	14	

	0	1	2	3	4	5	6	7	8	9	10	11	12	13	14	15
pool	T	e	X	t	r	o	f	f	S	c	r	i	b	e		

Fig. 3.22. String layout from a Pascal program.

$$pool\,[start\,[0]] = \text{'}\mathbf{T}\text{'}$$
$$pool\,[start\,[1]] = \text{'}\mathbf{t}\text{'}$$
$$pool\,[start\,[2]] = \text{'}\mathbf{S}\text{'}$$

The length of string s is given by

$$start\,[s+1] - start\,[s\,]$$

The disadvantage of storing integer index values in array *start*, rather than explicit pointers, is that the compiler cannot check that index values are used only to point to characters.

The actual array names in the code for TEX are *str_start* and *str_pool*.

The layout of strings in Fig. 3.23 shows how a C program might implement the approach of Fig. 3.22. By convention, the end of a string in C is marked by the constant **EOS**, defined to be '**\0**'. Elements of array **pool** hold the individual characters in the strings. A pointer to the first character in string **s** is held in **start[s]**. We see next that operations on pointers in C allow successive characters in a string to be accessed; the lack of such operations in Pascal (and Modula-2) is one of the reasons why array *start* in Fig. 3.22 holds integer index values rather than pointers.[5]

The pointer dereferencing operator in C is *****, and the operator **&** yields a pointer to its operand. The assignment

```
p = &x;
```

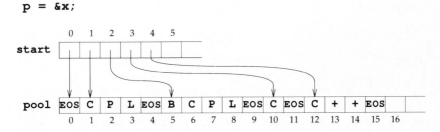

Fig. 3.23. String layout in a C program.

---

[5] Another tradeoff between the layouts in Fig. 3.22 and 3.23 is in the space required for the array *start*. For example, index values might be declared to be short integers, which fit into half a machine word, whereas a pointer might occupy a full machine word. The difference between using a half word or a full word is likely to be irrelevant for most programs.

makes **p** a pointer to **x**, so

```
*p = *p + 1;
```

has the same effect as

```
x = x + 1;
```

Arrays and pointers are intimately related in C. For all arrays **a**, if **p** points to **a[i]**, then **p+1** is a pointer to **a[i+1]**. In fact, an array name **a** is simply a pointer to the zeroth element **a[0]**. Thus, **a+1** points to **a[1]**; more generally, **a+i** points to **a[i]**.

The following linear search through a table

```
a[0] = x; i = n;
while( a[i] != x )
    --i;
return i;
```

can therefore be rewritten, using pointers, as

```
a[0] = x; p = a+n;
while( *p != x )
    --p;
return p-a;
```

Instead of using **i** as the index of element **a[i]**, the rewritten fragment maintains **p** as a pointer to **a[i]**. Instead of initializing **i** to **n**, the rewritten fragment initializes **p** to be a pointer to **a[n]**. Subsequently, instead of decrementing **i**, the rewritten fragment decrements **p**, since **p-1** points to **a[i-1]** if **p** points to **a[i]**. Finally,

```
return i;
```

changes into

```
return p-a;
```

If **p** is a pointer to **a[i]**, then **p** must equal **a+i**, so

```
i == p-a
```

The string layout in Fig. 3.23 cannot be used if the only operations on pointers are dereferencing and comparing two pointers for equality or inequality. Given a pointer to the first character of *s*, dereferencing and equality testing cannot extract the second and successive characters of *s*. Note that the individual characters in a string *s* must be accessed by an operation that compares *s* with a string in a buffer.

In C, the code for comparing string **s** with a string in array **buffer** can be written as follows:

```
p = start+s;
q = buffer;
while ( *p == *q ) {
    if ( *p == EOS )
        return 1;
    p++;
    q++;
}
return 0;
```

The comparison between the array of pointers in Fig. 3.23 and the array of integer index values in Fig. 3.22 shows how C is often used; type checking can catch some errors of indirection through array **start**. The motivation for the restrictions in Modula-2 will become more evident in Section 4.8, where we find that the restrictions prevent "dangling pointers" in Modula-2 programs.

3.8 TYPE NAMES AND TYPE EQUIVALENCE

In an assignment of the form

$\langle l\text{-}value \rangle := \langle expression \rangle$

the type of the left side must "equal" the type of the right side.
What does it mean for two types to be equal?

Example 3.5. Are the following two types equal?

array [0 .. 9] **of integer**
array [0 .. 9] **of integer**

In a larger context, if variables x, y, and z are declared as follows, are their types equal?

x, y : **array** [0 .. 9] **of integer**
z : **array** [0 .. 9] **of integer**

In Modula-2, x and y have the same type, because they are declared together, but z does not.
In the corresponding C fragments, x, y, and z all have the same type.   □

This example motivates a close look at type equivalence.

Structural Equivalence

Two type expressions are *structurally equivalent* if and only if they are equivalent under the following three rules:

SE1. A type name is structurally equivalent to itself.

SE2. Two types are structurally equivalent if they are formed by applying the same type constructor to structurally equivalent types.

SE3. After a type declaration, **type** $n = T$, the type name n is structurally equivalent to T.

By these rules, the types **integer** and **integer** are structurally equivalent, and so are the following array types:

> **array** [0..9] **of integer**
> **array** [0..9] **of integer**

More limited notions of type equivalence are obtained if we restrict the rules SE1-SE3. Some possibilities follow:

- Drop rule SE3. A type name can then be equivalent only to itself; however, some constructed types can still be equivalent to each other. A constructed type **pointer to** n remains equivalent to **pointer to** n because both are formed by applying the same constructor **pointer to** to the same type name n.

- Drop rules SE2 and SE3. Now, a type name is equivalent to itself, but no constructed type is equal to any other constructed type.

- Drop rule SE2 and restrict SE3 so that a type name can be equivalent only to other type names. Then, the following types s, t, and u are equivalent to themselves and to **integer**:

> **type** s = **integer**;
> t = s;
> u = t;

Type Equivalence in Modula-2

Modula-2 defines two types to be *compatible* if

C1. they are the same name, or
C2. they are s and t, and $s = t$ is a type declaration, or
C3. one is a subrange of the other, or
C4. both are subranges of the same basic type.

Furthermore, two types are *assignment compatible* if they are compatible, or if one is **cardinal** or a subrange of **cardinal** and the other is **integer** or a subrange of **integer**.

Type Equivalence in C

C uses structural equivalence for all types except records, which are called structures in C. The examples in this chapter have dealt primarily with arrays. Other data types, such as records or structures will be examined in later chapters.

EXERCISES

3.1 Write a conditional statement to assign **true** to variable *leap* if the value of variable *year* corresponds to a leap year. The rules for determining leap years are based on a decree by Pope Gregory XIII, which was eventually adopted in Great Britain and its colonies for years following 1752. Every fourth year is a leap year, so 1756, 1760, $\cdots$ are leap years. But 1800, 1900, $\cdots$ —years divisible by 100—are not leap years. Finally, years divisible by 400 are leap years, so 2000, 2400, $\cdots$ are leap years.

3.2 Characterize the output of the RAM program in Fig. 3.1, page 70, as a function of its input.

3.3 Write a RAM program to compute the sum of a sequence of integers. The program must read integers into successive memory locations, starting with **M[0]** and stopping as soon as a 0 is read into a memory location. Test your program by simulating it in a programming language of your choice.

3.4 Draw flow diagrams for the following Modula-2 program fragments (examples of flow diagrams appear in Fig. 3.5, page 76):

a) **if** E_1 **then** SL_1
    elsif E_2 **then** SL_2
    else SL_3
    end

b) **repeat** SL **until** E

c)   **repeat**
            SL_1;
            if E **then goto** 10; **end**;
            SL_2
        until false;
    10: ;   (∗ label 10 is attached to an empty statement ∗)

d) **repeat**
   SL_1;
   if E **then**
       done := **true**
   else
       SL_2
   end
   until *done*

3.5 Compare the program fragments in Exercise 3.4(c) and (d). How are they similar? How do they differ?

3.6 Draw flow diagrams for the following C program fragments containing the short-circuit boolean operators **&&** and **||**, corresponding to **and** and **or**, respectively.

a) ```
   if (E && F) S
   else T
   ```

b) ```
   if ( E || F ) S
   else T
   ```

c) ```
   if (d[1] < '0' || d[1] > '7')
       S
   else if (d[2] >= '0' && d[2] <= '7'
           && d[3] >= '0' && d[3] <= '7')
       T
   else
       error();
   ```

**3.7** Rewrite the pseudo-code in Fig. 3.24 so that no **if** part is nested within the **then** part of another **if**. Feel free to use empty statements and to replace any boolean expression by an equivalent one.

**3.8** Suppose that the statement list *SL* in

   **for** $i := E_1$ **to** $E_2$ **do** *SL* **end**

does not change the value of *i*.
   a) Rewrite this fragment using the other constructs of Modula-2. Use extra variables as needed.
   b) An assignment to *i* is said to be *safe* if it assigns *i* a value no smaller than that of $E_1$ and no greater than the initial value of $E_2$. Rewrite this fragment as in (a) using only safe assignments.
   c) Rewrite this fragment as in (b) without using **exit** statements.

**3.9** Develop a program for binary search from the description in Example 3.2, page 74.
   ```

```
(1)  if  character is printable  then
(2)        if  p ≤ mem_end  then
(3)              if  font ≠ normal  then
(4)                    if  font is unknown  then
(5)                          print '*'
(6)                    else
(7)                          print name of font
(8)                    end;
(9)                    print ' '
(10)             end;
(11)             print the character
(12)       end
(13) else
(14)       print a message
(15) end
```

Fig. 3.24. Pseudo-code for a conditional from a typesetting program.

3.10 Develop a program to find the kth occurrence of x, from left to right, $k \geq 0$, in a subarray $A[i..n]$.

3.11 In the imperative language of your choice, write a program to implement the pseudo-code

> **loop**
>   copy characters up to "(*";
>   throw away characters until "*)" is seen;
> **end**

  a) Use break and continue statements as needed. Goto statements may be used only to simulate break and continue by sending control to empty statements just after and just before a loop, respectively.

  b) Use only assignments, conditionals, statement lists, and while-loops.

3.12 Sketch an efficient implementation of case statements in which subranges can appear as case constants.

  a) Use a jump table and place an upper bound on the size of a subrange to be included in the table.

  b) Suppose there are fixed run-time costs for setting up each case and for making a test. How can tradeoffs between these costs be used to tailor the implementation of individual case statements.

3.13 The heart of Quicksort, an elegant and efficient sorting algorithm, is a partitioning algorithm that uses a value v to rearrange the elements of a subarray $A[m..n]$. Informally, the subarray is partitioned into two parts, consisting of elements smaller and larger than v:

Develop a program based on the following invariant:

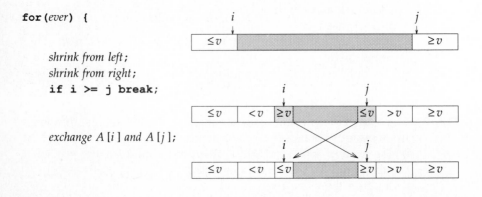

The subarray $A[m..i]$ consists of elements that are now known to be less than v. The middle subarray $A[i+1..k-1]$ consists of elements that are greater than or equal to v. And, the grey area $A[k..n]$ consists of the elements that remain to be partitioned. The idea is to shrink the grey area from the left by incrementing k and then reestablishing the invariant if $A[k]<v$. When $A[k]<v$, the invariant can be reestablished by exchanging $A[k]$ and $A[i+1]$.

3.14 Use the code skeleton in Fig. 3.25 to implement a partitioning algorithm (see Exercise 3.13). The skeleton shrinks the grey area alternately from the left and from the right. Initially, $A[m]\le v$ and $A[n]\ge v$ are known. The shrinkage from the left stops with $A[i]\ge v$. The shrinkage from the right stops with $A[j]\le v$.

```
for (ever) {

    shrink from left;
    shrink from right;
    if i >= j break;

    exchange A[i] and A[j];

}
```

Fig. 3.25. Code skeleton for partitioning an array.

*3.15 A *multi-level* break statement **break**(n) sends control out of n enclosing loops. Thus, **break**(0) has no effect and **break**(1) is a normal **break** statement. Modify the flow diagram in Fig. 3.26 to make the edges represent flow of control set up by **if, while, break**(1), and **break**(2) statements. Mark the edges that represent break statements. (Hint: Cut the flow diagram at the entrances to E_{12} and E_{21}.)

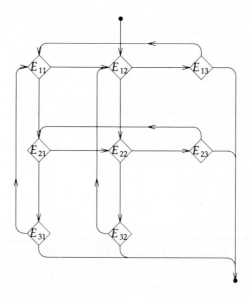

Fig. 3.26. Flow diagram that can be implemented using **break**(2).

BIBLIOGRAPHIC NOTES

Wirth [1983] is the original reference for Modula-2; King [1988] is designed to be a complete guide. Useful examples accompany the description of the ANSI standard version of C in Kernighan and Ritchie [1988].

Language facilities for organizing data show up clearly in the Plankalkül, designed by Konrad Zuse in 1945, because bits were its only atomic values. Zuse [1980] recalls, "The first principle of the Plankalkül is: data processing begins with the bit." All other types of values were built up from the individual bits. Arbitrary data structures were built up by construcing tuples, arrays, and sequences of simpler structures. The Plankalkül remained a "theoretical investigation"; it was never implemented.

Fortran, which became available in 1957, was based on the concepts of assignments, arrays, and **DO** statements, which are a precursor of **for** statements. Backus [1981] traces the history of Fortran and mentions that the language was developed specifically for use on the IBM 704, with no expectation of using it on other machines.

Shepherdson and Sturgis [1963] introduced random-access machines as a more convenient alternative than Turing machines for theoretical studies of computation; the instruction set in Section 3.2 is from Cook and Reckhow [1972].

Modula-2 and C belong to the Algol family of languages, named after Algol 60 (Naur [1963a]). A separate language, Algol 68 (van Wijngaarden et al. [1975]) provided data structuring facilities similar to those in Section 3.4.

Although Algol 60 provided structured control flow constructs, the examples in the Algol 60 report do contain **goto** statements. Knuth [1974] traces the historical background of the avoidance of goto statements; he credits Naur [1963b] with the first published remarks on the harmful nature of **goto** statements and Dijkstra [1968a] with making "the most waves."

With respect to structured statement constructs, experiments by Gannon and Horning [1975] suggest that fewer programming errors occur if statements are terminated rather than separated by semicolons. The case statement is the language design proposal that Hoare [1981] is "still most proud of."

A Soviet compiler, ПП 2, by Kamynin et al. was probably the first to use short-circuit evaluation of boolean expressions; see Minker and Minker [1980] for the historical development of this topic.

Zuse's Plankalkül had both break and continue statements (Knuth and Trabb Pardo [1977]). Since the Plankalkül lay forgotten until it was rediscovered in the 1970s these constructs must have been reinvented several times.

Floyd [1967] used invariant assertions to prove properties of individual programs; he attached invariants to points in the flow diagram for a program. Hoare [1969] introduced formulas of the form

$$\{\langle precondition \rangle\} \quad \langle statement \rangle \quad \{\langle postcondition \rangle\}$$

where $\langle precondition \rangle$ and $\langle postcondition \rangle$ are invariants attached to program points just before and just after the statement. Rules for manipulating such formulas are called "proof rules." Apt [1981] surveys the extensive literature on proof rules.

Dijkstra [1976] advocates the systematic development of programs from assertions. He gives numerous small examples, using statement constructs that differ from the ones in this chapter because they allow nondeterminism (see the bibilographic notes for Chapter 9). Additional examples of program development are given by Gries [1981]. Bentley [1986] makes informal use of invariants to develop a program for binary search. Kernighan and Plauger [1978] give rules for good programming style and then apply the rules to rewrite fragments taken from published programs.

Sentinels, in Section 3.3, are an old idea, going back to "tags" in Wilkes, Wheeler, and Gill [1951]. The description of string handling in TEX, in Section 3.7, is adapted from Knuth [1986], as is the pseudo-code in Exercise 3.7.

Quicksort by Hoare [1962] has been studied extensively. The program fragment in Exercise 3.14 is close to one studied by Sedgewick [1978].

Exercise 3.15 is based on Kosaraju [1974]; see also Baker and Kosaraju [1979]. Böhm and Jacopini [1966] show that every flow diagram can be implemented using conditionals and while-loops if auxiliary boolean variables can be added. The program fragment in Exercise 3.4(d) uses an auxiliary variable *done* to implement the goto statement in Exercise 3.4(c). See also Cooper [1967] and Bruno and Steiglitz [1972].

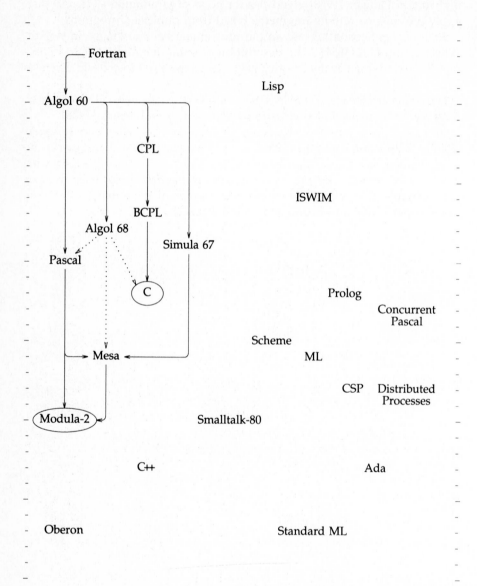

Pascal and Modula-2 retain the notion of block structure from Algol 60, with nested procedure declarations. C has a simpler structure.

Procedure
Activations

What C calls a "function," Modula-2 calls a "procedure." The only difference between functions and procedures in imperative languages is that functions return values and procedures do not. Since the word procedure evokes imperative languages, this chapter uses the terms *function procedure* and *proper procedure* when precision is needed, abbreviated where convenient to function and procedure.

The emphasis in this chapter is on how procedures work. What happens when a procedure is called? What does a name in a procedure refer to? How is the value of a variable accessed?

The run-time treatment of names in C programs is simpler than that of names in Modula-2 programs, so we consider C before Modula-2. Names in C are either local to some procedure or are global and visible in all procedures. Modula-2 and Pascal, in the tradition of Algol 60, allow procedure declarations to be nested, so the "right" declaration of a name could be at any one of several levels.

4.1   ON NAMES IN PROCEDURES

The main purpose of this section is to formulate principles for the use of names in imperative languages. Terms like activation and binding introduced in Chapter 2, are reviewed next in the context of procedures.

Terminology

A procedure declaration has four parts:

1. the name of the declared procedure,
2. the formal parameters of the procedure,
3. a body consisting of local declarations and a statement list, and
4. an optional result type.

The C function procedure **succ**, declared by

```
int  succ(int i)  { return (i+1) % size; }
```
(4.1)

has one formal parameter **i**. Its body is the statement

```
{ return (i+1) % size; }
```

The leading **int** in the declaration gives the type of the result. The **%** operator corresponds to **mod**; it returns the remainder after integer division.

A declaration of a name is also called a *binding* of the name; it introduces a new use of the name. All occurrences of the name to which a binding applies are said to be within the *scope* of the binding. The scope of formal parameters and of names declared within a procedure is contained within the procedure body. Such names are said to be *local to* or *bound within* the procedure. A binding of a name x is *visible* at a point in a program if an occurrence of x at the point would be within the scope of the binding. When a specific binding b of x is clear from the context, it is common practice to say "name x is visible," instead of the more precise "binding b of name x is visible."

In C, a nonlocal name is said to be *global* because it is then visible in all procedures. We use *locals* as an abbreviation for local variables, *globals* as an abbreviation for global variables, and so on.

In the declaration (4.1) of **succ**, parameter **i** is local and variable name **size** is global.

The use of a procedure is referred to as a *call* of the procedure. Prefix notation is the rule for procedure calls:

⟨*procedure-name*⟩ **(** ⟨*actual-parameters*⟩ **)**

Function procedures are called from within expressions, as in the call of **succ** within the inequality

```
succ(front) != rear
```

Proper procedures are treated as atomic statements; an example is a call

```
enter(c);
```

which is executed for its effect on the state of the computation.

Each execution of a procedure body is referred to as an activation of the procedure. A procedure is recursive if it can be activated from within its own procedure body, either directly by calling itself, or indirectly through calls to other procedures.

Environments and Stores

Does an occurrence of x refer to the name itself, to its l-value, or to its r-value? The answer to this question determines the treatment of parameters in procedure calls. The l-value of x is the storage associated with x, and the r-value consists of the contents of that storage. In the assignment

$$i := i + 1$$

the occurrence of variable i on the left side denotes an l-value, and its occurrence on the right side denotes an r-value.

The correspondence between variable names, l-values, and r-values can be made precise in terms of two mappings, called environments and stores. An *environment* maps a variable name to an l-value. A *store* maps an l-value to its contents. Together, an environment and a store completely specify a mapping from variables to r-values, as in Fig. 4.1. A store is just one component of the state of a computation; other components might deal with input and output as the computation proceeds.

In general, the term "environment" refers to any mapping from names to whatever the names represent, including names for procedures, types, constants, and so on.

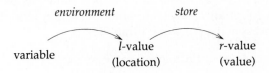

Fig. 4.1. Mappings from variables to l-values to r-values.

Principles for the Use of Names

The following informally stated principles set the direction for this chapter.

It seems reasonable to suppose that the meaning of a program is independent of the actual names of local variables. It should not matter whether a function uses x or n as the name of a formal parameter. Let us state this supposition as a principle because some languages deviate from it some of the time:

> *Renaming of local variables.* The computation set up by a program is unaffected if local variables in the source text are consistently renamed.

The *lexical environment* of a procedure is the environment in which the procedure body appears. A *calling environment* is the environment at a point of call of the procedure. An unobvious consequence of the renaming principle is that nonlocals in a procedure body refer to their values in the lexical environment. This rule on the treatment of nonlocals is called the *lexical scope rule.* Lisp has traditionally used a *dynamic scope rule,* under which nonlocals are evaluated in the calling environment. Dynamic scope leaves the meaning of a program sensitive to the names of local variables. Modern Lisps tend to use lexical scope.

The second principle deals with storage. Compilers for imperative languages often use a stack to organize storage for local variables, an organization made possible by the following principle:

> *Lifetimes of local variables.* Local variables are local to a procedure activation.

Each activation of a procedure gets its own local variables, and once it ends, there should be no need for the locals. Thus, storage for the locals is allocated when an activation begins, and is deallocated when the activation ends. When P calls Q and Q calls R, storage is therefore used in a last-in-first-out or stack-like manner. The stack in Fig. 4.2 grows downward, as activations are set up for P, Q, and R. Then the stack shrinks as control returns from R to Q to P. Each box in the figure represents storage for the locals of an activation.

A third assumption, often made implicitly, is that procedures can call themselves recursively. We state this too as a principle, because there are exceptions to it. Fortran 77 does not allow recursion (also, the lifetimes of locals persist across activations in Fortran 77).

> *Recursion assumption.* Procedures can be recursive.

The bulk of this chapter explores storage allocation strategies that are consistent with the above principles.

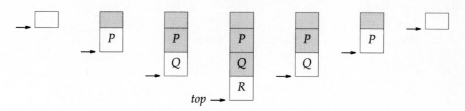

Fig. 4.2. Stack-like storage allocation for activations.

4.2   PROCEDURE DECLARATIONS IN C

C is geared to function procedures, declared by

⟨*result-type*⟩ ⟨*name*⟩ **(** ⟨*formal-parameter-declarations*⟩ **)**   **{**
    ⟨*declaration-list*⟩
    ⟨*statement-list*⟩
}

All of the nonterminals in this syntax, except ⟨*name*⟩, are optional. The smallest complete C program is

main() {}

A missing result type is taken by default to be **int**. A special type name **void** indicates the absence of a value. A result type **void** indicates that a ''function'' is a proper procedure with no result.

A more fully specified variant of the smallest program is

int   main(void)   { return 0; }

Execution of a C program begins in a function **main**, which returns a termination status. A zero status conventionally indicates normal termination.

The next two examples examine the complete C program in Fig. 4.3, which uses several little procedures to implement operations on a buffer. The main procedure treats these operations as atomic actions. The structure of the program will become more explicit in Chapter 5, where the buffer and its procedures are grouped and encapsulated.

Example 4.1. Binding occurrences of names are highlighted in Fig. 4.3.
    The declaration

int   notempty(void) { return front != rear; }

says that the parameterless procedure **notempty** returns an integer. Proper procedure **enter**, declared by

```c
#define MAXBUF 4
char buf[MAXBUF+1];
int  size = MAXBUF+1, front = 0, rear = 0;

int  succ(int i)     { return (i+1) % size; }
int  notempty(void) { return front != rear; }
int  notfull(void)   { return succ(rear) != front; }
void enter(int x)  {
    buf[rear] = x; rear = succ(rear);     /* no check for full! */
}
int leave(void) {
    int x;
    x = buf[front]; front = succ(front); /* no check for empty! */
    return x;
}

#include <math.h>
#include <stdio.h>
int main(void) {
    int c;
    for(;;) {
        if( frand() >= 0.5 && notempty() ) {
            putchar(leave());                /* consume a character */
        }
        else if( notfull() ) {
            c = getchar();
            if( c == EOF ) break;
            enter(c);                        /* produce a character */
        }
    }
    while( notempty() )                      /* flush the buffer */
        putchar(leave());
    return 0;
}
```

Fig. 4.3. A complete C program that copies characters through a buffer.

```c
void enter(int x) {
    buf[rear] = x; rear = succ(rear);
}
```

has one parameter **x** of type **int**. Within the procedure body, **x** is a local variable because it is a formal parameter. The remaining names **buf, rear**, and **succ** must be global because they are not declared within the procedure.

Parameterless procedure **leave**,

```
int leave(void) {
    int x;
    x = buf[front];  front = succ(front);
    return x;
}
```

has a local variable **x** and returns an integer.

Using darker type for binding occurrences, as in Fig. 4.3, the only occurrence of **succ** and the first occurrence of **i** (within parentheses) are binding occurrences in

```
int  succ(int i)  { return (i+1) % size; }
```

The scope of the binding of formal parameter **i** is the procedure body.

The scope of the binding of a procedure name like **succ** is the rest of the program. This procedure can then be called from within other procedure bodies. The body of **notfull** calls **succ**:

```
int  notfull(void)  { return succ(rear) != front; }
```

In words, the procedure returns true if the result of evaluating **succ(rear)** is not equal to the value of **front**.   □

Example 4.2. The program in Fig. 4.3 simulates a producer, which reads characters, and a consumer, which writes characters, as in Fig. 4.4. The library functions **getchar** and **putchar** are used for reading and writing. The producer and consumer interact with the buffer only through the procedures **notempty**, **notfull**, **enter**, and **leave**. The implementation and size of the buffer can therefore be changed without affecting the code for the producer and the consumer.

In more detail, procedure **main** uses a random-number generator **frand** to choose between running the producer or the consumer. If **frand** returns a value greater than or equal to **0.5**, then the consumer checks to see whether the buffer is not empty.[1] Provided the buffer is not empty, the consumer executes **putchar(leave())** to take a character out of the buffer and place it in the output. Otherwise, the producer checks to see if

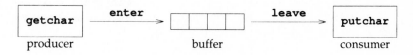

Fig. 4.4. Setting for the program in Fig. 4.3.

_____

[1] The standard integer-valued function **rand** can be used instead of the nonstandard **frand** by substituting **(float)rand()/32767.0** for the call **frand()**.

the buffer is not full. Provided the buffer is not full, the producer calls **getchar()** to read a character, with the intent of entering it into the buffer. The program stops when **EOF** is read, signifying the end of the input. The consumer then flushes the buffer.   □

4.3 PARAMETER-PASSING METHODS

When control reaches a procedure call, the statements in the procedure body are executed as if they appeared at the point of call. The effect of the highlighted call of **enter** in Fig. 4.5(a) is illustrated in (b) by pretending that the body of **enter** is inserted in place of the call (a compiler does not normally rewrite a program in this way).

The effect of a procedure call in a programming language depends on the answer to the following question:

What is the correspondence between the actual parameters in a procedure call and the formal parameters in the procedure body?

The answers examined in this section are motivated by differing interpretations of what a parameter stands for. Does an actual parameter $A[j]$ in a procedure call $P(A[j])$ represent its r-value, its l-value, or the program text $A[j]$ itself? Some interpretations are

- *Call-by-value.* Pass the r-value of $A[j]$.
- *Call-by-reference.* Pass the l-value of $A[j]$.
- *Call-by-name.* Pass the text $A[j]$ itself, avoiding "name clashes."

Another variant, examined later, is *call-by-value-result.* We say *value parameter* for a parameter that is passed by value, *reference parameter* for a parameter that is passed by reference, and so on for other methods.

C uses call-by-value. A parameter in Modula-2 is normally passed by-value. It is passed by reference, however, if the keyword **var** appears before the declaration of the formal parameter.

```
int main(void) {              int main(void) {
    int c;                        int c;
        . . .                         . . .

            enter(c);                     x = c; {
                                              buf[rear] = x;
                                              rear = succ(rear);
                                          }

        . . .                         . . .

}                             }
        (a)                           (b)
```

Fig. 4.5. Conceptual effect of a procedure call.

Call-by-Value

Call-by-value was introduced in Section 2.4, by considering a function *successor*:

    fun *successor* $(n) = n + 1$;

The value 6 of an expression *successor* (2+3) was obtained by evaluating the actual parameter 2+3 and using the result 5 for n in the body $n+1$.

    An imperative variant of *successor* is

```
int   succ(int i)   { return (i+1) % size; }
```

Under call-by-value, a formal like **i** corresponds to the r-value of an actual like **2+3**. The expression **succ(2+3)** is therefore evaluated as follows:

```
i = 2+3;              pass the value of 2+3 to i
t = (i+1) % size;     compute a result in temporary t
return t;             return the value of t
```

    A standard example for illustrating parameter-passing methods is a procedure *swap* (x, y), which exchanges the values of x and y.

Example 4.3. An abortive attempt at *swap* in C is

```
void swap1(int x, int y) {
    int z;
    z = x; x = y; y = z;      /* actuals are undisturbed */
}
```

A call **swap1(a,b)** does nothing to **a** and **b**. To see why, consider the effect of this call:

```
x = a;
y = b;
z = x; x = y; y = z;
```

This program fragment does not change **a** and **b**, although the values of **x** and **y** are indeed exchanged.   □

    Procedure *swap* (x, y) can be implemented in C by using pointers to pass l-values, as in the following program fragment:

```
void swap(int *px, int *py) {
    int z;
    z = *px; *px = *py; *py = z;
}
```

The parameters of **swap** are pointers to integers. A prefix "*****" is the pointer dereferencing operator in C. The parameter declarations

    int *px, int *py

say that ***px** and ***py** denote integers, hence **px** and **py** must denote pointers to integers.

A prefix **&** is the "address of" operator in C, so a call

    swap(&a, &b)

passes the *l*-values of **a** and **b**. The effect of **swap(&a, &b)** is given by

    px = &a;   px is assigned the l-value of a
    py = &b;   py is assigned the l-value of b
    z = *px;
    *px = *py;   indirect assignment to a through px
    *py = z;   indirect assignment to b through py

Call-by-Reference

Keyword **var** says that y is a reference parameter in the following Modula-2 declaration:

procedure $P(x : T_x;$ **var** $y : T_y);$ $\cdots$ **end** P ;

By default, x is a value parameter. The call $P(a+b, c)$ has the following effect:

assign x the *r*-value of $a+b$;
make the *l*-value of reference parameter y the same as that of c;
execute the body of procedure P;

An actual value parameter can be an expression, but an actual reference parameter must have an *l*-value; that is, it must be either a variable name or an assignable component of a data structure.[2]

Here is a Modula-2 version of *swap* (x, y):

---

[2] Early versions of Fortran did not check whether actual reference parameters were assignable. Consequently, a call *swap* (1, 2) might have swapped the constants 1 and 2. Each constant is held in some location in the machine, and since *swap* interchanges the values of its parameters, it would interchange the constants as well. Some languages avoid such problems by using call-by-value for actuals that are constants or expressions without *l*-values.

```
procedure swap (var x : integer;   var y : integer);
   var z : integer;
begin
   z := x ;   x := y ;   y := z ;
end swap ;
```

Both x and y are reference parameters, so a call $swap\,(i, A\,[i\,])$ does the following:

> make the l-value of x the same as that of i;
> make the l-value of y the same as that of $A\,[i\,]$;
> $z := x ;\ x := y ;\ y := z$

If i is 2 and $A\,[2]$ is 99, the effect of these statements is

> $z := 2;\ i := 99;\ A\,[2] := z$

Call-by-Value-Result

Call-by-value-result is also known as *copy-in/copy-out* because the actuals are initially copied into the formals and the formals are eventually copied back out to the actuals. Actuals like 2+3 that do not have l-values are passed by value. Actuals with l-values are treated as follows:

1. *Copy-in phase.* Both the r-values and the l-values of the actual parameters are computed. The r-values are assigned to the corresponding formals, as in call-by-value, and the l-values are saved for the copy-out phase.

2. *Copy-out phase.* After the procedure body is executed, the final values of the formals are copied back out to the l-values computed in the copy-in phase.

 Legal Ada programs are expected to have the same effect under call-by-reference and copy-in/copy-out, so an implementation can choose to use either one. Ada supports three kinds of parameters:

1. **in** parameters, corresponding to value parameters,

2. **out** parameters, corresponding to just the copy-out phase of call-by-value-result, and

3. **in out** parameters, corresponding to either reference parameters or value-result parameters, at the discretion of the implementation.

 A call $swap\,(i, A\,[i\,])$ does indeed exchange the values of i and $A\,[i\,]$ under call-by-value-result. The following pseudo-code borrows from C the address-of operator & and the dereferencing operator * to make explicit the initial computation of l-values for the actuals.

$px := \&i$; $py := \&(A[i])$;	save l-values of i and $A[i]$
$x := i$;	copy into x
$y := A[i]$;	copy into y
$z := x$; $x := y$; $y := z$;	exchange
$*px := x$;	copy out x
$*py := y$;	copy out y

Suppose, again, that i is initially 2 and that $A[2]$ is initially 99. Since the l-values of the actuals i and $A[i]$ are computed at the start, the copy-out phase affects $A[2]$ even though the final value of i is 99.

Programs that produce different results under call-by-reference and copy-in/copy-out can be contrived with the help of aliases—two expressions with the same l-value are said to be *aliases* for each other. Ada views programs that use aliases as being erroneous.

Example 4.4. Procedure *foo* in this example has two ways of changing the value of a variable i: (1) directly through an assignment to i and (2) indirectly through the copy-out of a formal x. The indirect change will undo the effect of the direct assignment.

A contrived program fragment is

```
program
    . . .
    procedure foo (x, y);  begin  i := y  end;
    . . .
begin
    i := 2;  A[i] := 99;
    foo (i, A[i]);
end.
```

The body of procedure *foo* is the assignment $i := y$, which mentions i explicitly. Since i is also passed as an actual in the call *foo* $(i, A[i])$, x becomes an alias for i. The call *foo* $(i, A[i])$ leaves both i and $A[i]$ unchanged because the copy-out phase restores their values:

$px := \&i$; $py := \&(A[i])$;	
$x := i$;	copy into x
$y := A[i]$;	
$i := y$;	change value of i
$*px := x$;	copy out x, thereby restoring i
$*py := y$;	

Call-by-reference, on the other hand, will change the value of i. □

Macro Expansion: Actuals as Program Text

A *macro processor* does the following:

1. Actual parameters are textually substituted for the formals.

2. The resulting procedure body is textually substituted for the call.

Textual substitution means that a string is literally substituted, as is.

C uses a macro preprocessor to support language extensions such as named constants and file inclusion. Preprocessor lines begin with a **#**. The C program on page 124 has three such lines. The line

```
#define MAXBUF 4
```

defines **MAXBUF** to be the string **4**. Every occurrence of **MAXBUF** is replaced by **4** before the program is compiled.

The other preprocessor lines,

```
#include <math.h>
#include <stdio.h>
```

are replaced by the contents of the standard files **math.h** and **stdio.h**. These files allow the program to use function **frand** from a library of mathematical functions and function **printf** from a library of input/output functions.

Example 4.5. Unfortunately, **swap(i,A[i])** does not simply exchange the values of **i** and **A[i]** under macro expansion. Textual substitution of the actuals into the procedure body yields

```
z = i;   i = A[i];   A[i] = z;
```

If **i** is initially 2 and **A[2]** is initially 99, this sequence is equivalent to

```
z = 2;   i = 99;   A[i] = 2;
```

The final assignment uses the modified value of **i**, so **A[99]** and not **A[2]** is set to the initial value of **i**.   □

Macro processors ignore "naming conflicts" that arise during substitution.

Call-by-Name: Resolution of Naming Conflicts

Although call-by-name is now primarily of historical interest, it is a convenient setting for studying conflicts between uses of the same name in the calling and lexical environments. Informally, a naming conflict occurs during substitution if the scope of an occurrence of the name changes.

A *naming conflict* occurs during the substitution of text T into S if some nonlocal name in T comes under the scope of a binding in S.

Example 4.6. The renaming principle says that the two program fragments in Fig. 4.6 are equivalent. The only difference between them is in the name of the local variable in procedure **out**; in (a) the variable is **y** and in (b) the variable is **x**.

Substitution of the body of procedure **P** for the call **P()** in Fig. 4.6(a) yields

```
int out(void) {
    int y;
    y = buf[m];
    m = (m+1) % x;
    return y;
}
```

No naming conflicts arise during this substitution because neither **m** nor **x** has a binding in procedure **out**.

A naming conflict arises, however, if the body of **P** is substituted, as is, for the call in Fig. 4.6(b), resulting in

```
int out(void) {
    int x;
    x = buf[m];
    m = (m+1) % x;     /* wrong, need x == (MAXBUF+1) */
    return x;
}
```

Here, nonlocal **x** in the body of **P** has fallen into the scope of the local binding of **x** in procedure **out**.   □

```
int   x = MAXBUF+1;                    int   x = MAXBUF+1;
int   m = 0;                           int   m = 0;
...                                    ...

void P(void){ m = (m+1) % x; }         void P(void){ m = (m+1) % x; }
...                                    ...

int out(void) {                        int out(void) {
    int y;                                 int x;
    y = buf[m];                            x = buf[m];
    P();                                   P();
    return y;                              return x;
}                                      }

            (a)                                    (b)
```

Fig. 4.6. The local in procedure **out** is **y** in (a) and **x** in (b).

The Algol 60 report describes call-by-name as follows (the examples are in the syntax of Algol 60):

1. Actual parameters are textually substituted for the formals. Possible conflicts between names in the actuals and local names in the procedure body are avoided by renaming the locals in the body. Suppose that name i appears in a procedure call $P(A[i])$, and that the body of P contains a local i:

   procedure $P(x)$; **begin integer** i; $\cdots$ $i := i + n$; $x := x + n$; $\cdots$ **end**;

   Then the local i in the body of P would be renamed. Using j instead, the body after substitution of actual $A[i]$ is

   begin integer j; $\cdots$ $j := j + n$; $A[i] := A[i] + n$; $\cdots$ **end**;

2. The resulting procedure body is substituted for the call. Possible conflicts between nonlocals in the procedure body and locals at the point of call are avoided by renaming the locals at the point of call. Above, n appears as a nonlocal in the procedure body; suppose now that at the point of call, n is local:

   begin integer n; $\cdots$ $n := n - 1$; $P(A[i])$; $\cdots$ **end**;

   Then, the local n at the point of call would be renamed. Using m instead, the calling program fragment becomes

   begin integer m;
       $\cdots$
     $m := m - 1$;
     begin integer j; $\cdots$ $j := j + n$; $A[i] := A[i] + n$; $\cdots$ **end**;
       $\cdots$
   end;

4.4   ACTIVATIONS HAVE NESTED LIFETIMES

The normal flow of control between procedure activations in imperative languages can be summarized by a tree. If P calls Q, then P is a parent of Q in the tree. This section uses a toy example to illustrate the flow of control between activations.

Activation Trees

Control flows between procedure activations in a last-in-first-out manner. If

   P calls Q, and Q calls R,

control returns

   from R back to Q, and from Q back to P.

Similarly, with activations of a recursive procedure P, if

activation P_1 sets up P_2, and P_2 sets up P_3,

then control returns

from P_3 back to P_2, and from P_2 back to P_1.

The *lifetime* of an activation begins when control enters the activation and ends when control returns from the activation. When P calls Q, the lifetime of Q is nested within the lifetime of P.

The flow of control between activations can be depicted by a tree, called an *activation tree*. Nodes in the tree represent activations. When activation P calls activation Q, the node for P has the node for Q as a child.

In the activation tree in Fig. 4.7, **main** calls **P**, which first calls **M**. The arguments passed to activations of **M** are shown for clarity.

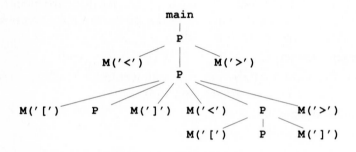

Fig. 4.7. An activation tree.

The tree in Fig. 4.7 summarizes the activity in Fig. 4.8, where each snapshot shows only the live activations. The snapshots correspond to a particular execution of the program in the next example; each occurrence of the letter **P** in the snapshots represents a call of procedure **parens** in the example.

Example 4.7. Procedure **parens** in Fig. 4.9 matches strings like

```
[]
<[]<[]>>
() ()
```

It checks whether an input string is balanced; that is, if each opening parenthesis has a matching closing parenthesis. For the purposes of this example, brackets, **[** and **]**, and the symbols **<** and **>** will also be referred to as parentheses. Any enclosed substrings must themselves be balanced. The surrounding program text for the procedure is in Fig. 4.10. Read

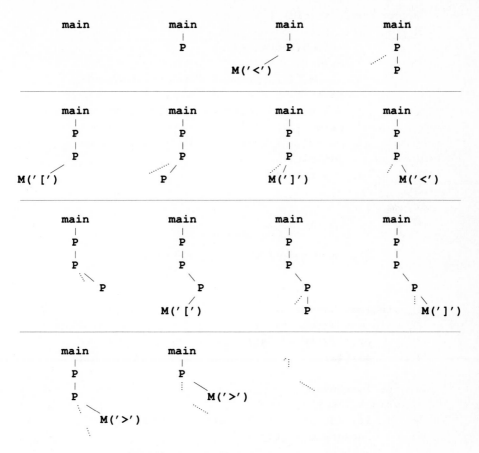

Fig. 4.8. Control flow between activations.

"match" for **M**; the shorter name makes it easier to draw activation trees.

The procedure calls on line 15 match balanced strings enclosed between
(and **)**:

(15)   **M(' ('); parens(); M(')'); continue;**

First, **M** is called to match **(**. A recursive call of **parens** then looks for
nested parentheses. Finally, **M** is called to match a balancing **)**.

Similarly, line 17 matches strings that begin with **<** and end with **>**, and
line 19 matches strings that begin with **[** and end with **]**.

Execution begins on line 26 in Fig. 4.10, where the next input character is
read into variable **lookahead**. Each call **M(t)** checks whether **t** is the
same as the lookahead character; if so, the next input character is read into
lookahead.

```
(11)   void parens(void) {
(12)       for(;;) {
(13)           switch(lookahead) {
(14)           case '(' :
(15)               M('('); parens(); M(')'); continue;
(16)           case '<' :
(17)               M('<'); parens(); M('>'); continue;
(18)           case '[' :
(19)               M('['); parens(); M(']'); continue;
(20)           default:
(21)               return;
(22)           }
(23)       }
(24)   }
```

Fig. 4.9. Procedure to parse balanced parentheses.

```
(1)    #include <stdio.h>
(2)    void error(char *s) {
(3)        printf("%s\n", s);
(4)        exit(1);
(5)    }
(6)    int lookahead;
(7)    void M(int t) {
(8)        if( lookahead != t ) error("syntax error");
(9)        lookahead = getchar();
(10)   }

           . . .

(25)   int main(void) {
(26)       lookahead = getchar();
(27)       parens();
(28)       if( lookahead != '\n' ) error("expected newline");
(29)       return 0;
(30)   }
```

Fig. 4.10. Context for procedure **parens** in Fig. 4.9.

The following tree shows the activations that are set up to read an input line containing **[]**; the program terminates after reading the newline character '**\n**' that implicitly appears at the end of a line.

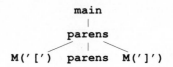

In more detail, **main** calls **parens**. Since the lookahead character is **[**, control reaches line 19, where **M** is called to match **[** and read the next lookahead character.

The recursive activation of **parens** sees lookahead **]**, and simply returns to its caller, through the default case on line 20 in the switch statement statement.

The parent activation of **parens** then calls **M** to match the balancing **]** and read **\n** as the next lookahead character. Control soon returns to line 28 in the body of **main**, where the endmarker **\n** is expected as the look-ahead, and the program terminates.   □

4.5 LEXICAL SCOPE IN C

Data needed for an activation of a procedure is collected in a record called an *activation record* or *frame*. Since control flows between activations in a stack-like manner, a stack can be used to hold frames. For this reason, frames are sometimes referred to as *stack frames*.

This section looks at stack frames for procedures in C. C does not allow procedure bodies to be nested, one inside the other, so stack-frame management for C is simpler than for Modula-2.

Alternatively, this section looks at the implementation of lexical scope in C—more specifically, at the storage to which a name in a procedure body refers.

The Scope of a Local Declaration

A C program consists of a sequence of global declarations of procedures, types, and variables. Types and variables can also be declared local to a procedure; however, a procedure cannot be declared local to another.

Local declarations can appear within any grouping of statements. A *compound* statement can have a sequence of optional declarations just after the opening brace **{**:

> **{** ⟨*declaration-list*⟩ ⟨*statement-list*⟩ **}**

Declarations within a statement allow variables to be declared where they are needed. Variable **c** is declared inside the then-part of the conditional in the following:

```
      else if( notfull() ) {
          int c;
          c = getchar();
          if( c == EOF ) break;
          enter(c);
      }
```

If such declarations are not permitted, then all variables must be declared at the beginning of the procedure body, even if they are needed only in a small fragment of the procedure.

The syntax of statements ensures that compound statements are nested one inside the other. Each compound statement begins with an opening brace, {, and ends with a matching close brace, }. The compound statements in Fig. 4.11(a) are boxed to emphasize their nesting. Statement nesting is usually shown by indentation in the source text. A more deeply nested statement is indented more than a less deeply nested one.

Just as statements nest one inside the other, scopes nest one inside the other. The scope of a declaration of x in a statement is that statement,

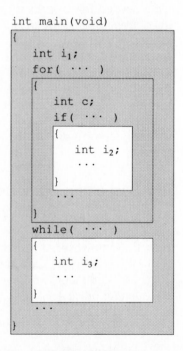

(a) Nested compound statements.   (b) Scope of i_1.

Fig. 4.11. Nesting of statements and scopes.

including any nested statements, provided x is not redeclared in the nested statements.

A redeclaration of x creates a *hole* in the scope of any outer bindings of x. The shaded portion of Fig. 4.11(b) shows the scope of the binding of i_1. The subscripts on the occurrences of i in Fig. 4.11(b) are not part of the program text; they simply allow us to talk about the three occurrences. The declarations of i_2 and i_3 create holes in the scope of i_1. By contrast, there are no holes in the scope of c, since c is not redeclared.

Another way of looking at the scope of a binding of a name x is from the viewpoint of an occurrence of x in its scope. This viewpoint leads to the *most closely nested rule*: an occurrence of a name is in the scope of the innermost enclosing declaration of the name.

Storage for Local Variables

A variable declared in a compound statement is local to an execution of the statement. Thus, when control leaves the statement, there is no further use for the local. This property allows variables with disjoint scopes to share storage because they are not needed simultaneously.

C compilers tend to allocate storage for all the variables in a procedure all at once when the procedure is called. One possible layout for the variables in Fig. 4.11 appears in Fig. 4.12. The scope of variable i_1 overlaps that of the other variables so it needs a distinct *l*-value of its own. Variables c and i_3 appear in disjoint compound statements, so the same *l*-value can be used for both of them. As long as control is in the statement containing c, the *l*-value belongs to c. As soon as control leaves this statement, the *l*-value can be used for other purposes, such as for holding the value of i_3. The *l*-value of i_2 must be distinct from those of i_1 and c because its scope is nested within those of i_1 and c.

Memory Layout for C Programs

The elements of a running C program are illustrated in the memory layout in Fig. 4.13. A machine register called a *program counter* keeps track of the flow of control through the code for the program. The code does not change during execution. Global data is held in statically allocated memory locations. Local data is held on a stack that grows and shrinks as activations start and end. At the other end of memory is an area called a

i_1
c, i_3
i_2

Fig. 4.12. *L*-values for local variables in Fig. 4.11.

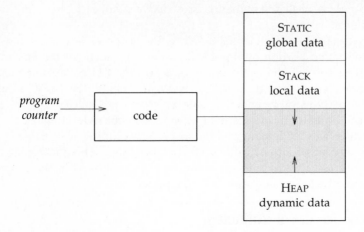

Fig. 4.13. Memory layout for C programs.

heap, which holds dynamic data that is allocated and deallocated through library procedures.

Procedure Call and Return in C

The basic frame layout in Fig. 4.14 is from Johnson and Ritchie [1981]; it has been adapted to implement C on several machine architectures.

The following actions occur when a procedure in C is called:

1. C uses call-by-value, so the caller evaluates the actual parameters for the call and places their values in the activation record for the callee. Consider the call **enter(c)** within **main** in Fig. 4.15. Variable **c** is local to the caller **main**, so it is the caller's responsibility to evaluate it.

2. Information needed to restart execution of the caller is saved. This information includes the address to which control must return on completion of the procedure call.

3. The callee allocates space for its local variables. Temporary storage for partial results during expression evaluation is also reserved. An expression like **(i+1)%size** is implemented by a sequence of instructions of the form

    $t_1 := i + 1; \quad t_2 := t_1 \% size;$

    where t_1 and t_2 are compiler-generated names. The values of compiler-generated names are held in temporary storage.

4. The body of the callee is executed. Additional activations may occur during this execution; in Fig. 4.15, **main** calls **enter**, and the body of **enter** calls **succ**. The field for outgoing parameters in Fig. 4.14 is

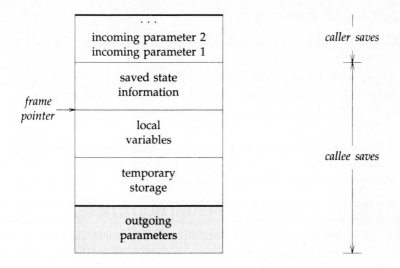

Fig. 4.14. Layout of activation records for C.

shaded because the outgoing parameters of one procedure become the incoming parameters of another.

5. Control returns to the caller. A return value, if any, is placed where the caller can find it, and the machine registers are restored, as needed, to their status when the call began. Control then goes to the saved return address.

```
char buf[MAXBUF+1];
int  size = MAXBUF+1, front = 0, rear = 0;
int  succ(int i)      { return (i+1) % size; }
 . . .
void enter(int x)   { buf[rear] = x; rear = succ(rear); }
 . . .
int main(void) {
     int c;
            . . .
          enter(c);
            . . .

}
```

Fig. 4.15. Program to illustrate procedure call and return.

Procedures as Parameters

Some examples of the use of procedures as parameters in C programs are as follows:

- A program to sort lines of text takes a comparison function as a parameter. With one comparison function, it treats the lines as strings to be sorted into dictionary order; with another, it treats the lines as numbers to be sorted in numeric order.

- An interactive program responds to commands selected from a menu. Associated with each menu item is a procedure that the menu manager takes as a parameter and calls when the item is selected.

The passing of procedures as parameters in C is facilitated by the two-level classification of names into those that are global and those that are local to some procedure. Globals are taken from the lexical environment of a procedure. Their l-values are known at compile time, so the code for a procedure body knows where to find them.

Name **y** in the declaration of **add_y** is global:

```
void add_y(int x) {  ···  x+y  ···  }
```

The program in Fig. 4.16 passes **add_y** as a parameter to **map**, which calls **add_y** on each element of an array **A**. Procedure **add_y** adds the value of global **y** to its parameter **x** and prints the resulting value. The output of the program is

```
101 102 103 104 105
```

This output does not change if **y** appears as a local in either **main**, which passes **add_y** to **map**, or in **map**, which calls **add_y**. For example, there is no change if local **i** in **map** is renamed **y**:

```
void map(int2void * f) {
    int y;
    for(y = 0; y < 5; ++y)
        f(A[y]);
}
```

The reason is that under lexical scope, the occurrence of **y** in **add_y** continues to refer to the global **y** in its lexical environment.

Functions are passed in C by passing pointers to them, so formal **f** of **map** is declared to be a pointer to type **int2void**. The first line of the program declares type name **int2void** to be the type of a function that takes an integer argument and returns a result of type **void**.

```
typedef void int2void(int);        /* type int 2void = integer → void */
#include <stdio.h>
int A[5] = { 1, 2, 3, 4, 5 };

int  y = 100;
void add_y(int x) { printf("%d ", x+y); }      /* add_y declared */

void map(int2void *f) {
    int i;
    for(i = 0; i < 5; ++i)
        f(A[i]);                               /* add_y called */
}

int main(void) {
    map(add_y); printf("\n");                  /* add_y passed */
    return 0;
}
```

Fig. 4.16. Procedure **add_y** is passed as a parameter to **map**.

Dangling Pointers

A *dangling pointer* refers to storage whose lifetime has passed. Function **f**

```
    int *f(void) { int x = 1; return &x; }
```

returns a dangling pointer because the lifetime of local **x** ends when control returns from **f**. An attempt to dereference a dangling pointer produces unpredictable results.

Tail-Recursion Elimination

When the last statement executed in the body of a procedure P is a recursive call, the call is said to be *tail recursive*. A procedure as a whole is *tail recursive* if all its recursive calls are tail recursive.

Tail-recursive calls can be eliminated and replaced by control flow within the procedure, thereby avoiding the overhead of a call. Not only is tail-recursion elimination interesting in its own right, its justification clarifies storage allocation for procedure activations.

Example 4.8. The binary search procedure **search** in Fig. 4.17 is tail recursive. It looks for **T** in a sorted array **X[lo..hi]** by comparing **T** with the middle element of the range. If the range is empty because **lo>hi**, it returns **no**. If the middle element is **T**, it returns **yes**. Otherwise, it discards half the range and calls itself recursively on the smaller range. As soon as either of the two recursive calls **search(lo,k-1)** or

```
#include <stdio.h>
int yes = 1, no = 0;
#define N 7
int X[] = { 0, 11, 22, 33, 44, 55, 66, 77 };
int T;
int search(int lo, int hi) {
    int k;
    if( lo > hi ) return no;
    k = (lo + hi) /2;
    if( T == X[k] ) return yes;
    else if( T < X[k] ) return search(lo, k-1);
    else if( T > X[k] ) return search(k+1, hi);
}
int main(void) {
    scanf("%d", &T);
    if( search(1,N) )
        printf("found\n");
    else
        printf("notfound\n");
    return 0;
}
```

Fig. 4.17. A tail-recursive binary search procedure.

search(k+1,hi) is completed, control flows back to the caller of **search(lo,hi)**. For more on binary search, see Example 3.2, page 74.

In more detail, **main** uses the library function **scanf** to read an integer into the *l*-value of **T**. It then calls **search(1,N)**, which returns either **yes** or **no**.   □

A tail-recursive call **P(a,b)** of a procedure **P** with formals **x** and **y** can be replaced by

    x = a; y = b;
    goto the first executable statement in **P**;

Suppose label **L** is attached to the first executable statement in procedure **search** in Fig. 4.17. Then, the call **search(lo,k-1)** can be replaced by

    lo = lo; hi = k-1;
    goto L;

Redundant assignments like **lo=lo** are omitted from the nonrecursive binary search procedure in Fig. 4.18, obtained from Fig. 4.17 by eliminating tail recursion and rearranging the goto statements.

```
#include <stdio.h>
int yes = 1, no = 0;
#define N 7
int X[] = { 0, 11, 22, 33, 44, 55, 66, 77 };
int T;
int search(int lo, int hi) {
    int k;
L:  if( lo > hi ) return no;
    k = (lo + hi) /2;
    if( T == X[k] ) return yes;
    else if( T < X[k] ) hi = k-1;
    else if( T > X[k] ) lo = k+1;
    goto L;
}
int main(void) {
    scanf("%d", &T);
    if( search(1,N) )
        printf("found\n");
    else
        printf("notfound\n");
    return 0;
}
```

Fig. 4.18. After eliminating tail recursion from the **search** in Fig. 4.17.

The snapshots in Fig. 4.19 show how a search for **55** proceeds. The initial call **search(1,7)** results in the creation of an activation record with

$$lo_1 = 1;\ hi_1 = 7;\ k_1 = 4;$$

Subscripts are used here to distinguish among the locals in the first, second, and third activations of **search**. Since **55** is greater than **X[k]**, a recursive activation is set up with

$$lo_2 = 5;\ hi_2 = 7;\ k_2 = 6;$$

Now **55** is less than **X[k]**, so a third and final activation occurs with

$$lo_3 = 5;\ hi_3 = 5;\ k_3 = 5;$$

Since **55** equals **X[k]**, the result **yes** is copied back up to **main** as the recursion unwinds.

Each activation of **search** executes the same code. The first activation finds parameter lo_1 at the same position relative to its frame pointer fp_1 as the second activation finds lo_2 with respect to fp_2, and so on. Once a tail-recursive call occurs, the locals in the calling activation just sit there, waiting to be deallocated when the recursion unwinds.

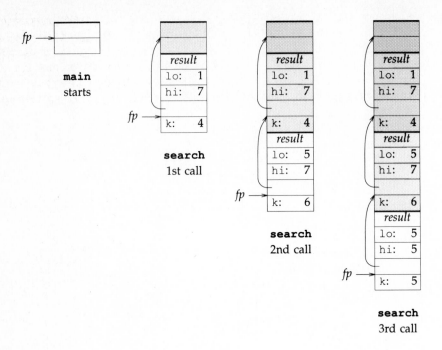

Fig. 4.19. An execution of the recursive binary search program in Fig. 4.17.

The snapshots in Fig. 4.20 show a nonrecursive search for **55**. Instead of setting up tail-recursive activations, the new program overwrites the affected fields in place, in the same activation record.

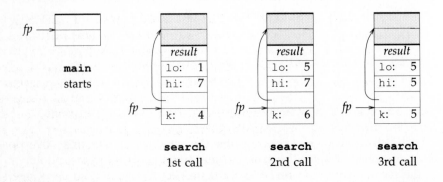

Fig. 4.20. After tail-recursion elimination, with the program of Fig. 4.18.

4.6   BLOCK STRUCTURE IN MODULA-2

A *block* consists of a sequence of declarations, including procedure declarations, and a sequence of statements. A language is said to be *block structured* if it allows blocks to be nested. This section examines the implementation of block structure in Modula-2, paying special attention to the treatment of nonlocal names in a block.

Blocks in Modula-2 serve as procedure and module bodies, as in the following syntax for procedure declarations:

> **procedure** ⟨*name*⟩ ⟨*formals*⟩ ; ⟨*block*⟩ ⟨*name*⟩

Here ⟨*formals*⟩ includes the formal parameters, if any, within parentheses, and a result type, if any.

The syntax of blocks themselves is given by

> ⟨*declaration-list*⟩ **begin** ⟨*statement-list*⟩ **end**

The blocks in Fig. 4.21 are enclosed within boxes. Nested within module *calc* is procedure *expr*, which has variable *temp* and procedure *term* declared within it. Nested inside *term* is another declaration of variable *temp* and a procedure *factor*.

Purpose of Block Structure

The declarations in a block are visible only within the block; the visibility rules are similar to those for compound statements in Section 4.5. The scope of a declaration in a block consists of that block and any nested blocks, except for holes due to nested redeclarations. Alternatively, a nonlocal occurrence of a name is in the scope of the most closely nested declaration of the name.

These visibility rules apply to procedure names as well. In Fig. 4.21, consider the nonlocal occurrence of *expr* in the innermost block for *factor*. The binding of *expr* is found by proceeding inside out, looking for the most closely nested block containing a declaration. The only declaration of *expr* in the figure is in module *calc*.

The procedure nesting in Fig. 4.21 is representative of those found in Pascal programs, where block structure is the only mechanism for controlling the visibility of names. The module facility of Modula-2 decouples visibility control from procedure nesting. Nevertheless, Modula-2 allows procedures to be nested, so the implementation of block structure in this section is needed for Modula-2 as well.

The procedure nesting from a desk calculator program is shown by indentation in the following:

module *calc* ;

. . .

> **procedure** *expr* () : **integer;**
>> **var** *temp* : **integer;**
>> **procedure** *term* () : **integer;**
>>> **var** *temp* : **integer;**
>>> **procedure** *factor* () : **integer;**
>>>> **var** *temp* : **integer;**
>>> **begin** (* *factor* *)
>>>
>>>   . . .
>>>
>>>   *temp* := *expr* ();
>>>
>>>   . . .
>>>
>>> **end** *factor* ;
>> **begin** (* *term* *)
>>
>>   . . .
>>
>>   *temp* := *temp* * *factor* ();
>>
>>   . . .
>>
>> **end** *term* ;
> **begin** (* *expr* *)
>
>   . . .
>
>   *temp* := *temp* + *term* ();
>
>   . . .
>
> **end** *expr* ;

. . .

end *calc.*

Fig. 4.21. Procedure *expr* with nested procedures *term* and *factor*.

calc

> *scan*
>> *getch*
>> *digitval*
> *expr*
>> *term*
>>> *factor*

Module *calc* uses *scan* to read and group the input into tokens and *expr* to evaluate expressions. Procedure *scan* happens to use *getch* to read individual characters and *digitval* to map digits to numeric values, but *getch* and *digitval* are not visible from within *expr*. Similarly, the code for *scan* cannot see *term* and *factor*, which *expr* happens to use.

Unfortunately, block structure has some problems:

- *Readability.* Block-structured programs can be hard to read because the statements in a procedure body appear after all the declarations in the procedure, so they could appear several pages after the procedure heading. In Fig. 4.21, the nested procedures *factor* and *term* separate the heading of *expr* from its statements.

- *Run-time overhead.* As we see next, there can be some overhead associated with access to nonlocals in a nested procedure body.

Access to Nonlocals: Control and Access Links

Suppose that memory is divided into areas for the code, static data, a run-time stack, and a heap, as in Section 4.5. Each block has an activation record with fields for parameters, saved state information, local variables, and compiler generated temporaries.

The essential difference between storage management for Modula-2 and storage management for C is in the way nonlocal names are accessed. A nonlocal refers to storage that is in some other activation record. The question is, which one?

Access to nonlocals will be illustrated by considering the program outline in Fig. 4.22. Procedures P, Q, and R are patterned after *expr*, *term*, and *factor* in Fig. 4.21. A real program, however, is unlikely to use its variables in the way the outline uses x, y, and z.

In the program text, the bindings of nonlocals y in Q and z in R appear in the enclosing procedure P. Thus, at run time, the *l*-values of y and z appear in an activation record for P.

A direct technique for implementing block structure is to maintain two kinds of links, included within the saved state information in an activation record:

1. A *control link*, also called a *dynamic link*, points to the activation record of the run-time caller.

2. An *access link*, also called a *static link*, points to the most recent activation of the lexically enclosing block.

The snapshots of the run-time stack in Fig. 4.23 correspond to an execution of the program in Fig. 4.22. Subscripts distinguish between activations of a procedure. After

M calls P, P calls Q, and Q calls R,

the stack is as in Fig. 4.23(a). In each of these calls, the callee is lexically nested within the caller, so both the control and the access links point from the callee to its caller.

In (b), R has just called P. That is, activation R_1 has made a recursive call to P_2. The control link from P_2 points to its caller R_1; the access link points to M, the most recent activation of the lexically enclosing block.

```
    module M ;
        procedure P ();
                var x, y, z;
                procedure Q ();
                        procedure R ();
                        begin (* R *)
                                · · · z := P (); · · ·
                        end R ;
                begin (* Q *)
                        · · · y := R (); · · ·
                end Q ;
            begin (* P *)
                    · · · x := Q (); · · ·
            end P ;
    begin (* M *)
            · · · P (); · · ·
    end M ;
```

Fig. 4.22. Illustration of nonlocal access within nested procedures.

Access links are used as follows. Each activation of P gets its own locals x, y, and z. Thus, in activation Q_1 nonlocal y refers to an l-value in P_1, and in activation Q_2 nonlocal y refers to an l-value in P_2. Similarly, z in R_1 refers to an l-value two access links away in P_1, and z in R_2 refers to an l-value two access links away in P_2.

The number of links to be followed to access a nonlocal can be computed at compile time, from the *nesting depth* of a block. Let the nesting depth of the block for a module be 1. The nesting depth of an enclosed block is 1 greater than the nesting depth of its enclosing block.[3] The *distance* between two blocks is the absolute value of the difference between their nesting depths.

In general, the address for a nonlocal occurrence of a name n has two parts:

1. the distance between the nonlocal and its binding specifying the number of access links to be traversed, and

2. the relative address of n within the activation record reached.

The distance between blocks is also needed to set up access links when a nonlocal procedure is called. For example, 3 is the distance between the

---

[3] This section ignores local modules declared inside another module. Wirth [1988] notes, "Experience with Modula over the last eight years has shown that *local modules* were rarely used. Considering the additional complexity of the compiler required to handle them, and the additional complications in the visibility rules of the language definition, the elimination of local modules [from Oberon] appears justified."

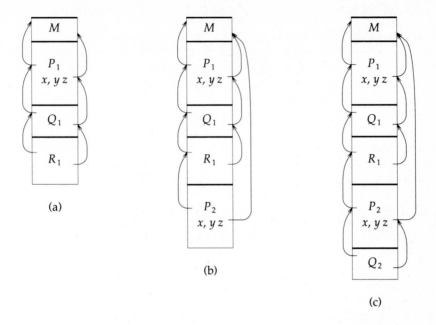

Fig. 4.23. Control links are to the left and access links are to the right.

block for R containing a call to nonlocal P and the block for M where P is declared. Also, 3 is the number of access links that take us from R_1 to the activation record for M. In more detail, when R_1 calls P_2,

1. we follow 3 access links from R_1 to find the activation record for M, and

2. set the access link in P_2 to point to M.

Access links for local procedures simply point to their callers, as when M calls P_1, P_1 calls Q_1, Q_1 calls R_1, and P_2 calls Q_2 in Fig. 4.23.

Procedures as Parameters

A procedure that is passed as a parameter carries its lexical environment along with it. That is, when a procedure X is passed as a parameter an access link a goes with it. Later, when X is called, a is used as the access link for its block.

The issues that arise with procedure parameters are similar to those that arise in functional languages, where functions can be passed freely. For more information, see the discussion of "closures" in Section 11.2.

Displays in the Absence of Procedures as Parameters

Displays are an optimization technique for obtaining faster access to nonlocals. A *display* is an array d of pointers to activation records, indexed by nesting depth. Array element $d[i]$ is maintained so that it points to the most recent activation of the block at nesting depth i.

The display in Fig. 4.24(a) is an array $d[1..4]$ with $d[1]$ pointing to the activation record M, $d[2]$ pointing to P_1, and so on. In (b) only the display elements $d[1]$ and $d[2]$ are shown, since P_2 can refer only to names declared in enclosing blocks. On return from P_2 to R_1, the display must be restored to its status in Fig. 4.24(a).

With a display, a nonlocal n can be found as follows:

1. Use one array access to find the activation record containing n.

2. Use the relative address within the activation record to find the *l*-value for n.

A general technique for maintaining a display is store the entire array within the activation record of the caller. The callee can then use the array for its own display. The size of the array is the maximum nesting depth in the program, which is usually small. For the running example of this section the maximum nesting depth is 4. This technique handles procedures that are passed as parameters, but it increases the overhead of a procedure call because the entire display has to be stored.

An alternative technique, illustrated in Fig. 4.25, works well when procedures are not passed as parameters, and can be made to work when they are. The idea is to save only $d[i]$ when an activation at nesting depth i occurs. The old value of $d[i]$ is saved within the activation record.

In Fig. 4.25, R_1 has called P_2. Since P_2 is at nesting depth 2, display element $d[2]$ points to P_2. The old value of $d[2]$ is saved within the activation record for P_2; it is shown by a heavy line. Display elements $d[3]$ and $d[4]$ are inaccessible. They remain in place, however, for use upon return from P_2 to R_1.

In summary, the part of the calling sequence for maintaining the display is

1. Save $d[i]$ in the activation record of the callee at nesting depth i.

2. Make $d[i]$ point to the callee.

Display maintenance in the return sequence from callee to caller is done simply by restoring $d[i]$ from the saved value in the callee.

The complication with procedures as parameters is that the parameter needs the entire display to set up its lexical environment.

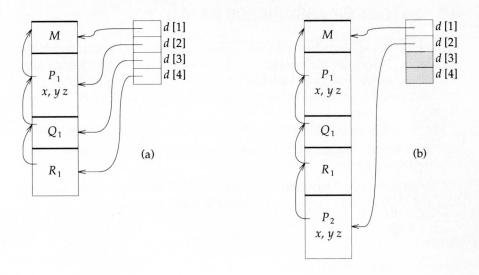

Fig. 4.24. Display elements, indexed by nesting depth, point to visible blocks.

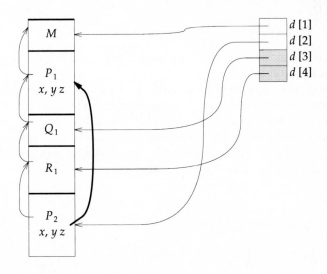

Fig. 4.25. Display maintenance in the absence of procedures as parameters.

4.7   LAYOUT OF ASSIGNABLE DATA TYPES

Besides their use for checking the consistency of a program, types in imperative languages determine the layout of data in the underlying machine. Storage for local variables is on the run-time stack, within the activation record for a procedure. Data allocated dynamically at run time is held in the heap.

The following principle allows us to go from a type to its storage layout:

> *Static layout principle.* The size and layout of the storage for each type are known statically.

One implication of the layout principle is that data structures such as lists and trees must be implemented using records and pointers.

Array Layout

After the variable declaration

var A : **array** $[0..4]$ **of integer**

the elements of array A appear in consecutive locations, as in Fig. 4.26. Let w be the *width* of each array element; that is, each element occupies w locations. Then, if $A[0]$ begins at location *base*, $A[1]$ begins at *base* $+w$, $A[2]$ at *base* $+2 \times w$, and so on.

A formula for the address of $A[i]$ is

$$i \times w + (base - low \times w) \tag{4.2}$$

where *low* is the lower bound of the array. In Fig. 4.26, *low* = 0, so the formula simplifies to $i \times w + base$.

The number of instructions needed to compute the formula (4.2) is independent of the value of i. Each element can therefore be accessed in constant time, providing random access to array elements.

We can do even better than the formula (4.2). The expression $(base - low \times w) = c$ can be precomputed and stored at compile time. The address of $A[i]$ can therefore be computed as

$$i \times w + c \tag{4.3}$$

Arrays of arrays can be defined as well:

var M : **array** $[1..3]$ **of** $[1..2]$ **of integer**

Now $M[1]$, $M[2]$, and $M[3]$ are subarrays; each subarray is indexed by values in the subrange $[1..2]$. If we write $M[i][j]$ as m_{ij}, then $M[1]$, $M[2]$, and $M[3]$ can be viewed as the rows of the following matrix:

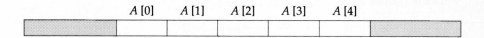

$A\,[0]$ $A\,[1]$ $A\,[2]$ $A\,[3]$ $A\,[4]$

Fig. 4.26. Consecutive locations for array elements.

$$\begin{bmatrix} m_{11} & m_{12} \\ m_{21} & m_{22} \\ m_{31} & m_{32} \end{bmatrix}$$

The layout in Fig. 4.27 is called *row-major layout* because the "rows" $M\,[1]$, $M\,[2]$, and $M\,[3]$ appear side by side. In other words, in row-major layout, the elements $M\,[i\,][j\,]$ are laid out with the last subscript j varying faster than the first subscript i.

A formula for the address of $A\,[i_1][i_2]$ is

$$i_1 \times w_1 + i_2 \times w_2 + (base - low_1 \times w_1 - low_2 \times w_2) \tag{4.4}$$

where w_1 is the width of the row $A\,[i_1]$, w_2 is the width of the row element $A\,[i_1][i_2]$, and low_1 and low_2 are the lower bounds for a row and an element of a row, respectively. Incidentally, w_1, the width of a row, is $n_2 \times w_2$, where n_2 is the number of elements in a row; that is, $n_2 = high_2 - low_2 + 1$.

Again, precomputation of $(base - low_1 \times w_1 - low_2 \times w_2) = d$ at compile time reduces the run-time address computation of (4.4) to

$$i_1 \times w_1 + i_2 \times w_2 + d \tag{4.5}$$

In *column-major layout*, the first subscript of the two subscripts in $M\,[i,j\,]$ varies fastest:

$$M\,[1,1],\ M\,[2,1],\ M\,[3,1],\ M\,[1,2],\ M\,[2,2],\ M\,[3,2]$$

Both row-major and column-major layout generalize to more than two levels of subscripts.

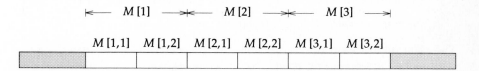

$\longmapsto\quad M\,[1]\quad\longrightarrow\!\!\longleftarrow\quad M\,[2]\quad\longrightarrow\!\!\longleftarrow\quad M\,[3]\quad\longrightarrow$

$M\,[1,1]\quad M\,[1,2]\quad M\,[2,1]\quad M\,[2,2]\quad M\,[3,1]\quad M\,[3,2]$

Fig. 4.27. Row-major array layout.

Variant Records

Suppose that objects in a set A can be classified into disjoint subsets $B_1, B_2, \ldots, B_k$, with $k > 1$. Such objects can be represented by a variant record with common information held in "fixed" fields and classification-specific information in optional "variant" parts. This classification into subsets is done more systematically using the concept of subtypes in Chapter 6.

Here are two examples of such objects from everyday life. All aircraft have a manufacturer and a price; however, a small commuter aircraft has just one engine and a certain wide-body jet has four engines. All employees have a home address; however, their marital status indicates whether they have a spouse.

For a programming example, consider the nodes in the following expression tree:

All nodes have a type; however, they can have different numbers of children. Such nodes can be classified into those for variables, constants, binary operators, and unary operators, with zero, zero, two, and one children, respectively.

We use the following simplified syntax to explore the layout of variant parts within a record (the complete syntax is similar to that of case statements, complete with default **else** parts):

case $\langle tag\text{-}name \rangle : \langle type\text{-}name \rangle$ **of**
$\langle constant \rangle_1 :$ $\langle name \rangle_1 : \langle type\text{-}expression \rangle_1$ ' | '
$\langle constant \rangle_2 :$ $\langle name \rangle_2 : \langle type\text{-}expression \rangle_2$ ' | '
       $\cdots$ ' | '
$\langle constant \rangle_v :$ $\langle name \rangle_v : \langle type\text{-}expression \rangle_v$
end

A variant part of a record is designed to be in one of a specified set of states; each state can have a distinct field layout. This syntax provides for v possible states, corresponding to the following distinct constants:

$\langle constant \rangle_1, \langle constant \rangle_2, \ldots, \langle constant \rangle_v$

The state depends on the value stored in a special field, called a *tag field*, with name $\langle tag\text{-}name \rangle$ and type given by $\langle type\text{-}name \rangle$.

The record type *node* in Fig. 4.28 is a representative example. It is defined in terms of *kind*, an auxiliary enumeration type. Fields c_1 and c_2

type $kind = (unary, \; binary)$;
      $node = $ **record**
                $c_1 : T_1$;
                $c_2 : T_2$;
                case $k : kind$ **of**
                    $unary :$ $child : T_3$; |
                    $binary :$ $lchild, \; rchild \; : \; T_4$;
                end;
          end;

Fig. 4.28. The variant part of record type $node$ begins with **case**.

are in the common fixed part of the type $node$. The variant part of $node$ has two distinct field layouts, corresponding to the constants $unary$ and $binary$ of type $kind$; the two layouts are separated by $|$. The choice between these two variant layouts depends on the value of the tag name k. If k has value $unary$, then the variant part has just one field, named $child$. If k has value $binary$, then the variant part has two fields, named $lchild$ and $rchild$.

The space reserved for a variant part is just enough to hold the fields in the largest variant. The layout for the fields of type $node$ in Fig. 4.28 is shown in Fig. 4.29. The fixed part consists of two fields c_1 and c_2. On the borderline between the fixed and variant part is the tag field k. It is present in all states, so it behaves like the fixed fields, yet it exists only because of the variant part. The value in the tag field is given by the two constants $unary$ and $binary$. If the variant part is in state $unary$, then only one field $child$ exists; otherwise, it is in state $binary$ and the two fields $lchild$ and $rchild$ exist. These two variant layouts can therefore share the same space.

Variant records introduce weaknesses into the type system for a language. Compilers do not usually check that the value in the tag field is consistent with the state of the record. Furthermore, tag fields are optional. The tag name can be dropped, as in the following declaration of type t:

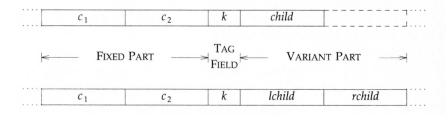

Fig. 4.29. Layout for record type $node$ from Fig. 4.28.

```
type  s = [1 .. 2];
      t = record
            case : s of
              1: (i : integer);
              2: (r : real)
            end;
          end;
var   x : t;
```

Record type *t* consists of only a variant part. The type name *s* after **case** says that the variant part can be in one of two states, given by constants 1 and 2 associated with *s*. Since a tag name does not appear between **case** and the type name *s*, there is no tag field; the state of the variant part therefore cannot be stored within the record. The only possible fields for variable *x* are *x.i* and *x.r*, only one of which exists at any given time. Since the state is not stored within the record, an implementation cannot check whether *x* is in state 1 when *x.i* is selected and whether *x* is in state 2 when *x.r* is selected. Unsafe program fragments like

```
x.r := 1.0;
WriteInt (x.i)
```

will therefore go undetected. An execution of such a program fragment produced the machine-dependent output

16512

The above weaknesses make variant records problematic as a language construct. Nevertheless, they can be a useful implementation concept.

4.8   POINTERS AND DYNAMIC ALLOCATION

Pointers in programming languages are motivated by indirect addresses in machine language, the main difference being that a pointer *p* must point only to objects of a specific type *T*. Pointers have a fixed size, independent of the type *T*; they typically fit into a single machine word.

If *p* is a pointer to an object of type *T*, then *p*↑ refers to the object pointed to by *p*. The design of Modula-2 and Pascal was governed by the following principle:

   Alias avoidance. A pointer must not be an alias for any variable name or for any component of a data structure denoted by a name.

From the syntax of Modula-2, a name in a declaration such as

   var ⟨*name*⟩ : ⟨*type-expression*⟩

is local to some module or procedure. Its storage, or the object it denotes, is therefore on the run-time stack. The alias avoidance principle implies that a pointer cannot refer to an object on the stack. Hence, dangling pointers cannot occur, except by explicit deallocation under program control, as discussed below.

Linked Data Structures

By the static layout principle, the size of the storage for each type must be known at compile time. Thus, data structures that grow or shrink during execution must be made up of fixed-size cells or nodes. The data structure grows when a cell is linked in and it shrinks when a cell is removed. The ability to grow is desirable in programs like compilers, which must handle source text ranging from a few lines to several thousand lines. The compiler's internal data structures can then start out at a size adequate for typical source text, growing only if a large program comes along.

Cells and links are also used to implement data structures such as lists and trees, which have recursively defined types. (See the definition of the ML datatypes *bitree* and *searchtree* in Section 2.8.) A cell in a singly linked list appears in Fig. 4.30.

In the following declarations, type *link* is a pointer to a *cell* and a *cell* is a record with an information field and a single link to the next cell:

type *link* = **pointer to** *cell*;
    cell = **record**
          info : **integer**;   (4.6)
          next : *link*;
      end;

The conceptual or logical organization of a linked data structure is separate from its physical layout in memory. The links between cells determine the logical organization. The connected cells need not be physically adjacent to each other; they can be anywhere in memory. As long as links between them are maintained, cells can even be moved without disturbing the data structure.

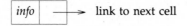

info   ⟶   link to next cell

Fig. 4.30. A cell in a linked-list data structure.

Operations on Pointers in Modula-2

Modula-2 tightly controls the objects to which a pointer can point by allowing only the following operations on pointers:

- *Dynamic creation of objects.* If p has type **pointer to** T, then execution of the statement **new**(p) leaves p pointing to a newly created object of type T. We call any object created by **new** a *dynamic* object.

- *Dereferencing.* The operator ↑ is called the *dereferencing* operator. As mentioned earlier, p↑ denotes the object pointed to by p.

- *Assignment.* Assignments are permitted between pointers of the same type.

- *Equality testing.* The equality relation = tests if two pointers of the same type point to the same object. An inequality test ≠ is allowed as well.

- *Deletion of objects.* A dynamic object exists until it is explicitly released by execution of a statement **dispose**(p), which leaves the pointer p dangling.

The above operations ensure that a pointer can point only to dynamic objects. To see why, note that only **new** and assignment can change what a pointer p points to. By definition, **new** leaves p pointing to a dynamic object. A little thought shows that an assignment can make p point only to an object created by a previous call to **new**.

Furthermore, dynamic objects are created only by **new**, so the converse is true as well; that is, a dynamic object is accessible only through a pointer.

A special pointer **nil** points to no object and belongs to all pointer types.[4]

Example 4.9. The transformation in Fig. 4.31 adds a cell at the front of a linked list. The new cell has 4 in its *info* field.

The transformation can be implemented as follows. Suppose that p has type *link*, declared as in (4.6). The statement **new**(p) leaves p pointing to a

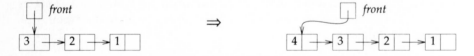

Fig. 4.31. Insert a cell at the front of a linked list.

---

[4] Modula-2 supports creation and deletion of objects, but the Pascal names **new** and **dispose** are not built into the language. Alternative names for these operations are **allocate** and **deallocate**.

newly created cell. An assignment $p\uparrow.info$ puts 4 in the $info$ field of the cell pointed to by p.

For illustration, suppose that the three cells in the initial list are called c_3, c_2, and c_1, from left to right, and that the newly allocated cell is called c_4. The subscript in c_i is a reminder that c_i is not a part of the program, and is for use only within the remarks in the right-hand column:

PROGRAM	REMARK
new(p);	allocate a new cell c_4; p points to c_4
$p\uparrow.info := 4$;	$c_4.info := 4$;
$p\uparrow.next := front$;	$c_4.next$ points to c_3
$front := p$;	$front := p$;

Transformations like the one in Fig. 4.31 are needed to enter elements into a stack implemented as a linked list.   □

Circular Types

Linked data structures give rise to recursive or circular types. The following fragment is repeated from earlier in this section:

```
type  link = pointer to cell;
       cell = record
                   info : integer;
                   next : link;
               end;
```

Type $link$ is defined in terms of type $cell$ because a link is a pointer to a cell. Furthermore, type $cell$ is defined in terms of $link$ because a cell is a record with a field holding a link. Thus $link$ and $type$ are defined circularly, in terms of each other.

The circular dependency between $link$ and $cell$ can be seen from the types of the following expressions (assume that p is declared to have type $link$):

EXPRESSION	TYPE
p :	$link$
$p\uparrow$:	$cell$
$p\uparrow.next$:	$link$
$p\uparrow.next\uparrow$:	$cell$
$p\uparrow.next\uparrow.next$:	$link$
$p\uparrow.next\uparrow.next\uparrow$:	$cell$

. . .

This progression continues indefinitely.

Circular dependencies between types occur only through pointer types in Modula-2 and C. In the declarations of $link$ and $cell$ just given, the first occurrence of $cell$ is on the right side of

> **type** *link* = **pointer to** *cell*;

At this point, *link* depends on *cell*, but *cell* has yet to be declared. Subsequently, type *cell* is defined in terms of *link*, thereby setting up a circular dependency.

EXERCISES

4.1 Rewrite the function **main** in the C program in Fig. 4.3, page 124, to eliminate all procedure calls except those to **getchar**, **putchar**, and **frand**.

4.2 Give a single program fragment that produces different results under each of the following parameter-passing methods:
a) call-by-value,
b) call-by-reference,
c) call-by-value-result,
d) call-by-name.

4.3 Suppose procedure *swap* 2 is declared as follows:

> **procedure** *swap* 2(*x*, *y* : **integer**);
>   **procedure** *f* () : **integer**;
>   **var** *z* : **integer**;
>   **begin** (∗ *f* ∗)
>   *z* := *x* ; *x* := *y* ; **return** *z*
>   **end** *f* ;
>   **begin** (∗ *swap* 2 ∗)
>   *y* := *f* ()
>   **end** *swap* 2;

Describe the effect of the procedure call *swap* 2(*i*, *A* [*i*]) under each of the following parameter-passing methods:
a) call-by-value,
b) call-by-reference,
c) call-by-value-result,
d) macro expansion.

4.4 Suppose that the call-by-name method is used to pass parameters to the procedure *swap* 2 in Exercise 4.3. Suppose also that an assignment $E_1 := E_2$ is implemented as follows:

> compute the *l*-value of E_1;
> compute the *r*-value of E_2;
> place the *r*-value of E_2 into the *l*-value of E_1

a) Explain why *swap* 2(*i*, *A* [*i*]) exchanges the values of *i* and *A* [*i*].

b) Under what conditions will the call *swap* 2(*i*, *A* [*p* ()]) fail to simply exchange the values of *i* and the array element *A* [*p* ()], where function *p* is declared by

> **procedure** *p* () : **integer**;
> **begin**
>> *i* := *i* + 1; **return** *i*
> **end** *p*

4.5 The dynamic scope rule specifies that nonlocals must be evaluated in the calling environment. Explain why macro expansion of procedure calls produces the same result as would be obtained under the dynamic scope rule.

4.6 Quicksort is an algorithm for sorting the elements of a subarray *A* [*m* .. *n*] in place. It works as follows (see Fig. 4.32):

1. If the subarray has at most one element, there is nothing to be done. The remaining steps assume that the subarray has at least two elements.

2. Choose some element of the subarray, and call it a *pivot*. In Fig. 4.32, the pivot is **31**, enclosed within dashed lines.

3. Rearrange the elements of the subarray so that elements less than or equal to the pivot appear to its left, and elements greater than or equal to the pivot appear to its right (use the algorithm from either Exercise 3.13 or 3.14).

4. Apply Quicksort to recursively sort the smaller and larger elements in place.

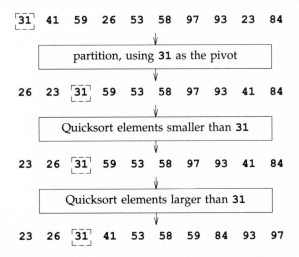

Fig. 4.32. An illustration of Quicksort.

Implement Quicksort in the language of your choice. Insert print statements on entry and exit to each procedure to show the activations that occur when Quicksort is applied to the initial subarray in Fig. 4.32.

4.7 Procedure **parens** in Example 4.7, page 134, matches strings with the following EBNF syntax:

$$Parens ::= \{ \ '(' \ Parens \ ')' \ | \ '<' \ Parens \ '>' \ | \ '[' \ Parens \ ']' \ \}$$

Modify the procedure to match the syntax

a) $Parens ::= \ '(' \ Parens \ ')' \ | \ '<' \ Parens \ '>' \ | \ '[' \ Parens \ ']'$

b) $E ::= \ '(' \ '+' \ E \ E \ ')' \ | \ '<' \ '*' \ E \ E \ '>' \ | \ '[' \ 'n' \ ']'$

c) $E ::= \ '+' \ E \ E \ | \ '*' \ E \ E \ | \ 'n'$

4.8 Expressions with the syntax

$$
\begin{aligned}
E &::= T \ \{ \ '+' \ T \ | \ '-' \ T \ \} \\
T &::= F \ \{ \ '*' \ F \ | \ '/' \ F \ \} \\
F &::= \ '(' \ E \ ')' \ | \ \mathbf{number}
\end{aligned}
$$

can be evaluated by setting up procedures corresponding to the nonterminals E, T, and F. The body of the procedure for a nonterminal is constructed from the right side of the production as follows:

- The braces { and } correspond to loops.

- Alternatives separated by | lead to a case statement. An alternative is selected if the leading token in the alternative equals the lookahead token.

- A token in the right side matches the lookahead token in the input; procedure **parens** in Example 4.7 calls **M** for this purpose.

- A nonterminal results in a call to its procedure.

The version of the procedure for E in Fig. 4.33 combines evaluation with matching. The procedures for E, T, and F return an integer representing the value of the subexpression matched by an activation of the procedure. An activation of procedure **E** in Fig. 4.33 matches a sequence of terms separated by $+$ or $-$ signs, and returns the value of this sequence.

In the language of your choice, implement an evaluator for infix expressions like **(512-487)*2**. Feel free to use or adapt the extracts from a desk-calculator program in Section 3.5 (see page 94).

```
int E(void) {
    int value;
    value = T();
    for(;;) {
        switch(lookahead) {
        case '+':
            M('+'); value = value + T(); continue;
        case '-':
            M('-'); value = value - T(); continue;
        default:
            return value;
        }
    }
}
```

Fig. 4.33. Procedure for evaluating a sequence of terms separated by + or − signs.

4.9 The procedure call and return sequence for C must be capable of handling the standard function **printf**, which presents the following problem: the number and type of its arguments can vary from call to call. The first argument of **printf** specifies the output format for the remaining arguments. The **%d** within the first argument string in the call

   printf("found %d ", n);

tells us that there must be a second argument of type integer, whose value must be printed in decimal notation. Adapt the procedure call and return sequence in Section 4.5 to handle **printf**. Note that the caller of **printf** knows the arguments at compile time, but that the callee needs to examine the first argument of a call to determine the number and types of the remaining arguments of that call.

4.10 The snapshots of the stack of activation records in Fig. 4.19 and 4.20 illustrate recursive and nonrecursive binary searches for **55**. Draw corresponding snapshots to illustrate searches for **40**, which is not in the table.

4.11 The pseudo-code in Fig. 4.22, page 150, contains nested procedures with nonlocal variables. For each assignment in the pseudo-code, describe the actions that occur every time the assignment is executed. Be explicit about the procedure call and return sequences and the use and maintenance of the control and access links.

4.12 Redo Exercise 4.11 to use a display instead of access links.

4.13 The lower and upper bounds of a *dynamic array* are computed on procedure entry. Thus, if dynamic array A is declared in procedure P, then the lower and upper bounds of A can be given by expressions whose values are recomputed for every activation of P.

a) Adapt the layout of activation records in Section 4.5 to include space for dynamic arrays. Indicate any changes to the procedure call and return sequence.

b) Assuming row-major layout, give a formula for computing the address of $A[i_1][i_2] \cdots [i_k]$, where $k \geq 1$. Precompute expressions where possible to reduce run-time address computation.

c) Assuming column-major layout, give a formula as in (b).

4.14 With cells and linked lists as in Section 4.8, give a program fragment that removes an element from the front of one list and inserts it at the front of another list.

4.15 A binary search tree is a data structure for maintaining sets of values like integers, which can be compared using a $\leq$ relation. A binary search tree is either empty, or it consists of a node with two binary search trees as subtrees. Each node holds an integer element. Binary search trees satisfy the following invariant: The elements held in the left subtree of a node are smaller than the element n at the node, and the elements held in the right subtree of the node are larger than n. (For more information see Example 2.5, page 57.)

a) Describe an implementation of binary search trees in terms of records and pointers.

b) Write a function *member* to determine if an integer is held at some node in a binary search tree.

c) Write a function *insert* to add an integer to a binary search tree.

d) Write a function *print* that prints the elements within a binary search tree, in increasing order.

BIBLIOGRAPHIC NOTES

Naur [1981] notes, "Recursive procedures were becoming known just barely at the time [when Algol 60 was defined], and mostly through McCarthy's work on LISP." The treatment of activation records in this chapter is suitable for a language in the Algol family, but not for a language like Lisp; scope rules for nonlocals in functional languages are examined in Section 11.2. Exception handling, another topic that is related to the material in this chapter, is discussed in Section 7.6.

Recursion was added almost as an afterthought to Algol 60, by the addition of a clarifying sentence, "Any occurrence of the procedure identifier
within the body of the procedure other than in a left part in an assignment
statement denotes activation of the procedure (Naur [1963a])." An
immediate consequence of recursion is that more than one activation of a
procedure can be alive at the same time, ruling out the possibility of static
or compile-time allocation of storage for variables. The techniques in Section 4.6 for handling block structure were developed soon thereafter.
Dijkstra [1960] discusses the use of displays for accessing nonlocals in a
lexically scoped block-structured language. Randell and Russell [1964]
describe a compiler for Algol 60, complete with stack allocation, displays,
and dynamic arrays (see Exercise 4.13). For more information, see textbooks on compilers, such as Aho, Sethi, and Ullman [1986].

The benefits of block structure and procedure nesting have been ques-
tioned from time to time. See Wulf and Shaw [1973], Clarke, Wileden, and
Wolf [1980], and Hanson [1981].

Exercises 4.3 and 4.4 are motivated by Fleck [1976], who discusses the
difficulties of implementing a *swap* procedure using call-by-name.

The expression evaluator outlined in Exercise 4.8 is based on an
approach to syntax analysis, called "recursive-descent parsing." The outline in Exercise 4.8 is geared to productions in which alternatives separated
by | begin with tokens. The choice between alternatives can then be
made by a case statement that compares the lookahead symbol with the
tokens. Techniques for handling more grammars can be found in textbooks on compilers.

Johnson and Ritchie [1981] discuss the nuances of procedure call and
return sequences for C, including the handling of the standard function
printf (Exercise 4.9).

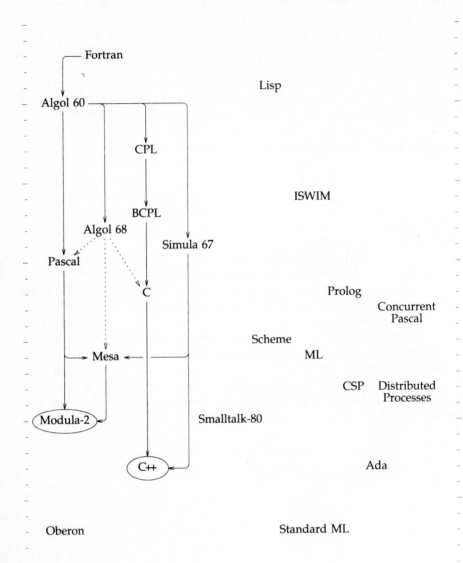

Fortran

Lisp

Algol 60

CPL

ISWIM

BCPL

Algol 68

Simula 67

Pascal

C

Prolog

Concurrent
Pascal

Scheme

Mesa

ML

CSP   Distributed
Processes

Modula-2

Smalltalk-80

C++

Ada

Oberon

Standard ML

Simula 67 is a general-purpose programming language, motivated by simulation models. The class construct of Simula directly influenced classes in C++ and Smalltalk-80, and indirectly influenced, through Mesa, modules in Modula-2.

```
┌─────────────────────────────────────────────────────────────────┐
│  Five                                                             │
└─────────────────────────────────────────────────────────────────┘
```

Data
Encapsulation

Language constructs for structuring programs are found under various names, including class, cluster, flavor, form, module, package, and structure. Along with so many names go so many viewpoints on how programs should be organized and developed.

The two key ideas in this chapter are as follows:

1. Data belongs together with the operations on it.

2. Information hiding can make programs easier to read and maintain.

5.1 CONSTRUCTS FOR PROGRAM STRUCTURING

The idea that data and operations go together was one of the early lessons of the Simula project. Nygaard and Dahl [1981] recall seeing many useful applications in which collections of variables and procedures served as "natural units of programming."

This section considers the difference between modules and classes, both of which can be used to collect variables and procedures. Simply stated, modules partition the static program text, whereas classes can be used, in addition, to describe dynamic objects that exist at run time.

Procedures

Before we examine any new constructs, let us recapitulate the role of procedures, which have been in use since the earliest days of computing.
Function procedures extend the built-in operators of a language, and
proper procedures extend the built-in actions.

Among the benefits of procedures are the following:

- *Abstractions of operations.* The user of a procedure needs to know only
  what a procedure does, not how the procedure is implemented. Procedures can be used to partition a program so that the operations in it
  can be understood in isolation.

- *Language extensions.* Standard collections of useful procedures are a
  way of extending a language. Both C and Modula-2 rely on libraries
  of procedures for such essential operations as input/output.

Modules Partition the Static Program Text

A *module* partitions the text of a program into manageable pieces.
Modules are static. We cannot create new modules or copies of existing
modules dynamically as a program runs.

A module serves as a black box with which the rest of the program
interacts through an interface. The *interface* of a module is a collection of
declarations of types, variables, procedures, and so on. An implementation
of the module consists of everything else about the module, including the
code for the procedures. Interfaces and implementations are also referred
to as the *public* and *private* views, respectively, of the module.

The public and private views of two modules, *table* and *buffer*, appear in
Fig. 5.1; the private views are shaded. The interface of module *table* consists of procedures *insert* and *find*. The interface of module *buffer* consists
of the procedures *enter* and *leave* and the constant *nul*.

A module is said to have a *local state* because its variables retain their
values even when control is not in the module. For example, consider a
program made up of three modules:

The variables in *buffer* retain their values even when control is in one of the
other modules, *producer* or *consumer*.

MODULE *table*

procedure *insert* ;
procedure *find* ;
const *limit* ;
var *tab, avail* ;
· · ·
procedure bodies
· · ·
initialization

MODULE *buffer*

procedure *enter* ;
procedure *leave* ;
const *nul* ;
const *maxbuf* ;
var *size, front,* · · ·
procedure *succ* ;
· · ·
procedure bodies
· · ·
initialization

Fig. 5.1. Pseudo-code for two modules.

Classes Describe Dynamic Objects

A *class* corresponds to a type. The term class is an abbreviation of "class of objects," as in class of stacks, class of trees, or class of circles. *Objects* are dynamic. We can create and delete objects as a program runs.

The preceding remarks about modules extend to classes of objects because each module has a corresponding object that exists at run time. No distinction was made earlier between the static text of modules *table* and *buffer* in Fig. 5.1 and their dynamic counterparts because each of these modules sets up a single object.

To give some perspective on objects, the next example considers a simulation problem, typical of those for which Simula was designed.

Example 5.1. The scene is an airport. Passengers wait in line to check in for a flight. During check-in, a ticket agent assigns each passenger a seat on the flight.

The problem is to study the queue of waiting passengers: how it builds up before a flight, how long a passenger has to wait, how much it shrinks if an extra ticket agent is put to work.

This problem can be studied by writing a program that simulates the airport scene. Some assumptions are made about the rate at which passengers arrive and the time taken by a ticket agent to check in a passenger. When the program runs, it plays a game in which objects representing passengers, ticket agents, and queues are created. As the game progresses, passenger objects arrive, wait in queues, and depart.

Data about the behavior of the queues is gathered by playing the game over and over again.   □

The following observations are motivated by Example 5.1:

- The objects in a program depend on the problem to be solved. In the airport example, it is natural to design objects representing passengers, queues, and ticket agents. If we choose to implement a queue as a linked list, then additional objects are needed to represent lists and linked cells.

- Objects can be created and deleted at run time. Passengers arrive, wait for a ticket agent, and then leave for a flight. Arriving can be simulated by creating a passenger object and leaving can be simulated by deleting it.

- A class can be thought of as the type of an object; objects in a class hold similar data and support similar operations. All queues of passengers have similar properties.

Pseudo-code for two classes of objects appears in Fig. 5.2. Each class has a *constructor* procedure, which is called to initialize a newly created object of the class, and a *destructor* procedure, which is called just before the object disappears. Code for cleanup or "last-rites" can be put in the destructor. A class is just like a record type with fields for the data in the class. Class *cell* is like a record type with fields named *info* and *next*. The dashed cell next to the cell object in Fig. 5.2 is included to suggest that *next* points to another cell.

The interface of class *queue* consists of a constructor and three procedures *enter*, *leave*, and *empty*. A queue is implemented using two pointers to cells, called *front* and *rear*. The dashed cells pointed to by *front*

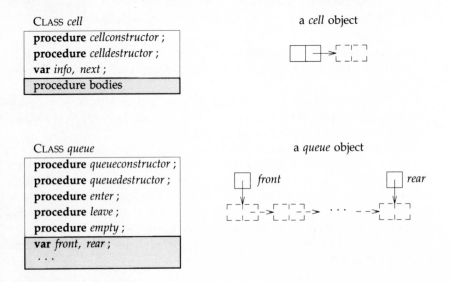

Fig. 5.2. Pseudo-code for two classes of objects.

and *rear* are allocated and deallocated as elements enter and leave the queue. A queue object is therefore implemented using cell objects.

Discussion

Despite the philosophical differences behind their design, modules and classes have been applied to solve similar problems. Classes in C++ can specify one-of-a-kind objects as easily as they specify objects that are copies of each other. We see in Section 5.6 that modules in Modula-2 can be used to create uninitialized objects at run time.

5.2 REPRESENTATION INDEPENDENCE

An *abstract specification* tells us the behavior of an object independently of its implementation; that is, an abstract specification tells us what an object does independently of how it works. A *concrete representation* tells us how an object is implemented, how its data is laid out inside a machine, and how this data is manipulated by its operations.

For example, the abstract notion of the sequence of primes from 7 through 47 can be written concretely as

$$7, 11, 13, 17, 19, 23, 29, 31, 37, 41, 43, 47$$

or it can be laid out in consecutive array elements, or it can be held in cells in a linked list. The array and linked-list layouts are concrete implementations.

Information Hiding

The creation of truly abstract specifications, or *data abstraction*, is an ideal that is rarely attained. Instead, as terms like *implementation hiding, encapsulation*, and *representation independence* suggest, objects are packaged so that details of a concrete representation, such as data layouts, are not visible from the outside. We state this as an informal principle:

> *Representation independence*. A program should be designed so that the representation of an object can be changed without affecting the rest of the program.

Scope rules, which control the visibility of names, are the primary tool for achieving representation independence. The implementation of an object can be hidden by carefully choosing the names that go into an interface and the names that remain private. Private names can be changed without affecting the rest of the program.

Example 5.2. Consider a buffer that behaves as a queue. Elements leave it in the order that they enter. The buffer's interface consists of three names:

1. *enter* (*x*). A procedure to enter elements into the buffer. Returns **true** if *x* is entered successfully; returns **false** otherwise.

2. *nul.* A constant.

3. *leave* (). A procedure to extract elements from the buffer in a first-in-first-out order. Returns *nul* if the buffer is empty and there are no elements to return.

This public interface says nothing about the implementation of the buffer.[1]

The private view of the buffer includes the data structures needed to hold elements inside the buffer. In Fig. 5.3, the buffer is implemented as an array with two indices *front* and *rear*.

A sequence of snapshots of the public and private views of the buffer appears in Fig. 5.4. After *enter* (*a*), the buffer holds just one element *a*, and after *enter* (*b*), the buffer has two elements *a b*. From the outside, the buffer behaves as a first-in-first-out queue. This public view is more abstract than the underlying array with indices to mark the front and rear.

In the implementation, the buffer contents wrap around the right end of the array. In the snapshot with buffer contents *d e f*, element *f* is held in the leftmost array element.   □

Modula-2 and C++ hide the private names of an object from the rest of the program. In Example 5.2, the rest of the program cannot see, and hence cannot change, the array or the front and rear indices into the array. It cannot, therefore, corrupt the buffer contents, either maliciously or inadvertently.

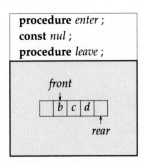

Fig. 5.3. Interface and implementation of a circular buffer.

---

[1] An abstract specification of the buffer must specify what happens when an attempt is made to enter an element into a full buffer and when an attempt is made to extract an element from an empty buffer. Exceptions are a useful language construct for managing such situations. See Section 7.6 for more information.

OPERATION	PUBLIC VIEW Buffer Contents	PRIVATE VIEW Implementation
enter (a)	a	a
enter (b)	a b	a b
enter (c)	a b c	a b c
leave ()	b c	b c
enter (d)	b c d	b c d
enter (e)	b c d e	b c d e
leave ()	c d e	c d e
leave ()	d e	d e
enter (f)	d e f	f d e
enter (g)	d e f g	f g d e
leave ()	e f g	f g e
leave ()	f g	f g

Fig. 5.4. Public and private views of a buffer.

Information Hiding and Program Development

Techniques like information hiding are no substitute for clean design. In fact, they make clean design more critical. Modules and classes formalize the structure of a program and allow a language to prevent attempts to compromise the structure. If the structure is inappropriate, then information hiding stands in the way.

Unfortunately, the hardest task of program design is discovering the right modules, the right objects, the right viewpoint from which to view a computation. Program development is therefore likely to involve periodic adjustments to the structure of the program. This expectation reinforces Jackson's [1975] two fundamental rules for program optimization:

Rule 1. Don't do it.

Rule 2. Don't do it yet.

Parnas [1972] suggests that the structure of a program be chosen to encapsulate "difficult design decisions or decisions that are likely to change." Since design decisions often revolve around the representation of objects, this approach is likely to lead to implementations that can be changed more readily.

Example 5.3. Information hiding can help not only with changes in algorithms and data structures, but also with small changes to refine, debug, or tune the performance of an implementation. An example of a change in data structures is the replacement of the fixed-size array implementation of a queue in Example 5.2 by a linked list. The linked list can grow as needed.

Simply saying that a queue is represented as a linked list is not enough to spell out the details of its implementation. Two variations on this theme appear in Fig. 5.5. Since elements enter a queue at the rear and leave from the front, the variant in Fig. 5.5(a) uses two pointers to locate the two ends. The other variant in Fig. 5.5(b) is based on the subtle observation that a single rear pointer suffices if the list is circularly linked, because the data structure satisfies the invariant:

$rear\uparrow.next$ is the front cell

An initial implementation can use the more direct layout in Fig. 5.5(a). Later, if desired, the implementation can be refined to use the trickier layout in Fig. 5.5(b).   □

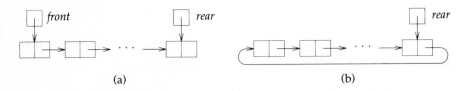

(a)   (b)

Fig. 5.5. Data layouts for implementing queues.

5.3   DATA INVARIANTS

It was stated earlier in this chapter that a module has a local state, consisting of the values of its variables. More precisely, the object represented by a module has a local state, since state is a property of a computation, not of the program text. Objects described by classes also have a local state.

A *data invariant* for an object is a property of its local state that holds whenever control is not in the object. The following are data invariants for the buffer implemented using an array in Example 5.2:

> The buffer is empty if array index *front* equals index *rear*.
> The buffer is full if the next element after *rear* is *front*.
> The elements between *front* and *rear* are in the order they entered.

A counterpart of the structured programming principle is

Data invariant principle. Design an object around a data invariant.

The rest of this section considers language facilities that bear on data invariants.

Initialization of Private Data

The private data of an object is inaccessible from the outside, so initialization of this data belongs with the code for the object. Initialization is needed to set up data invariants when the object is created. An implementation of a queue must set up front and rear pointers before any elements are entered into the queue. These remarks are independent of whether an object is specified by a module or a class.

It is most convenient if initialization is done automatically, by executing programmer-supplied initialization code. If a language does not help with initialization, then errors can occur if private data is inadvertently used before the expected data invariants are established.

Should Data Be Public?

Assignments to public variables can change the local state of an object. It is up to the programmer to ensure that such assignments do not disturb the desired data invariants.

For example, consider a desk-calculator program consisting of two modules *lex* and *eval*. Each call to a procedure in the lexical analyzer *lex* reads enough input characters to isolate the next token. This token is then held in a variable *lookahead*, and the value of the token is held in a variable *lookvalue*. If *lookahead* and *lookvalue* are public, then the other module *eval* can change their values, disturbing the invariant that *lookahead* represents the next token.

If variables are not made public, then all interactions with an object must be through the object's public operations. Read and write access to the value of a variable v can be provided using two operations, one for returning the value of v and the other for assigning a value to v:

> *getV* ()   returns the value of v
> *setV* (*a*)   equivalent to $v := a$

Note that *getV* (), by itself, provides read-only access to the value of *v*.

A benefit of allowing variables to appear in an interface is that a programmer can then choose whether to make a variable visible. Outside code can read and write a public variable directly, so the code is not cluttered with operations of the form *getV* and *setV*.

Should Operations Be Private?

Both Modula-2 and C++ allow private procedures that are not in the interface. Since these procedures cannot be called from the outside, we do not have to insist that they preserve data invariants.

Returning to the desk-calculator example, the lexical analyzer uses a procedure *getch* to read individual characters. As the individual characters in a number **487** are being read, the values of *lookahead* and *lookvalue* temporarily violate the data invariants of the lexical analyzer. If *getch* were public, then it could be called from the outside by *eval*, thereby perhaps inadvertently disturbing the data invariants of *lex*.

It therefore seems useful to allow operations to be private to an object. Furthermore, public procedures must be designed to preserve data invariants.

5.4   PROGRAM STRUCTURE IN MODULA-2

A module in Modula-2 establishes a scope for the declarations within it. A name crosses a module boundary only through an explicit *import* or *export* declaration.

Definition and *implementation* modules set up public and private views:

- An interface or definition module consists of a set of declarations. The declarations describe constants, variables, procedures, and types that are accessible from outside the module. Code for procedures does not appear in the interface.

- An implementation module contains the code behind an interface, including private constants, types, variables, and procedures. In more detail, an implementation consists of private data structures, code to initialize the data structures, code for the procedures in the interface, and private procedures, if any.

Execution of a Modula-2 program is controlled by a *program* or *main module*. The programs in earlier chapters consist solely of main modules. A *local module* appears within another module or procedure. Its lifetime is determined by the lifetime of its enclosing construct. The lifetime of a nonlocal module extends from the beginning to the end of a program.

A Definition Module

The complete Modula-2 program that follows reads integers and inserts them into a table to help it recognize duplicates as they are read. It has two parts:

1. A main module, *duplicates*, to read integers and write out duplicates.

2. A *table* to keep track of the integers that have been seen.

Since *duplicates* uses the *table*, it is called a client of *table*. When it reads an integer n, the client asks *table* whether n has been seen before. If so, n is a duplicate. Otherwise, n is added to the table of the integers that have been seen.

The interface to the table is

```
(1a)    DEFINITION MODULE table;
(2a)      EXPORT QUALIFIED insert, find;
(3a)      PROCEDURE insert(x: INTEGER) : BOOLEAN;
(4a)      PROCEDURE find(x: INTEGER) : BOOLEAN;
(5a)    END table.
```

Procedure names *insert* and *find* must be explicitly exported, as on line 2a, for them to be visible to a client of *table*. Keyword **qualified** means that the exported names can be referred to as *table.insert* and *table.find*, in case some other module happens to export the same names.

The correspondence between the interface and the implementation of *table* is sketched in Fig. 5.6. The interface mentions the names, *insert* and *find*, of the procedures on the table and the types of their parameters and results. Both *insert* and *find* have one integer parameter, called x, and both return a boolean value (that is, both return **true** or **false**).

The implementation, enclosed in a box in the figure, is private. It consists of the data structure to hold elements that have been seen, code to initialize the data structure, and code to implement *insert* and *find*.

A Main Module

The main module explicitly imports *insert* and *find* from *table*. It separately imports input/output procedures and a status variable *Done* from module *InOut*. All names must be explicitly imported, as on lines 2b-4b, for them to be visible within the body of *duplicates*.

```
(1b)    MODULE duplicates;
(2b)      FROM table IMPORT insert, find;
(3b)      FROM InOut IMPORT ReadInt, WriteInt,
(4b)            WriteLn, WriteString, Done;
(5b)      VAR n: INTEGER;
```

definition module *table* ;
  export qualified *insert*, *find* ;
 	
  procedure *insert* (*x* : **integer**) : **boolean**;
 	
  procedure *find* (*x* : **integer**) : **boolean**;
 	
end *table*.
	implementation module *table* ;
	
	  data structure to hold elements
	
	  procedure *insert* (*x* : **integer**) : **boolean**;
	    implementation of *insert*
	  end *insert* ;
	
	  procedure *find* (*x* : **integer**) : **boolean**;
	    implementation of *find*
	  end *find* ;
	
	begin
	  initialization of the data structure
	end *table*.

Fig. 5.6. Two views of *table*.

The body of *duplicates* calls *ReadInt* on line 8b to read an integer into *n*. If the reading is done successfully, module *InOut* sets the status variable *Done* to true. Control then reaches line 11b, where *find* (*n*) is used to check if *n* is in the table; if not, *insert* (*n*) on line 13b enters it into the table. Module *duplicates* has no idea of how elements are represented in the table.

```
(6b)     BEGIN
(7b)        LOOP
(8b)           ReadInt(n);
(9b)           IF NOT Done THEN
(10b)             EXIT
(11b)          ELSIF find(n) THEN
(12b)             WriteInt(n,6); WriteLn;
(13b)          ELSIF NOT insert(n) THEN
(14b)             WriteString("Table Full, "); WriteLn;
(15b)          END
(16b)       END
(17b)    END duplicates.
```

Implementation of the Table

For completeness, we show an implementation of the table based on the organization in Fig. 5.7 (see also Section 3.3). Elements are inserted in sequence, starting at position 1 of array *A*. Variable *n* marks the last used position in the array. Initially, *n* is 0.

The symbolic constant *limit* on line 2c is a parameter that determines the maximum number of elements to be held in the table. The use of a symbolic constant allows the table size to be changed by touching only the

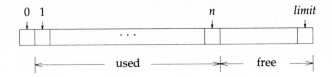

Fig. 5.7. Table organization for linear search.

definition of *limit*. The small value 5 for *limit* makes it easier to test the behavior of a full table.

```
(1c)    IMPLEMENTATION MODULE table;
(2c)    CONST limit = 5;
```

The data in the implementation module consists of the array *A* and variable *n*:

```
(3c)    VAR A : ARRAY [0..limit] OF INTEGER;
(4c)        n : CARDINAL;
```

Function procedure *insert* (*x*) returns **false** if the table is full; otherwise, it inserts *x* into the table and returns **true**.

```
(5c)    PROCEDURE insert(x: INTEGER) : BOOLEAN;
(6c)    BEGIN
(7c)      IF n >= limit THEN
(8c)        RETURN FALSE;
(9c)      ELSE
(10c)       n := n + 1;
(11c)       A[n] := x;
(12c)       RETURN TRUE;
(13c)     END;
(14c)   END insert;
```

Operation *find* (*x*) implements a linear search for *x* with a sentinel in *A* [0]. The search begins at the most recently inserted element *A* [*n*]. The search ends successfully if *x* is found within the table, at position $i \geq 1$, or unsuccessfully if the sentinel *A* [0] is the only occurrence of *x*.

```
(15c)      PROCEDURE find(x: INTEGER): BOOLEAN;
(16c)        VAR i: CARDINAL;
(17c)      BEGIN
(18c)        A[0] := x; i := n;
(19c)        WHILE A[i] <> x DO
(20c)          i := i - 1;
(21c)        END;
(22c)        RETURN i >= 1;
(23c)      END find;
```

The data is initialized by the assignment in the body of the implementation module:

```
(24c)      BEGIN
(25c)        n := 0;
(36c)      END table.
```

5.5   LOCAL MODULES

The boxes in Fig. 5.8 illustrate scope boundaries set up by nested modules. For a name to cross a boundary, it must be imported or exported within the nested module. In Fig. 5.8, *producer* exports *produce* and *consumer* exports *consume* to the containing module *buffertest*.

In more detail, the program module *buffertest* imports names from three outside modules *buffer*, *InOut*, and *MathLib1*. Of these names, local module *producer* chooses to import *enter* and *Read*, and local module *consumer* chooses to import *leave*, *nul*, and *Write*. Names not explicitly imported are not visible in the local modules.

Local module *producer* exports *produce* and local module *consumer* exports *consume* to the containing module *buffertest*.

Besides visibility control, local modules are useful for initialization. Module *producer* in Fig. 5.8 uses a variable *nextch* to hold the next input character. This data invariant is established at the outset by initialization code in the module body.

5.6   MULTIPLE INSTANCES IN MODULA-2

The informal equation

modules = visibility + initialization

summarizes the use of modules to partition the text of a program statically. Can we use modules to simulate classes of objects? This section shows how uninitialized objects can be created and deleted dynamically.

```
module buffertest ;
    from buffer import enter, leave, nul ;
    from InOut import Read, Write, WriteLn, WriteString ;
    from MathLib1 import random ;
    module producer ;
        import enter, Read ;  export produce ;
        var nextch : char;
        procedure produce () : boolean;
        begin
            (* Maintains nextch as next character to be entered. *)
            (* Returns false only when nothing more to produce. *)
        end produce ;
    begin (* initialization for producer *)
        Read (nextch);
    end producer ;

    module consumer ;
        import leave, nul, Write ;  export consume ;
        procedure consume () : boolean;
            var ch : char;
        begin
            (* Extracts a character from the buffer and writes it. *)
            (* Returns false if it gets nul from an empty buffer. *)
        end consume ;
    begin (* empty initialization for consumer *)
    end consumer ;
begin
    (* Randomly call produce () and consume () until nothing more to produce. *)
    (* Use consume () to flush the buffer *)
end buffertest.
```

Fig. 5.8. Import and export of names across module boundaries.

Opaque Export of Types

Opaque export of a type occurs when the type is exported by mentioning only its name in a definition module, as in

    type *Complex* ;

An importer of *Complex* knows nothing about the structure of *Complex*. The only operations provided by the language on such opaque types are assignment and tests for equality and inequality. All other operations have to be exported along with the opaque type for them to be available to an importer.

Complex Numbers

A complex number corresponds to a point in a plane. Two ways of specifying a complex number appear in Fig. 5.9. In Cartesian coordinates, a complex number is represented by a pair (x, y), where x is its horizontal displacement and y is its vertical displacement from the origin. In polar coordinates, a complex number is represented by a pair (r, θ), where r is its distance from the origin and θ is an angle.

Module *complexnumbers* manages complex numbers. It exports a type *Complex*, procedure *cartesian* for creating a complex number from its Cartesian coordinates, procedures *xpart* and *ypart* for extracting the Cartesian coordinates from a complex number, and procedures *add* and *multiply* for mapping two complex numbers to a complex result:

> **definition module** *complexnumbers* ;
>
> > **export qualified** *Complex, cartesian, xpart, ypart, add, multiply* ;
> >
> > **type** *Complex* ;
> >
> > **procedure** *cartesian* (*x*, *y* : **real**) : *Complex* ;
> >
> > **procedure** *xpart* (*c* : *Complex*) : **real**;
> > **procedure** *ypart* (*c* : *Complex*) : **real**;
> > **procedure** *add* (*c*, *d* : *Complex*) : *Complex* ;
> > **procedure** *multiply* (*c*, *d* : *Complex*) : *Complex* ;
>
> **end** *complexnumbers*.

A module *complextest* can now declare variables of type *Complex* and use the above operations to create and manipulate complex numbers:

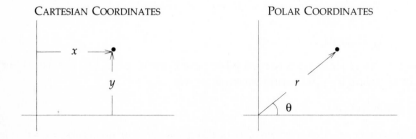

Fig. 5.9. A complex number in Cartesian and polar coordinates.

```
module complextest ;
    from complexnumbers import Complex, cartesian, · · · ;
    var northeast, northwest, a, b : Complex ;
    . . .
begin
    . . .
    northeast := cartesian (1.0, 1.0);   northwest := cartesian (−1.0, 1.0);
    a := add (northeast, northwest);
    b := northwest ;
    . . .
end complextest.
```

One difficulty with this approach is that a declaration

```
    var northeast, northwest, a, b : Complex ;
```

declares the variables *northeast*, *northwest*, *a*, and *b*, but it does not initialize them. In the above fragment, *northeast* and *northwest* are initialized explicitly by calling a procedure *cartesian* that is exported along with type *Complex*.

Implementation of Complex Numbers

Dynamically allocated data is accessed only through pointers in Modula-2, so type *Complex* must be implemented as a pointer to a record holding the local data for a complex number. Implementation module *complexnumbers* therefore begins with

```
implementation module complexnumbers ;
    from Storage import allocate, deallocate;
    type Complex = pointer to record
                        xx, yy : real;
                    end;
```

Being pointers, objects of type *Complex* can be passed freely. Procedure *cartesian* allocates a record by calling **new**(*p*), saves its arguments in the fields of the record, and returns pointer *p*:

```
procedure cartesian (x, y : real) : Complex ;
    var p : Complex ;
begin
    new(p);
    p↑.xx := x ;  p↑.yy := y ;
    return p ;
end cartesian ;
```

The implementation of the remaining procedures is omitted.

5.7   CLASSES IN C++

This section introduces classes in C++ as a generalization of records, called structures in C and C++. A structure is traditionally a grouping of data; C++ allows both data and functions to be structure members. We consider a sequence of three structures **bx**, **by**, and **bz**, where **bz** is close to the class **buffer** in Fig. 5.10. The program in Fig. 5.10 sets up a single buffer object.[2]

Relationship with C

The purpose of C++ is to extend C to support information hiding and a style of programming that emphasizes classes of objects.

Compatibility with C, efficiency, and strict compile-time checking were the primary design goals for C++:

- Compatibility with C allows existing C code to continue to be used. Most implementations of C++ are even "link compatible" with C, which means that separately compiled C++ code can be linked with existing C libraries, without recompiling the C libraries.

- Efficiency was stressed so there would be no penalty for using C++ instead of C. Operations for accessing private data can result in lots of little functions; "in-line expansion" eliminates overhead from function calls.

- Strict compile-time checking gives the programmer an early warning of potential errors. Changes can be made more freely because checking exposes any incompatibilities introduced by the change. Type information also helps the compiler to generate code.

The similarity between C++ and C is deceptive, however, because a fresh approach to programming is needed to realize the benefits of classes and objects in C++. Stroustrup [1986] warns, "The better one knows C, the harder it seems to avoid writing C++ in C style, and thereby lose some potential benefits of C++."

---

[2] The program in Fig. 5.10 treats empty and full buffers differently from the program in Fig. 4.3, page 124. Function **enter** of class **buffer** returns 1 when a character is entered into a buffer and 0 when it is not. Function **leave** of class **buffer** returns a null character '\0' when a buffer is empty. Since the null character has value zero, the program fragment

```
while( (ch = b.leave()) != '\0' ) putchar(ch);
```

can be written more succinctly as

```
while( (ch = b.leave()) ) putchar(ch);
```

because a nonzero value is treated as true in C.

```
const int MAXBUF = 4;
class buffer {
public:
        buffer()      { size = MAXBUF+1; front = rear = 0; }
    int  enter(char);
    char leave();
private:
    char buf[MAXBUF+1];
    int  size, front, rear;
    int  succ(int i) { return (i + 1) % size; }
};

int  buffer::enter(char x) {
    if( succ(rear) == front ) return 0;
    buf[rear] = x; rear = succ(rear);
    return 1;
}

char buffer::leave() {
    if( front == rear ) return '\0';
    int x = buf[front]; front = succ(front);
    return x;
}

#include <stdio.h>
#include <math.h>
main() {
    buffer b;
    int ch, nextch = getchar();
    while( nextch != EOF ) {
        if( frand() >= 0.5 && ((ch = b.leave()) != '\0') )
            putchar(ch);
        else if( b.enter(nextch) )
            nextch = getchar();
    }
    while( (ch = b.leave()) != '\0' )
        putchar(ch);
    return 0;
}
```

Fig. 5.10. A C++ program to copy characters through a buffer.

Start with Structures

A structure declaration begins with **struct** and consists of a sequence of declarations enclosed within braces { }. The declaration of a structure **bx** with four members **buf**, **size**, **front**, and **rear** is

```
struct bx {
    char buf[MAXBUF+1];
    int  size;
    int  front;
    int  rear;
};
```

Now **bx** can be used as a type name to declare variables **b1** and **b2**:

```
bx b1, b2;
```

Structures in C++ differ from C in that functions can be structure members. A special member function called a constructor is called automatically to initialize an object upon creation. A constructor has the same name as the structure in which it appears. The constructor in **by** initializes members **size**, **front**, and **rear**:

```
struct by {
        by() { size = MAXBUF+1; front = rear = 0; }
    char buf[MAXBUF+1];
    int  size;
    int  front;
    int  rear;
};
```

Another example of a structure with member functions is

```
struct bz {
        bz() { size = MAXBUF+1; front = rear = 0; }
    int  succ(int i) { return (i + 1) % size; }
    int  enter(char);
    char leave();
    char buf[MAXBUF+1];
    int  size;
    int  front;
    int  rear;
};
```

The body of a member function can be included within the structure declaration, or it can appear outside. The body of **succ** appears in this declaration, but the bodies of **enter** and **leave** do not.

When a function body appears separately, the *name-resolution* operator : : connects the member to its structure. The following pseudo-code shows how members **enter** and **leave** of **bz** might be declared:

```
int  bz::enter(char x) { /* body of enter */ }
char bz::leave()       { /* body of leave */ }
```

Member functions have access to the data and functions in a structure.

Public and Private Class Members

Structures and classes are closely related in C++, to the point that a declaration

```
struct x { ⟨member-declarations⟩ };
```

is just shorthand for

```
class x { public: ⟨member-declarations⟩ };
```

The only difference between structures and classes is that, by default, all members of a structure are public, whereas, by default, all members of a class are private. Thus, a declaration

```
class x { ⟨member-declarations⟩ };
```

is just shorthand for

```
struct x { private: ⟨member-declarations⟩ };
```

The keywords **public, private**, and **protected** control the visibility of member names in a class declaration. Public members are visible to code outside a class, but private members are not. Protected members behave like private members, except with "derived classes," introduced in Section 5.9.

Class **buffer** has the same members as structure **bz**, but only the constructor, **enter**, and **leave** are public in **buffer**:

```
class buffer {
public:
        buffer() { size = MAXBUF+1; front = rear = 0; }
    int  enter(char);
    char leave();
private:
    char buf[MAXBUF+1];
    int  size, front, rear;
    int  succ(int i) { return (i + 1) % size; }
};
```

A variable denoting a buffer object is declared by

```
buffer b;
```

Dot notation is used to select a member of an object, so function **enter** of **b** is referred to as **b.enter**, as in

```
 ···  else if( b.enter(nextch) )  ···
```

In-line Expansion of Function Bodies

Implementation hiding can result in lots of little functions that manipulate private data. Function-call overhead can be avoided by using an implementation technique called *in-line expansion*, which replaces a call by the function body, taking care to preserve the semantics of the language. Thus, in-line expansion in C++ differs from macroexpansion in C because in-line expansion preserves the semantics of call-by-value parameter passing.

Suppose we were to add public functions **notempty** and **notfull** to class **buffer**:

```
int notempty() { return front != rear; }
int notfull()  { return succ(rear) != front; }
```

These functions return results computed from private data. The client of a buffer object **b** might use **notempty** in a test :

```
if( frand() >= 0.5 && b.notempty() )  ···
```

In-line expansion implements this test as if it were written

```
if( frand() >= 0.5 && (b.front != b.rear) )  ···
```

Since the expanded expression refers directly to the members **b.front** and **b.rear**, it can be executed more efficiently than can the original expression.

In-line expansion eliminates the overhead of function calls at run time, so it encourages free use of functions, even small functions. It also encourages data hiding, because private data can be accessed efficiently through in-line public functions. The original expression uses public function **notempty** to access the private data of **b**. Inside the machine, away from the eyes of the programmer, the implementation refers directly to the private data.

Functions declared within a class declaration are expanded in-line, at the discretion of the compiler. For functions declared outside the class declaration, keyword **inline** is a hint to the compiler to expand a function in-line.

Header Files

C and C++ programmers conventionally partition a program into files corresponding loosely to modules. The conventions are not a part of C or C++, yet their use is so prevalent that they deserve mention. A *header* file, with a `.h` suffix, corresponds to a definition module; it is a collection of declarations. A corresponding implementation file, with a `.c` suffix, contains additional declarations and code needed for the names declared in the header file.

The buffer example might be partitioned into three files, called **buf.h**, **buf.c**, and **buftest.c** in Fig. 5.11.

File buf.h:

```
const int MAXBUF = 4;
class buffer {
public:
     public member declarations
private:
     private member declarations
};
```

File buf.c:

```
#include "buf.h"
int   buffer::enter(char x) {
     body of enter appears here
}
char buffer::leave() {
     body of leave appears here
}
```

File buftest.c:

```
#include "buf.h"
#include <stdio.h>
#include <math.h>
main() {
     buffer    b;
     rest of the code for main appears here
}
```

Fig. 5.11. Static subdivision of the program in Fig. 5.10 into files.

The implementation file **buf.c** begins with

```
#include "buf.h"
```

which a preprocessor replaces by the contents of the file **buf.h**, making the declaration of class **buffer** visible in file **buf.c**.

File **buftest.c** "includes" the contents of three files, **buf.h**, an input/output library **stdio.h**, and a library of mathematical functions **math.h**. The difference between the quotes in **"buf.h"** and the enclosing brackets, **< >**, in **<stdio.h>** lies in where the operating system looks for the files.

5.8   CLASSES OF OBJECTS IN C++

Linked lists are a convenient vehicle for illustrating the creation and deletion of objects in C++ because they involve both objects and pointers. Dynamic allocation and deallocation in C++ are done using pointers.

The following points are illustrated in this section:

- A constructor is called automatically when an object is created.
- Function names can be overloaded.
- Objects created by **new** exist until they are deallocated by **delete**.
- A class can allow a "friend" to access its private members.

Review of Pointers

As in C, the pointer-dereferencing operator is a prefix *****. Read the declaration

```
cell *p;
```

as "we get an object of type **cell** when we apply ***** to **p**." In the following declaration

```
class cell {
    int    info;
    cell *next;
};
```

member **next** is a pointer to another cell object.

Pointers to structures are used so frequently that there is special syntax for accessing members. The syntax **p->info** refers to member **info** of the structure pointed to by **p**. It is an abbreviation of **(*p).info**, which explicitly uses ***** to dereference **p** and then uses dot notation to select member **info**.

The address-of operator **&** creates a value that points to an object. At the end of the following fragment, cell **c** is linked to **d**:

```
cell c, d;
c.next = &d;              now c.next points to cell d
```

A null pointer, pointing to no object, is written as **0**—zero is heavily overloaded in C and C++. Within the code for an object, the special name **this** denotes a pointer to the object itself.

Constructors for Automatic Initialization

A constructor in a class is called automatically when a variable is declared. Suppose that class **cell** is declared by

```
class cell {
        cell(int i, cell *n) { info = i; next = n; }
    int    info;
    cell *next;
};
```

Actual parameters for the constructor appear in parentheses to the right of a declared variable. The sequence of two declarations

```
cell a(1, 0);       declare a and call a.cell(1,0)
cell b(2, &a);      declare b and call b.cell(2,&a)
```

leaves variables **a** and **b** initialized as follows:

The same name can be given to more than one function in a class, provided we can tell the overloaded functions apart by looking at the number and types of their parameters. Constructor **cell** is overloaded in

```
class cell {
        cell(int i) { info = i; next = this; }
        cell(int i, cell *n) { info = i; next = n; }
    int    info;
    cell *next;
};
```

The new constructor is called in declarations with a single parameter. The declaration

```
    cell c(7);
```

leaves **c** initialized as follows:

Allocation and Deallocation

C++ provides two operators **new** and **delete** for allocation and deallocation, respectively. Execution of the expression

```
new cell(1, 0)
```

creates an object of class **cell**, initializes the object by passing **(1,0)** to
its constructor, and then returns a pointer to the newly created object. The
statements

```
cell *front;                   declare front
front = new cell(1, 0);        create a new cell object
front = new cell(2, front);    insert a new cell; update front
```

create the following list:

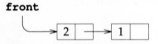

Objects created by **new** exist until they are explicitly deallocated. The
first cell in the above linked list is deallocated by the statements

```
cell *temp = front;        declare temp and save front
front = front->next;
delete temp;
```

The resulting list is:

Friends Have Access to Private Members

The members of a class are private unless they are explicitly declared to be
public. A *friend* declaration within a class gives nonmember functions
access to the private members of the class.

The declaration of class **cell** in Fig. 5.12 declares **circlist** to be a
friend, so the functions of class **circlist** can access the private members
of **cell**. Since **public** does not appear in the declaration of class **cell**,
its members are hidden from all other code.

```
class cell {
friend class circlist;
        cell(int i)          { info = i; next = this; }
        cell(int i, cell *n) { info = i; next = n; }
    int    info;
    cell *next;
};
class circlist {
    cell *rear;
public:
        circlist()   { rear = new cell(0); }
    int    empty()    { return rear == rear->next; }
    void   push(int);
    int    pop();
    void   enter(int);
};
```

Fig. 5.12. Class **cell** lets class **circlist** be a friend.

Circularly Linked Lists

The data structure implemented by class **circlist** is illustrated in Fig.
5.13. Member **rear** points to one of a sequence of circularly linked cells.
The constructor function

```
circlist()   { rear = new cell(0); }
```

initializes **rear** by allocating a new cell. The new cell is initialized by the
call **cell(0)**, which puts 0 in the **info** field and links the cell to itself.
   Member **push** of **circlist** adds a cell to the front of the list and
member **enter** adds a cell at the rear of the list. Member **pop** deletes a
cell from the front of the list and returns its value. The behavior of **pop** on
an empty list is somewhat unsatisfactory, because it simply returns 0.
   For completeness, the code for the members of **circlist** appears in
Fig. 5.14.

Fig. 5.13. Data structure for implementing stacks and queues.

```
void circlist::push(int x) {
    rear->next = new cell(x, rear->next);
}
void circlist::enter(int x) {
    rear->info = x;
    rear = rear->next = new cell(0, rear->next);
}
int circlist::pop() {
    if( empty() ) return 0;
    cell *front = rear->next;
    rear->next = front->next;
    int x = front->info;
    delete front;
    return x;
}
```

Fig. 5.14. Code for member functions in Fig. 5.12.

5.9   DERIVED CLASSES AND INFORMATION HIDING

Inheritance mechanisms define objects as extensions of previously defined objects. The extension is said to inherit the variables and operations of the previous object. This section examines the interaction between inheritance and information hiding in C++. Chapter 6 considers subtypes, another key issue raised by inheritance.

The main example in this section is motivated by the observation that class **circlist** in Fig. 5.12 can be used to implement both stacks and queues. The list behaves as a stack when elements are added at the front using **push** and removed from the front using **pop**. On the other hand, the list behaves as a queue when elements are added at the rear using **enter** and removed from the front using **pop**. Both stacks and queues will be derived from lists.

Base and Derived Structures

A class D can be defined as an extension of a class B by mentioning only the changes from B. In C++ terminology, the starting point B is called a *base* class and the extension D is called a *derived* class.

Structures allow the concept of extension to be introduced separately from information hiding—by default, all members of a structure are public. Remarks about base and derived structures carry over to base and derived classes.

The following syntax can be used to define a derived structure:

```
struct ⟨derived⟩ : ⟨base⟩ {
    ⟨added-members⟩
};
```

A derived structure inherits all the members of its base structure, except the base constructor. An abstract example is

```
struct B {                      declaration of structure B
    int   x;                    public data member
    char  f();                  public member function
          B() { x = 1; }
};
struct D : B {                  D derived from B
    int   g();                  added member function
};
```

Objects of the derived structure **D** have three members: **x** and **f**, inherited from the base structure **B**, and **g**, added in the declaration of **D**.

A member added by a derived structure **D** can have the same name as a member of its base structure **B**. If the same member name **m** appears in both, then the full name **B::m** can be used to refer to the member **m** of **B**. Similarly, **D::m** is the full name of member **m** of **D**.

Information Hiding

C++ has three keywords—**public**, **private**, and **protected**—for controlling the visibility of member names in a class declaration. As in earlier sections, public members are visible to outside code, and private members are not. Protected members are visible through inheritance to derived classes, but not to other code.

A derived class is said to have a *public base class* if the derived class maintains the visibility of all inherited members. Otherwise, the derived class is said to have a *private base class*.

The default visibility of inherited members can be specified by writing the keywords **public** and **private** before the name of the base class. In the following syntax, keyword **public** says that, by default, members inherited by ⟨derived⟩ from ⟨base⟩ retain the visibility they had in ⟨base⟩:

```
class ⟨derived⟩ : public ⟨base⟩ {
    ⟨member-declarations⟩
};
```

That is, a public member of ⟨base⟩ is by default a public member of ⟨derived⟩, and similarly for protected and private members.

Keyword **private** says that, by default, all members inherited by ⟨derived⟩ from ⟨base⟩ become private members of ⟨derived⟩:

```
class ⟨derived⟩ : private ⟨base⟩ {
    ⟨member-declarations⟩
};
```

Nonprivate inherited members can be made visible by writing their full names in the derived class.

Example 5.4. Most of the members in the following redeclaration of **circlist** are protected because **circlist** will be used as a base for derived classes:

```
class circlist {
public:
    int    empty();
protected:
            circlist();
    void   push(int);
    int    pop();
    void   enter(int);
private:
    cell *rear;
};
```

Function **empty** tests for emptiness without changing the data structure.

Class **queue** is derived from **circlist**, as follows:

```
class queue : private circlist {
public:
            queue();
    void enterq(int);
    int  leaveq();
            circlist::empty;
};
```

This declaration adds functions **queue**, **enterq**, and **leaveq**, and says that inherited member **empty** is public: The visibility of an inherited member is declared by writing its full name, without type information. The full name of inherited member **empty** is **circlist::empty**. A listing of the members of class **queue** appears in Fig. 5.15.

Since variable **rear** is private in the base class, it is hidden from **queue**, **enterq**, and **leaveq**, but **rear** is visible to the inherited functions **circlist**, **empty**, **push**, and **pop**.

We now repeat the declaration of class **queue** to show the bodies of the member functions:

Public Functions

queue	added constructor function
enterq	added
leaveq	added
empty	inherited and explicitly made public

Private Functions

push	inherited
pop	inherited
enter	inherited

Private Variables (accessible to functions added by **queue**)
          none

Private Variables (accessible only to inherited functions)
     rear   inherited

Fig. 5.15. A complete listing of the members of class **queue**.

```
class queue : private circlist {
public:
        queue()            {}
    void enterq(int x)  { enter(x); }
    int  leaveq()       { return pop(); }
        circlist::empty;
};
```

The constructor **queue** implicitly calls the constructor **circlist** of the base class; its body has no statements because it does nothing beyond what **circlist** does.

Added functions **enterq** and **leaveq** simply call the inherited functions **enter** and **pop** respectively. In-line expansion would result in direct calls to the inherited functions.

A derived stack is

```
class stack : private circlist {
public:
        stack()             {}
    void push(int x)        { circlist::push(x); }
    int  pop()              { return circlist::pop(); }
        circlist::empty;
};
```

This time, the prefix **circlist::** is needed to refer to the inherited functions **circlist::push** and **circlist::pop** because derived class **stack** overrides these names with functions of its own.

A trivial program that uses classes **stack** and **queue** can be constructed along the following lines:

```
main() {
    stack   s;
    queue   q;

    s.push(1);   s.push(2);   s.push(3);
    q.enter(7);  q.enter(8);  q.enter(9);
    . . .

}
```

Privacy Principle

Functions in the derived class cannot see the private members of its base class. This restriction may seem surprising at first, but to do otherwise would violate the following principle:

Privacy principle. The private members of a class are inaccessible from code outside the class.

For perspective on this principle, let us reexamine class **stack**:

```
class stack : private circlist {
public:
          stack()             {}
    void push(int x)     { circlist::push(x); }
    int  pop()           { return circlist::pop(); }
          circlist::empty;
};
```

The base class members **circlist::push** and **circlist::pop** are protected. Yet **stack** makes them indirectly accessible by declaring new functions **stack::push** and **stack::pop**, which simply call the underlying protected functions.

If a derived class could see private members, then the same approach could be used to make private members accessible, in violation of the privacy principle.

EXERCISES

5.1 Design a program that uses an auxiliary stack to evaluate postfix expressions. Such an evaluator is described in Section 2.3.

5.2 What are the data invariants for the table in Section 5.4?

5.3 Outline a C++ version of the Modula-2 program in Section 5.4 for finding duplicates.

5.4 Modify the program in Section 5.4 to count the number of times an integer is seen.

5.5 Modify the program in Section 5.4 to recognize duplicate words instead of integers, where a word is any maximal sequence of characters that does not include a blank, a tab, or a newline or end-of-line character.

5.6 Change the implementation of the table in Section 5.4 to use a binary search tree (see Example 2.5, page 57) instead of linear search.

5.7 Give implementations for the operations *xpart*, *ypart*, *add*, and *multiply* on complex numbers in Section 5.6.

5.8 Implement a noncircular variant of class **circlist** in Section 5.8.
   a) Call the new class **linklist**, and use pointers to the front and rear cells in the list.
   b) Derive classes for queues and stacks with **linklist** as a base.

5.9 Redo Exercise 5.8 using modules instead of classes for cells, lists, queues, and stacks. *Hint.* Instead of being derived from lists, queues and stacks can be implemented by lists.

5.10 The approach to creating and manipulating uninitialized objects in Section 5.6 can also be used in Pascal and C, although we lose the information-hiding benefits of modules and classes. Complex numbers were manipulated in Section 5.6 by declaring type *Complex* to be a pointer to a record containing the data for a complex number. Redo Exercise 5.8 in C, using pointers and structures to implement cells, lists, queues, and stacks.

5.11 Design an array implementation of a first-in-first-out buffer, based on the following invariants:

   The buffer is empty when *holds* = 0.
   The buffer is full when *holds* = *size*.
   The first-in element is in *buf* [*front*].
   The last-in element is in *buf* [*rear*].
   The elements wrap around the right end of the array.

5.12 Design a lexical analyzer for expressions—a lexical analyzer groups characters into tokens. Expressions are made up of tokens corresponding to names, integers, parentheses, and the operators **+**, **−**, *****, **DIV**, and **MOD**. A name begins with a letter and consists of a sequence of letters and digits. Every time the lexical analyzer sees a new name, it assigns a sequence number to the name.

a) Design a client that asks for and displays tokens. Integers, parentheses, and operators must be displayed as is. Display names by writing **NAME[s]**, where *s* is the sequence number for the name. Thus, **b*b−4*a*c** must be displayed as

NAME[1] * NAME[1] − 4 * NAME[2] * NAME[3]

b) Modify the lexical analyzer to maintain a window on the input, consisting of the up to *windowsize* most recently read characters. The lexical analyzer must support an operation to display the window. Such windows are sometimes used to show the context in which an error is detected.

5.13 A *directed graph* consists of a set of *nodes* and a set of *edges* of the form $x \rightarrow y$, where *x* and *y* are nodes (see Fig. 5.16). Edge $x \rightarrow y$ is said to be *from x to y*. The set of all nodes reachable by zero or more edges from a starting node *start* can be computed using a data structure, called a *closure-set*, that supports the following operations:

- *create* (). Creates and initializes a closure-set with no nodes in it.

- *insert* (*x* : *Node*). Enters *x* as an unmarked node into the closure-set.

- *find* (*x* : *Node*) : **boolean**. Returns **true** if node *x* was previously inserted; otherwise, returns **false**.

- *worktodo* () : **boolean**. Returns **true** if a previously inserted node has not yet been marked.

- *marknext* () : *Node*. Returns and marks a previously inserted and as yet unmarked node.

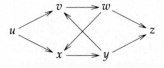

Fig. 5.16. A directed graph.

Nodes reachable from *start* can now be computed by the pseudo-code

```
create ();
insert (start);
while worktodo () do
    x := marknext ();
    for each edge x →y  do
        if not find (y) then
            insert (y)
        end if
    end for
end while
(* the closure-set now contains the reachable nodes *)
```

a) Operations *insert* and *find* correspond directly to operations of the same name supported by the table in Section 5.4. Adapt the table organization in Fig. 5.7 to implement closure-sets.

b) Design a derived class **closureset** based on a class **table**, which corresponds to the table organization in Fig. 5.7.

c) Design a program that reads in a start node and a set of edges and prints out the nodes reachable from the start node. Use node numbers for input/output, so a node can be read by reading an integer and an edge can be read by reading a pair of integers.

d) Implement your design in C++.

5.14 A *keyword-in-context* (KWIC) index, or *permuted index*, consists of a sequence of lines, sorted by keywords appearing within the lines; the lines are circularly shifted so that the keywords line up. For each keyword in a line, the index contains a copy of the line. The lines

```
Ask not what your country can do.
Ask what you can do.
```

lead to the index entries in Fig. 5.17.

a) Design a program to produce a permuted index.

b) How would your design change if a sorting program were available?

BIBLIOGRAPHIC NOTES

Wirth [1979] discusses the design decisions behind modules in Modula-2, and notes, "A module is effectively a bracket around a group of (type, variable, procedure, etc.) declarations establishing a scope of identifiers."

```
country can do.          Ask not what your
do.                      Ask what you can
    what your country    can do.          Ask not
        Ask what you     can do.
    Ask not what your    country can do.
        your country can do.          Ask not what
        Ask what you can do.
can do.           Ask    not what your country
                  Ask    what you can do.
can do.       Ask not    what your country
        Ask what         you can do.
do.       Ask not what   your country can
```

Fig. 5.17. A permuted index.

At the time it seemed as if nested modules would be more useful than the ability to define classes of objects. For perspective on the design decisions, see Wirth [1988].

Stroustrup [1986], the primary reference for C++, contains the historical note, "C is retained as a subset, and so is C's emphasis on facilities that are low-level enough to cope with the most demanding systems programming tasks. ... The other main source of inspiration was Simula67; the class concept (with derived classes and virtual functions) was borrowed from it." Subsequent extensions to the language, including provisions for protected members, are described in Stroustrup [1987b].

The groundwork for many of the ideas in this chapter was laid by the Simula project; Nygaard and Dahl [1981] trace its history. Simula I was primarily a language for describing and programming simulations. Experience with Simula I led to the recognition that data belongs together with the operations upon it, and that programming effort could be saved if common properties of objects could be preprogrammed. Classes of objects emerged as the central concept of a new general-purpose programming language, Simula 67, designed in 1967. The counterpart of a derived class in C++ could be defined by "prefixing," where common properties appeared in a prefix (a similar approach can be used to implement derived classes). Note, however, that "it took several years of slowly growing understanding ... until the fundamental difference between the internal ('concrete') view of an object and an external ('abstract') one finally was made clear by Hoare [1972]." Birtwistle et al. [1979] is a comprehensive textbook on Simula 67.

The concepts of modules and objects are natural ones and were clearly developed independently in several contexts, including assembly language. The AED project exploited the idea of grouping operations with data (Ross and Rodriguez [1963]). Parnas [1972] begins with, "The major advancement in the area of modular programming has been the development of coding techniques and assemblers which (1) allow one module to be written with little knowledge of the code in another module, and (2) allow modules to be reassembled and replaced without reassembly of the whole system." Parnas's thrust is to present criteria for decomposing a system into modules, using permuted-index programs as running examples. See also the permuted-index programs in Kernighan and Plauger [1981], Morris, Schmidt, and Wadler [1980], and Aho, Kernighan, and Weinberger [1988].

In the 1970s, constructs in the spirit of modules and classes were designed into a number of languages, such as Mesa (Geschke, Morris, and Satterthwaite [1977]) and CLU (see Liskov and Guttag [1986]). Mesa influenced the module facility of Modula-2.

For an algebraic approach to data abstraction, see Goguen, Thatcher, and Wagner [1978]; Liskov and Zilles [1974] is an early reference.

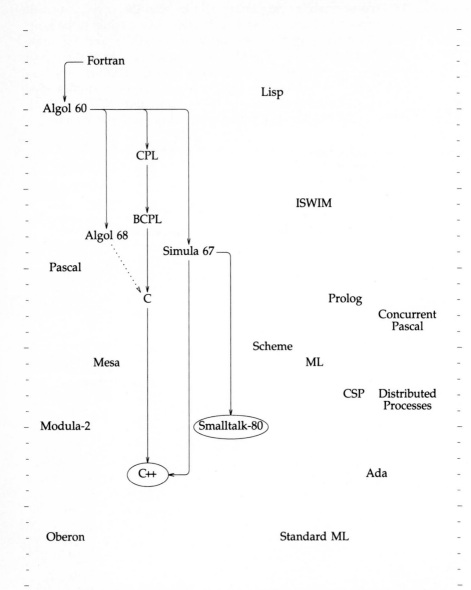

The popular term *object-oriented programming* refers to a programming style that relies on the concepts of inheritance and data encapsulation. Smalltalk-80 and C++, the working languages of this chapter, illustrate that object-oriented programming can be practiced in languages that differ in essential ways. For example, Smalltalk is usually interpreted, whereas C++ is compiled; there is no mention of types in a Smalltalk program, whereas C++ requires type declarations and performs strict static type checking.

Six

Inheritance

Inheritance is a language facility for defining a new class of objects as an extension of previously defined classes. The new class inherits the variables and operations of the previous ones.

This chapter begins with the Smalltalk-80 language and its inheritance mechanism. We then consider inheritance in C++. C++ has flexible facilities for information hiding, and these facilities allow us to distinguish between inheritance and the related concept of subtypes.

Object-oriented programming creates a setting in which dynamic objects interact by sending messages to each other. Messages correspond to procedure calls. In the running example of Section 6.1, objects are shapes such as lines and circles, and message *draw* asks a shape to draw itself. When we send a message *draw* to a shape, we do not know or care whether it is a line or a circle. All we want the shape to do is to draw itself.

The traditional classification of objects into types leads to disjoint sets of objects, as in Fig. 6.1(a). An integer is quite different from an array of characters, so the set of integers does not overlap with the set of objects associated with the type array of characters. Subranges are an exception to the traditional classification; for example, 37 belongs at the same time to the subrange [10..99], to the subrange [0..100], and to the set of all integers. In particular, 37 can appear anywhere an integer is expected. Subranges are a form of subtype.

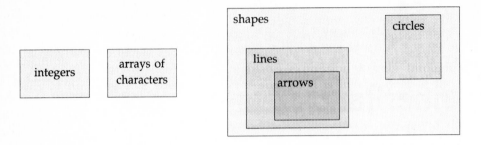

(a) Disjoint sets of objects.   (b) Nested sets of objects.

Fig. 6.1. Classification of objects.

A *subtype S* of a type *T* is such that any *S*-object is at the same time a *T*-object; that is, an object of type *S* also has type *T*. Any operation that can be applied to a *T*-object can also be applied to an *S*-object. *T* is called a *supertype* of *S*.

The terms subtype and supertype are motivated by the terms subset and superset. Associated with each type is a set of values. The set of values associated with a subtype *S* of *T* is a subset of the set of values associated with *T*. The nested sets in Fig. 6.1(b) correspond to the types shape, line, arrow, and circle, where line, arrow, and circle are subtypes of shape, and arrow is a subtype of line.

A distinguishing feature of object-oriented programming is captured by the following seemingly innocuous principle:

> *Subtype principle.* An object of a subtype can appear wherever an object of a supertype is expected.

The nested classification of objects in Fig. 6.1(b) results from *single inheritance*, where a class of objects is defined as a subtype of a larger class. Under *multiple inheritance*, a class can be a subtype of more than one class. Inheritance can be exploited to customize existing code and avoid code duplication.

This chapter concentrates on single inheritance, although the working languages, Smalltalk-80 and C++, also support multiple inheritance.

Single inheritance leads to a class hierarchy; Fig. 6.2 depicts a small fragment of the class hierarchy provided by the Smalltalk system. Set, LinkedList, and Array are subclasses of Collection, and an object of a subclass can appear wherever an object of a superclass is expected.

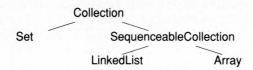

Fig. 6.2. An excerpt from the Smalltalk class hierarchy.

6.1 INTRODUCTION

The running example in this section builds figures out of basic shapes, say lines, rectangles, and circles:

Let a figure consist of a list of shapes. The following figure consists of four circles, a line, and a rectangle:

Programming with Procedures

A procedure-oriented approach to managing figures is to structure a program around the operations on shapes. We can imagine operations for drawing, rotating, and scaling a figure. A procedure to draw a figure might look like the following pseudo-code:

```
void draw(figure f) {
    for( shape s in f ) {
        switch(s.kind) {
        case LINE:        code to draw a line; break;
        case RECTANGLE:   code to draw a rectangle; break;
        case CIRCLE:      code to draw a circle; break;
        default:          code to emit an error message; break;
        }
    }
}
```

For each shape **s** in a figure **f**, this procedure classifies **s** and then executes code that is appropriate to drawing that kind of shape. Suppose that type **shape** is a variant record with a tag field **kind** for distinguishing among the shapes. If the value of **s.kind** equals a constant **LINE**, then the code for drawing a line is executed, and so on for rectangles and circles.

A problem with this procedure-oriented approach is that the code for manipulating shapes is spread across the various procedures. If a new shape is added, then code for handling the new shape has to be added to each procedure. For example, suppose that a new shape *arrow* is added, consisting of an arrowhead attached to an end of a line, as in

Procedure **draw** can be modified to draw arrows by adding a case of the form

> **case ARROW:**   *code to draw an arrow;* **break;**

Even if the amount of new code is small, it is spread across procedures, each of which must be studied before the new code is added.

Programming with Subtypes

Now consider a different approach, one that collects all the information about an object in one place. A line-drawing program can be organized by setting up the class hierarchy in Fig. 6.3(a), which says that a shape can be a line, a rectangle, or a circle. Class *shape* collects common properties, such as the height, the width, the position, and an operation for moving the shape. Properties that are specific to lines, rectangles, and circles appear in the appropriate subclasses. For example, lines, rectangles, and circles have their own **draw** procedures.

A figure now draws itself by asking each shape on its list to draw itself. Since each shape has its own **draw** procedure, the figure does not need to classify the shapes on its list:

```
    void figure::draw() {
        for( shape s  in this figure )
            s.draw();
    }
```

```
                 shape                          shape
               ⁄   |   ＼                     ⁄   |   ＼
         line  rectangle  circle         line  rectangle  circle
                                                  ⋮
                                                arrow

              (a)                              (b)
```

Fig. 6.3. Adding a new shape by extending lines to arrows.

The C++ notation **figure::draw** is made up of a class name **figure** and a member **draw** of that class. The code for drawing the basic shapes is still needed, but it now appears with the rest of the information about that shape.

Inheritance allows arrows to be added by extending lines, without touching the code for the other objects. The new hierarchy appears in Fig. 6.3(b). An arrow inherits all the properties of a line, so the only additional code needed to draw it is the code for drawing an arrowhead. The following pseudo-code first calls **line::draw** to draw a line, and then adds an arrowhead:

```
void arrow::draw() {
    line::draw();
    code to draw the arrowhead;
}
```

Furthermore, arrows can immediately appear within figures, along with the other shapes. The same "pre-arrow" code for drawing the list of shapes in a figure will handle arrow shapes as well because it continues to ask each shape to draw itself.

When programming with subtypes, the code for each individual operation is often small and seems to simply "pass the buck" by invoking operations in other objects. The power of such programs becomes evident only when we examine a program as a whole or when we try to solve the same problem using a different approach.

6.2 THE SMALLTALK-80 VOCABULARY

Smalltalk, the language, is just one part of the Smalltalk system. The system has a sophisticated user interface, through which programs are entered, viewed, and edited. Tools called "browsers" selectively display portions of the program text, a procedure at a time.

On the printed page, where possible, we collect all the information about a class in one place, using different fonts or typefaces to highlight portions of the program text. Instead of the normal program font, a bold font will sometimes be used as an attention-getting device.

This chapter deals only with the programming language aspects of Smalltalk-80. The language emphasizes the uniform application of a small number of concepts, cloaked in unusual terminology. A large number of system classes are available for use in Smalltalk programs; an inheritance mechanism allows system classes to be customized.

The Smalltalk vocabulary reflects the view of a running program as a collection of interacting objects. The objects interact by sending messages to each other. The five basic words of the vocabulary are:

object	Collection of private data and public operations.
class	Description of a set of objects.
instance	An instance of a class is an object of that class.
method	A procedure body implementing an operation.
message	A procedure call. Request to execute a method.

In informal usage, object and instance are synonyms, as are operation and method. A message tells an object to perform one of its operations, so a message corresponds to a procedure call; more precisely, a message name corresponds to a procedure name and the act of sending a message corresponds to a procedure call. A method describes how an operation is to be performed, so a method corresponds to a procedure body.

A message is written to the right of its recipient. A message without arguments, called a *unary message*, consists simply of a name, as in message pop to s:

    s pop

Messages that carry arguments are built of names that end in a colon; such names are called *keywords*. The expression

    s push: 80

sends message push: with argument 80 to s.

The general form of a message in Smalltalk, called a *keyword message*, consists of a sequence of keyword-argument pairs. The expression

    elements at: top put: 'celebrate'

sends elements a message consisting of two keywords. Keyword at: carries argument top and keyword put: carries argument 'celebrate'.

We talk of a message by concatenating its keywords together. In the preceding expression, an at:put: message is sent to object elements.

The Use of Objects in Smalltalk

The view of class Stack in Fig. 6.4 shows its data and operations.[1] The instance variables spelling and top hold the data of an instance of class Stack. Note the absence of type constraints; elements is assigned an array that can hold objects of any type.

The instance methods implement the operations supported by an instance of Stack. The operations are used in the following sequence of expressions (separated by dots):

[1] Smalltalk-80 does not have a textual representation. All code is entered and displayed through a programming environment provided by the system. The view in Fig. 6.4 collects information that need not be displayed at the same time. For simplicity, the Smalltalk examples in this chapter omit the grouping of related messages into "categories."

class **Stack**
instance variables
    elements
    top

instance methods
    pop
        | temp |
        temp ← elements at: top.
        top ← top − 1.
        ↑ temp

    push: anElement
        top ← top + 1.
        elements at: top put: anElement

    initialize
        elements ← Array new: 99.
        top ← 0

Fig. 6.4. A view of a class Stack in Smalltalk.

| s | *introduce temporary variable* s
s ← Stack new.   *assign* s *a new uninitialized stack*
s initialize.   *explicitly initialize* s
s push: 'Smalltalk'.   *push string* 'Smalltalk'
s push: 80   *push number* 80

Temporary variables are introduced by writing them between vertical bars. An uninitialized instance of a class is created by sending a new message to the class, as in

    Stack new

The class description in Fig. 6.4 provides an explicit initialize operation to prepare the instance variables of a stack object.

    The above program text therefore assigns a new stack to s, initializes it, and pushes two elements of different types onto it.

6.3   ELEMENTS OF SMALLTALK-80

The syntax and semantics of Smalltalk-80 are introduced in this section using a variant of class Stack. A Smalltalk tradition is to use unabbreviated descriptive names. When two or more words are put together to form a name, the first letter of an embedded word is capitalized, as in anElement.

Variables

Variables must be "declared" before they are used. A declaration specifies whether a variable is temporary or whether it belongs to an instance, a class, or larger grouping. Smalltalk declarations say nothing about the type of a variable.

A fresh temporary variable is created for each evaluation of a code fragment. Temporary variables are declared by writing them within vertical bars at the beginning of the code fragment.

An instance variable belongs to an instance. Its value can be changed only by operations belonging to the instance. It exists as long as the instance does.

This chapter uses only temporary variables and instance variables. Incidentally, a single copy of a "class variable" is shared by all instances of a class, and a single copy of a "global variable" is shared by all instances of all classes.

Class Methods and Instance Methods

Most classes respond to the message new, as in

    Stack new

sent to the class Stack. Here new is a *class method* because it belongs to the class.

Class methods are used primarily to create objects. The view of class Stack in Fig. 6.5 shows a class method new:. Note that keyword message new:, ending in a colon, is different from the unary message new. Class method new is provided by the language for creating uninitialized objects; we use new: with an argument aSize to create and initialize a stack.

An instance method belongs to an object. Several instance methods are mentioned in Fig. 6.5.

To summarize: Messages for class methods are sent to the class, and messages for instance methods are sent to the individual instances of the class.

Expressions

Expressions have a unique syntax in Smalltalk (see Fig. 6.6). Evaluation proceeds from left to right.

All arithmetic operators have the same precedence, so the addition in the expression 2 + 3 * 5 is done before the multiplication; that is, the following equivalences hold:

    2 + 3 * 5 ≡ (2 + 3) * 5 ≡ 25

class **Stack**

instance variables
  elements   An array to hold elements.
  size   Maximum number of elements.
  top   Index of the top element.

class methods
  new: aSize   Return an initialized stack of size aSize

instance methods
  isEmpty   Are there any elements in the stack?
  isFull   Is the stack full?
  pop   Remove and return the top element.
  push: anElement   Make anElement the new top of stack.
  initialize: aSize   Called by class method new:

Fig. 6.5. A view of class Stack.

The assignment operator is ←. The left side of an assignment must be a variable; changes to components of a data structure are made by sending an appropriate message to that data structure.

Arrays support both at: and at:put: messages. An at: message looks up the value of an array element, while an at:put: changes the value of an array element. Thus,

A at: i

corresponds to $A[i]$, the value of the element of array A at position i. On the other hand,

SMALLTALK	COMMENT
$a	character a
$$	character $
'string'	string 'string' of six characters
top ← 0	$top := 0$
A at: i put: x	$A[i] := x$, where A is an array
y ← A at: i	$y := A[i]$, where A is an array
#(2 3 5)	unnamed array with elements 2, 3, 5
#(2 $3 'five')	unnamed array of number 2, character 3, and string 'five'
2 + 3 * 5	note left-to-right evaluation: $(2 + 3) * 5 \equiv 25$
s pop	message pop to object s
s push: 10	message push: with argument 10 to object s
self isEmpty	message isEmpty from an object to itself

Fig. 6.6. Syntax of expressions in Smalltalk.

    A at: i put: x

corresponds to $A[i] := x$; the value of x is assigned to the element of array
A at position i.

By convention, at: and at:put: messages are supported by all Smalltalk
objects that store information in components; examples are arrays, dictionaries, and tables.

Returning Values

Each method returns a value. An explicit return value is preceded by ↑;
the default is to return the object itself if no explicit return value is
specified. The following implementation of instance method isEmpty is
taken from Fig. 6.7:

isEmpty
     ↑ top = 0

An instance of class Stack responds to message isEmpty by evaluating the
expression ↑ top = 0. The return value operator ↑ has lower precedence
than other operators and messages, so the expression is equivalent to

    ↑ (top = 0)

In words, return the value of the test top = 0; the value returned is true if
top equals 0 and false otherwise.

Messages to self

Classes and objects can invoke one of their own operations by sending a
message to the special name self. Thus, self within a class method refers
to the class itself and self within an instance method refers to the instance
itself. Smalltalk's inheritance mechanism, introduced in Section 6.4, generalizes this notion of "self."

A stack object can use

    self isFull

to check if it has room for any more elements. Method push: in Fig. 6.7
uses self

    push: anElement
        self isFull ifTrue: [· · ·] ifFalse: [· · ·]

The effect of the message isFull to self is to evaluate expression top >= size
in the body of method isFull.

Class method new: in Fig. 6.7 uses self to refer to class Stack itself:

class **Stack**

instance variables

> **elements**
> **top**
> **size**

class methods

> **new: aSize**
>> ↑ self new initialize: aSize

instance methods

> **isEmpty**
>> ↑ top = 0
>
> **isFull**
>> ↑ top >= size
>
> **push: anElement**
>> self isFull
>>> ifTrue: [self error: 'stack full']
>>> ifFalse: [top ← top + 1.
>>>> elements at: top put: anElement]
>
> **pop**
>> | temp |
>> self isEmpty
>>> ifTrue: [self error: 'stack empty']
>>> ifFalse: [temp ← elements at: top.
>>>> top ← top − 1.
>>>> ↑ temp]
>
> **initialize: aSize**
>> top ← 0.
>> size ← aSize.
>> elements ← Array new: (aSize + 1)

Fig. 6.7. Implementation description of a class Stack.

new: aSize
> ↑ ((self new) initialize: aSize)

Parentheses have been added here to show how this class method creates, initializes, and returns a stack instance:

1. The value of subexpression (self new) is an uninitialized instance, just as the value of Stack new would be.

2. The uninitialized instance receives the initialize: message with argument aSize. We see next that initialize: initializes the instance and returns it.

3. The explicit ↑ in class method new: further returns the initialized instance.

Expression Sequences

A sequence of expressions is separated by dots, as in the body of instance method initialize: in Fig. 6.7:

initialize: aSize
>   top ← 0.   size ← aSize.   elements ← Array new: (aSize + 1)

In the absence of an explicit return operator ↑, method initialize: returns the instance itself.

A semicolon has a special meaning: it separates multiple messages to the same object. Evaluation of the expression sequence

>   s push: 'Smalltalk'.   s push: 80.   s push: 'system'

sends three push: messages to object s. These messages to s can be written alternatively as

>   s push: 'Smalltalk';   push: 80;   push: 'system'

Multiple or *cascaded* messages to the same object can sometimes eliminate the need for temporary variables.

Blocks

A *conditional* has the following syntax:

>   ⟨test-expression⟩
>   ifTrue: [⟨expression-sequence⟩₁]
>   ifFalse: [⟨expression-sequence⟩₂]

An expression sequence enclosed within square brackets, [and], is called a *block*.

The following conditional implements method push: in Fig. 6.7:

push: anElement
>   self isFull
>   ifTrue: [self error: 'stack full']
>   ifFalse: [top ← top + 1.
>   elements at: top put: anElement]

The test self isFull returns one of the boolean values true and false. If true is returned, then the expressions in the block following ifTrue: are evaluated, otherwise, false is returned and the expressions in the block following ifFalse: are evaluated.

A *while* loop has one of the following two forms:

⟨*test-expression*⟩   whileTrue: [⟨*expression-sequence*⟩]

⟨*test-expression*⟩   whileFalse: [⟨*expression-sequence*⟩]

No surprises here. In the whileTrue: case, the test expression and the expression sequence are evaluated alternately, while the test is true. In the whileFalse: case, the test expression and the expression sequence are evaluated alternately, while the test is false.

The conventional behavior of conditionals and while-loops hides an unusual aspect of blocks. Blocks are objects. They can be assigned to variables and passed as arguments. The expression sequence in a block is evaluated only when the block receives the message value.

Variable bumpX is assigned a block [x ← x+1] by

bumpX   ←   [x ← x + 1]

This assignment affects variable bumpX, but x is unaffected because the block is treated as data. Now, the expression sequence

x ← 0.	*assign 0 to* x
bumpX value.	*evaluate the block* bumpX
bumpX value	*evaluate the block* bumpX

leaves x with value 2.

6.4 INHERITANCE IN SMALLTALK

Smalltalk encourages the use of inheritance to define a new class *B* as an extension of a previous class *A*. The extension *B* is called a *subclass* of *A*; conversely, *A* is called a *superclass* of *B*.

Subclasses/superclasses in Smalltalk parallel subtypes/supertypes and subsets/supersets. The inheritance rules ensure that an object of a subclass *B* can appear wherever an object of a superclass *A* is expected. Informally, the objects of subclass *B* are a subset of the objects of superclass *A*.

The inheritance rules are as follows:

- Single inheritance sets up a hierarchy as in Fig. 6.8. Single inheritance means that each class has at most one superclass, although it can have several subclasses. At the root of the hierarchy is class Object. All classes except Object have exactly one superclass.

- A subclass inherits variables and methods from its superclass. Thus, instance variables of the superclass automatically become instance

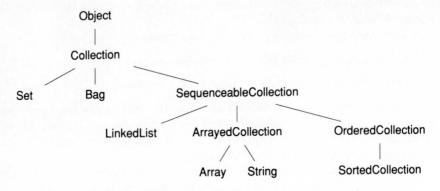

Fig. 6.8. A portion of the Smalltalk class hierarchy.

variables of the subclass, instance methods are inherited as instance methods, class methods are inherited as class methods, and so on.

- In addition to the inherited variables, a subclass can declare fresh variable names, different from the inherited variables.
- Methods in the subclass override inherited methods. We noted earlier that a method is an implementation of an operation. Suppose that for some operation *op*, both the superclass and subclass provide methods. In this case, the method provided by the subclass is used. (Rules for the special names self and super appear later in this section.)

Inheritance is central to programming in Smalltalk. The system provides a large number of existing classes that can be adapted, through inheritance, to the needs of a particular application. All classes in the Smalltalk system, including user-defined classes, are part of the subclass-superclass hierarchy. A portion of the hierarchy appears in Fig. 6.8; Goldberg and Robson [1983] devote several chapters to system classes.

Example 6.1. Smalltalk's inheritance rules will be illustrated by considering a class GrammarSymbol with two subclasses, Token and Nonterminal (see Fig. 6.9). These classes are taken from an extended example in Section 6.5, where the motivation for them is presented.

GrammarSymbol is a subclass of Object, the root of the Smalltalk class hierarchy. GrammarSymbol has one class method new: for creating initialized objects. Instances of GrammarSymbol have one instance variable spelling, and two instance methods spell and setSpelling:.

Subclass Token inherits variable spelling and the class and instance methods of GrammarSymbol. It adds an instance method isNullable.

Subclass Nonterminal of GrammarSymbol overrides new:. Both Nonterminal and GrammarSymbol have a class method new:, and the method in

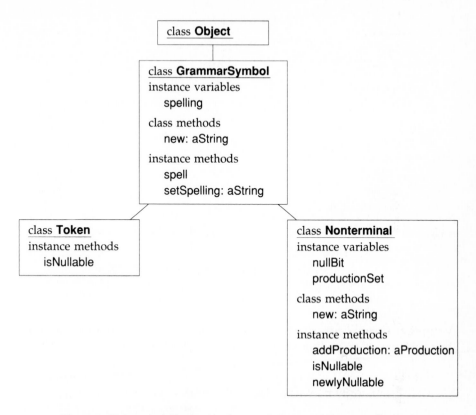

Fig. 6.9. Token and Nonterminal are subclasses of GrammarSymbol.

the subclass is used whenever a clash occurs. A complete listing of the variables and methods for Nonterminal appears in Fig. 6.10.

The rest of this example considers some expressions that use the classes in Fig. 6.9. Explanatory remarks appear on the right.

Subclass Nonterminal overrides class method new:, but Token does not:

>   Token new: 'begin'   *use* new: *from* GrammarSymbol
>   Nonterminal new: 'statement'   *use* new: *from* Nonterminal

Neither subclass overrides instance method spell. A token or nonterminal object x therefore responds to message spell by using the inherited method:

>   x spell   *use instance method* spell *of* GrammarSymbol

Both subclasses add an instance method isNullable. An instance x of one of the subclasses uses the method defined in that subclass:

instance variables	
spelling	inherited
nullBit	added
productionSet	added

class methods	
new: aString	overrides new: in GrammarSymbol

instance methods	
spell	inherited
setSpelling: aString	inherited
addProduction: aProduction	added
isNullable	added
newlyNullable	added

Fig. 6.10. A complete listing of the variables and methods of class Nonterminal.

| x |	*introduce temporary variable* x
x ← Token new: 'begin'.	*create a token and assign it to* x
x isNullable.	*use instance method* isNullable *of* Token

A run-time error occurs if x is an instance of GrammarSymbol because only the subclasses have methods for the message isNullable:

| x |	*introduce temporary variable* x
x ← GrammarSymbol new: 'begin'.	*create a grammar symbol and assign it to* x
x isNullable.	*error:* x *does not understand message* isNullable □

Operations on Collection Classes

Class Collection in Smalltalk supports several messages to carry out iterations of the form (see Fig. 6.11):

for each element x of a collection **do**
    something with x
end

Subclasses of Collection, such as Set, Array, and Dictionary, inherit these messages.

The Smalltalk counterpart of "do something with x" is a block that takes an argument x. The notation for such a block is

    [:⟨variable⟩ | ⟨expression-sequence⟩]

The value of a block is the value of its last expression.

<u>class **Collection** superclass Object</u>
instance methods

select: aBlock	Evaluate aBlock for each element of this collection. Return a collection consisting of the elements for which the block evaluates to true.
reject: aBlock	Evaluate aBlock for each element of this collection. Return a collection consisting of the elements for which the block evaluates to false.
do: aBlock	Evaluate aBlock for each element of this collection.
collect: aBlock	Evaluate aBlock for each element of this collection. Return a collection formed from the results of the successive evaluations of the block.

Fig. 6.11. Operations on elements in a collection.

Example 6.2. The select: operation in

   productionSet select: [:p | p isNullable]

evaluates the block [:p | p isNullable] for each element p of productionSet; all elements that return true in response to message isNullable are returned as a collection.

   A reject: operation complements select:. Nullable elements of rightSide are thrown away by

   rightSide reject: [:s | s isNullable]

The expression

   aSet collect: [:s | s spell]

collects and returns the results of sending message spell to each element s of aSet.   □

Messages to self

A message to self is a message to the object itself. Even within an inherited method, self refers to the object itself. An inherited method is treated as if it were defined in the subclass, so instances of self in the inherited method refer to the subclass.

Example 6.3. Subclass B in Fig. 6.12 has two methods:

   instance methods
      meShow   inherited from A
      show   overrides show in A

class **A**
instance methods
    show
        ↑ '1A'
    meShow
      ↑ self show

class **B** superclass A
instance methods
    show
       ↑ '2B'

Fig. 6.12. Method meShow sends a message to self.

The occurrence of self in

meShow
    ↑ self show

refers to the object that uses meShow. Expression b meShow, following, therefore evaluates to '2B' and expression a meShow evaluates to '1A':

a ← A new.   *assign* a *an instance of* A
b ← B new.   *assign* b *an instance of* B
a show.   *result* '1A'
b show.   *result* '2B'
a meShow.   self *refers to* a; *result* '1A'
b meShow.   self *refers to* b; *result* '2B'   □

Messages to super

When a subclass overrides an inherited method, the special name super allows the overridden method to be used. Within the subclass, a message to super invokes the method that the superclass would use for that message.

Example 6.4. The only difference between Fig. 6.13 and Fig. 6.12 is the addition to B of method bypass.

    bypass
      ↑ super show

The discussion in Example 6.3 carries over to the modified classes in Fig. 6.13. In addition, we have

b ← B new.   *assign* b *an instance of* B
b bypass.   *result* '1A'

```
class  A
instance methods
    show
        ↑ '1A'
    meShow
        ↑ self show

class  B  superclass  A
instance methods
    show
        ↑ '2B'
    bypass
        ↑ super show
```

Fig. 6.13. Method bypass sends a message to super.

Instance method bypass in subclass B uses super show to refer to method show in the superclass, which returns '1A'.   □

6.5   AN EXTENDED SMALLTALK EXAMPLE

This section develops a program to manipulate grammars. We proceed as follows:

1. Identify the objects in a representation of a grammar.

2. Design messages to extract a property of the grammar.

3. Write a Smalltalk program.

The program uses Smalltalk system classes for sets, arrays, and dictionaries. A dictionary is a set of key-value pairs; one of the operations on dictionaries retrieves the value associated with a key.

To obtain the most benefit from this section, think about what a corresponding program in another language would look like.

Objects in a Representation of Grammars

As noted in Section 1.5, the heart of a grammar is a set of rules called productions. The production

$\langle block \rangle$ ::= $\langle declaration\text{-}list \rangle$ **begin** $\langle statement\text{-}list \rangle$ **end**

can be read as: A $\langle block \rangle$ can consist of a $\langle declaration\text{-}list \rangle$, the token **begin**, a $\langle statement\text{-}list \rangle$, and the token **end**. A token is an atomic symbol in the syntax.

Here ::= separates the left and right sides of a production. The left side is a variable called a nonterminal. The right side is a sequence of zero or more nonterminals and tokens. Productions with the same left side can be combined and written with | separating the alternative right sides, as in the following ten productions with left side ⟨digit⟩:

⟨digit⟩   ::=   0 | 1 | 2 | 3 | 4 | 5 | 6 | 7 | 8 | 9

Any program to manipulate grammars must choose a representation for the objects of a grammar; that is, for productions, nonterminals, and tokens. An informal description of these objects is as follows

- A *grammar symbol* is either a *token* or a *nonterminal*.

- A *production* has a left side consisting of a nonterminal and a right side consisting of a sequence of zero or more grammar symbols.

- A *grammar* has three parts: a set of nonterminals, a starting nonterminal, and a set of tokens. In the program in this section, each nonterminal keeps track of its own set of productions, the productions that it is the left side of.

These objects motivate the class hierarchy in Fig. 6.14. The root is Object because all Smalltalk classes must directly or indirectly be subclasses of Object. We collect common properties of tokens and nonterminals into class GrammarSymbol, with subclasses Token and Nonterminal.

Class Production is a subclass of Object. It has an instance variable leftSide to keep track of the nonterminal on the left side of a production, and an instance variable rightSide to keep track of the sequence of grammar symbols on the right side of the production. The value of rightSide will be an array of grammar symbols.

Class Grammar is also a subclass of Object. It has several instance variables to keep track of the nonterminals, the tokens, and the starting nonterminal; the details are given later in this section.

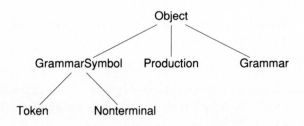

Fig. 6.14. Class hierarchy for representing grammars.

Nullable Nonterminals

Now, on to something for the objects to work on. The problem of finding "nullable" nonterminals is representative of grammar-manipulation problems faced by compiler writers. Nullable nonterminals correspond to optional syntactic constructs that can be missing or null.

Let ⟨empty⟩ denote the absence of grammar symbols. Alternatively, ⟨empty⟩ denotes a sequence of zero grammar symbols. Thus, the two productions

> ⟨optional-fraction⟩ ::= ⟨empty⟩
> | . ⟨digit-sequence⟩

say that an optional fraction can be missing or that it can consist of a point "." followed by a sequence of digits.

If a production has ⟨empty⟩ as its right side, then it is nullable. Other productions can be nullable as well; the following is a recursive definition of nullable nonterminals and productions:

- A nonterminal is *nullable* if it is the left side of a nullable production.

- A production is *nullable* if its right side is ⟨empty⟩ or if the right side consists entirely of nullable nonterminals.

Example 6.5. The following grammar is for numbers like 365, 3.142, and .25, with optional integer and fractional parts. (Although it illustrates nullable nonterminals, this grammar is not good for describing numbers because it allows ⟨number⟩ itself to be null or to be a single dot.)

> ⟨number⟩ ::= ⟨digit-sequence⟩ ⟨optional-fraction⟩
>
> ⟨digit-sequence⟩ ::= ⟨empty⟩ | ⟨digit⟩ ⟨digit-sequence⟩
>
> ⟨digit⟩ ::= 0 | 1 | 2 | 3 | 4 | 5 | 6 | 7 | 8 | 9
>
> ⟨optional-fraction⟩ ::= ⟨empty⟩ | . ⟨digit-sequence⟩

Nonterminals ⟨digit-sequence⟩ and ⟨optional-fraction⟩ are nullable because they have productions with right side ⟨empty⟩. Consequently, the production

> ⟨number⟩ ::= ⟨digit-sequence⟩ ⟨optional-fraction⟩

must be nullable, and so must the nonterminal ⟨number⟩ on its left side. Nonterminal ⟨digit⟩, however, is not nullable because each of its productions has a token on its right side.

Discovery of a nullable nonterminal can lead to the discovery of others, so an iterative algorithm will be used to find them.

class **Token** superclass GrammarSymbol
instance methods
    isNullable
        ↑ false

class **Nonterminal** superclass GrammarSymbol
instance methods for Nonterminal
    isNullable
        ↑ nullBit   "Return value of status bit"

    newlyNullable
        nullBit ifTrue: [↑ false].
        nullBit ← (productionSet select: [:p | p isNullable]) isNonEmpty.
        ↑ self isNullable

class **Production** superclass Object
instance methods
    isNullable
        ↑ (rightSide reject: [:s | s isNullable]) isEmpty

class **Grammar** superclass Object
instance methods
    findNullable
        | newInformation newNulls |
        newInformation ← true.
        [newInformation]
            whileTrue:
                [newNulls ← nonterminalSet select: [:n | n newlyNullable].
                  newInformation ← newNulls isNonEmpty].
        ↑ (nonterminalSet select: [:n | n isNullable]) collect: [:n | n spell]

Fig. 6.15. Operations for finding nullable nonterminals.

Messages for Finding Nullable Nonterminals

The messages illustrated in Fig. 6.15 are designed for the following iterative approach to finding nullable nonterminals:

    while there is new information **do**
        ask each nonterminal if its status now changes to nullable;
    end

This while-loop is the heart of method **findNullable** of class **Grammar** in
Fig. 6.15. It implements the pseudo-code:

```
procedure findNullable ();
    var newInformation, newNulls;
begin
    newInformation := true;
    while newInformation do
        newNulls := set of newly nullable nonterminals;
        newInformation := isNonEmpty (newNulls);
    end;
    return set of spellings of nullable nonterminals;
end findNullable ;
```

Method findNullable uses the following code to find the set of newly null-able nonterminals:

    newNulls ← nonterminalSet select: [:n | n newlyNullable].

In words, from the set of nonterminals of the grammar, select the subset of nonterminals n for which the expression

    n newlyNullable

is true. Assign this subset to newNulls.

A nonterminal has a status bit, called nullBit, initially false, that is assigned true when we discover that the nonterminal is nullable. A non-terminal responds to message isNullable by returning the value of its status bit. A token cannot disappear, so it responds to message isNullable by returning false.

Instance method newlyNullable checks whether the status of a nontermi-nal is now ready to change from false to true. If nullBit is already true, then the status cannot change and the method returns false. Otherwise, each production in productionSet is asked to check whether it is nullable:

    productionSet select: [:p | p isNullable]

If this set is nonempty, then nullBit is set to true and its value is returned.[2]

A production is nullable if each grammar symbol on its right side is nullable—put differently, if the set of non-nullable symbols on its right side is empty. This set is given by

    rightSide reject: [:s | s isNullable]

---

[2] This program was run by adding instance method isNonEmpty to class Collection:

```
class Collection superclass Object
instance methods
    isNonEmpty
        ↑ self isEmpty not
```

User Interface for Setting up a Grammar

The rest of this section is a detailed description of the classes for representing grammars; it can be skipped on first reading. Section 6.6 starts on page 235.

To minimize the code for entering grammars, class Grammar uses a crude user interface. First, the spellings of the nonterminals, the starting nonterminal, and the spellings of the tokens are entered. Then the productions are entered, one at a time. The declarations allow any string to be used as the spelling of a grammar symbol, obviating the need for conventions, such as enclosing brackets ⟨ and ⟩ for nonterminals.

The following is an array of strings representing the spellings of the nonterminals in the grammar of Example 6.5:

> #('number' 'digit-sequence' 'optional-fraction' 'digit')

A similar array for the spellings of the tokens is

> #('0' '1' '2' '3' '4' '5' '6' '7' '8' '9' '.')

The grammar of Example 6.5 might be entered as follows:

```
| G |
G ← Grammar
        nonterminals: #('number' 'digit-sequence' 'optional-fraction' 'digit')
        start: 'number'
        tokens: #('0' '1' '2' '3' '4' '5' '6' '7' '8' '9' '.').

G   left: 'number'   right: #('digit-sequence' 'optional-fraction').

G   left: 'digit-sequence'   right: #().

G   left: 'digit-sequence'   right: #('digit' 'digit-sequence').
        . . .
```

Keyword nonterminals: is followed by an array of the spellings of the nonterminals. Keyword tokens: is accompanied by a similar array for tokens. Each production is entered using a left:right: message.

Implementation of Grammar Symbols and Productions

Implementation details for GrammarSymbol, Token, Nonterminal, and Production appear next, interspersed with comments.

The external interface of a grammar symbol is its spelling. Class method new: creates a grammar symbol initialized with a string as its spelling. The initialization is done by setSpelling and the string is retrieved by spell:

class **GrammarSymbol** superclass Object
instance variables
    spelling

class methods for GrammarSymbol
    new: aString
        ↑ self new setSpelling: aString

instance methods for GrammarSymbol
    setSpelling: aString
        spelling ← aString
    spell
        ↑ spelling

Class Token has one method and no variables:

class **Token** superclass GrammarSymbol
instance methods
    isNullable
        ↑ false

Subclass Nonterminal adds two instance variables to GrammarSymbol: nullBit is a status bit and productionSet holds the set of productions with this nonterminal on the left side.

class **Nonterminal** superclass GrammarSymbol
instance variables
    nullBit
    productionSet

Class Nonterminal reimplements new: to initialize the added variables nullBit and productionSet:

class methods for Nonterminal
    new: aString
        ↑ super new: aString initialize

In more detail, message new: to super creates an instance and initializes the inherited variable spelling. This instance then receives message initialize to initialize nullBit and productionSet.

The grammar is read in a production at a time, and message addProduction: is used each time to add the production to productionSet.

instance methods for Nonterminal
initialize
```
productionSet ← Set new.
nullBit ← false
```

addProduction: aProduction
```
productionSet  add: aProduction
```

isNullable
```
↑ nullBit
```

newlyNullable
```
nullBit ifTrue: [ ↑ false].
nullBit ← (productionSet  select: [:p | p isNullable]) isNonEmpty.
↑ self  isNullable
```

A production has instance variables to hold a left side and a right side. Class method left:right: creates an instance and sends it a setLeft:setRight: message.

class **Production** superclass Object

instance variables
    leftSide
    rightSide

class methods
left: aNonterminal right: aSequence
```
↑ self  new  setLeft: aNonterminal  setRight: aSequence
```

instance methods
setLeft: aNonterminal setRight: aSequence
```
leftSide ← aNonterminal.
rightSide ← aSequence
```

isNullable
```
↑ (rightSide  reject: [:s | s isNullable]) isEmpty
```

Implementation of Grammar Objects

As mentioned earlier, a grammar is entered by declaring the nonterminals, the starting symbol, and the tokens, and then entering the productions one by one. Most of the code for class Grammar deals with grammar entry. The code is shown for completeness; it does more work and so is harder to read than the code seen so far in this section.

We want the following to assign G a grammar object:

```
G ← Grammar
        nonterminals: #('number' 'digit-sequence' 'optional-fraction' 'digit')
        start: 'number'
        tokens: #('0' '1' '2' '3' '4' '5' '6' '7' '8' '9' '.').
```

The declared nonterminals are held in a dictionary nonterminalDictionary, which maps nonterminal spellings to the corresponding internal objects. There is a similar dictionary for tokens.

<u>class **Grammar** superclass Object</u>
instance variables
    nonterminalDictionary
    nonterminalSet
    startSymbol
    tokenDictionary

The class method for creating grammar objects creates an uninitialized object and sends it a setNonterminals:setStart:setTokens: message, telling the object to initialize itself:

class methods for Grammar
    nonterminals: nStrings start: aString tokens: tStrings
        ↑ self new
            setNonterminals: nStrings
            setStart: aString
            setTokens: tStrings

The spelling of a grammar symbol is its external user interface, which is used for input/output. During initialization, for each external spelling, an internal grammar symbol object with that spelling is created. Dictionaries map spellings to the corresponding objects:

instance methods for Grammar
    setNonterminals: nStrings setStart: aString setTokens: tStrings
        nonterminalDictionary ← Dictionary new.
        nStrings do: [:n | nonterminalDictionary at: n put: (Nonterminal new: n)].
        startSymbol ← nonterminalDictionary associationAt: aString.
        nonterminalSet ← nonterminalDictionary values asSet.
        tokenDictionary ← Dictionary new.
        tStrings do: [:t | tokenDictionary at: t put: (Token new: t)]

In words, nonterminalDictionary is assigned a newly created dictionary. For each string n in the array nStrings of nonterminal spellings, a new nonterminal is created by

Nonterminal new: n

The key n and this new nonterminal are then entered into the dictionary by an at:put: message. The starting nonterminal is looked up in the dictionary by sending an associationAt: message accompanied by its spelling aString. Message values extracts the value portion of the key-value pairs from the nonterminal dictionary, and message asSet converts the extracted values into a set. Tokens are then created and entered into a token dictionary.

Productions are added one at a time. We want the following expression to add a production to grammar G:

   G   left: 'optional-fraction'   right: #('.' 'digit-sequence').

The method for this message, given next, looks up 'optional-fraction' in the nonterminal dictionary and assigns its corresponding nonterminal object to lhs. The sequence of strings accompanying right: must also be mapped to an appropriate sequence of tokens and nonterminals. Each string s is looked up first in the token dictionary, and if absent, is looked up next in the nonterminal dictionary, by

   tokenDictionary at: s ifAbsent: [nonterminalDictionary at: s]

The grammar symbol objects extracted from the dictionaries are collected and the collection assigned to rhs. Only then can a production object be created and given to the left side lhs, to be added to its productionSet.

```
left: aString right: stringSequence
    | lhs rhs |
    lhs ← nonterminalDictionary associationAt: aString.
    rhs ← stringSequence
            collect:    [:s | tokenDictionary at: s
                                    ifAbsent: [nonterminalDictionary at: s]
                         ].
    lhs addProduction: (Production left: lhs right: rhs)
```

Finally, we repeat the method for finding nullable nonterminals:

```
findNullable
    | newInformation   newNulls |
    newInformation ← true.
    [newInformation]
        whileTrue:
            [newNulls ← nonterminalSet select: [:n | n newlyNullable].
             newInformation ← newNulls isNonEmpty].
    ↑ (nonterminalSet select: [:n | n isNullable])  collect: [:n | n spell]
```

6.6 INHERITANCE IN C++

In C++ terminology, the extension of a base class is called a derived class. The base-class/derived-class relationship in C++ is more general than the subtype/supertype relationship because derived classes can be used even in situations where subtypes are not appropriate. Informally, a derived class is a subtype if it does not interfere with the visibility of inherited members.

Review of C++

Since C++ has already been introduced in Section 5.7, we use the following class declaration to remind us of some of its features:

```
class buffer {
public:
        buffer() { size = MAXBUF+1; front = rear = 0; }
    int  enter(char);
    char leave();
private:
    char buf[MAXBUF+1];
    int  size;
    int  front;
    int  rear;
    int  succ(int i) { return (i + 1) % size; }
};
```

Classes in C++ generalize records or structures by allowing functions to be class members. The body of a function can appear within the class declaration, or it can appear separately. The bodies of functions **buffer** and **succ** appear in the declaration of **buffer**, and the bodies of functions **enter** and **leave** must appear separately. A special function called a constructor, with the same name as the class, is called automatically when an object of the class is created. Initialization code for the variables in the class declaration belongs in the constructor.

The types of all members must be fully declared because their usage is strictly checked at compile time.

C++ has three keywords—**public**, **private**, and **protected**—for controlling the visibility of member names in a class declaration. As in Section 5.9, public members are visible to outside code, and private members are not. Protected members are visible through inheritance to derived classes, but not to other code.

This chapter deals primarily with classes derived according to the following syntax:

```
class ⟨derived⟩ : public ⟨base⟩ {
    ⟨member-declarations⟩
};
```

Class ⟨derived⟩ inherits all the members of class ⟨base⟩. Keyword **public**
before ⟨base⟩ says that, by default, the inherited members have the same
visibility in class ⟨derived⟩ that they do in ⟨base⟩.

Virtual Functions

Object-oriented programming in C++ relies on virtual functions. Informally, the keyword **virtual** before a function declaration says: Use the
function body in the derived class, whenever possible.

The only difference between functions **f** and **g** in the following pseudo-
code is that keyword **virtual** appears before the declaration of **f**:

```
class B {
public:
virtual char  f()      { return 'B'; }
        char  g()      { return 'B'; }
        char  testF()  { return f(); }
        char  testG()  { return g(); }
};
```

The distinction between **f** and **g** will be tested using the following derived
class, which redeclares **f** and **g**:

```
class D : public B {
public:
        char  f()      { return 'D'; }
        char  g()      { return 'D'; }
};
```

B::f and **B::g** return character ′**B**′, and **D::f** and **D::g** return character
′**D**′.

The **main** function is

```
main() {
        D d;
        print d.testF(), d.testG();
}
```

What are the values of the expressions **d.testF()** and **d.testG()**? Functions **testF** and **testG** are declared in the base class **B** and remain public in the derived class **D**. The expressions **d.testF()** and **d.testG()** call **f** and **g**, respectively.

Virtual functions are taken from the derived class where possible, so the body of **B::testF** calls **D::f** and returns **'D'**. On the other hand, **g** is not a virtual function, so the body of **B::testG** calls **B::g** and returns **'B'**.

Subtypes in C++

The subtype principle can be restated for C++ as follows:

A derived class can appear wherever a public base class is expected.[3]

From the definition in Section 5.9, a derived class is said to have a public base class if the derived class maintains the visibility of all inherited members. Otherwise, the derived class is said to have a private base class.

Example 6.6. Subtypes and virtual functions can be used to completely separate the implementation of a class from its public interface. Since virtual functions are slightly less efficient than nonvirtual functions, the separation exacts a run-time cost.

The declaration of class **buffer** earlier in this section mentions both the public and private members. Thus, the declaration mentions not only the interface of the buffer, but also its implementation in terms of an array **buf** and indices **front** and **rear**. Although private members like **buf** and **front** are inaccessible from outside the class, their presence in the declaration nevertheless fixes the implementation of buffers.

The following variant mentions only the public members of **buffer**:

```
class bufdef {
public:
  virtual int  enter(char x) { }
  virtual char leave()       { }
};
```

The bodies of the member functions are empty because they will never be used. The functions are virtual and are expected to be redefined by derived classes like **fixbuf**:

---

[3] Early versions of C++ recognized subtypes only for pointer types. The reference manual in Stroustrup [1986] states, "A pointer to a class may be converted to a pointer to a public base class of that class."

```
class fixbuf : public bufdef {
public:
        fixbuf() { size = MAXBUF+1; front = rear = 0; }
   int   enter(char);
   char leave();
private:
   char buf[MAXBUF+1];
   int   size, front, rear;
   int   succ(int i) { return (i + 1) % size; }
};
```

Any client that wishes to use a buffer need know only about **bufdef**. An example is a function **copy**, which expects to be called with a pointer to an object of class **bufdef**:

```
void copy(bufdef *b) {
    ··· b->enter(c); ···
}
```

Since **fixbuf** is a subtype of **bufdef**, function **copy** can be passed a pointer to a **fixbuf** instead of a pointer to a **bufdef**. In the following fragment, **copy** is passed a pointer to **f**, created by the address-of operator, **&**:

```
main() {
    fixbuf f;
    copy(&f);
    return 0;
}
```

This approach allows us to change the implementation of buffers without changing function **copy**. For example, suppose that a subtype **linkbuf** of **bufdef** uses linked lists to implement an unbounded buffer. Function **copy** will happily accept a pointer to a **linkbuf**.   □

Code Reuse without Subtypes

We can prevent a derived class from being a subtype by making its base class private, as in the following syntax:

```
class D : private B { ··· }
```

The keyword **private** makes **B** a private base class in this declaration. An object of class **D** cannot simply appear in place of an object of class **B**.

Example 6.7. Consider a base class with the properties of both stacks and queues:

```
class hybrid {
public:
        hybrid();
    void push(int);
    int  pop();
    void enter(int);
    int  leave();
};
```

Derived class **stack** explicitly names the inherited members **push** and **pop** to make them public, and, by default, it hides **enter** and **leave**:

```
class stack : private hybrid {
public:
        stack()         {}
        hybrid::push;
        hybrid::pop;
}
```

The constructor of the base class **hybrid** is called automatically before the constructor **stack** in the derived class is called. Here, constructor **stack** has an empty body, so it does nothing.

Class **stack** is derived from **hybrid**, but should a stack object be allowed to appear anywhere a hybrid object can? Clearly not, because the **enter** and **leave** functions allow a hybrid object to be used as queue. Class **stack**, however, hides these operations, so a stack cannot be used as a queue. Thus, a pointer to **stack** should not be, and is not, a subtype of pointer to **hybrid**.   □

6.7   AN EXTENDED C++ EXAMPLE

This section illustrates inheritance in C++ by developing a program to find prime numbers. A prime number is divisible only by itself and 1; alternatively, n is a prime if its only factors are 1 and n itself. The prime numbers smaller than 50 are

2 3 5 7 11 13 17 19 23 29 31 37 41 43 47

The program in this section can be transliterated directly into Smalltalk.

A Prime Number Sieve

The Greek philosopher Eratosthenes is credited with the *sieve method* for computing primes. The underlying idea is that n is a prime if n is not a multiple of any prime p smaller than n. Thus, 3 is a prime because it is not a multiple of 2. 5 is a prime because it is a multiple neither of 2 nor of 3.

A variant of the sieve method begins with the sequence of integers, starting with 2 (see the top of Fig. 6.16). Primes and their multiples are repeatedly removed from the sequence. First, 2 is a prime, so 2 is output, and all multiples of 2 are removed from the sequence. Then, 3 is a prime, so 3 is output, and all multiples of 3 are removed from the sequence. In general, if a number is output, then it must be a prime.

	2	3	4	5	6	7	8	9	10	11	12	13	14	15	$\cdots$
2 is a prime	2̸	3	4̸	5	6̸	7	8̸	9	1̸0̸	11	1̸2̸	13	1̸4̸	15	$\cdots$

	3	5	7	9	11	13	15	17	19	21	23	25	27	29	$\cdots$
3 is a prime	3̸	5	7	9̸	11	13	1̸5̸	17	19	2̸1̸	23	25	2̸7̸	29	$\cdots$

	5	7	11	13	17	19	23	25	29	31	35	37	41	43	$\cdots$
5 is a prime	5̸	7	11	13	17	19	23	2̸5̸	29	31	3̸5̸	37	41	43	$\cdots$

Fig. 6.16. At each step, the leftmost surviving number is a prime.

The program in this section is motivated by McIlroy [1968]. The approach of Fig. 6.16 will be implemented by assembling a network out of two kinds of objects, called *counters* and *filters*. A counter emits integers, starting from some initial value; *counter* (2) in Fig. 6.17 starts from 2, and emits 2, 3, 4, $\cdots$. A filter *filter* (n) removes multiples of n from its input. Thus *filter* (2) allows only odd numbers to get through and *filter* (3) allows only numbers that are not divisible by 3 to get through. Sample inputs and outputs for these filters appear in Fig. 6.17.

Counters and filters will be put together dynamically, as in Fig. 6.18. On demand, *counter* (2) emits the integers 2, 3, 4, 5, $\cdots$, starting with the prime 2. On seeing 2, the *sieve* outputs it and immediately spawns a filter

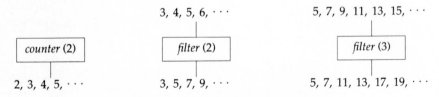

Fig. 6.17. Components for computing primes.

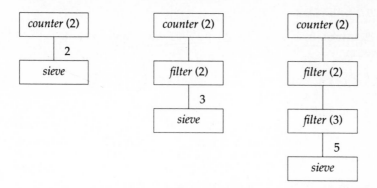

Fig. 6.18. Each prime *n* reaching *sieve* spawns a filter that removes multiples of *n*.

to remove subsequent multiples of 2. In general, if an integer *n* survives to reach the *sieve*, then it must be a prime. For each new prime *n*, the *sieve* spawns *filter* (*n*) to remove multiples of *n*.

A Base Class

The rest of this section consists of a C++ program, interspersed with commentary. Line numbers in parentheses show how the pieces of the program fit together; the numbers are not part of the program.

Counters, filters, and the sieve in Fig. 6.18 will be derived from class **item**, declared on lines 2-7:

```
(1) #include      <stdio.h>
(2) class item {
(3) public:
(4)          item *source;
(5)                  item(item *src) { source = src; }
(6) virtual int   out()                { return 0; }
(7) };
```

Each item has a member **source**, pointing to the source of its input. In Fig. 6.18, *filter* (2) gets its input from *counter* (2), and *filter* (3) gets its input from *filter* (2). The source for *sieve* changes every time a new filter is spawned. The only component without a source is *counter* (2). The absence of a source can be implemented by assigning the null pointer **0** to **source**.

The keyword **virtual** on line 6 makes member **out** a placeholder for functions of the same name to be provided later in derived classes. Each class in this section has a member **out**.

Derived Classes

Class **counter** has **item** as its public base class. We now examine the
declaration

```
(8) class counter: public item {
(9)        int   value;
(10) public:
(11)       int   out ()                      { return value++; }
(12)             counter(int v) : item(0) { value = v; }
(13) };
```

Class **counter** uses a member, **value,** to keep track of the next value to
be produced by the counter. Member **out** returns this value and then uses
the **++** operator to increment variable **value** by 1. Since **value** will be
initialized to 2, successive calls of member **out** return 2, 3, 4, · · · , as
desired (see Fig. 6.17).

Initialization of Derived and Base Classes

Before considering the constructor declaration on line 12 let us examine the
members inherited by class **counter**. The class has the following
members

source	pointer to an item, inherited from the base class
value	integer counter value, added
counter::out	output function for the derived class, added
item::out	inherited virtual output function
counter	constructor for the derived class

The constructor declaration on line 12

```
counter(int v) : item(0) { value = v; }
```

has three parts:

1. **counter(int v)** says that counter takes an integer argument.

2. **: item(0)** passes the null pointer **0** as an argument to the constructor, **item,** of the base class. C++ ensures that the base-class constructor
   is executed before the constructor of the derived class. The base class
   name is optional in **: item(0)**; earlier versions of C++ required **: (0)**
   instead, without the name **item.**

3. **{ value=v; }** is the body of the constructor in the derived class.

In other words, initialization information for the base class appears
between the colon and the body of the derived constructor.

Class **sieve** also has **item** as its public base class:

```
(14) class sieve: public item {
(15) public:
(16)         int       out();
(17)                   sieve(item *src): item(src) {};
(18) };
```

The body of added member function **out** appears separately.

The constructor on line 17

```
sieve(item *src): item(src) {};
```

results in the following initialization

call constructor **item** of the base class with argument **src**;
execute the empty body **{ }** of constructor **sieve** of the derived class;

Class **filter** is declared by

```
(19) class filter: public item {
(20)     int factor;
(21) public:
(22)     int out();
(23)         filter(item *src, int f): item(src)
                                          { factor = f; }
(24) };
```

Subtypes and Supertypes

All counters are items.
c is a counter.
Hence, **c** is an item.

Alternatively, an object of derived class **counter** (a subtype) can appear where an object of public base class **item** (its supertype) is expected.

The notion of subtypes is needed to explain the declarations on lines 26-27 in the main function:

```
(25) main() {
(26)         counter c(2);
(27)         sieve   s(&c);
(28)         int     next;
(29)         do {
(30)             next = s.out();
(31)             printf("%d ", next);
(32)         } while (next < 61);
(33)         printf("\n");
(34) }
```

For readability, we repeat the declarations of the constructors **counter**, **sieve**, and **item**:

```
counter(int v)  : item(0) { value = v; }
sieve(item *src): item(src) {};
item(item *src) { source = src; }
```

The declaration on line 26,

```
counter c(2);
```

creates a counter. The base class constructor, **item**, is called with the null pointer **0**, so the inherited member **source** is initialized to the null pointer. The constructor **counter** uses the argument 2 to initialize **value**.
The declaration on line 27

```
sieve(&c);
```

creates a sieve. The argument **&c**, a pointer to the counter **c**, is passed to the base class constructor, so inherited member **source** is initialized to point to **c**. In more detail, the constructor **sieve** expects its argument to be a pointer to an item. Instead, it is passed a subtype: pointer to counter. A pointer to a counter can appear where a pointer to an item is expected.[4]

Virtual Functions

The keyword **virtual** on line 6 before the declaration of **out** in class **item** is crucial. Without it, the output of the program in this section changes from

2 3 5 7 11 13 17 19 23 29 31 37 41 43 47 53 59 61

to

0 0 0 0 0 ⋯

A blow-by-blow description of the **out** functions of classes **sieve** and **counter** shows the use of virtual functions. The algorithm illustrated in Fig. 6.18 requires the sieve to spawn a filter as a side effect, each time a prime reaches it:

---

[4] The converse, however, is not permitted in C++; that is, an object of a base class cannot appear in place of an object of a derived class. At compile time, the compiler has no way of knowing whether a particular item is a counter or a sieve. A dynamically checked implementation could check whether an item is a counter or a sieve.

```
(35) int sieve::out() {
(36)        int n = source->out();
(37)        source = new filter(source, n);
(38)        return n;
(39) }
```

On line 36, function **sieve::out** gets a prime from its source by calling **source->out()**. A filter is spawned on line 37.

How does the call **source->out()** get a number?

The declarations on lines 26-27

```
counter c(2);
sieve   s(&c);
```

initialize **s.source** to **&c**. The function call **s.source->out** therefore calls one of the two **out** functions belonging to **c**; that is, either the inherited function **item::out** or the added function **counter::out**. The keyword **virtual**, on line 6 in the base class **item** says that given a choice between **item::out** and **counter::out**, the function to be used is **counter::out**.[5]

Spawning Filters

The rest of the story is anticlimactic.

The first filter is spawned when the prime 2 reaches the sieve directly from the counter. This prime arrives when control returns from the call **source->out()** on line 36. The assignment on line 37 that spawns a filter can be rewritten as follows to show the current values of the variables:

$$s.source = new filter(\&c, 2); \tag{6.1}$$

Informally, the right side creates a new filter with counter **c** as its source and 2 as its factor. The left side **s.source** is assigned a pointer to the newly created filter.

Rest of the Program

Here is how filters work:

---

[5] Although **s.source** points to **c**, the type of **s.source** is "pointer to **item**." Had **out** not been **virtual** in the base class, the C++ compiler would take **s.source->out()** to be a call of **c.item::out**. Virtual functions eliminate such ambiguities.

```
(40) int filter::out() {
(41)         while(1) {
(42)             int n = source->out();
(43)             if (n % factor)
(44)                 return n;
(45)         }
(46) }
```

Control can flow out of the while-loop on lines 41-45 only through the
return on line 44. Each execution of the loop gets a number **n** from its
source and returns it only if **n** mod **factor** is nonzero; that is, if **n** is not a
multiple of **factor**.

EXERCISES

6.1 Describe a class of queues, using the description of the Smalltalk
class Stack in Fig. 6.7, page 217, as a guide.

6.2 Implement the Smalltalk classes Node and MyTree described in
Fig. 6.19. Additional methods are needed to create initialized
nodes and trees. These classes are motivated by binary trees that
are either empty or consist of a root with a left and a right subtree,
both of which are binary trees. Use nil as the value of an empty
tree—nil is a constant corresponding to a null or empty object, and
is the value of an uninitialized variable. The predicate isNil tests if
a value is nil. At each node *n* in a tree, an *in-order* traversal visits
the nodes in the left subtree of *n*, visits *n*, and then visits the nodes
in the right subtree of *n*.
a) How would you compute the number of nodes in a tree?
b) How would you compute the *height* of a tree, where the height
of an empty tree is 0 and the height of any other tree is 1 plus
the maximum of heights of the left and right subtrees of its
root?

6.3 Define a subclass WordNode of Node in Fig. 6.19, which extends
each node with a string.
a) Provide a method for creating an initialized object of class
WordNode.
b) How would you create a set consisting of the strings at the
nodes in a tree?

6.4 Use pseudo-code to describe the effect of the following Smalltalk
program fragments from Section 6.5:

class **Node** superclass Object
instance variables
    leftNode   The root of the left subtree.
    rightNode   The root of the right subtree.

class methods
    left: lNode right: rNode   Return an initialized node.

instance methods
    isLeaf   Are both leftNode and rightNode nil?
    left   Return the value of leftNode.
    right   Return the value of rightNode.
    do: aBlock   Evaluate aBlock at each node during
                                   an in-order traversal.

class **MyTree** superclass Object
instance variables
    root   The root of this tree.

instance methods
    isEmpty   Is the root nil?
    do: aBlock   Evaluate aBlock at each node during
                                   an in-order traversal.

Fig. 6.19. Partial description of classes for implementing binary trees.

  a) newnulls ← nonterminalSet select: [:n | n newlyNullable]

  b) (nonterminalSet select: [:n | n isNullable]) collect: [:n | n spell]

  c) rhs ← stringSequence
            collect: [:s | tokenDictionary at: s
                      ifAbsent: [nonterminalDictionary at: s]]

  d) nonterminalDictionary ← Dictionary new.
     nStrings do: [:s | nonterminalDictionary at: s put:
                      (Nonterminal new: s)].
     nonterminalSet ← nonterminalDictionary values asSet

6.5 Use the operations select:, reject:, do:, and collect: described in Fig.
    6.11, page 223, to do the following:
    a) Count the number of elements in a collection.
    b) Construct the set of elements that appear more than once in a
       collection.
    c) Determine the number of times each element appears in a col-
       lection.
    d) Construct the union of two sets.

e) Construct the intersection of two sets.

6.6 Messages and methods in Smalltalk correspond to function calls and function bodies, respectively, in C++. Compare the rules in Smalltalk (C++) for determining the method (function body) to be executed in response to a message (function call). Illustrate your answer by giving
  a) C++ counterparts of the Smalltalk classes in Fig. 6.13, page 225, which use self and super to influence the search for a method.
  b) Smalltalk counterparts of the C++ classes **B** and **D** on page 236, which use virtual functions to influence the function body to be used in response to a function call.

6.7 Implement a prime-number sieve in Smalltalk.

6.8 Implement binary trees in C++, using the discussion of linked lists in Section 5.8 as a guide. Design a class **node** corresponding to **cell** and a class **bitree** corresponding to **circlist**.
  a) Implement a member **size** of **bitree** to compute the number of nodes in a tree.
  b) Implement a member **height** of **bitree** to compute the height of a binary tree (height is defined in Exercise 6.2(b)).

6.9 The following expression tree has three kinds of nodes:

The three kinds of nodes are: (1) leaves with an integer value, (2) unary nodes with an operator and a single subtree, and (3) binary nodes with an operator and two subtrees. The goal is to construct and print expression trees in parenthesized prefix notation, where parentheses enclose an operator and its operands. For example, the above tree must be printed as

    (* (− 5) (+ 3 4))

Develop the fragment in Fig. 6.20 into a C++ program. Note that a tree prints itself by asking its root node to print itself. Function **print** in class **node** is virtual, so a derived class can supply a function body to be executed when **print** is called.

6.10 Redo Exercise 6.9 using variant records. Treat nodes as records with three variants, corresponding to leaves, unary nodes and binary nodes.

```
#include <stdio.h>
class node {
public:
virtual void  print() {}
};
 . . .
class tree {
        node *root;
public:
                tree(int);
                tree(char *op, tree *p);
                tree(char *op, tree *l, tree *r);
        void  print() { root->print(); }
};
main() {
    tree t1("-", new tree(5));
    tree t2("+", new tree(3), new tree(4));
    tree t("*", &t1, &t2);
    t.print();
    printf("\n");
}
```

Fig. 6.20. Program for constructing and printing expression trees.

6.11 Suppose that we need to manipulate an array, **A**, whose elements
are pointers to objects of either class **D** or class **E**. For simplicity,
suppose that each object has two members: **id**, an identifying
integer, and **print**, a function that prints the name of the class the
object belongs to.

  a) Derive **D** and **E** as subtypes of a base class **B**, and declare the
     array elements to be pointers to **B**. Check your work by
     evaluating **A[i]->print()** for each array element **A[i]**.

  b) Let **dp** be a pointer to **D**—the type of **dp** is a subtype of the
     type of **A[i]**. C++ allows the assignment **A[i]=dp**, but not
     dp=A[i] because, at compile time, we cannot tell whether
     A[i] points to an object of class **D**. Modify your solution to
     part (a) to simulate variant records by adding a tag to each
     object; the value of the tag specifies the class of the object.
     Check your work by evaluating **A[i]->print()** only if the
     run-time value of **A[i]** denotes a pointer to class **D**.

  c) Suppose that instead of two classes **D** and **E**, we want to allow
     for additional subtypes **F**, **G**, **H**, · · · . Add a virtual function
     isa to class **B** from (a), which takes a class name as an argu-
     ment and returns true if the object belongs to that class. Note

that a subtype of **B** must be independent of all other subtypes of **B**. Check your work by executing the following program fragment, where **A[i]->print()** must be executed only if **A[i]** denotes an object of class **D**:

```
for(i = 0; i < MAX; i++)
    if( A[i]->isa('D') )
        A[i]->print();
```

For simplicity, class names are taken to be single characters in this fragment. Extend the solution to allow strings to be class names—the library function **strcmp** can be used to compare strings.

6.12 The syntax for derived classes in Section 6.6 extends to allow multiple inheritance, where a class is derived from more than one base class. The following declaration makes **complexcell** a subtype of both **complex** and **cell**:

```
class complexcell : public complex, public cell {
public:
    complexcell(double x, double y)
        : complex(x,y), cell(0) {}
};
```

The constructor **complexcell** is called with two arguments **x** and **y**, which it passes to the base class constructor **complex** (for complex numbers); the constructor of the other base class **cell** is passed the null pointer **0**.

a) Declare a class **cell** with a member **next** pointing to a **cell**; the constructor simply initializes **next**. Declare a class **list** with the following members:

front	Points to the first of a sequence of cells.
link	Inserts a cell at the front of the list.
unlink	Removes the front cell, and returns a pointer to it.

b) Since **complexcell** is a subtype of **cell**, we can form a list of complexcells without changing the code for **list** from (a). Write a program that repeatedly uses **link** to build a list of complexcells, and then repeatedly uses **unlink** to remove complexcells. Since **complexcell** is at the same time a subtype of **complex**, your program should treat complexcells as complex numbers and print out the real and imaginary parts of a complexcell as it is unlinked.

BIBLIOGRAPHIC NOTES

Inheritance and data encapsulation are a response to Hamming's [1969] complaint: "whereas Newton could say, 'If I have seen a little farther than others it is because I have stood on the shoulders of giants,' I am forced to say, 'Today we stand on each other's feet.' Perhaps the central problem we face in all of computer science is how we are to get to the situation where we build on the work of others rather than redoing so much of it in a trivially different way."

A significant fraction of the book by Goldberg and Robson [1983] describes the class hierarchy that comes with the Smalltalk-80 system. They note, "The Smalltalk-80 system is based on ideas gleaned from the Simula language and from the visions of Alan Kay, who first encouraged us to try to create a uniformly object-oriented system." Exercises 6.2 and 6.3 are motivated by examples in their book. Deutsch [1984] presents techniques for the efficient implementation of Smalltalk. Borning and Ingalls [1982] extend Smalltalk to allow multiple inheritance; that is, to allow a class to have multiple superclasses. Ingalls [1978] describes Smalltalk-76, an earlier version of the system.

Stroustrup [1987b] mentions some of the extensions to C++ that came after the publication of the book on C++ (Stroustrup [1986]). Stroustrup [1987a] describes the design and efficient implementation of multiple inheritance in C++. Exercise 6.9 is from Koenig [1988].

For a glimpse of the extensive literature on object-oriented programming, see the proceedings of the annual *ACM SIGPLAN Conference on Object-Oriented Programming, Systems, and Languages*. Inheritance is just one of the many concepts explored in the thorough survey of types by Cardelli and Wegner [1985]. See also the papers in the collection Shriver and Wegner [1987].

The example of class **hybrid** with derived classes (but not subtypes) **stack** and **queue** in Section 6.6 is attributed to Peter Canning by Snyder [1986]. Snyder explores the relationship between encapsulation and inheritance and argues that "subtyping should not be tied to inheritance."

Object-oriented extensions have been developed for a number of languages. Moon [1986] describes the Flavors system, an extension of Lisp. The original Flavors system was developed in 1979.

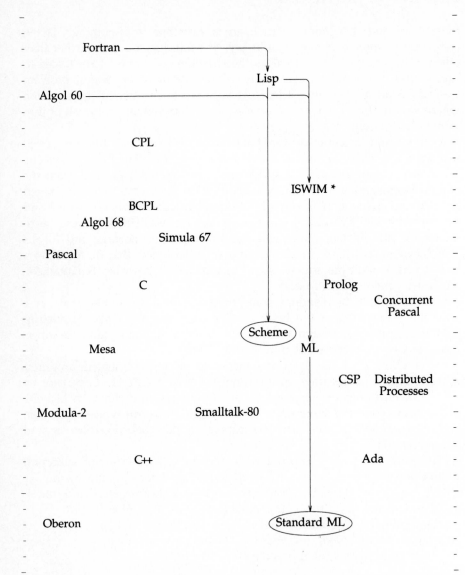

The name Lisp is a contraction of "List Processor." Lisp's primitives for manipulating lists were inspired by those of an extension of Fortran called FLPL, for Fortran List Processing Language. Lisp was designed in part because FLPL did not have recursion and conditionals within expressions. Mathematical elegance came later.

Functional Programming

Pure functional programming is characterized by the following informally stated principle:

> The value of an expression depends only on the values of its subexpressions, if any.

The value of an expression like $a+b$ is simply the sum of the values of a and b. This principle rules out side effects within expressions, so pure functional programming can alternatively be characterized as programming without assignments. In the absence of side effects, an expression has the same value every time it is evaluated.

Most functional languages are impure because they do provide assignments. Nevertheless, their programming style is dominated by the pure part of the language. This chapter deals with pure functional programming.

Another characteristic of functional languages is that users do not have to worry about managing storage for data:

> *Implicit storage management.* Built-in operations on data allocate storage as needed. Storage that becomes inaccessible is automatically deallocated.

The absence of explicit code for deallocation makes programs simpler and shorter. A consequence of this approach is that the language implementation must perform "garbage collection" to reclaim storage that has become inaccessible.

Finally, functional programming treats functions as "first-class citizens":

> *Functions are first-class values.* Functions have the same status as any other values. A function can be the value of an expression, a function can be passed as an argument, and a function can be put in a data structure.

The treatment of functions as first-class values permits the creation of powerful operations on collections of data, as we see in Section 7.3.

The working languages of this chapter are Scheme, a dialect of Lisp, and Standard ML, introduced in Chapter 2.

7.1   SCHEME, A DIALECT OF LISP

This section introduces a functional subset of Scheme; we stay away from assignments. The list data structure is explored in Section 7.2, and functions are considered further in Section 7.3.

Why Lisp?

Lisp is widely available, has a devoted following, and is the language of choice for applications such as artificial intelligence.

Functional languages in general, and Lisp in particular, have played a special role in language definition. A language definition must itself be written in some notation, called a *meta-language* or *defining language*, and defining languages tend to be functional. In fact, the first implementation of Lisp arose, almost by accident, when Lisp was used to define itself.

The basic concepts of functional programming originated with Lisp. It was designed by John McCarthy in 1958, making it probably the second oldest major language, after Fortran. It is surely the first to provide recursion, first-class functions, garbage collection, and a formal language definition (in Lisp itself). Lisp implementations also led the way in integrated programming environments, which combine editors, interpreters, and debuggers.

With all these benefits, why doesn't everybody use Lisp? First, Lisp has a unique syntax, leading to irreverent remarks such as "LISP stands for Lots of Silly Parentheses." The parentheses, however, do have a silver lining: The uniformity of Lisp syntax makes it easy to manipulate programs as data.

Second, Lisp programs are untyped; that is, Lisp does not associate types with expressions. Programming errors that could be caught by a type checker therefore go unnoticed until a problem occurs at run time. Experience with ML shows that we can have the benefits of type checking without sacrificing flexibility.

Third, Lisp implementations have been inefficient in the past. In the early 1960s, Lisp was "ultraslow" for numerical computations. Good implementations are now available.

Why Scheme?

Scheme is a relatively small language that provides constructs at the core of Lisp. It has two characteristics that make it especially suited for this chapter: lexical scope and true first-class functions. Earlier Lisps did not fully support first-class functions, and used dynamic scope rules, which leave a program sensitive to the choice of local names within functions.

Interacting with a Scheme Interpreter

A good way to learn Scheme is to interact with an interpreter and study its responses. We consider two kinds of interactions with Scheme:

1. Supply an expression to be evaluated.

2. Bind a name to a value.

Note that a value can be a function.

A transcript of an interactive session with an interpreter winds through this section. Responses from the interpreter will consistently be indented and shown in italics. When we type

```
3.14159                    ; a number evaluates to itself
```

the interpreter responds with

```
3.14159
```

Comments begin with a semicolon and continue to the end of the line.
Name **pi** is bound to **3.14159** by

```
(define pi 3.14159)        ; bind a variable to a value
    pi
```

Now **pi** evaluates to **3.14159**:

```
pi                         ; a variable evaluates to its value
    3.14159
```

Within names, Scheme ignores the distinction between uppercase and lowercase letters, so **pi**, **Pi**, **pI**, and **PI** are all the same name:

```
    pI                              ; respond with value bound to pi
         3.14159
```

Names in Scheme can contain special characters, but not parentheses, as in **long-name**, **research!emlin**, and **back-at-5:00pm**. In general, a name can begin with any character that cannot begin a number.

Parenthesized Prefix Expressions

Dialects of Lisp, including Scheme, use a form of prefix notation for expressions in which parentheses surround an operator and its operands. The arithmetic expression $5 * 7$ is written as

```
(* 5 7)
     35
```

The general form of an expression in Scheme is

$$(E_1 \ E_2 \ \cdots \ E_k)$$

Here, expression E_1 represents an operator to be applied to the values of $E_2, \ldots, E_k$. The order of evaluation of the subexpressions $E_1, E_2, \ldots, E_k$ is unspecified; however, all the subexpressions are evaluated before the value of E_1 is applied to its operands. In other words, Scheme uses innermost or call-by-value evaluation.

Arithmetic expressions with several operators can be translated into Scheme by following their subexpression structure. The expression $4+5*7$ is the sum of 4 and $5*7$:

```
(+ 4 (* 5 7))
     39
```

The uniform use of parenthesized prefix notation gives Scheme a simple syntax—at the expense of a proliferation of parentheses. Fig. 7.1 summarizes some of the constructs used in this chapter. ML counterparts of the constructs are included as comments.

Quoting

Quoting is needed to treat expressions as data. A quoted item evaluates to itself. Quoting syntax will be introduced by considering symbols.

A *symbol* is an object with a spelling. Quoting is used to choose whether a spelling is treated as a symbol or as a variable name.

An item can be quoted in one of two equivalent ways:

```
(quote ⟨item⟩)
' ⟨item⟩
```

Unquoted, **pi** is a variable name, bound to a value:

`(define pi 3.14159)`	*; give name* **pi** *to* **3.14159**
`(define (sq x) (* x x))`	*;* **fun** *sq* $(x) = x * x$
`(define sq (lambda (x) (* x x)))`	*;* **fun** *sq* $(x) = x * x$
`(lambda (x) (* x x))`	*; unnamed function value* *; parameter* x, *body* $x * x$
`(* `E_1` `E_2`)`	*;* $E_1 * E_2$
`(`E_1` `E_2` `E_3`)`	*; apply the value of* E_1 *as a* *; function to arguments* E_2 *and* E_3
`(if `P` `E_1` `E_2`)`	*; if* P **then** E_1 **else** E_2
`(cond (`P_1` `E_1`) (`P_2` `E_2`) (else `E_3`))`	*; if* P_1 **then** E_1 *;* **else if** P_2 **then** E_2 *;* **else** E_3
`(let ((`x_1` `E_1`) (`x_2` `E_2`)) `E_3`)`	*; evaluate* E_1 *and* E_2; *then* *; evaluate* E_3 *with* x_1 *and* x_2 *; bound to their values*
`(let* ((`x_1` `E_1`) (`x_2` `E_2`)) `E_3`)`	*;* **let val** $x_1 = E_1$ *;* **val** $x_2 = E_2$ *;* **in** E_3 *;* **end**
`(quote blue)`	*; symbol* **blue**
`(quote (blue green red))`	*; list* **(blue green red)**
`(list `E_1` `E_2` `E_3`)`	*; list of the values of* E_1, E_2, E_3

Fig. 7.1. Some Scheme constructs.

> **pi**
> *3.14159*

We can treat **pi** as the spelling of a symbol by quoting it:

> `(quote pi)`
>   *pi*
> `'pi`
>   *pi*

Unquoted, `*` represents the multiplication function:

```
(define f *)                          ; defines f to be a function
    f
(f 2 3)
    6
```

Quoted, `'*` represents the symbol with spelling `*`:

```
(define f '*)                         ; defines f to be a symbol
    f
(f 2 3)
    ERROR: Bad procedure *
```

Scheme refers to functions as procedures.

Function Definitions

The following syntax is one way of defining functions:

>   (**define** (⟨*function-name*⟩ ⟨*formal-parameters*⟩) ⟨*expression*⟩)

An example is

```
(define (square x) (* x x))       ; fun square (x) = x * x
    square
(square 5)                        ; apply function square to 5
    25
```

This definition associates a function value with name **square**. The function takes a parameter and multiplies the parameter by itself.

The binding of a function name to a function value is clearer from the syntax

>   (**define** ⟨*function-name*⟩ ⟨*function-value*⟩)

In order to use this syntax, we need a notation for function values. Scheme provides the notation

>   (**lambda** (⟨*formal-parameters*⟩) ⟨*expression*⟩)

for an unnamed function value. Thus, a function with formal parameter **x** and body **(* x x)** is written as

>   (**lambda** (x) (* x x))

The tradition of using **lambda** to write functions goes back to Church's lambda calculus, discussed in Chapter 12.

Now **square** can be defined by

```
(define square (lambda (x) (* x x)))
    square
```

Scheme allows an unnamed function to appear in the operator position in an expression:

```
(square 5)
    25

((lambda (x) (* x x)) 5)    ; unnamed function applied to 5
    25
```

Further examples of the use of **lambda** appear in Section 7.3.

Conditionals

The boolean values **true** and **false** are written as **#t** and **#f**, respectively. Within conditional expressions, only **#f** is treated as false; all other values are treated as true.[1]

Predicates are expressions that evaluate to true or false. By convention, the names of Scheme predicates end in "?," as in

number?	Test whether argument is a number.
symbol?	Test whether argument is a symbol.
equal?	Test whether arguments are structurally equal.

Conditional expressions come in two forms. One form is

```
(if  P  E₁  E₂)                ; if  P  then  E₁  else  E₂
```

The other form corresponds to a sequential choice:

```
(cond  (P₁  E₁)              ; if  P₁  then  E₁
       . . .                 ;  . . .
       (Pₖ  Eₖ)              ; else if  Pₖ  then  Eₖ
       (else  Eₖ₊₁) )        ; else  Eₖ₊₁
```

Conditionals are needed for recursive functions, such as the following definition of the factorial function:

```
(define (fact n)             ; fun  fact(n)  =
   (if (= n 0)               ;      if  n = 0
       1                     ;      then  1
       (* n (fact (- n 1))) ));     else  n * fact(n − 1)
```

---

[1] Following Lisp tradition, some Scheme implementations treat () as being equivalent to **#f**.

The Let-Construct

The syntax of the **let** construct is

> **(let ((** x_1 E_1 **) (** x_2 E_2 **)** $\cdots$ **(** x_k E_k **)) ** F **)**

Its value is determined as follows. The expressions $E_1, E_2, \ldots, E_k$ are all evaluated. Then expression F is evaluated, with x_i representing the value of E_i. The result is the value of F.

The **let** construct allows subexpressions to be named. The expression

> **(+ (square 3) (square 4))**
>   *25*

can be rewritten as follows, with name **three-sq** for **(square 3)** and **four-sq** for **(square 4)**:

> **(let ((three-sq (square 3))**
>   **(four-sq (square 4)))**
>   **(+ three-sq four-sq))**
>   *25*

The **let** construct can also be used to factor out common subexpressions. The recomputation of the common subexpression **(square 3)** in

> **(+ (square 3) (square 3))**
>   *18*

can be avoided by rewriting the expression as

> **(let ((three-sq (square 3)))**
>   **(+ three-sq three-sq))**
>   *18*

A sequential variant of the **let** construct is written with keyword **let***. Unlike **let**, which evaluates all the expressions $E_1, E_2, \ldots, E_k$ before binding any of the variables, **let*** binds x_i to the value of E_i before E_{i+1} is evaluated. The syntax is

> **(let* ((** x_1 E_1 **) (** x_2 E_2 **)** $\cdots$ **(** x_k E_k **)) ** F **)**

The distinction between **let** and **let*** can be seen from the responses in

> **(define x 0)**
>   *x*
> **(let ((x 2) (y x)) y)**   ; *bind* **y** *before redefining* **x**
>   *0*
> **(let* ((x 2) (y x)) y)**   ; *bind* **y** *after redefining* **x**
>   *2*

7.2 LISTS

Programs and data look alike in Lisp dialects. Both are represented as lists.

List Elements

A *list* is a sequence of zero or more values. Any value can be a list element. Among potential list elements in Scheme are booleans, numbers, symbols, other lists, and functions (this chapter ignores characters, strings, and vectors).

A list is written by enclosing its elements within parentheses. The *empty* or *null* list, with zero elements, is written as **()**.[2] The list

>   **(it seems that)**

has the symbols **it**, **seems**, and **that** as its three elements. The list

>   **((it seems that) you (like) me)**

has four elements, the first and third of which are lists.

Parentheses are important: **like** is a symbol, but **(like)** is a list with one element.

The structure of a list can be seen more easily from a tree representation, such as the one in Fig. 7.2 for the following lists:

>   **(it seems that you like me)**
>   **((it seems that) you (like) me)**

The relationship between lists and trees is made precise later in this section.

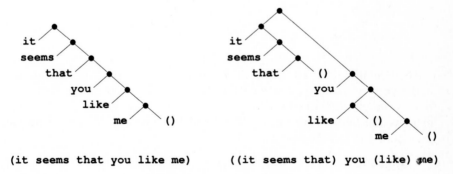

(it seems that you like me)   ((it seems that) you (like) me)

Fig. 7.2. Examples of lists.

---

[2] Other Lisp dialects treat **nil** as a synonym for **()**, but Scheme treats **nil** as a name that can be bound to something else, if desired.

Note that the list

(a ())

has two elements, the first, **a**, being a symbol, and the second, **()**, being the empty list. Thus, **(a)** with just one element **a** differs from **(a ())**.

Is **(+ 2 3)** an expression or a list? The answer is both. The Scheme interpreter treats

(+ 2 3)
    5

as an expression and responds with its value. Quoting tells the interpreter to treat **(+ 2 3)** as a list:

' (+ 2 3)
    (+ 2 3)

A leading single quote is sufficient to say that the construct immediately following the quote stands for itself:

' (no quotes at (nested levels))
    (no quotes at (nested levels))

The matching closing parenthesis delimits the construct affected by a leading single quote.

Operations on Lists

With any grouping of elements, operations are needed to inspect the elements and to construct a new grouping. So it is with lists. The basic operations on lists are summarized in Fig. 7.3.

The predicate **null?** returns true if it is applied to the empty list, and false otherwise:

(null? ())
    #t

The operations for extracting the components of a nonempty list are **car** and **cdr** (pronounced "could-er"); these names are part of the Lisp tradition. Car extracts the head, or first element, of a nonempty list. Cdr extracts the tail, consisting of all but the first element. These operations are applied in Fig. 7.4 to a list **x** defined by

(define x ' ((it seems that) you (like) me))
    x

The first line of Fig. 7.4 shows list **x**. The remaining lines use **car** and **cdr** to take **x** apart. For ease of comparison, the expressions in the figure are written so that their **x**s line up.

Lists in Scheme are written between parentheses **(** and **)**, with white space separating list elements. The empty list is written as **()**. The operations on lists are

(null? x)   True if **x** is the empty list and false otherwise.

(car x)   The first element of a nonempty list **x**.

(cdr x)   The rest of the list **x** after the first element is removed.

(cons a x)   A value with car **a** and cdr **x**; that is,

$$(car (cons a x)) = a$$
$$(cdr (cons a x)) = x$$

Fig. 7.3. Lists in Scheme.

Lisp provides a shorthand for expressions like

```
(car (cdr x))
```

consisting of successive applications of **car** and **cdr**. This expression can be abbreviated and written as **(cadr x)** using a single operator **cadr** formed by writing an opening **c**, a sequence of **as** and **ds** corresponding, from left to right, to the original **car** and **cdr** operators, and a trailing **r**.

The **cons** operation builds lists; **(cons a x)** creates a value with head **a** and tail **x**. An alternative "dotted" notation for **(cons a x)** is **(a . x)**.

EXPRESSION	SHORTHAND	VALUE
x	**x**	*((it seems that) you (like) me)*
(car x)	**(car x)**	*(it seems that)*
(car (car x))	**(caar x)**	*it*
(cdr (car x))	**(cdar x)**	*(seems that)*
(cdr x)	**(cdr x)**	*(you (like) me)*
(car (cdr x))	**(cadr x)**	*you*
(cdr (cdr x))	**(cddr x)**	*((like) me)*

Fig. 7.4. Use of **car** and **cdr** to take list **x** apart.

The dots in the tree representation

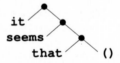

of list **(it seems that)** correspond to **cons** operations. These operations appear explicitly as dots in

    '(it . (seems . (that . ())))
        (it seems that)

More precisely, a **cons** operation builds a *pair*, sometimes called a *dotted pair*, from its operands. The name *list* is reserved for a chain of pairs ending in an empty list; that is, **x** is a list if repeated application of **cdr** eventually results in the empty list **()**.

A list with several elements can alternatively be built by applying the **list** operator to the elements. Thus,

    (list 'it 'seems 'that)
        (it seems that)

is equivalent to

    (cons 'it (cons 'seems (cons 'that '())))
        (it seems that)

7.3   SOME USEFUL FUNCTIONS

This section develops a small library of functions for list manipulation. The functions are tools that either solve common problems or can be adapted to do so. For example, a function that copies list elements, one by one, can be adapted to process the elements during copying.

The equations in Fig. 7.5 describe the functions in the library. (Equations appear in a lighter font in this section.) The equations

    (length nil)   ≡ 0
    (length (cons a y)) ≡ (+ 1 (length y))

say that the length of the empty list **nil** is **0** and the length of the list **(cons a y)** is **1** more than the length of the list **y**.

Scheme implementations of the functions in Fig. 7.5 appear in this section. The equations for **length** motivate the following definition:

    (define (length x)
      (cond ((null? x) 0)
            (else (+ 1 (length (cdr x))))))

```
(length nil)                    ≡ 0
(length (cons a y))             ≡ (+ 1 (length y))

(rev nil z)                     ≡ z
(rev (cons a y) z)              ≡ (rev y (cons a z))

(append nil z)                  ≡ z
(append (cons a y) z)           ≡ (cons a (append y z))

(map f nil)                     ≡ nil
(map f (cons a y))              ≡ (cons (f a) (map f y))

(remove_if f nil)               ≡ nil
(remove_if f (cons a y))  ≡ (remove_if f y)              if (f a) is true
(remove_if f (cons a y))  ≡ (cons a (remove_if f y)) otherwise

(reduce f nil v)                ≡ v
(reduce f (cons a y) v)   ≡ (f a (reduce f y v))
```

Fig. 7.5. Functions for list manipulation.

Reverse versus Append

Functions that treat lists as sequences of elements are often linear recursive. They wind down a list until they reach the end, and then unwind back to the beginning. As noted in Section 2.5, the evaluation of a linear-recursive function has

1. a winding phase in which new recursive activations are initiated, and

2. a subsequent unwinding phase in which control returns from the activations in a last-in-first-out manner.

When a function constructs a list, the order of the elements depends on the phase in which the list is constructed. We now consider why function **rev** in Fig. 7.5 can be used to reverse a list, but **append** cannot. Informally, a list is reversed if it is copied during the winding phase, but remains in order if it is copied during the unwinding phase.

Function **rev** is related to the standard function **reverse** in Scheme by

```
(reverse x)   ≡   (rev x nil)
```

The difference between **rev** and **append** lies in the following equations:

```
(rev (cons a y) z)     ≡   (rev y (cons a z))
(append (cons a y) z)  ≡   (cons a (append y z))
```

These equations capture the distinction between functions **rev** and **append**:

```
(define (rev x z)
  (cond ((null? x) z)
        (else (rev (cdr x) (cons (car x) z))) ))

(define (append x z)                    ; a version of append
  (cond ((null? x) z)
        (else (cons (car x) (append (cdr x) z))) ))
```

The **cons** operation in **rev** is done during the winding phase. On arguments **(b c d)** and **(a)**, the winding phase is suggested by the following equalities (see Fig. 7.6):

```
(rev '(b c d) '(a))   ≡   (rev '(c d) '(b a))

                      ≡   (rev '(d) '(c b a))

                      ≡   (rev nil '(d c b a))

                      ≡   '(d c b a)
```

The resulting list is built up as the second argument of the successive calls of **rev**. As mentioned in Section 2.5, tail-recursive functions have a trivial unwinding phase, during which a result is simply carried back. Tail-recursive functions, such as **rev**, are implemented efficiently in Scheme.

On the same arguments, the winding phase of **append** consists of the successive calls

```
(append '(b c d) '(a))  calls  (append '(c d) '(a))

 (append '(c d) '(a))   calls  (append '(d) '(a))

  (append '(d) '(a))    calls  (append nil '(a))
```

The resulting list is built up during the unwinding phase:

Fig. 7.6. Steps during the reversal of a list.

$$(\text{append nil '(a))} \equiv \text{'(a)}$$

$$(\text{append '(d) '(a))} \equiv \text{'(d a)}$$

$$(\text{append '(c d) '(a))} \equiv \text{'(c d a)}$$

$$(\text{append '(b c d) '(a))} \equiv \text{'(b c d a)}$$

Map a Function across List Elements

A *filter* is a function that copies a list, making useful changes to the elements as they are copied. The simplest filter is **copy**, which simply copies list elements without change:

$$(\text{copy nil)} \equiv \text{nil} \tag{7.1}$$
$$(\text{copy (cons a y))} \equiv \text{(cons a (copy y))}$$

Filter **copy-sq** squares list elements as it copies them:

$$(\text{copy-sq nil)} \equiv \text{nil} \tag{7.2}$$
$$(\text{copy-sq (cons a y))} \equiv \text{(cons (square a) (copy-sq y))}$$

Here, think of **square** as a "change function" because it makes changes to list elements as they are copied.

Scheme provides a function **map** to apply a function **f** to each element of a list **x**. Thus, **map** is a tool for building a filter out of **f**. For example,

(map square '(1 2 3 4 5))
   (1 4 9 16 25)

The difference between the following equations for **map** and the pairs of equations (7.1) and (7.2) is that **map** takes a change function as an argument:

$$(\text{map f nil)} \equiv \text{nil} \tag{7.3}$$
$$(\text{map f (cons a y))} \equiv \text{(cons (f a) (map f y))}$$

Function **map** can be defined by

```
(define (map f x)
   (cond ((null? x) nil)
         (else (cons (f (car x)) (map f (cdr x)))) ))
```

Example 7.1. Lambda notation is helpful for adapting existing functions so they can be used together with **map**. In particular, **map** expects a change function to be unary; that is, to take one argument. This example uses lambda notation to adapt the binary function *****.

We have seen

(map square '(1 2 3 4 5))

in which **map** applies the unary function **square** to each element of a list. Instead of squaring each element of the list, suppose that we want to multiply each element by **2**. A unary function that multiplies its argument by **2** can be created from *****, using lambda notation:

```
(lambda (x) (* 2 x))
```

This anonymous doubling function takes an argument **x** and applies ***** to **2** and **x**. The doubling function is the first argument of **map** in

```
(map (lambda (x) (* 2 x)) '(1 2 3 4 5))
    (2 4 6 8 10)
```

Another use of the anonymous doubling function occurs on the second line of

```
(define (double-all z)              ; to double each element
  (let ((f (lambda (x) (* 2 x))))   ; create a function and
    (map f z) ))                    ; map it across the list
```

where the **let**-construct makes **f** an abbreviation for the anonymous function.   □

A standard Scheme extension is to allow **map** to apply a function to corresponding elements of $k \geq 1$ lists. In

```
(map f x y z)
```

the three-argument function **f** is applied to the corresponding elements of the lists **x**, **y**, and **z**.

Higher-Order Functions

A function is called *higher order* if either its arguments or its results are themselves functions. Tools that build new functions out of simpler ones are higher-order functions.

An *iterator* is a function that loops or iterates through the elements of a list and does something with each element. An example is the higher-order function **map** just described. Another is a function **remove-if** that removes elements from a list if some condition holds. More precisely, **remove-if** copies list elements, unless predicate **f** is true on **a**:

```
(define (remove-if f x)
  (cond ((null? x) nil)
        ((f (car x)) (remove-if f (cdr x)))
        (else (cons (car x) (remove-if f (cdr x)))) ))
```

We can now use the Scheme predicate **odd?** to remove odd numbers

```
(remove-if odd? '(0 1 2 3 4 5))
    (0 2 4)
```

or the Scheme predicate **even?** to remove even numbers

```
(remove-if even? '(0 1 2 3 4 5))
    (1 3 5)
```

Lambda notation can be used to adapt existing predicates. The anonymous function

```
(lambda (n) (equal? 0 n))
```

adapts **equal?** to test whether an element equals **0**. It is used to remove 0s in

```
(remove-if (lambda (n) (equal? 0 n)) '(0 7 0 4 0))
    (7 4)
```

Accumulate a Result

We begin with two special cases that motivate the function **reduce**. The special cases compute the sum and product, respectively, of a list of integers.

The sum of an empty list **x** is **0**, and the sum of a nonempty list **x** is computed by adding the first element to the sum of the remaining elements:

$$
\begin{aligned}
&(\text{sum-all nil}) \equiv 0 \\
(\text{sum-all (cons a y)}) &\equiv (+ \text{ a (sum-all y)})
\end{aligned}
$$

Similarly, the product of an empty list **x** is **1**, and the product of a nonempty list **x** is computed by multiplying the first element with the product of the remaining elements:

$$
\begin{aligned}
&(\text{product-all nil}) \equiv 1 \\
(\text{product-all (cons a y)}) &\equiv (* \text{ a (product-all y)})
\end{aligned}
$$

The following equations describe a generalization of **sum-all**, **product-all**, and a host of related functions. The three parameters of **reduce** are a binary operator **f**, a list, and an initial value **v**. If the list is empty, the initial value **v** is returned. Otherwise, **f** is applied to the first element and the result obtained from the rest of the list:

$$
\begin{aligned}
&(\text{reduce f nil v}) \equiv \text{v} \\
(\text{reduce f (cons a y) v}) &\equiv (\text{f a (reduce f y v)})
\end{aligned}
$$

An implementation of **reduce** is

```
(define (reduce f x v)
  (cond ((null? x) v)
        (else (f (car x) (reduce f (cdr x) v))) ))
```

Function **sum-all** can be simulated by applying **reduce** to **+**, a list **x**, and **0**:

```
(reduce + '(1 2 3 4 5) 0)
    15
```

Similarly, **product-all** can be simulated by applying **reduce** to *, a list **x**, and **1**:

```
(reduce * '(1 2 3 4 5) 1)
    120
```

Example 7.2. Function **reduce** and an extension of **map** will now be used to "zip" two lists into one. Given two lists

> **x**
> (a b c)

and

> **y**
> (1 2 3)

the list **(a 1 b 2 c 3)** can be constructed as in Fig. 7.7:

```
(reduce append (map list x y) nil)
    (a 1 b 2 c 3)
```

The subexpression **(map list x y)** applies **list** to the corresponding elements of **x** and **y**. In

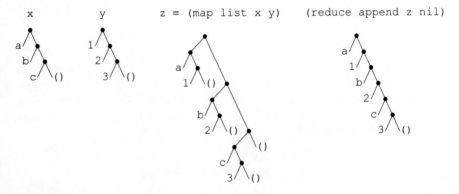

Fig. 7.7. Use of **map** and **reduce**.

```
(map list '(a b c) '(1 2 3))
    ((a 1) (b 2) (c 3))
```

the function **list** is applied to **a** and **1**, yielding the list **(a 1)**, to **b** and **2**, yielding the list **(b 2)**, and to **c** and **3**, yielding the list **(c 3)**.

Now **reduce** can be used to flatten these sublists.   □

7.4   A MOTIVATING EXAMPLE: DIFFERENTIATION

Several of Lisp's, and hence Scheme's, characteristic features were motivated by the problem of differentiating expressions like $x * (x + y + z)$. The differentiation program in this section illustrates the following:

- syntax-directed translation,
- the representation of expressions as data, and
- the use of higher-order functions.

The expressions produced by the differentiation program will be simplified by applying rules of the following form:

$$x + 0 = x$$
$$x * 1 = x \qquad (7.4)$$

This section concludes with a small expression simplifier; in general, simplification is a difficult problem.

Syntax-Directed Differentiation

What might a differentiation program look like? The following pseudo-code uses the syntax of expression E to compute the derivative of E with respect to variable x.

> **fun** $d(x, E) =$
>   **if** E is a constant **then** $\cdots$
>   **else if** E is a variable **then** $\cdots$ (7.5)
>   **else if** E is the sum $E_1 + E_2 + \cdots + E_k$ **then** $\cdots$
>   **else if** E is the product $E_1 * E_2 * \cdots * E_k$ **then** $\cdots$

This pseudo-code (7.5) motivates the function

```
(define (d x E)
  (cond ((constant? E) (diff-constant x E))
        ((variable? E) (diff-variable x E))
        ((sum? E) (diff-sum x E))
        ((product? E) (diff-product x E))
        (else (error "d: cannot parse" E)) ))
```

The predicates **constant?**, **variable?**, **sum?**, and **product?** determine whether expression **E** is a constant, a variable, a sum, or a product. In each case, the actual work of computing the derivative is delegated to a function devoted to that case.

The differentiation routine **d** manipulates expression **E** only through pairs of functions like **sum?** and **diff-sum**, so it is independent of the representation of expression **E**.

Constants

Let constants be represented as numbers. Predicate **constant?** is then the same as the Scheme predicate **number?**:

```
(define constant? number?)
```

The derivative of a number is zero. Since **diff-constant** is called only when expression **E** is a constant, it always returns **0**:

```
(define (diff-constant x E) 0)
```

Variables

Let variables be represented as symbols. Predicate **variable?** is then the same as the Scheme predicate **symbol?**:

```
(define variable? symbol?)
```

The derivative of a variable **x** with respect to **x** itself is **1**. Function **diff-variable** therefore returns **1** if expression **E** equals the variable **x**; otherwise, **diff-variable** returns **0** because it expects **E** to be some other variable.

```
(define (diff-variable x E)
  (if (equal? x E) 1 0) )
```

Lists of Subexpressions

Before continuing with the differentiation example, we reexamine sums and products. Lists representing binary sums and products have three elements, the operator and its two operands, as in

```
(+ 2 3)            ; 2 + 3  =  5
   5
(* 2 3)            ; 2 * 3  =  6
   6
```

Lisp dialects, including Scheme, allow **+** and ***** to take any number of arguments:

```
(+ 2 3 5)              ; 2 + 3 + 5  =  10
    10
(+ 2)                  ; 2  =  2
    2
(+)                    ; adding nothing yields 0
    0

(* 2 3 5)              ; 2 * 3 * 5  =  30
    30
(* 2)                  ; 2  =  2
    2
(*)                    ; multiplying nothing yields 1
    1
```

McCarthy's 1958 differentiation program dealt with sums and products containing lists of subexpressions. The need to manipulate such lists motivated function **map**. McCarthy [1981] recalls that **map** "was obviously wanted for differentiating sums of arbitrarily many subterms, and with a slight modification, it could be applied to differentiating products."

Differentiation Rules for Sums and Products

Informally, the derivative of sum $E_1 + E_2$ is the sum of the derivatives of the subexpressions E_1 and E_2.

The following equalities are for binary sums and products:

$$d (x, E_1 + E_2) = d (x, E_1) + d (x, E_2) \tag{7.6}$$

$$d (x, E_1 * E_2) = d (x, E_1) * E_2 + E_1 * d (x, E_2) \tag{7.7}$$

A generalization to sums with k subexpressions is

$$d (x, E_1 + E_2 + \cdots + E_k) = \\ d (x, E_1) + d (x, E_2) + \cdots + d (x, E_k) \tag{7.8}$$

For ease of programming, the equality for products with k subexpressions is adapted from the binary case. It is

$$d (x, E_1 * E') = d (x, E_1) * E' + E_1 * d (x, E') \\ \textbf{where } E' = E_2 * \cdots * E_k \tag{7.9}$$

Differentiation of Sums

Let a sum be represented as a list consisting of the operator **+** and $k \geq 0$
subexpressions. Scheme has an essential predicate **pair?** that tests
whether its operand is a pair created by a **cons** operation. Predicate **sum?**
returns true if its argument **E** is a pair with car **+**:

```
(define (sum? E)
  (and (pair? E)
       (equal? '+ (car E)) ))
```

The body of **sum?** relies on short-circuit evaluation of boolean expressions
from left to right. That is, the subexpression

```
(equal? '+ (car E))
```

is evaluated only if **(pair? E)** is true.

Function **diff-sum** does not manipulate sums directly; it uses two com-
plementary functions **args** and **make-sum**. Given a sum

$$(+ \ E_1 \ E_2 \ \cdots \ E_k)$$

args extracts the list of subexpressions

$$(E_1 \ E_2 \ \cdots \ E_k)$$

and **make-sum** does the converse:

```
(define (args E) (cdr E))

(define (make-sum x) (cons '+ x))
```

From equality (7.8), the derivative of $E_1 + E_2 + \cdots + E_k$ is the sum of the
derivatives of the subexpressions. Function **diff-sum** uses Scheme's
essential function **map** to differentiate each subexpression:

```
(define (diff-sum x E)
  (make-sum
   (map (lambda (expr) (d x expr))
        (args E) )))
```

This use of lambda notation to adapt **d** for use with **map** is similar to its
use in Example 7.1, page 267, where the binary multiplication function *****
was adapted to form a doubling function. The anonymous function

```
(lambda (expr) (d x expr))
```

is a unary function for differentiating an expression with respect to a fixed
x.[3]

---

[3] Variable **x** is free in this anonymous function because it is not bound within the anonymous
function. Under the lexical scope rules of Scheme, **x** refers to the parameter **x** of **diff-sum**,
no matter where the anonymous function is applied. The treatment of free variables is faced
in Chapter 11, where an interpreter for a subset of Scheme is developed.

Example 7.3. Suppose that **s** is the sum of **u**, **v**, and **w**:

```
(define s (make-sum '(u v w)))
   s
```

The explanation of the interaction

```
(d 'v s)
   (+ 0 1 0)
```

is as follows. Since **s** is a sum, the differentiation function **d** calls **diff-sum** with symbol **v** and expression **s**. The body of **diff-sum** creates an anonymous function equivalent to

```
(lambda (expr) (d 'v expr))
```

and uses **map** to apply this function to each element of **(args s)**; that is, to **(u v w)**, resulting in the list **(0 1 0)**. Finally, **make-sum** converts this list into a sum.   □

Differentiation of Products

Predicate **product?** is similar to **sum?**:

```
(define (product? E)
  (and (pair? E)
       (equal? '* (car E)) ))
```

Function **diff-product** returns **0** if it is applied to the trivial expression **(*)** with zero subexpressions; it returns the derivative of E_1 if it is applied to **(* E_1)** with one subexpression; and it calls **diff-product-args** to differentiate all other expressions. The number of subexpressions of **E** is computed by using **args** to extract the list of subexpressions of **E**, and then taking the length of the list.

```
(define (diff-product x E)
  (let* ((arg-list (args E))
         (nargs (length arg-list)) )
     (cond ((equal? 0 nargs) 0)
           ((equal? 1 nargs) (d x (car arg-list)))
           (else (diff-product-args x arg-list)) )))
```

The sequential **let*** construct is needed because **nargs** is defined in terms of **arg-list**.

For convenience, equality (7.9) is repeated here:

$$d\,(x,\ E_1 * E') \ = \ d\,(x,\ E_1) * E' \ + \ E_1 * d\,(x,\ E')$$
$$\text{where} \ \ E' = E_2 * \cdots * E_k \tag{7.9}$$

Function **diff-product-args** implements this equality, using the following names:

E1	for	E_1
EP	for	E'
DE1	for	$d\,(x,\ E_1)$
DEP	for	$d\,(x,\ E')$
term1	for	$d\,(x,\ E_1) * E'$
term2	for	$E_1 * d\,(x,\ E')$

The code for **diff-product-args** is

```
(define (diff-product-args x arg-list)
  (let* ((E1 (car arg-list))
         (EP (make-product (cdr arg-list)))
         (DE1 (d x E1))
         (DEP (d x EP))
         (term1 (make-product (list DE1 EP)))
         (term2 (make-product (list E1 DEP))) )
    (make-sum (list term1 term2)) ))
```

Summary of the Differentiation Program

The differentiation program of this section consists of function **d** and its auxiliary routines to manipulate the various kinds of expressions. Function **d** sets up a syntax-directed translation because it uses the syntax of an expression **E** to translate **E** into the differentiated result.

The following examples use **d** to find derivatives with respect to a variable **v**.

```
(d 'v 'v)
    1

(d 'v 'w)
    0

(d 'v ' (+ u v w))
    (+ 0 1 0)

(d 'v ' (* v (+ u v w)))
    (+ (* 1 (* (+ u v w))) (* v (+ 0 1 0)))
```

Simplification of Expressions

The results of the differentiation program can be made more readable by removing occurrences of **0** from sums, occurrences of **1** from products, and "flattening" sums and products. The sum

    (+ a (+ b c) d)

can be rewritten as

    (+ a b c d)

Further simplifications arise from the representation of expressions as lists. For example, **(+)** simplifies to **0** and **(*)** to **1**.

The rest of this section implements a function **simplify** capable of simplifying

    (+ (* 1 (* (+ u v w))) (* v (+ 0 1 0))))

into

    (+ u v w v)

Function **simplify** delegates the work of simplifying sums and products; other expressions are left unchanged:

```
(define (simplify E)
  (cond ((sum? E) (simplify-sum E))
        ((product? E) (simplify-product E))
        (else E) ))
```

The rules for simplifying sums and products are symmetric; **0** is for sums what **1** is for products. Thus, **simplify-sum** and **simplify-product** call a common routine **simpl** with suitable parameters:

```
(define (simplify-sum E)
  (simpl sum? make-sum 0 E))

(define (simplify-product E)
  (simpl product? make-product 1 E))
```

The actions of function **simpl** on the product

    (* 1 (* a (+ 0 b 0)))

are illustrated in Fig. 7.8. Call this product **E**. The figure illustrates the evaluation of

    (simpl product? make-product 1 E)

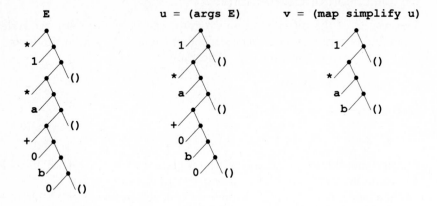

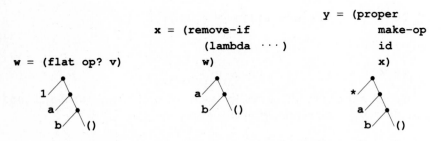

Fig. 7.8. Simplify (* 1 (* a (+ 0 b 0))) into (* a b).

The evaluation proceeds in six parts:

1. The subexpressions of **E** are extracted, using

    (args E)

2. Let the result of part 1 be a list **u**. Each subexpression in **u** is simplified, using

    (map simplify u)

    In Fig. 7.8, **1** simplifies to itself, and **(* a (+ 0 b 0))** simplifies to **(* a b)**.

3. Let the result of part 2 be a list **v**. An auxiliary function **flat** is called to flatten the list of subexpressions, using

    (flat op? v)

    In Fig. 7.8, **op?** is **product?** and **(1 (* a b))** flattens to **(1 a b)**.

4. Let the result of part 3 be a list **w**. All occurrences of **id** are removed from **w**, using

    (remove-if (lambda (z) (equal? id z)) w)

See page 269 for more on this use of **remove-if**. In Fig. 7.8, **id** is **1**, and the result of removing **1** from **(1 a b)** is **(a b)**.

5. Let the result of part 4 be **x**. An auxiliary function **proper** is called to convert **x** into an expression. Function **proper** ensures that **0** is returned instead of **(+)** and that **expr** is returned instead of **(+ expr)**; similarly, **1** is returned instead of **(*)** and **expr** is returned instead of **(* expr)**. In Fig. 7.8, **proper** converts **(a b)** into **(* a b)**.

6. Let the result of part 5 be **y**. Finally, **y** is returned.

These parts are put together in the following code:

```
(define (simpl op? make-op id E)
  (let* ((u (args E))
         (v (map simplify u))
         (w (flat op? v))
         (x (remove-if (lambda (z) (equal? id z)) w))
         (y (proper make-op id x)) )
    y))
```

The behavior of the auxiliary function **flat** can be seen from

```
(flat sum? nil)
    ()

(flat sum? '(2 (+ 3 4) 5 (* 6 7)))
    (2 3 4 5 (* 6 7))
```

The sum **(+ 3 4)** is flattened; all other list elements are copied. The code for **flat** is as follows:

```
(define (flat op? x)
  (cond ((null? x) nil)
        ((op? (car x))
         (append (args (car x))
                 (flat op? (cdr x)) ))
        (else (cons (car x) (flat op? (cdr x)))) ))
```

Finally, function **proper** is defined by

```
(define (proper make-op id x)
  (cond ((null? x) id)
        ((null? (cdr x)) (car x))
        (else (make-op x)) ))
```

7.5 ML: STATIC TYPE CHECKING

A fundamental difference between Standard ML and Scheme is that ML is strongly typed and Scheme is untyped. Otherwise, both are lexically scoped, treat functions as first-class values, rely on implicit storage management, and can be used to solve the same problems. All of the Scheme examples in this chapter can be restated in ML without changing their spirit.

This section considers some features that endow ML with a uniquely powerful type system.

A function in ML is applied by writing it next to its argument. Thus, $f(x)$ and $f\ x$ are equivalent. Function application associates to the left, so $d\ x\ E$ corresponds to $(d\ x)\ E$; that is, the result of applying d to x is a function that is applied to E.

Type Inference

Where possible, ML infers types without help from the user. The inferred type *int* for integer is included in the response to the expression

>   **2+2;**
>   *val it = 4 : int*

An expression like **2+2** is the implicit declaration of the variable **it**. Keyword **val** marks a value declaration, keyword **fun** marks a function declaration, and a semicolon terminates a declaration.

Returning to type inference, the response to the function declaration

>   **fun successor(n) = n+1;**
>   *val successor = fn : int -> int*

can be read as, "The value of **successor** is a function from integers to integers." In the expression **n+1**, variable **n** must have type integer because **1** is an integer and the built-in operator **+** can be applied either to a pair of integers or to a pair of reals.

Types can be supplied explicitly by using the notation

>   ⟨*expression*⟩ : ⟨*type-expression*⟩

Explicit types are needed sometimes to resolve overloading, as in

>   **fun add(x,y) = x + y;**
>   *Error: overloaded variable "+" cannot be resolved*

Any hint about the type of **x**, **y**, or **x+y** is enough for ML to infer the type of this function:

```
fun add(x,y):int = x + y;              (*  result is an integer *)
    val add = fn : int * int -> int
fun add(x,y) = x + (y:int);            (*  y  is an integer *)
    val add = fn : int * int -> int
```

Comments appear between (* and *).

What is the type of an identity function **I**, which maps its argument to itself?

```
fun I(x) = x;
    val I = fn : 'a -> 'a
```

The leading quote in **'a** identifies it as a type parameter. Type parameters **'a**, **'b**, $\cdots$ are written as the Greek letters α, β, $\cdots$ in publication notation. The type of **I** can be read as, "function from any type α to α." Indeed, **I** can be applied to integers, strings, functions, even to itself.

Parametric Polymorphism

A *polymorphic* function can be applied to arguments of more than one type. We concentrate on a special kind of polymorphism called *parametric polymorphism* in which type expressions are parameterized. An example is the type expression $\alpha \rightarrow \alpha$ with parameter α. (Overloading, another kind of polymorphism, is sometimes referred to as *ad-hoc polymorphism*.)

Polymorphic functions arise naturally when lists are manipulated. Lists are written between brackets [and], so parentheses can be used purely for grouping expressions. Commas separate the elements of a list. The empty list is written equivalently as [] or as **nil**. The basic functions for list manipulation are

null	Test for emptiness.
hd	Return head or first element.
tl	Return tail or all except the first element.
: :	Infix constructor, pronounced "cons."

All elements of a list must have the same type. If this type is **'a**, then the type of the list itself is **'a list**. A list of integers has type **int list**:

```
[0,1,2];
    val it = [0,1,2] : int list
```

A list of strings has type **string list**:

```
["zero", "one", "two"];
    val it = ["zero","one","two"] : string list
```

An example of a polymorphic function is

```
fun length(nil) = 0
  | length(a::y) = 1 + length(y);
      val length = fn : ('a list -> int)
```

Function **length** is defined by cases that are checked in sequence. If the argument is **nil**, then the length is **0**. Otherwise, if the argument has the form **a::y** with head **a** and tail **y**, then its length is one greater than the length of **y**.

Now **length** can be applied to a list of strings:

```
length(["hello", "world"]);
      val it = 2 : int
```

or it can be applied to a list of elements of any other type

```
length([true, true]);
      val it = 2 : int
```

ML is unusual because it allows user-defined functions to be polymorphic. Other typed languages like Modula-2 and C++ have built-in polymorphic operators for manipulating arrays, records, and pointers of any type but user-defined functions cannot be polymorphic.

Datatype Declarations

Since all elements of a list have the same type, we cannot use the Lisp approach of representing expressions as lists. The Scheme term

```
(* v (+ u v w))
```

has elements of three different types: ***** is an operator, **v** is a variable, and **(+ u v w)** is another expression. Such mixing of types makes it difficult to track down errors, caused, say, by passing a list of expressions instead of a list of lists of expressions.

Datatype **expr** can be used to represent expressions:

```
datatype expr = constant of int
              | variable of string
              | sum of expr list
              | product of expr list;
      datatype  expr
      con constant : int -> expr
      con variable : string -> expr
      con product : expr list -> expr
      con sum : expr list -> expr
```

The prefix *con* stands for "constructor." The value constructor **constant** creates an **expr** out of an integer argument; note the type in the following value declaration:

```
val zero = constant(0);
    val zero = constant 0 : expr

val one = constant(1);
    val one = constant 1 : expr
```

Similarly, the value constructor **variable** constructs an **expr** out of a string:

```
val u = variable("u")
val v = variable("v")
val w = variable("v");
    val u = variable "u" : expr
    val v = variable "v" : expr
    val w = variable "v" : expr
```

A counterpart of the Scheme expression **(* v (+ u v w))** is

```
product [v, sum [u,v,w]]
```

Since several introductory examples of the use of datatypes appear in Section 2.8, we now consider the more challenging example in Fig. 7.9; it is a counterpart of the Scheme differentiation procedure in Section 7.4.

```
fun d x (constant _) =
      zero
  | d (variable s) (variable t) =
      if s = t then one else zero
  | d x (sum Elist) =
      sum(map (d x) Elist)
  | d x (product []) =
      zero
  | d x (product [E]) =
      d x E
  | d x (product (E1::Elist)) =
      let val EP = product(Elist)
          val term1 = product [d x E1, EP]
          val term2 = product [E1, d x EP]
      in sum [term1, term2]
      end
```

Fig. 7.9. A differentiation function in ML.

Value constructors are used in two ways by the differentiation function **d** in Fig. 7.9: for analyzing the structure of an expression and for constructing an expression. In words, the derivative of a constant is zero:

```
fun d x (constant _) =
        zero
```

The symbol _ stands for "don't care," and **zero** was just defined to be **constant(0)**.

An instructive case in the definition of **d** is

```
 | d x (sum Elist) =
        sum(map (d x) Elist)
```

This case applies to expressions of the form **sum Elist**. In words, the individual expressions in **Elist** are differentiated and their sum is returned. In more detail, **(d x)** is a function that differentiates a single expression with respect to **x**. The built-in iterator **map** applies this function to each element of **Elist** and returns a list of differentiated subexpressions. Constructor **sum** converts the returned list into an expression.

As an aside, the construct

let val $x_1 = E_1$ **val** $x_2 = E_2 \cdots$ **val** $x_k = E_k$ **in** F **end**

binds x_i to the value of E_i before E_{i+1} is evaluated. Thus, in the last case for the product, **EP** is bound to **product(Elist)** before **term1** and **term2** are bound.

7.6 EXCEPTION HANDLING IN ML

Exceptions are a mechanism for handling special cases or failures that occur during the execution of a program. Consider a function *phone* that normally returns a telephone number if there is an entry for *person* in a database. What if a special case occurs during execution because there is no entry for *person*? Lisp programs often return the empty list to signal such cases.

The exception mechanism in ML allows failures to be made explicit. The simplest form of an exception declaration consists of the keyword **exception** followed by the name of an exception:

```
exception Nomatch;
      exception Nomatch : exn
```

An exception is *raised* by writing

raise ⟨*exception-name*⟩

The following function **member** looks for an element **a** in a list **x** and raises exception **Nomatch** if the list is empty:

```
fun member(a, x) =
  if null(x) then raise Nomatch
  else if a = hd(x) then x
  else member(a, tl(x));
```

The normal behavior of **member** is to return the portion of a list from the first occurrence of **a** to the end:

```
member(3, [1,2,3,1,2,3]);
    val it = [3,1,2,3] : int list
```

The special case occurs in

```
member(4, []);
    uncaught exception Nomatch
```

Exceptions can be caught or handled by using the following syntax:

$$\langle expression \rangle_1 \ \mathbf{handle} \ \langle exception\text{-}name \rangle \ \Rightarrow \ \langle expression \rangle_2$$

This construct behaves like $\langle expression \rangle_1$ except if $\langle exception\text{-}name \rangle$ is raised during the evaluation of $\langle expression \rangle_1$; control then passes to $\langle expression \rangle_2$ and its value is returned.

Suppose that **Oops** and **Other** are exceptions:

```
exception Oops; exception Other;
    exception Oops : exn
    exception Other : exn
```

Since **2+3** evaluates to 5, the handler in the following construct is ignored and the construct behaves like **2+3**:

```
2+3 handle Oops => 0;
    val it = 5 : int
```

Control flows to the exception handler in the following construct, so the result is **0**:

```
(raise Oops) handle Oops => 0;
    val it = 0 : int
```

Finally, an exception handler for **Oops** has no effect on other exceptions:

```
(raise Other) handle Oops => 0;
    uncaught exception Other
```

Exceptions are handled dynamically. If *f* calls *g*, *g* calls *h*, and *h* raises an exception, then we look for handlers along the call chain, *h*, *g*, *f*. The first handler along the chain catches the exception.

Example 7.4. Exception handling will be illustrated by writing an integer subtraction function that returns $m-n$ if $m \geq n$ and returns 0 otherwise.

One of the building blocks is a function **s** that raises exception **Neg** instead of returning a negative result:

```
exception Neg;
    exception Neg : exn
fun s(m,n) : int =
  if m >= n then m-n else raise Neg;
    val s = fn : ((int * int) -> int)
s(5,3);
    val it = 2 : int
s(5,15);
    uncaught exception Neg
```

Function **subtract** provides a handler for exception **Neg**. If the exception is raised during the evaluation of **s(m,n)**, the handler returns **0** instead:

```
fun subtract(m,n) =
  s(m,n) handle Neg => 0;
    val subtract = fn : ((int * int) -> int)
subtract(5,3);
    val it = 2 : int
subtract(5,15);
    val it = 0 : int                                         □
```

For a more realistic example of exceptions, consider a pattern-matching program that checks its argument **a** against a list of patterns in a database. Suppose that a function **match** checks **a** against an individual pattern and returns the pattern number if they match; otherwise, the function raises exception **Nomatch**.

Function **fetch** tries the patterns in the database one by one:

```
fun fetch(a, nil) =
      raise Notfound
  | fetch(a, pat::rest) =
      match(a, pat) handle Nomatch => fetch(a, rest)
```

If the list of patterns is empty, then **fetch** raises exception **Notfound**. Otherwise, let the list of patterns be **pat::rest**. If **match(a,pat)** raises exception **Nomatch**, then **fetch** catches this exception and calls itself recursively to try the next pattern on the list.

7.7 STORAGE ALLOCATION FOR LISTS

By design, programs in functional languages like Scheme and ML can be understood independently of the underlying allocation and deallocation of storage. Nevertheless, some familiarity with storage management is helpful for assessing the cost of storage management.

Is it expensive to pass lists as parameters to functions? No—we see in this section that a pointer is all that is passed. This section considers the traditional implementation of lists in Lisp dialects, using cells as in Fig. 7.10. The operation to examine closely is the list constructor **cons**.

Cons Allocates Cells

Lists are built out of cells capable of holding pointers to the head and tail, or car and cdr, respectively, of a list. The **car** operation is named after "Contents of the Address part of Register" and **cdr** is named after "Contents of the Decrement part of Register." Words on the IBM 704, a machine long gone, could hold two pointers in fields called the *address* part and the *decrement* part. When Lisp was first implemented on the IBM 704, the **cons** operation allocated a word and stuffed pointers to the head and tail in the address and decrement parts, respectively.

The empty list **nil** is a special pointer; Lisp tradition is to use 0, but any address can be reserved as the value of **nil**. Think of **nil** as a special address that is not used for anything else.

Each execution of **cons** returns a pointer to a newly allocated cell. The list in Fig. 7.11(a) is built by applying **cons** three times:

```
(cons 'it (cons 'seems (cons 'that nil)))
```

Reading inside out, **cons** is first applied to a pointer to the symbol **that** and the empty list. The second application is for the symbol **seems** and the pointer returned from the first application.

As for the remaining operations on lists, **null** simply compares its argument for equality with **nil**, **car** returns the pointer in the first field, and **cdr** returns the pointer in the second field.

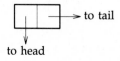

Fig. 7.10. Lists are built out of cells with pointers to the head and tail.

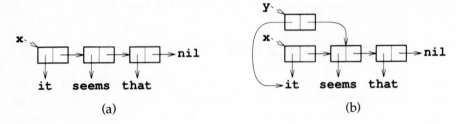

Fig. 7.11. Each cons operation constructs a cell.

Notions of Equality

The distinction between the standard Scheme functions **equal?** and **eq?** reveals the underlying representation of lists as pointers to cells. The **eq?** function checks whether its two arguments are identical pointers, so it is fussier than **equal?**, which recursively checks whether its two arguments are lists with "equal" elements.

On symbols, the two predicates **equal?** and **eq?** agree:

```
(equal? 'hello 'hello)
    #t
(eq? 'hello 'hello)
    #t
```

As might be expected, **equal?** returns **#t**, for **true**, with the following arguments:

```
(equal? '(hello world) '(hello world))
    #t
```

The implementation of quoted lists has to be studied to explain why the following expression is false in some Scheme implementations:

```
(eq? '(hello world) '(hello world))
    #f
```

This expression may be easier to understand after working out a simpler example.

Example 7.5. The list pointed to by **x** in Fig. 7.11 prints out as

```
(it seems that)
```

So does the list pointed to by **y** in part (b) of the figure. Yet **x** and **y** point to different cells.

The situation in Fig. 7.11(a) is set up by the following definition of **x**:

```
(define x '(it seems that))
     x
```

Each execution of **cons** allocates a cell, so the following definition sets up the situation in Fig. 7.11(b):

```
(define y (cons (car x) (cdr x)))
     y
```

Now **(car x)** and **(car y)** are identical pointers and **(cdr x)** and **(cdr y)** are identical pointers. But **y** is bound to a different cell from **x**, a cell created by applying **cons** to the head and tail of **x**. Hence, the responses in

```
(equal? x y)
     #t
```

```
(eq? x y)
     #f
```
□

Returning to the list

```
'(hello world)
```

each occurrence of this list is an abbreviation for

```
(cons 'hello (cons 'world nil))
```

As in Fig. 7.12, four cells are allocated to hold the arguments of **eq?** in

```
(eq? '(hello world) '(hello world))
```

The two separate occurrences of **(hello world)** are therefore equivalent under **equal?**, but not under **eq?**.

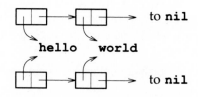

Fig. 7.12. Two lists with the same elements.

Allocation and Deallocation

Cells that are no longer in use have to be recovered or deallocated; otherwise, we eventually run out of memory. A cell is no longer in use if nothing points to it.

A standard technique for allocating and deallocating cells is to link them on a list called a *free list*. The free list acts as a stack of cells; a pop operation on the stack returns a freshly allocated cell and a push operation returns a cell back onto the stack. A language implementation performs *garbage collection* when it returns cells to the free list automatically, without explicit instructions from a program.

What happens to the lists created during the interactions

```
(cons 'short-lived nil)
    (short-lived)
(let ((x '(short-lived))) x)
    (short-lived)
```

In each case, a cell, **(short-lived)**, with head **short-lived** and tail **nil** is allocated. After the response, the cell is no longer reachable, and can therefore be deallocated. By contrast, the cell created by **cons** in

```
(define x (cons 'saved nil))
    x
```

can subsequently be accessed through **x**:

```
x
    (saved)
```

Two of the numerous approaches to deallocation of cells are as follows:

1. *Lazy approach.* Wait until memory runs out and only then collect dead cells. If enough memory is available, the need for collecting cells may never arise. Since it takes time to examine a cell or manipulate a pointer, a disadvantage of this approach is that all other work comes to a halt when the garbage collector has control of the machine.

2. *Eager approach.* Each time a cell is reached, check whether the cell will be needed after the operation; if not, deallocate the cell by placing it on the free list. A standard technique is to set aside some space with each cell for holding a *reference count* of the number of pointers to the cell. If the reference count ever drops to zero, the cell can be deallocated.

Having looked at when garbage collection occurs, we now turn to how it can be implemented.

A simple approach to garbage collection, called the *mark-sweep* approach, is as follows:

1. *Mark phase.* Mark all the cells that can be reached by following pointers. Think of pouring colored ink through all the pointers into the cell area. The ink follows pointers from cell to cell, eventually coloring all reachable cells.

2. *Sweep phase.* Sweep through memory, looking for unmarked cells. Unlike the mark phase, which hops through memory along pointers, the sweep phase starts at one end of memory and looks at every cell. Unmarked cells are returned to the free list.

A *copying collector* avoids the expense of the sweep phase, which looks at every cell, by dividing memory into two halves, the *working* half and the *free* half. Cells are allocated from the working half. When the working half fills up, the reachable cells are copied into consecutive locations in the free half. The roles of the free and working halves are then switched. A copying collector looks only at the reachable cells, the cells that would be marked by a mark-sweep collector. Copying collectors are particularly effective in a virtual memory system.

EXERCISES

7.1 Write Scheme or ML functions that compare adjacent list elements and respond with a list, as described in each case. The sample responses are all with the input list

(a b a a a c c)

a) Remove the second and succeeding adjacent duplicates, yielding

(a b a c)

b) Leave only the elements that are not repeated, yielding

(a b)

c) Leave only one copy of the repeated elements, yielding

(a c)

d) Count the number of repeated occurrences, yielding

((1 a) (1 b) (3 a) (2 c))

7.2 The following tail-recursive or iterative version of the **length** function uses an extra parameter in which it accumulates the result:

```
        (len nil res)   ≡   res
    (len (cons a y) res)   ≡   (len y (+ 1 res))
```

For any list **x**, **(length x)** is equivalent to **(len x 0)**. Use this technique to construct tail-recursive versions of the following functions:

a) a function that adds together all the elements in a list.

b) a function that multiplies together all the elements in a list.

c) the factorial function.

7.3 Implement a variant of Quicksort for lists. That is, sort a list as follows. Pick an element and call it the pivot. Partition the list into two sublists of elements smaller than and larger than the pivot. Recursively sort the sublists. Combine the sorted sublists and the pivot together into a sorted list.

a) Define a function that sorts lists of integers.

b) Define a function that takes two arguments: a predicate **p** for comparing elements, and a list of elements to be sorted.

7.4 Suppose that sets are implemented as lists, where each element of a set appears exactly once in its list. Define functions that implement the following operations:

a) Test whether an element is a member of a set.

b) Construct the union of two sets.

c) Construct the intersection of two sets.

d) Construct the difference of two sets; that is, the set of elements that are in the first set, but not in the second set.

e) How would your implementations change if sets were implemented by sorted lists without repeated elements?

7.5 Suppose that sets are implemented as lists, and that the union of two sets is implemented by simply appending their lists. Note that the same element can appear more than once in the list for a set. Implement the member, intersection, and difference operations on sets.

7.6 Implement the following functions based on the Scheme report:

a) **(append** $list_1$ $list_2$ $list_3$**)**, which appends the elements of the three lists.

b) **(list-tail** $list$ n**)**, which returns the remaining sublist after the first n elements of a list are removed.

c) **(list-ref** $list$ n**)**, which returns the nth element of a list.

d) **(map** f $list_1$ $list_2$ $list_3$**)**, which applies function f to corresponding elements of three lists of the same length.

7.7 We get a *flattened* form of a list if we ignore all but the initial opening and final closing parenthesis in the written representation of a list. The flattened form of

```
((a) ((b b)) (((c c c))))
```

is

(a b b c c c)

Alternatively, the flattened form can be thought of as the list read off the leaves of a tree representation of a list.

a) Implement a function **flatten** to construct flattened forms.

b) Implement a function **same-leaves** to tests whether two lists have the same flattened form.

*c) Give an efficient implementation of **same-leaves** that avoids flattening two huge lists, only to discover that their flattened forms differ in some prefix.

7.8 Fill in the blanks in the following equivalences (see Section 7.3 for properties of the functions):

a) `(reduce ___ x ___ )` $\equiv$ `(length x)`

b) `(reduce ___ x ___ )` $\equiv$ `(append x z)`

c) `(reduce ___ x ___ )` $\equiv$ `(remove-if f x)`

d) `(reduce ___ x ___ )` $\equiv$ `(map f x)`

7.9 The list-manipulation function in this exercise is motivated by a rule for differentiating products. Let E' represent the derivative with respect to x of an expression E. The rule is

$$(E_1 * E_2 * \cdots * E_k)' \equiv \begin{array}{l} E_1' * E_2 * \cdots * E_k \\ + E_1 * E_2' * \cdots * E_k \\ \cdots \\ + E_1 * E_2 * \cdots * E_k' \end{array}$$

a) Define a function **foo** that applies a function **f** to each element of a list **x** and returns a list of sublists. The ith element of the ith sublist is formed by applying **f** to the ith element of **x**; the remaining elements of the ith sublist are as in **x**.

b) Modify the differentiation program in Section 7.4 so that it differentiates products using the rule in this exercise.

7.10 Pattern matching and transformation rules occur frequently in symbolic computation. The following patterns and corresponding response templates can be used to generate "conversations" like the one in Fig. 7.13 (responses are in italics):

PATTERN	RESPONSE TEMPLATE
___₁ **my** *single* ___₂ **me** ___₃	*tell me about your single*
___₁ **i am** ___₂	*i am sorry to hear you are* ___₂
___₁ **am i** ___₂	*do you believe you are* ___₂
___₁ **you** ___₂ **me**	*why do you think i* ___₂ *you*
___₁	*in what way*

well my friend made me come here
   tell me about your friend

he says i am depressed
   i am sorry to hear you are depressed

i think i need help
   in what way

oh am i making sense so far
   do you believe you are making sense so far

you are making fun of me
   why do you think i are making fun of you

Fig. 7.13. Responses generated using pattern matching.

The blank spaces in a pattern, denoted by subscripted dashes, can be filled in with any sequence of words. A single word is filled in for *single*. Write a program that uses patterns and response templates to simulate a conversation.

BIBLIOGRAPHIC NOTES

McCarthy [1981] recalls the early history of Lisp, including the role of differentiation in motivating the following: recursive functions defined using conditional expressions, a version of **map**, the use of the λ-notation of Church [1941] to write anonymous functions, and garbage collection. "No solution [for erasure of abandoned list structure] was apparent at the time, but the idea of complicating the elegant definition of differentiation with explicit erasure was unattractive."

The Scheme dialect of Lisp was developed in 1975 by Steele and Sussman [1975]. Abelson and Sussman [1985] is a textbook that uses the dialect to introduce programming concepts. The Scheme report (Rees and Clinger [1986]) notes, "Scheme has influenced the evolution of Lisp. ... Scheme was the first major dialect of Lisp to distinguish procedures from lambda expressions and symbols, to use a single lexical environment for all variables, and to evaluate the operator position of a procedure call in the same way as an operand position." Scheme also provides "first class escape procedures." Some of Scheme's innovations have been adopted in Common Lisp (Steele [1984]).

ML, for meta language, began as the programming language for a machine-assisted system for formal proofs. The initial design was done by Robin Milner, in collaboration with the other authors of Gordon et al. [1978]. The application to proofs motivated the emphasis on type checking. Harper, Milner, and Tofte [1988] is the defining document for Standard ML, the language used in this book. The composite report by Harper, MacQueen, and Milner [1986] includes a tutorial on the language and a preliminary description of the module facility. Modules in ML are much more general than the modules considered in Chapter 5.

Backus's impassioned critique of "conventional von Neumann languages" drew popular attention to functional programming. The style of programming advocated by Backus has come to be called FP; see the paper by John Williams in the collection Darlington, Henderson, and Turner [1982]. This collection consists of lecture material compiled for a course on various aspects of functional programming.

Exercise 7.10 is based on a program called Eliza due to Weizenbaum [1966]. Eliza conversed by simply rearranging the sentences that were presented to it. Weizenbaum [1976], "was startled to see how quickly and how deeply people conversing with [Eliza] became emotionally involved" in the interchange. They talked to Eliza as if it were a person, even when they knew it to be a program.

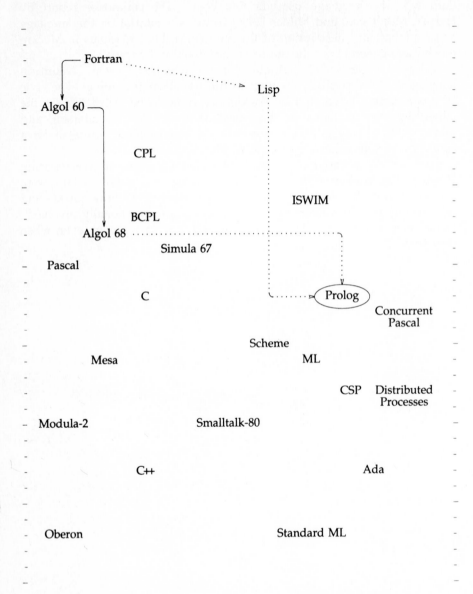

Prolog was influenced primarily by prior work on mechanical theorem proving and syntax analysis. Prolog borrows lists from Lisp. The dotted line from Algol 68 to Prolog represents the influence not of Algol 68 itself, but of W-grammars, a notation proposed for describing Algol 68. Work with W-grammars led to an ancestor of Prolog called System Q.

296

Logic Programming

The concept of logic programming is linked historically to a language called Prolog, developed in 1972 and still the only widely available language of its kind. Prolog was first applied to natural language processing. It has since been used for specifying algorithms, searching databases, writing compilers, building expert systems—in short, all the kinds of applications for which a language like Lisp might be used. Prolog is especially suited to applications involving pattern matching, backtrack searching, or incomplete information.

Prolog is a practical tool. It reduces logic programming to practice. However, it introduces a few impurities that are put into perspective if we distinguish between Prolog, the language, and logic programming, the concept. This chapter therefore begins with an informal discussion of logic programming.

8.1 COMPUTING WITH RELATIONS

Logic programming deals with relations rather than functions. It is based on the premise that programming with relations is more flexible than programming with functions, because relations treat arguments and results uniformly. Informally, relations have no sense of direction, no prejudice about who is computed from whom.

The running example in this section is a relation *append* on lists. Although Prolog itself is not introduced until Section 8.2, we anticipate its notation for lists. Lists are written between brackets [and], so [] is the empty list and [b, c] is a list of two symbols b and c. If H is a symbol and T is a list, then [H | T] is a list with head H and tail T. Hence

$$[a, b, c] = [a \mid [b, c]]$$

Relations

A concrete view of a *relation* is as a table with $n \geq 0$ columns and a possibly infinite set of rows. A tuple $(a_1, a_2, \ldots, a_n)$ is *in* a relation if a_i appears in column i, $1 \leq i \leq n$, of some row in the table for the relation.

Relation *append* is a set of tuples of the form (X, Y, Z), where Z consists of the elements of X followed by the elements of Y. A few of the tuples in *append* are as follows:

append		
X	Y	Z
[]	[]	[]
[a]	[]	[a]
...	...	...
[a, b]	[c, d]	[a, b, c, d]
...	...	...

Relations are also called *predicates* because a relation name *rel* can be thought of as a test of the form

Is a given tuple in relation *rel*?

For example, ([a], [b], [a, b]) is in relation *append*, but ([a], [b], []) is not.

The rest of this section uses pseudo-English to talk informally about relation *append*.

Rules and Facts

Relations will be specified by *rules*, written in pseudo-code as

$$P \textbf{ if } Q_1 \textbf{ and } Q_2 \textbf{ and } \cdots \textbf{ and } Q_k.$$

for $k \geq 0$.[1] Such rules are called *Horn clauses*, after Horn [1951], who studied them. Languages have tended to work with Horn clauses because Horn clauses lead to efficient implementations.

---

[1] Looking ahead to Section 8.2, P, Q_1, Q_2, $\ldots$, Q_k are terms. A *term* is either a constant or a variable or has the form $rel(T_1, T_2, \ldots, T_n)$, for $n \geq 0$, where *rel* is the name of a relation and $T_1, T_2, \ldots, T_n$ are terms. By convention, variable names begin with uppercase letters; constant and relation names begin with lowercase letters.

A *fact* is a special case of a rule, in which $k=0$ and P holds without any conditions, written simply as

   P.

The *append* relation is specified by two rules. The first is a fact stating that triples of the form $([\,], Y, Y)$ are in relation *append*. A pseudo-English statement of this fact is

   append $[\,]$ and Y to get Y.

The second rule for *append* is shown for completeness. It uses the notation $[H \mid T]$ for a list with head H and tail T:

   append $[H \mid X_1]$ and Y to get $[H \mid Z_1]$ **if**
      append X_1 and Y to get Z_1

It follows from this rule that

   append $[a, b]$ and $[c, d]$ to get $[a, b, c, d]$ **if**
      append $[b]$ and $[c, d]$ to get $[b, c, d]$

Here $H=a$, $X_1=[b]$, $Y=[c, d]$, and $Z_1=[b, c, d]$. Note that $[a \mid [b]]$ is the same list as $[a, b]$ and that $[a \mid [b, c, d]]$ is the same list as $[a, b, c, d]$.

Queries

Logic programming is driven by queries about relations. The simplest queries ask whether a particular tuple belongs to a relation. The query

   append $[a, b]$ and $[c, d]$ to get $[a, b, c, d]$?   (8.1)
      Answer : yes

asks whether the triple $([a, b], [c, d], [a, b, c, d])$ belongs to relation *append*.

   Horn clauses cannot represent negative information; that is, we cannot directly ask whether a tuple is not in a relation. Queries in this chapter will therefore have yes/fail answers rather than yes/no answers. By "fail" is meant failure to deduce a yes answer. Section 8.6 considers a limited form of negation based on failure.

   Queries containing variables are much more interesting:

   Is there a Z such that
      append $[a, b]$ and $[c, d]$ to get Z?   (8.2)
      Answer : yes, when $Z = [a, b, c, d]$

What seems like a yes/fail query is really a request for suitable values for the variables in it. The query (8.2) is a request for a Z such that $([a\ b], [c, d], Z)$ is in the relation *append*.

   A benefit of working with relations is that if we append X and Y to get Z, then any one of X, Y, and Z can be computed from the other two. This property motivates the earlier remark that relations are flexible because they have no prejudice about who is computed from whom. X can be computed from Y and Z:

> Is there an X such that
>   append X and $[c, d]$ to get $[a, b, c, d]$? (8.3)
>   *Answer*: yes, when $X = [a, b]$

Or Y can be computed from X and Z:

> Is there a Y such that
>   append $[a, b]$ and Y to get $[a, b, c, d]$? (8.4)
>   *Answer*: yes, when $Y = [c, d]$

Queries (8.1)-(8.4) illustrate several different ways of using the same relation *append*. New relations can be defined from old. In the following three rules for *prefix*, *suffix*, and *sublist*, the variables S, X, Y, and Z refer to portions of a list (see Fig. 8.1):

> prefix X of Z **if**
>   for some Y, append X and Y to get Z.

> suffix Y of Z **if**
>   for some X, append X and Y to get Z.

> sublist S of Z **if**
>   for some X, prefix X of Z **and** suffix S of X.

What is Logic Programming?

The term *logic programming* refers loosely to

- the use of facts and rules to represent information, and
- the use of deduction to answer queries.

These two aspects reflect a division of labor between us as programmers and a language for logic programming. We supply the facts and rules, and the language uses deduction to compute answers to queries. Kowalski [1979b] illustrates this division of labor by writing the informal equation

algorithm = logic + control

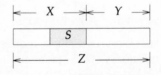

Fig. 8.1. Variable names referring to portions of a list.

Here logic refers to the facts and rules specifying what the algorithm does, and control refers to how the algorithm can be implemented by applying the rules in a particular order. We supply the logic part, and the programming language supplies the control.

Prolog has spawned numerous dialects, some with their own notions of control. This chapter uses Edinburgh Prolog, a de facto standard dialect. Nonsyntactic differences between dialects can be illustrated by writing a family of equations

$$\text{algorithm}_D = \text{logic} + \text{control}_D$$

where D is a dialect and control_D represents its notion of control.

Control in Edinburgh Prolog proceeds from left to right; see Section 8.5 for details. The rule

$$P \ \text{ if } \ Q_1 \text{ and } Q_2 \text{ and } \cdots \text{ and } Q_k.$$

$k \geq 0$, can be read as

> to deduce P,
>   deduce Q_1;
>   deduce Q_2;
> $\cdots$
>   deduce Q_k;

This simple strategy is surprisingly versatile and flexible. Unfortunately, it sometimes gets stuck in infinite loops, and it can produce anomalies involving negation.

8.2 INTRODUCTION TO PROLOG

This section introduces Prolog by considering relations on atomic objects. Data structures are considered in the next section; programs that benefit from Prolog's unique abilities appear in Section 8.4.

The examples in this section are motivated by the arrows or *links* in Fig. 8.2.

Terms

Facts, rules, and queries are specified using terms; see Fig. 8.3 for the basic syntax of Edinburgh Prolog.

A *simple term* is a *number*, a *variable* starting with an uppercase letter, or an *atom* standing for itself. Examples of simple terms are

```
0   1972   X   Source   lisp   algol60
```

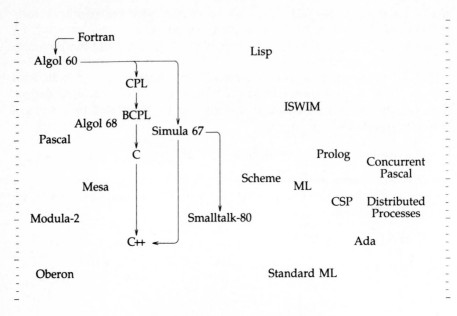

Fig. 8.2. Links between languages.

Here **0** and **1972** are numbers, **X** and **Source** are variables, and **lisp** and **algo160** are atoms.

A *compound term* consists of an atom followed by a parenthesized sequence of subterms. The atom is called a *functor* and the subterms are called *arguments*. In

    link(bcpl, c)

the functor is **link**, and the arguments are **bcpl** and **c**.

A few extensions to the syntax of compound terms will be introduced as needed. Some operators can be written in infix as well as prefix notation; for example, the prefix notation **=(X, Y)** can equivalently be rewritten as **X=Y**.

The special variable "**_**" is a placeholder for an unnamed term. All occurrences of _ are independent of each other.

    ⟨*fact*⟩   ::= ⟨*term*⟩ .
    ⟨*rule*⟩   ::= ⟨*term*⟩ : – ⟨*terms*⟩ .
    ⟨*query*⟩ ::= ⟨*terms*⟩ .

    ⟨*term*⟩ ::= ⟨*number*⟩ | ⟨*atom*⟩ | ⟨*variable*⟩ | ⟨*atom*⟩ **(** ⟨*terms*⟩ **)**

    ⟨*terms*⟩ ::= ⟨*term*⟩ | ⟨*term*⟩ **,** ⟨*terms*⟩

Fig. 8.3. Basic syntax of facts, rules, and queries in Edinburgh Prolog.

Interacting with Prolog

A snapshot of an interactive session winds its way through the rest of this section. As in Chapter 7, system responses appear in italic letters. When started, the system responds with the "prompt" characters

    ?–

to indicate that a query is expected.

The *consult* construct reads in a file containing facts and rules, and adds its contents at the end of the current database of rules.[2] Thus,

```
?- consult(links).
      links consulted  · · ·
      yes
```

reads file **links**; its contents are in Fig. 8.4. A sequence of facts starting with

```
link(fortran, algol60).
```

specifies a relation **link** on atoms. This fact says that the pair (**fortran, algol60**) belongs to **link**.

```
link(fortran,  algol60).
link(algol60,  cpl).
link(cpl,      bcpl).
link(bcpl,     c).
link(c,        cplusplus).
link(algol60,  simula67).
link(simula67, cplusplus).
link(simula67, smalltalk80).

path(L, L).
path(L, M) :- link(L, X), path(X, M).
```

Fig. 8.4. Facts and rules in a file **links**.

---

[2] Use *reconsult* to override rules in the database. Some implementations allow rules to be entered directly by consulting the special file name *user*.

Existential Queries

A query

$$\langle term \rangle_1 \; , \; \langle term \rangle_2 \; , \quad \cdots \quad , \; \langle term \rangle_k \; .$$

for $k \geq 1$, corresponds to the following pseudo-code:

$$\langle term \rangle_1 \text{ and } \langle term \rangle_2 \text{ and } \cdots \text{ and } \langle term \rangle_k \; ?$$

Queries are also called *goals*. It is sometimes convenient to refer to the individual terms in a query as "subgoals." There is no formal distinction between a goal and a subgoal, however, just as there is no formal distinction between a term and a subterm.

Since there are no variables in the query

```
?- link(cpl,bcpl), link(bcpl,c).
    yes
```

the response is simply *yes*.

A variable in a query refers to the existence of some appropriate object. The query

```
?- link(algol60,L), link(L,M).
```

can therefore be read as

> Are there *L* and *M* such that
> *link* (*algol* 60, *L*) **and** *link* (*L*, *M*)?

A *solution* to a query is a binding of variables to values that makes the query true.[3] A query with solutions is said to be *satisfiable*. The system responds with a solution to a satisfiable query:

```
?- link(algol60,L), link(L,M).
    L = cpl
    M = bcpl
```

We now have two choices:

- Type a carriage return. Prolog responds with *yes* to indicate that there might be more solutions. It then immediately prompts for the next query.

- Type a semicolon and a carriage return. Prolog responds with another solution, or with *no* to indicate that no further solutions can be found.

The semicolons in the following interaction keep asking for further solutions:

---

[3] Technically, all variables in a query are implicitly existentially quantified. With the quantifiers in place, this query becomes

> ∃*L*, *M*. *link* (*algol* 60, *L*) **and** *link* (*L*, *M*)?

```
?- link(algol60,L), link(L,M).
    L = cpl
    M = bcpl ;

    L = simula67
    M = cplusplus ;

    L = simula67
    M = smalltalk80 ;

    no
```

Variables can appear anywhere within a query. The query

```
?- link(L, bcpl).
```

asks for an object with a link to **bcpl**, and the query

```
?- link(bcpl, M).
```

asks for an object to which **bcpl** has a link.

Universal Facts and Rules

A rule

$$\langle term \rangle \quad :- \quad \langle term \rangle_1 \ , \ \langle term \rangle_2 \ , \ \cdots \ , \ \langle term \rangle_k \ .$$

for $k \geq 1$, corresponds to the following pseudo-code:

$$\langle term \rangle \quad \textbf{if} \quad \langle term \rangle_1 \ \textbf{and} \ \langle term \rangle_2 \ \textbf{and} \ \cdots \ \textbf{and} \ \langle term \rangle_k.$$

The term to the left of the :- is called the *head* and the terms to the right of the :- are called *conditions*.

A fact is a special case of a rule. A fact has a head and no conditions.

The following fact and rule specify a relation **path**:

```
path(L, L).                                                    (8.5)
path(L, M) :- link(L, X), path(X, M).                          (8.6)
```

The idea is that a path consists of zero or more links. We take a path of zero links to be from **L** to itself. A path from **L** to **M** begins with a link to some **X** and continues along the path from **X** to **M**.

Any object can be substituted for a variable in the head of a rule. Fact (8.5) can therefore be read as

> For all L,
> $path (L, L)$.

Rule (8.6) has a variable **X** that appears in the conditions, but not in the head. Such variables stand for some object satisfying the conditions.[4] Rule (8.6) can therefore be read as

> For all L and M,
> $path(L, M)$ **if**
>   there exists X such that
> $link(L, X)$ **and** $path(X, M)$.

Negation as Failure

Prolog answers *no* to a query if it fails to satisfy the query. The *negation as failure* assumption is tantamount to saying, "If I can't prove it, it must be false."

The facts in Fig. 8.4 say nothing about a link from **lisp** to **scheme**, hence the *no* answer in the following:

```
?- link(lisp,scheme).
    no
```

Similarly, the **not** operator represents negation as failure, rather than true logical negation. A query **not** (P) is treated as true if the system fails to deduce P. Negation as failure works for simple cases; more complex cases are dealt with in Section 8.6. The following example contains an application for **not**.

Example 8.1. Are there two languages L and M in Fig. 8.2 with links to the same language N? A first attempt at this query is

```
?- link(L,N), link(M,N).
    L = fortran
    N = algol60
    M = fortran
```

Let us now add the requirement that variables **L** and **M** must have different values:

---

[4] Technically, all variables in facts and rules are implicitly universally quantified. With the quantifiers in place, the rule becomes

> $\forall L, M, X.\ path(L, M)$ **if** $(link(L, X)$ **and** $path(X, M))$

Since X does not appear in its head, the rule is logically equivalent to

> $\forall L, M.\ path(L, M)$ **if** $(\exists X.\ link(L, X)$ **and** $path(X, M))$

```
?- link(L,N), link(M,N), not(L=M).
    L = c
    N = cplusplus
    M = simula67 ;

    L = simula67
    N = cplusplus
    M = c ;

    no
```

These two solutions are different because the individual variables have different values.

As a rule of thumb, **not** can be used to test known values or values that become known before **not** is applied. The reordered query

```
?- not(L=M), link(L,N), link(M,N).
    no
```

fails because the values of variables **L** and **M** are not known at the start of the query. Unknown values could be equal, so **not(L=M)** fails.   □

Unification

How does Prolog solve equations of the following form

```
?- f(X,b) = f(a,Y).
    X = a
    Y = b
```

An *instance* of a term T is obtained by substituting subterms for one or more variables of T. The same subterm must be substituted for all occurrences of a variable.

Thus, **f(a,b)** is an instance of **f(X,b)** because it is obtained by substituting subterm **a** for variable **X** in **f(X,b)**. Similarly, **f(a,b)** is an instance of **f(a,Y)** because it is obtained by substituting subterm **b** for variable **Y** in **f(a,Y)**.

As another example, **g(a,a)** is an instance of **g(X,X)**, and so is **g(h(b),h(b))**. However, **g(a,b)** is not an instance of **g(X,X)** because we cannot substitute **a** for one occurrence of **X** and a different subterm **b** for the other occurrence of **X**.

Deduction in Prolog is based on the concept of unification; two terms T_1 and T_2 *unify* if they have a common instance U. If a variable occurs in both T_1 and T_2, then the same subterm must be substituted for all occurrences of the variable in both T_1 and T_2.

Terms **f(X,b)** and **f(a,Y)** unify because they have a common instance **f(a,b)**.

Unification occurs implicitly when a rule is applied. Suppose that the relation **identity** is defined by the fact

    identity(Z,Z).

Now unification is used to compute the response to the query

    ?- identity(f(X,b), f(a,Y)).
        X = a
        Y = b

The response is computed by unifying **identity(Z,Z)** with

    identity(f(X,b), f(a,Y))

which leads to the unification of **Z** with **f(X,b)** and with **f(a,Y)**. In effect, **f(X,b)** is unified with **f(a,Y)**.

Arithmetic

The **=** operator stands for unification in Prolog, so

    ?- X = 2+3.
        X = 2+3

simply binds variable **X** to the term **2+3**.

The infix **is** operator evaluates an expression:

    ?- X is 2+3.
        X = 5

Since the **is** operator binds **X** to **5**, the query

    ?- X is 2+3, X = 5.
        X = 5

is satisfied. However,

    ?- X is 2+3, X = 2+3.
        no

fails because **2+3** does not unify with **5**. Term **2+3** is the application of operator **+** to arguments **2** and **3**, whereas **5** is simply the integer **5**. Hence, **2+3** does not unify with **5**.

8.3   DATA STRUCTURES IN PROLOG

Prolog supports several notations for writing Lisp-like lists. After review-
ing the notations, we see that they are just syntactic sugar for ordinary
terms; that is, they sweeten the syntax without adding any new capabili-
ties.

The view of terms as data carries over from lists to other data structures,
particularly trees.

Lists in Prolog

The simplest way of writing a list is to enumerate its elements. The list
consisting of the three atoms **a**, **b**, and **c** can be written as

```
[a, b, c]
```

The empty list is written as **[]**.

We can also specify an initial sequence of elements and a trailing list,
separated by |. The list **[a,b,c]** can also be written as

```
[a, b, c | []]
[a, b | [c]]
[a | [b, c]]
```

A special case of this notation is a list with head **H** and tail **T**, written as
[H|T]. The head is the first element of a list, and the tail is the list con-
sisting of the remaining elements.

Unification can be used to extract the components of a list, so explicit
operators for extracting the head and tail are not needed. The solution of
the query

```
?- [H|T] = [a,b,c].
   H = a
   T = [b,c]
```

binds variable **H** to the head and variable **T** to the tail of list **[a,b,c]**.
The query

```
?- [a|T] = [H, b, c].
   T = [b,c]
   H = a
```

illustrates Prolog's ability to deal with partially specified terms. The term
[a|T] is a partial specification of a list with head **a** and unknown tail
denoted by variable **T**. Similarly, **[H,b,c]** is a partial specification of a
list with unknown head **H** and tail **[b,c]**. For these two specifications to
unify, **H** must denote **a** and **T** must denote **[b,c]**.

Example 8.2. The append relation on lists is defined by the following rules:

```
append([], Y, Y).
append([H|X], Y, [H|Z]) :- append(X, Y, Z).
```

These rules are Prolog counterparts of the pseudo-English rules in Section 8.1. In words, the result of appending the empty list `[]` and a list `Y` is `Y`. If the result of appending `X` and `Y` is `Z`, then the result of appending `[H|X]` and `Y` is `[H|Z]`.

The responses to the following queries show that the rules for **append** can be used to compute any one of the arguments from the other two:

```
?- append([a,b], [c,d], Z).
    Z = [a,b,c,d]

?- append([a,b], Y, [a,b,c,d]).
    Y = [c,d]

?- append(X, [c,d], [a,b,c,d]).
    X = [a,b]
```

The following query shows that inconsistent arguments are rejected

```
?- append(X, [d,c], [a,b,c,d]).
    no
```

Difference lists discussed in Section 8.4 lead to a faster implementation of append.   □

Terms as Data

The connection between lists and terms is as follows. `[H|T]` is syntactic sugar for the term `.(H,T)`:

```
?- .(H, T) = [a,b,c].
    H = a
    T = [b,c]
```

Thus, the dot operator or functor `"."` corresponds to cons in Lisp, and lists are terms. The term for the list `[a,b,c]` is

```
.(a, .(b, .(c, [])))
```

There is a one-to-one correspondence between trees and terms. That is, any tree can be written as a term and any term can be drawn as a tree. Any data structure that can be simulated using trees can therefore be simulated using terms. Using an example from Section 2.8, binary trees can be written as terms, using an atom **leaf** for a leaf and a functor **nonleaf** with two arguments for a nonleaf node, as in Fig. 8.5.

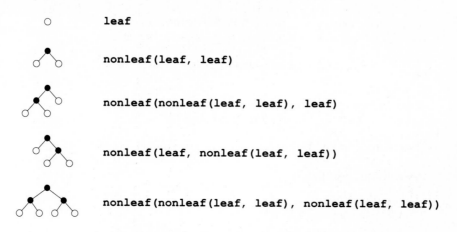

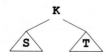

Fig. 8.5. Terms for representing binary trees.

Example 8.3. Example 2.5 on binary search trees, page 57, has a direct counterpart in Prolog. Let atom **empty** represent an empty binary search tree and let a term **node(K, S, T)** represent a tree

with an integer value **K** at the root, left subtree **S**, and right subtree **T**.

The rules in Fig. 8.6 define a relation **member** to test whether an integer appears at some node in a tree. The two arguments of **member** are an integer and a tree. The fact

    member(K, node(K,_,_)).

can be interpreted as saying that **K** appears in a tree if it appears at the root. Each occurrence of the special variable _ is a placeholder for a distinct unnamed term, so **node(K,_,_)** represents a binary search tree with **K** at the root and some unnamed left and right subtrees. We can emphasize that **member** is a relation on pairs consisting of an integer **K** and a tree **U** by restating the preceding rule as

    member(K, U) :- U = node(N,S,T), K = N.

The rule

    member(K, node(N,S,_)) :- K < N, member(K, S).

can be interpreted as

```
member(K, node(K,_,_)).
member(K, node(N,S,_)) :- K < N, member(K, S).
member(K, node(N,_,T)) :- K > N, member(K, T).
```

Fig. 8.6. Relation **member** on binary search trees.

K is in a tree *node* (N, S, _) **if**
    K < N **and** K is in the left subtree S.

We leave it to the reader to define a relation **insert** corresponding to

insert K into S to get T.

and a relation **delete** to remove an integer from a tree.   □

The atom **empty** and the functor **node** in Example 8.3 simulate the value constructors *empty* and *node* in the following datatype declaration, from Example 2.5:

datatype *searchtree* = *empty* | *node* **of int** * *searchtree* * *searchtree* ;

Other ML datatypes can be simulated similarly.

Beyond trees, variables in Prolog allow terms to represent data structures with sharing. The term **node(K,S,S)** represents a graph

Although this chapter does not explore the possibility, terms can also represent graphs with cycles.

8.4   PROGRAMMING TECHNIQUES

The programming techniques in this section exploit the strengths of Prolog; namely, backtracking and unification. Backtracking allows a solution to be found if one exists. Unification allows variables to be used as placeholders for data to be filled in later.

Careful use of the techniques in this section can lead to efficient programs. The programs in this section rely on the left-to-right evaluation of subgoals in Prolog. Therefore, variants of the programs may not work, for reasons that will become clear when control in Prolog is discussed in Section 8.5.

Guess and Verify

A *guess-and-verify* query has the form

> Is there an S such that
>   *guess* (S) **and** *verify* (S)?

where *guess* (S) and *verify* (S) are subgoals. Prolog responds to such a query by generating solutions to *guess* (S) until a solution satisfying *verify* (S) is found. Such queries are also called *generate-and-test* queries.

Similarly, a *guess-and-verify* rule has the following form:

> *conclusion* ($\cdots$) **if** *guess* ($\cdots, S, \cdots$) **and** *verify* ($\cdots, S, \cdots$)

Example 8.4. The guess-and-verify rule in this example is as follows:

```
overlap(X, Y) :- member(M, X), member(M, Y).
```

In words, two lists **X** and **Y** overlap if there is some **M** that is a member of both **X** and **Y**. The first goal **member(M,X)** guesses an **M** from list **X**, and the second goal **member(M, Y)** verifies that **M** also appears in list **Y**.

The rules for **member** are

```
member(M, [M |_]).
member(M, [_ |T]) :- member(M, T).
```

The first rule says that **M** is a member of a list with head **M**. The second rule says that **M** is a member of a list if **M** is a member of its tail **T**.

To see why

```
?- overlap([a,b,c,d], [1,2,c,d]).
    yes
```

produces a *yes* response, consider the query

```
?- member(M, [a,b,c,d]), member(M, [1,2,c,d]).
```

The first goal in this query generates solutions and the second goal tests to see whether they are acceptable. The solutions generated by the first goal are

```
?- member(M, [a,b,c,d]).
    M = a ;
    M = b ;
    M = c ;
    M = d ;
    no
```

The first two are not acceptable, but the third is

```
?- member(a, [1,2,c,d]).
     no

?- member(b, [1,2,c,d]).
     no

?- member(c, [1,2,c,d]).
     yes
```

                                                                    □

Hint. Since computation in Prolog proceeds from left to right, the order of the subgoals in a guess-and-verify query can affect efficiency. Choose the subgoal with fewer solutions as the guess goal.

As an extreme example of the effect of goal order on efficiency, consider the following two queries:

```
?- X = [1,2,3], member(a,X).
     no

?- member(a,X), X = [1,2,3].
     [ infinite computation ]
```

Relation **member** is as in Example 8.4. In

```
?- X = [1,2,3], member(a,X).
     no
```

the guess goal **X=[1,2,3]** has just one solution, and this solution does not satisfy **member(a,X)** because **a** is not in the list **[1,2,3]**. On the other hand, in

```
?- member(a,X), X = [1,2,3].
     [ infinite computation ]
```

the guess goal **member(a,X)** has an infinite number of solutions:

```
X = [a|_] ;          a can be the first element of X
X = [_,a,|_] ;       a can be the second element of X
X = [_,_,a,|_] ;     a can be the third element of X
   ...
```

none of which binds **X** to the list **[1,2,3]**. Hence, an infinite computation ensues as Prolog tries the solutions in turn, looking for one that satisfies **X=[1,2,3]**.

Variables as Placeholders

So far in this chapter, variables have been used in rules and queries, but not in terms representing objects. Terms containing variables can be used to simulate modifiable data structures; the variables serve as placeholders for subterms to be filled in later. Such terms will be used in Example 8.5 to implement queues efficiently.

Recall the use of terms to represent binary trees in Section 8.3:

leaf

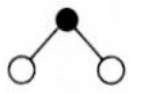

nonleaf(leaf, leaf)

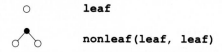

The terms **leaf** and **nonleaf(leaf,leaf)** are completely specified. By contrast, the list **[a,b|X]** containing a variable **X** is partially specified because we do not yet know what **X** represents. This list **[a,b|X]** has **a** as its first element, has **b** as its second element, and has a variable **X** representing the rest of the list. If **X** is subsequently unified with **[]**, then **[a,b|X]** will represent **[a,b]**, but if **X** is unified with **[c]**, then **[a,b|X]** will represent **[a,b,c]**, and so on, for other possible values for **X**.

An *open* list is a list ending in a variable, referred to as the *endmarker* variable of the list. An empty open list consists of just an endmarker variable. A list is *closed* if it is not open.

Internally, Prolog uses machine-generated variables, written with a leading underscore _ followed by an integer. In the following interaction, the machine-generated variable **_1** corresponds to the endmarker **X**:

```
?- L = [a,b|X].
     L = [a,b|_1]
     X = _1
```

Prolog generates fresh variables each time it responds to a query or applies a rule.

An open list can be modified by unifying its endmarker. The following query extends **L** into a new open list with endmarker **Y** (see Fig. 8.7):

```
?- L = [a,b|X], X = [c,Y].
     L = [a,b,c|_2]
     X = [c|_2]
     Y = _2
```

Unification of an endmarker variable is akin to an assignment to that variable. In Fig. 8.7, list **L** changes from **[a,b|_1]** to **[a,b,c|_2]** when **_1** unifies with **[c|_2]**.

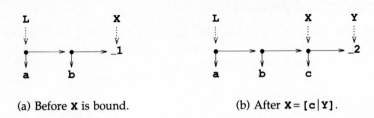

(a) Before **X** is bound.   (b) After **X** = [c|Y].

Fig. 8.7. Extending an open list by unifying its endmarker.

```
setup(q(X,X)).

enter(A, q(X,Y), q(X,Z))  :- Y = [A|Z].

leave(A, q(X,Z), q(Y,Z))  :- X = [A|Y].

wrapup(q([],[])).
```

Fig. 8.8. Rules for manipulating queues.

An advantage of working with open lists is that the end of a list can be accessed quickly, in constant time, through its endmarker. The following example uses open lists to implement queues.

Example 8.5. This example discusses the rules in Fig. 8.8 for manipulating queues. The relation **enter(a, Q, R)** is described informally by

When element **a** enters queue **Q**, we get queue **R**.

Similarly, **leave(a, Q, R)** is described by

When element **a** leaves queue **Q**, we get queue **R**.

When a queue is created, it is represented by a term of the form **q(L, E)**, where **L** is an open list with endmarker **E**. Subsequent operations will, in general, extend the list **L**, as in the following diagram:

Therefore, **L** in **q(L, E)** represents an open list, **E** represents some suffix of **L**, and the contents of the queue **q(L, E)** are the elements of **L** that are not in **E**.

The implementation of queues is illustrated in Fig. 8.9, which shows the effect of the query

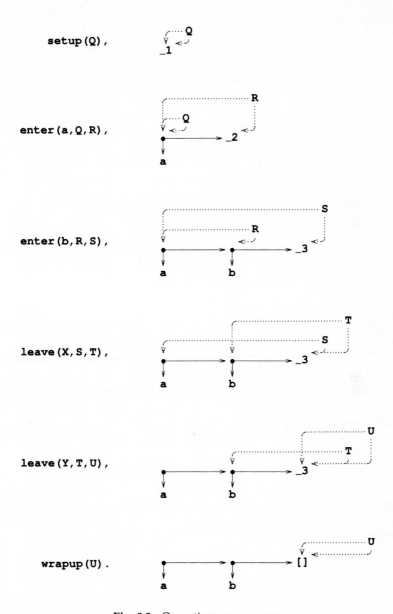

Fig. 8.9. Operations on a queue.

```
?- setup(Q), enter(a,Q,R), enter(b,R,S),
      leave(X,S,T), leave(Y,T,U), wrapup(U).
```

The first goal **setup(Q)** creates an empty queue:

```
?- setup(Q).
    Q = q(_1,_1)
```

In Fig. 8.9, a queue **q(L,E)** is marked by dotted arrows to **L** and **E**. The arrows from **Q** therefore go to the empty open list **_1** with endmarker **_1**.

Now consider the second goal **enter(a,Q,R)**. The rule

```
enter(A, q(X,Y), q(X,Z)) :- Y = [A|Z].
```

can be read as

> To enter A into a queue $q(X, Y)$,
>   bind Y to a list $[A \mid Z]$, where Z is a fresh endmarker,
>   and return the resulting queue $q(X, Z)$.

After **setup(Q)** initializes **Q** to **q(_1,_1)**, the second goal in

```
?- setup(Q), enter(a,Q,R).
    Q = ···
    R = q([a|_2],_2)
```

unifies **_1** with **[a|_2]**, where **_2** is a fresh endmarker.

The third goal **enter(b,R,S)** enters **b** into **q([a|_2],_2)** by unifying **_2** with **[b|_3]**, where **_3** is a fresh variable.

When an element leaves a queue **q(L,E)**, the resulting queue has the tail of **L** in place of **L**. Note in the diagram to the right of **leave(X,S,T)** that the open list for queue **T** is the tail of the open list for **S**. Similarly, in the diagram to the right of **leave(Y,T,U)**, the open list for **U** is the tail of the open list for **T**.

The final goal **wrapup(U)** checks that the enter and leave operations leave **U** in an initial state **q(L,E)**, where **L** is an empty open list with endmarker **E**. Otherwise, **q(L,E)** will not unify with **q([],[])** in the fact

```
wrapup(q([],[])).
```

In Fig. 8.9, **U** refers to **q(_3,_3)** and **wrapup(q(_3,_3))** unifies **_3** with **[]**.   □

Surprisingly, the rules for queues in Fig. 8.8 support "deficit" queues, which an element can leave before it enters. More precisely, an unspecified element represented by a variable can leave and be later filled in by an enter operation. In the following query, element **X** leaves the initial queue before we learn from the goal **enter(a,R,S)** that **X** represents **a**:

```
?- setup(Q), leave(X, Q, R), enter(a, R, S), wrapup(S).
      Q = q([a],[a])
      X = a
      R = q([],[a])
      S = q([],[])
```

Difference Lists

Applications that use lists can be adapted to use open lists instead. Open-list versions require more care, but they can be more efficient. Care is needed because an open list changes when its endmarker is unified (see Fig. 8.7). Difference lists are a technique for coping with such changes.

A *difference list* is made up of two lists **L** and **E**, where **E** unifies with a suffix of **L**. The contents of the difference list consist of the elements that are in **L** but not in **E**. We write this difference list as **dl(L,E)**. The lists **L** and **E** can be either open or closed. They are typically open.

Examples of difference lists with contents **[a,b]** are

```
dl([a,b], []).
dl([a,b,c], [c]).
dl([a,b|E], E).
dl([a,b,c|F], [c|F]).
```

In effect, the variables in **dl(L,E)** allow us to refer directly to the end-points of its contents. The append operation on difference lists can be implemented in constant time using a nonrecursive rule. An informal reading of the following rule is that if **X** extends from **L** up to **M** and **Y** extends from **M** to **N**, then **Z**, the result of appending **X** and **Y**, extends from **L** to **N**:

```
append_dl(X, Y, Z) :-
     X = dl(L,M), Y = dl(M,N), Z = dl(L,N).
```

We close this section with an example that leads into the discussion of control in Prolog in Section 8.5. It is tempting to define a rule

```
contents(X, dl(L,E)) :- append(X, E, L).
```

to formalize the notion that the contents of **dl(L,E)** are the elements that are in **L** but not in **E**. The following queries confirm that each of the following difference lists has contents **[a,b]**:

```
?- contents([a,b], dl([a,b,c], [c])).
   yes
```

```
?- contents([a,b], dl([a,b,c|F], [c|F])).
   F = _1
   yes
```

An attempt to ask for the contents of **dl([a,b|E],E)** leads to a response
that will be explained in Section 8.5:

```
?- contents(X, dl([a,b|E], E)).
   X = []
   E = [a,b,a,b,a,b,a,b,a,b,a,b,a,b,a,b,a,b,  ...
```

8.5   CONTROL IN PROLOG

In the informal equation

algorithm = logic + control

"logic" refers to the rules and queries in a logic program and "control"
refers to how a language computes a response to a query. The pseudo-
code in Fig. 8.10 is an overview of control in Prolog.
   Control in Prolog is characterized by two decisions in Fig. 8.10:

1. *Goal order.* Choose the leftmost subgoal.

2. *Rule order.* Select the first applicable rule.

The response to a query is affected both by goal order within the query
and by rule order within the database of facts and rules.

Example 8.6. The examples in this section use the rules in Fig. 8.11.
   A sublist S of Z

can be specified in the following seemingly equivalent ways:

```
start with a query as the current goal;
while the current goal is nonempty do
        choose the leftmost subgoal;
        if a rule applies to the subgoal then
                select the first applicable rule;
                form a new current goal
        else
                backtrack
        end if
end while;
succeed
```

Fig. 8.10. Control in Prolog.

```
append([], Y, Y).
append([H|X], Y, [H|Z]) :- append(X,Y,Z).

prefix(X,Z) :- append(X,Y,Z).

suffix(Y,Z) :- append(X,Y,Z).

appen2([H|X], Y, [H|Z]) :- appen2(X,Y,Z).
appen2([], Y, Y).
```

Fig. 8.11. Database of rules for examples in Section 8.5.

prefix X of Z **and** suffix S of X.
suffix S of X **and** prefix X of Z.

The corresponding Prolog queries usually produce the same responses. Their responses differ, however, if S is not a sublist of Z:

```
?- prefix(X,[a,b,c]), suffix([e],X).
   no

?- suffix([e],X), prefix(X,[a,b,c]).
   [ infinite computation ]
```

We look closely at the suffix-prefix goal order in this section.

Rule order can also make a difference. New solutions are produced on demand for

```
?- append(X, [c], Z).
   X = []
   Z = [c] ;

   X = [_1]
   Z = [_1,c] ;

   X = [_1,_2]
   Z = [_1,_2,c]

   yes
```

(Recall that the *yes* means there might be more solutions.)

Relation **appen2** in Fig. 8.11 has the same rules as **append**, but they are written in the opposite order. The response

```
?- appen2(X, [c], Z).
   [ infinite computation ]
```

is also explained in this section.   □

Unification and Substitutions

Since unification is central to control in Prolog, we now define it more formally than on page 307.

A *substitution* is a function from variables to terms. Let us write a substitution as a set of elements of the form $X \to T$, where variable X is mapped to term T. Unless stated otherwise, if a substitution maps X to T, then variable X does not occur in term T. An example of a substitution is $\{V \to [b,c], Y \to [a,b,c]\}$.

$T\sigma$ is a standard notation for the result of applying substitution σ to term T. The result of applying a substitution to a term is given by

$$X\sigma = U \qquad\qquad \text{if } X \to U \text{ is in } \sigma$$

$$X\sigma = X \qquad\qquad \text{otherwise, for variable } X$$

$$(f(T_1, T_2))\sigma = f(U_1, U_2) \qquad \text{if } T_1\sigma = U_1, \ T_2\sigma = U_2$$

This definition generalizes to functors f with $k \geq 0$ arguments. In words, if σ contains $X \to U$, then the result of applying σ to variable X is U; otherwise $X\sigma$ is simply X. The result of applying σ to a term $f(T_1, \ldots, T_k)$, for $k \geq 0$ is obtained by applying σ to each subterm. For example,

$$Y \{V \to [b,c], Y \to [a,b,c]\} = [a,b,c]$$

$$Z \{V \to [b,c], Y \to [a,b,c]\} = Z$$

$$(append([\,],Y,Y)) \{V \to [b,c], Y \to [a,b,c]\} = append([\,],[a,b,c],[a,b,c])$$

A term U is an *instance* of T, if $U = T\sigma$, for some substitution σ. Terms T_1 and T_2 unify if $T_1\sigma$ and $T_2\sigma$ are identical for some substitution σ; we call σ a *unifier* of T_1 and T_2. Substitution σ is the *most general unifier* of T_1 and T_2, if for all other unifiers σ', $T_1\sigma'$ is an instance of $T_1\sigma$.[5]

The terms $append([\,], Y, Y)$ and $append([\,], [a|V], [a,b,c])$ unify because they have a common instance $append([\,], [a,b,c], [a,b,c])$. Their most general unifier is the substitution $\{V \to [b,c], Y \to [a,b,c]\}$.

Applying a Rule to a Goal

The pseudo-code in Fig. 8.12 restates control in Prolog in terms of substitutions and unifiers. We explore it by first considering an example that succeeds without backtracking. Backtracking is then described in terms of a tree representation of a computation.

In Fig. 8.12, a rule $A :- B_1, \ldots, B_n$ *applies* to a subgoal G if its head A unifies with G. Variables in the rule are renamed before unification to keep them distinct from variables in the subgoal.

[5] In the definition of most general unifier, it is enough to say that $T_1\sigma'$ is an instance of $T_1\sigma$. Since σ and σ' are both unifiers, $T_2\sigma'$ is automatically an instance of $T_2\sigma$, because $T_1\sigma = T_2\sigma$ and $T_1\sigma' = T_2\sigma'$.

start with a query as the current goal;
while the current goal is nonempty **do**
      let the current goal be $G_1, \ldots, G_k$, where $k \geq 1$;
      choose the leftmost subgoal G_1;
      if a rule applies to G_1 **then**
          select the first such rule $A :- B_1, \ldots, B_j$, where $j \geq 0$;
          let σ be the most general unifier of G_1 and A;
          the current goal becomes $B_1\sigma, \ldots, B_j\sigma, G_2\sigma, \ldots, G_k\sigma$
    else
        backtrack
    end if
end while;
succeed

Fig. 8.12. Control in Prolog: restatement of Fig. 8.10.

Example 8.7. The response to the query

```
?- suffix([a],L), prefix(L,[a,b,c]).
    L = [a]
```

is computed without backtracking, as in Fig. 8.13. Initially, the current goal consists of the two subgoals in this query:

$$\texttt{suffix([a],L), prefix(L,[a,b,c])} \tag{8.7}$$

Choose the leftmost subgoal **suffix([a],L)**. Select the only rule that applies to this subgoal. Rename the variables in the rule to keep them distinct from any variables in the goal. With **X′**, **Y′**, and **Z′** as the renamed variables, the rule for **suffix** becomes

```
suffix(Y', Z') :- append(X', Y', Z').
```

The substitution $\{\texttt{Y}' \to \texttt{[a]}, \texttt{Z}' \to \texttt{L}\}$ unifies the rule head with the chosen subgoal. The rule as it applies to the subgoal **suffix([a],L)** is given by the pseudo-code:

suffix ([a], L) **if** *append* (_1, [a], L)

Here, [a] takes the place of **Y′**, L takes the place of **Z′**, and a Prolog-like name _1 takes the place of **X′**.

Replace the subgoal **suffix([a],L)** in (8.7) by the condition **append(_1, [a], L)** to get the new current goal:

$$\texttt{append(\_1,[a],L), prefix(L,[a,b,c])} \tag{8.8}$$

The fact **append([],Y″,Y″)** applies to the new leftmost subgoal **append(_1,[a],L)** because **[]** unifies _1 and **Y″** unifies with both **[a]**

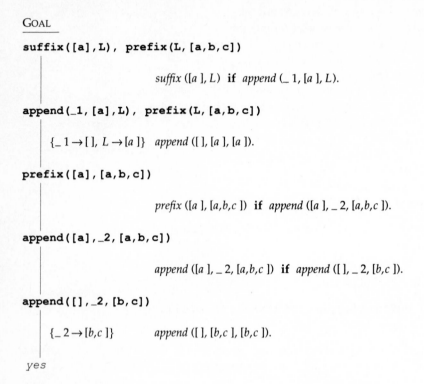

<small>GOAL</small>

`suffix([a],L), prefix(L,[a,b,c])`

suffix ([a], L) **if** append (_ 1, [a], L).

`append(_1,[a],L), prefix(L,[a,b,c])`

{_ 1 → [ ], L → [a]} append ([ ], [a], [a]).

`prefix([a],[a,b,c])`

prefix ([a], [a,b,c]) **if** append ([a], _ 2, [a,b,c]).

`append([a],_2,[a,b,c])`

append ([a], _ 2, [a,b,c]) **if** append ([ ], _ 2, [b,c]).

`append([],_2,[b,c])`

{_ 2 → [b,c]}   append ([ ], [b,c], [b,c]).

yes

Fig. 8.13. A computation that succeeds without backtracking.

and **L**. Since a fact consists of a head and no conditions, the new current goal is

$$\texttt{prefix([a],[a,b,c])} \qquad\qquad (8.9)$$

Note that **[a]** has been substituted for variable **L**.

The rest of the computation can be seen from Fig. 8.13.   □

Prolog Search Trees

The chain of goals in Fig. 8.13 generalizes into *Prolog search trees,* which depict computations that explore all possible solutions to a goal. Nodes in a Prolog search tree represent goals. A node has a child for each rule that applies to the leftmost subgoal at the node. The order of the children is the same as the rule order in the database of rules.[6]

A Prolog computation explores a Prolog search tree in a "depth-first" manner. It starts at the root and explores the subtrees at the children of each node from left to right. The computation produces a *yes* response each time it reaches a node in the subtree with an empty goal.

Example 8.8. A portion of the Prolog search tree for the query

```
?- suffix([b], L), prefix(L, [a,b,c]).
   L = [a,b]
```

appears in Fig. 8.14.

There is only one rule for **suffix**, so the root has only one child. The approach of Example 8.7 yields the following goal at the child of the root:

$$\texttt{suffix([b], L), prefix(L, [a,b,c])}$$
$$\texttt{append(\_1, [b], L), prefix(L, [a,b,c])}$$

$$\{\_1 \rightarrow [\,], L \rightarrow [b\,]\}$$

$$\texttt{prefix([b], [a,b,c])}$$
$$\texttt{append([b], \_2, [a,b,c])}$$

$$\texttt{backtrack}$$

$$\{\_1 \rightarrow [\_3 \mid \_4], L \rightarrow [\_3 \mid \_5]\}$$

$$\texttt{append(\_4, [b], \_5), prefix([\_3\mid\_5], [a,b,c])}$$

$$\{\_4 \rightarrow [\,], \_5 \rightarrow [b\,]\}$$

$$\texttt{prefix([\_3,b], [a,b,c])}$$
$$\texttt{append([\_3,b], \_6, [a,b,c])}$$

$$\{\_3 \rightarrow a\}$$ $$\cdots$$

$$\texttt{append([b], \_6, [b,c])}$$
$$\texttt{append([], \_6, [c])}$$

$$\{\_6 \rightarrow [c\,]\}$$

yes

Fig. 8.14. Portion of a Prolog search tree leading to a *yes* response.

[6] The definition of Prolog search trees presupposes that rules are applied to the leftmost subgoal. A more general definition of search trees would allow any subgoal to be chosen as the subgoal to which rules are applied. Furthermore, a more general definition would allow rules to be selected in any order.

$$\texttt{append(\_1, [b], L), prefix(L, [a,b,c])} \tag{8.10}$$

Both of the rules for append apply to the leftmost subgoal in (8.10). The node for (8.10) therefore has two children. Prolog tries rules in the order they appear in the database of rules. It therefore unifies `append(_1, [b], L)` with `append([], Y', Y')` to get the substitution

$$\{\_1 \rightarrow [], \ L \rightarrow [b]\}$$

Since the first rule for **append** is a fact, it has no conditions, so the new goal formed from (8.10) is

$$\texttt{prefix([b], [a,b,c])} \tag{8.11}$$

There is only one rule for **prefix**, and it leads to a new goal,

$$\texttt{append([b], \_2, [a,b,c])} \tag{8.12}$$

Now we have a problem. This subgoal does not unify with either of the rules for **append**. Prolog therefore backtracks to the nearest goal with an untried rule. Such a goal is (8.10), reproduced here:

$$\texttt{append(\_1, [b], L), prefix(L, [a,b,c])} \tag{8.10}$$

The first rule for **append** did not lead to success, so Prolog tries the second one. A suitable instance of the second rule is

$$\texttt{append([\_3|\_4], [b], [\_3|\_5]) :- append(\_4, [b], \_5).}$$

A new goal is formed from (8.10) using the substitution

$$\{\_1 \rightarrow [\_3|\_4], \ L \rightarrow [\_3|\_5]\}$$

The new goal is

$$\texttt{append(\_4, [b], \_5), prefix([\_3|\_5], [a,b,c])} \tag{8.13}$$

The computation now proceeds without backtracking to a *yes* response in Fig. 8.14.   □

See Fig. 8.15 for a final restatement of control in Prolog. Procedure *visit* calls itself recursively to try new subgoals. In terms of search trees, a recursive call corresponds to visiting one of the children of a node. The recursion can stop in one of two ways:

1. The goal G is empty and **succeed** is reached.

2. No rule applies to the leftmost subgoal of G and the activation ends.

Backtracking corresponds to the latter case, in which no rule applies to G and control returns to the caller.

procedure *visit* (G);
begin
      if the current goal G is nonempty **then**
          let G be $G_1, \ldots, G_k$, where $k \geq 1$;
          choose the leftmost subgoal G_1;
          for $i := 1$ **to** the number of rules **do**
              let rule i be $A :- B_1, \ldots, B_j$, where $j \geq 0$;
              if rule i applies to G_1 **then**
                 let σ be the most general unifier of G_1 and A;
                 let G' be $B_1\sigma, \ldots, B_j\sigma, G_2\sigma, \ldots, G_k\sigma$;
                 visit (G')
              end if
          end for
      else
          succeed
      end if
      { backtrack by returning to caller }
end *visit*

Fig. 8.15. Control in Prolog as a recursive procedure.

Goal Order Changes Solutions

The order of subgoals within a query affects the Prolog search tree for a query. The reason is that rules are always applied to the leftmost subgoal.

From Example 8.7 or from Fig. 8.13, the solution `L=[a]` to the following query is produced without backtracking. Note, however, that an infinite computation ensues if we ask for another solution.

```
?- suffix([a],L), prefix(L,[a,b,c]).
    L = [a] ;
    [ infinite computation ]
```

The leftmost subgoal

```
?- suffix([a],L).
    L = [a] ;
    L = [_1,a] ;
    L = [_1,_2,a] ;
    ...
```

has an infinite number of solutions, only the first of which satisfies `prefix(L,[a,b,c])`.

In other words, the Prolog search tree for the goal

```
suffix([a],L), prefix(L,[a,b,c])
```

has exactly one *yes* node that is reached without backtracking as in Fig. 8.13. A futile search through the rest of the infinite tree ensues if we ask for a further solution.

By contrast, the reordered query

```
?- prefix(X,[a,b,c]), suffix([a],X).
    L = [a] ;
    no
```

has a finite Prolog search tree. The portion leading up to the only *yes* node appears in Fig. 8.16. The same solution *L=[a]* is reached without backtracking in Fig. 8.13 and with backtracking in Fig. 8.16. Hence, a change in goal order leads to a change in the Prolog search tree.

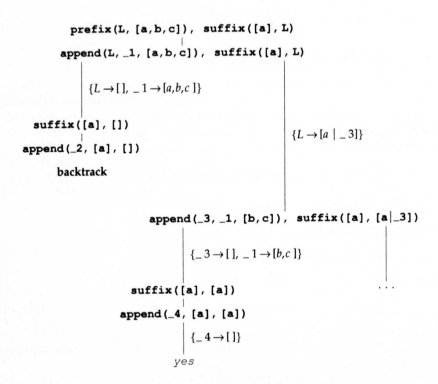

Fig. 8.16. Effect of changing goal order. Compare with Fig. 8.13.

Rule Order Affects the Search for Solutions

The rule order in the database of rules determines the order of the children of a node in a Prolog search tree. Rule order therefore changes the order in which solutions are reached by a Prolog computation.

The Prolog search trees in Fig. 8.17 are based on the following rule order:

```
append([], Y, Y).
append([H|X], Y, [H|Z]) :- append(X,Y,Z).

appen2([H|X], Y, [H|Z]) :- appen2(X,Y,Z).
appen2([], Y, Y).
```

The search tree for **appen2(X, [c], Z)** is a mirror image of the search tree for **append(X, [c], Z)**. Unfortunately, the Prolog computation for **appen2(X, [c], Z)** never reaches a solution because it keeps going deeper and deeper down an infinite path:

```
?- appen2(X, [c], Z).
    [ infinite computation ]
```

The computation for **append(X, [c], Z)**, on the other hand, goes from one solution to the next:

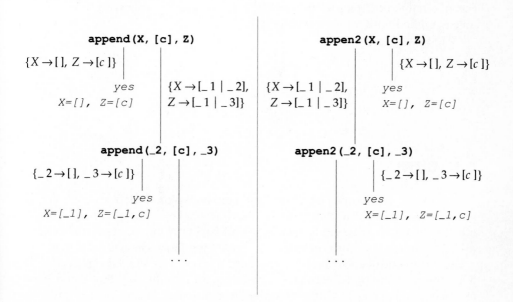

Fig. 8.17. Rule order determines the order of the children of a node.

```
?- append(X, [c], Z).
    X = []
    Z = [c] ;

    X = [_1]
    Z = [_1,c] ;
    ...
```

The Occurs-Check Problem

In the name of efficiency, Prolog neglects to check whether a variable X occurs in a term T before it unifies X with T; such checks are called *occurs checks*. When X does indeed occur in T, then unification of X and T can lead to a nonterminating computation. For example, consider

```
?- append([], E, [a,b|E]).
    E = [a,b,a,b,a,b,a,b,a,b,a,b,a,b,a,b,a,b, ···
```

For `append([],E,[a,b|E])` to unify with `append([],Y,Y)`, variable `Y` must unify with both `E` and with the term `[a,b|E]` containing `E`.

Prolog neglects to check whether `E` occurs within `[a,b|E]`. When we attempt to substitute `[a,b|E]` for `E`, we get

$$E = [a,b|E] = [a,b,a,b|E] = [a,b,a,b,a,b|E] = ···$$

Some variants of Prolog construct cyclic terms like the following if a variable is unified with a term containing it:

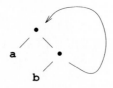

8.6   CUTS

Informally, a cut prunes or "cuts out" an unexplored part of a Prolog search tree. Cuts can therefore be used to make a computation more efficient by eliminating futile searching and backtracking. Cuts can also be used to implement a form of negation, something Horn clauses cannot do.

Cuts are controversial because they are impure. As we saw in Section 8.5, control in Prolog sometimes sends it into an infinite loop that could be avoided by choosing a different order of evaluation. Pure logic is order independent, so Prolog is an approximation of pure logic. Cuts make Prolog depart further from pure logic, to the point where a Prolog program must be read procedurally; that is, it must be read in terms of its computation.

A *cut*, written as **!**, appears as a condition within a rule. When a rule

$$B :- C_1, \ldots, C_{j-1}, !, C_{j+1}, \ldots, C_k$$

is applied during a computation, the cut tells control to backtrack past $C_{j-1}, \ldots, C_1, B$, without considering any remaining rules for them. We explore the implications of this remark before considering programming applications of cuts.

A Cut as the First Condition

Consider rules of the form $B :- !, C$, in which a cut appears as the first condition. If the goal C fails, then control backtracks past B without considering any remaining rules for B. Thus, the cut has the effect of making B fail if C fails.

To see the effect of a cut on a Prolog search tree, consider the following rules for **b**:

```
b :- c.
b :- d.
b :- e.
```

Since there are three rules for **b**, any node with **b** as the first subgoal has three children, one for each rule. Suppose that the condition at a node is b, G, where G represents some additional subgoals. Then the subtree rooted at the node has the following form:

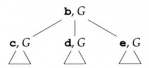

Now, suppose a cut is inserted in the second rule, changing it to

```
b :- !, d.
```

This cut eliminates the rule **b:-e** from ever being considered. The new Prolog search tree is as follows. (The dotted part is shown only for comparison; it is not part of the new search tree.)

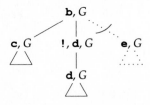

In more detail, a cut as the first subgoal in **!, d,** *G* is satisfied immediately, leaving **d,** *G* as the new goal. During backtracking, however, the cut has the side effect of eliminating the third rule **b :-e** from consideration.

Example 8.9. The following database of rules is designed specifically for the Prolog search tree in Fig. 8.18(a):

```
a(1)  :- b.
a(2)  :- e.
b  :- c.
b  :- d.
d.
e.
```

The query **a(X)** has two solutions:

```
?- a(X).
    X = 1 ;
    X = 2 ;
    no
```

If the rule **b:-c** is changed to **b:-!,c** by inserting a cut as the first condition, the Prolog search tree changes to the one in Fig. 8.18(b). The query **a(X)** then has just one solution:

```
?- a(X).
    X = 2 ;
    no                                                            □
```

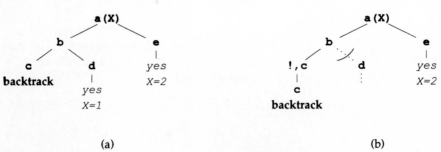

(a)   (b)

Fig. 8.18. Effect of a cut.

The Effect of a Cut

As mentioned earlier, when a rule

$$B :- C_1, \ldots, C_{j-1}, !, C_{j+1}, \ldots, C_k$$

is applied during a computation, the cut tells control to backtrack past $C_{j-1}, \ldots, C_1, B$, without considering any remaining rules for them.

The following example considers the effect of inserting a cut in the middle of a guess-and-verify rule. As discussed in Section 8.4, the right side of a guess-and-verify rule has the form *guess* (S), *verify* (S), where *guess* (S) generates potential solutions until one satisfying *verify* (S) is found. The effect of inserting a cut between them, as in

> *conclusion* (S) :– *guess* (S), !, *verify* (S)

is to eliminate all but the first guess.

Example 8.10. The search trees in Fig. 8.19 are based on the rules in Fig. 8.20. The computation depicted by Fig. 8.19(a) begins with the succession of goals:

a(Z)	*starting goal*
b(Z)	*from* a (X) :– b (X).
g(Z), v(Z)	*from* b (X) :– g (X), v (X).

The subgoal **g(Z)** generates values **1**, **2**, and **3** for **Z**. Each of these values leads to a solution of the original goal **a(Z)**.

The fourth solution $Z=4$ in Fig. 8.19(a) is obtained by backtracking and trying the alternative rule for **b**:

> **b(X)   :– X=4, v(X) .**

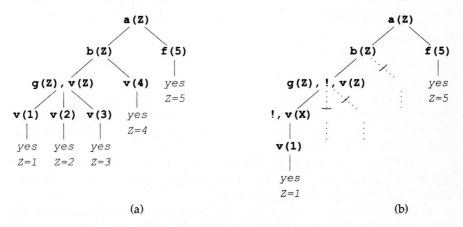

(a)   (b)

Fig. 8.19. Solutions eliminated by a cut.

```
a(X)  :- b(X).                  a(X)  :- b(X).
a(X)  :- f(X).                  a(X)  :- f(X).
b(X)  :- g(X), v(X).            b(X)  :- g(X), !, v(X).
b(X)  :- X = 4, v(X).           b(X)  :- X = 4, v(X).
g(1).                           g(1).
g(2).                           g(2).
g(3).                           g(3).
v(X).                           v(X).
f(5).                           f(5).

        (a)                             (b)
```

Fig. 8.20. Insertion of a cut in the third rule.

We get to the final solution $Z=5$ by backtracking all the way back to the original goal **a(Z)** and trying the rule

```
a(X)  :- f(X).
```

Now, consider the database of Fig. 8.20(b), where a cut appears in the first rule for **b**:

```
b(X)  :- g(X), !, v(X).
```

The insertion of this cut changes the Prolog search tree in Fig. 8.19(a) into the tree in Fig. 8.19(b). This cut tells control to backtrack past **g(X)** and **b(X)** without considering any remaining rules for **g** and **b**, as in Fig. 8.19(b). The goal **a(Z)** now has just two solutions.   □

Cuts in Prolog are frequently misunderstood, perhaps with good reason. From the search tree in Fig. 8.19(b), the query **a(Z)** has two solutions:

```
?- a(Z).
    Z = 1 ;
    Z = 5 ;
    no
```

We might expect from these responses that **a(2)**, **a(3)**, and **a(4)** are unsatisfiable. In fact, the search trees in Fig. 8.21 reach a *yes* response for each of **a(2)**, **a(3)**, and **a(4)**.

The queries **a(2)** and **a(3)** lead to a *yes* response without backtracking, as in Fig. 8.21(a-b). Since no backtracking is needed, the cut does not prevent the computation from reaching a *yes*.

Finally consider the query **a(4)**. The computation in Fig. 8.21(c) never reaches the cut, because **g(4)** is unsatisfiable. The cut therefore has no effect, and the computation reaches a *yes*.

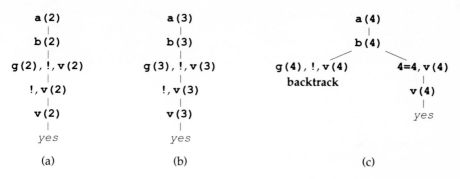

Fig. 8.21. Prolog search trees based on the rules in Fig. 8.20(b).

Programming Applications of Cuts

A relatively benign use of cuts is to prune parts of a Prolog search tree that cannot possibly reach a solution. Such cuts have been called *green* cuts; they make a program efficient without changing its solutions. Cuts that are not green are called *red*.

By restricting backtracking, cuts reduce the memory requirements of a program. Without cuts, every single rule application and unification has to be recorded until the overall computation succeeds or backtracking occurs.

Example 8.11. For an example of green cuts, consider the following rules for binary search trees, from Fig. 8.6, page 312:

```
member(K, node(K,_,_)).
member(K, node(N,S,_)) :- K < N, member(K, S).
member(K, node(N,_,T)) :- K > N, member(K, T).
```

These three rules are mutually exclusive because only one of **K=N**, **K<N**, and **K>N** can be true at a time. The cut in the second rule,

```
member(K, node(K,_,_)).
member(K, node(N,S,_)) :- K < N, !, member(K, S).
member(K, node(N,_,T)) :- K > N, member(K, T).
```

is therefore a green cut. It is reached only if **K<N**, so the third rule cannot possibly apply if the cut is reached. The cut makes the program more efficient in the following case: **K<N** but **member(K,S)** fails because **K** is not in the tree. Without the cut, Prolog will backtrack and try the third rule, only to fail on the test **K>N**—there could be many such futile tests during a single unsuccessful search.   □

Variants of the **lookup** relation in the following example have been used in compilers written in Prolog. The compilers use binary search trees.

For simplicity, however, the example uses linear search to look for a key in a list of key-value pairs.[7]

Example 8.12. The only difference between the rules for **lookup** and **install** is a cut in the first rule for **lookup**:

```
lookup(K,V, [(K,W)|_]) :- !, V = W.
lookup(K,V, [_|Z]) :- lookup(K,V,Z).

install(K,V, [(K,W)|_]) :- V = W.
install(K,V, [_|Z]) :- install(K,V,Z).
```

The **lookup** relation can be used to enter information into a table of key-value pairs. The table is maintained as an open list, ending in a variable.

```
?- lookup(p,72,D).
    D = [(p,72)|_1] ;
    no
```

(Recall that we type a semicolon to ask for more solutions. The *no* response means that there are no more solutions.) An attempt to enter two different values for the same key ends in failure:

```
?- lookup(p,72,D), lookup(p,73,D).
    no
```

The following query uses relation **lookup** both to enter pairs and to look up a value:

```
?- lookup(1,58,D), lookup(p,72,D), lookup(p,Y,D).
    D = [(1,58),(p,72)|_1]
    Y = 72 ;

    no
```

Lacking the cut, relation **install** behaves quite differently. The following query has an infinite number of solutions:

```
?- install(p,72,D).
    [(p,72)|_1] ;
    [_2,(p,72)|_3] ;
    [_2,_4,(p,72)|_5]

    yes
```

Relation **install** also allows two different values to be entered for the same key:

[7] The simplified syntax of terms in Section 8.2 does not allow terms of the form (K,V), but Prolog does. The term (K,V) is a pair with first component K and second component V.

```
?- install(p,72,D), install(p,73,D).
    [(p,72),(p,73)|_1] ;
```

The role of the cut can be seen more clearly from the following equivalent version of the above rules for **lookup**:

```
lookup(K,V,L)  :- L = [(K,W)|_], !, V = W.
lookup(K,V,L)  :- L = [_|Z], lookup(K,V,Z).
```

If **D** is a fresh variable, we get the following succession of goals:

```
lookup(p,72,D)                    starting goal
D=[(p,_1)|_2], !, 72=_1           apply first rule
!, 72=_1                          D unifies
72=_1
yes                               72 unifies with _1
```

The cut prevents further solutions by eliminating consideration of the second rule for **lookup**.

Now consider the query

```
?- lookup(p,72,D), lookup(p,73,D).
    no
```

As we just saw, the subgoal **lookup(p,72,D)** leaves **D** bound to a list [(p,72)|_2]. We therefore get the following succession of goals:

```
lookup(p,73,[(p,72)|_2])
[(p,72)|_2]=[(p,_3)|_4], !, 73=_3      apply first rule
!, 73=72                                the lists unify
73=72
```

The cut forces failure by preventing consideration of the second rule for **lookup**.   □

Negation as Failure

The **not** operator in Prolog is implemented by the rules

```
not(X)  :- X, !, fail.
not(_).
```

Informally, the first rule attempts to satisfy the argument **X** of **not**. If the goal **X** succeeds, then the cut and **fail** are reached. The construct **fail** forces failure and the cut prevents consideration of the second rule. On the other hand, if the goal **X** fails, then the second rule succeeds, because _ unifies with any term.

These rules for **not** explain the difference between the responses to

```
?- X = 2, not(X = 1).
    X = 2
```

and

```
?- not(X = 1), X = 2.
    no
```

In the first of these two queries, the subgoal **X=2** unifies **X** with **2** (see Fig. 8.22(a)), leaving **not(2=1)** as the current goal. The first rule for **not** yields the new goal

```
2=1, !, fail
```

Since **2=1** fails, the cut is not reached; hence, the cut is not shown in Fig. 8.22(a). Then, the second rule for **not** is tried and the goal **not(2=1)** succeeds.

The search tree for the second query appears in Fig. 8.22(b). The first rule for **not** yields the current goal

```
X=1, !, fail, X=2.
```

The subgoal **X=1** succeeds, the cut is satisfied, and **fail** is reached. The cut eliminates consideration of the other rule for **not** so the entire computation fails. Note that the subgoal **X=2** is never reached.

In general, it is safe to apply **not** to a term without variables because such terms have no variables to be changed by unification.

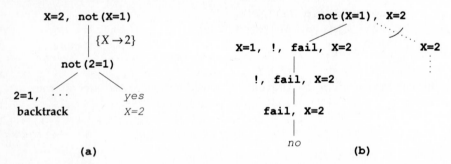

Fig. 8.22. Prolog search trees illustrating negation as failure.

EXERCISES

8.1 Given the relations

father(X, Y)	**X** is the father of **Y**
mother(X, Y)	**X** is the mother of **Y**
female(X)	**X** is female
male(X)	**X** is male

define relations for the following:
a) sibling.
b) sister.
c) grandson.
d) first cousin.
e) descendant.

8.2 Using only the **append** relation, formulate queries to determine the following:
a) the third element of a list.
b) the last element of a list.
c) all but the last element of a list.
d) whether a list is a concatenation of three copies of the same sublist.
e) whether a list **Y** is formed by inserting an element **A** somewhere in a list **X**.

8.3 Define relations to determine if a list
a) is a permutation of another.
b) has an even number of elements.
c) is formed by merging two lists.
d) is a palindrome; that is, it reads the same from left to right as it does from right to left.

8.4 Define relations corresponding to the following operations on lists:
a) Remove the second and succeeding adjacent duplicates.
b) Leave only the elements that do not have an adjacent duplicate.
c) Leave only one copy of the elements that have adjacent duplicates.

8.5 Complete Example 8.3, page 311, by defining relations **insert** and **delete** on binary search trees.

8.6 Arithmetic can be performed in Prolog by using subgoals of the form

⟨*variable*⟩ **is** ⟨*expression*⟩

This subgoal succeeds if the result of evaluating the expression unifies with the variable, as in

```
?- X is 2, Y is X+1.
     X = 2
     Y = 3
```

An error occurs if the expression after **is** contains any unbound variables, as in

```
?- Y is X+1, X is 2.
     Error
```

a) Define a relation corresponding to the factorial function.

b) Define a relation corresponding to a tail-recursive version of the factorial function.

8.7 Draw Prolog search trees for the query

```
?- reverse([a,b,c,d],W).
```

where **reverse** is defined by the rules:

a) ```
reverse([],[]).
reverse([A|X],Z) :- reverse(X,Y), append(Y,[A],Z).
```

b) ```
reverse(X,Z)  :- rev(X,[],Z).
rev([],Y,Y).
rev([A|X],Y,Z)  :- rev(X,[A|Y],Z).
```

8.8 Consider a relation **member** defined by the rules

```
member(M,  [M|_]).
member(M,  [_|T])  :- member(M, T).
```

Draw the portion of the Prolog search tree that corresponds to the responses in the following:

a) ```
?- member(b, [a,b,c]).
```
   *yes*

b) ```
?- member(d,  [a,b,c]).
```
   no

c) ```
?- member(b, X).
```
   $X = [b|\_]$ ;
   $X = [\_,b|\_]$ ;
   $X = [\_,\_,b|\_]$
   *yes*

**8.9** With the relation **member** as in Exercise 8.8, draw Prolog search trees for the following queries:

a) ```
X = [1,2,3],  member(a,X).
```

b) ```
member(a,X), X = [1,2,3].
```

**8.10** Except for the cut in the first rule, the following rules are as in Section 8.5:

```
append([], Y, Y)  :- !.
append([H|X],Y,[H|Z])  :- append(X,Y,Z).

prefix(X,Z)  :- append(X,Y,Z).

suffix(Y,Z)  :- append(X,Y,Z).
```

Compare the Prolog search trees for the following queries with the trees in Fig. 8.13 and 8.14:
```

a) **suffix([a],L), prefix(L,[a,b,c]).**
b) **suffix([b],L), prefix(L,[a,b,c]).**

BIBLIOGRAPHIC NOTES

Prolog, from *programmation en logique*, is the name of a programming language developed by Alain Colmerauer and Phillipe Roussel in 1972. Companion articles by Kowalski [1988] and Cohen [1988] provide a glimpse of its early history. The development of the language was influenced by W-grammars (van Wijngaarden et al. [1975]), the description language for Algol 68, and by Robinson's [1965] resolution principle for mechanical theorem proving.

Kowalski notes, "Looking back on our early discoveries, I value most the discovery that computation could be subsumed by deduction." His early examples included "computationally efficient axioms for such recursive predicates as addition and factorial." He continues, "For [Colmerauer], the Horn clause definition of appending lists was much more characteristic of the importance of logic programming."

Cohen offers reasons why Prolog developed slowly, relative to Lisp: (1) the lack of interesting examples illustrating the expressive power of the language, (2) the lack of adequate implementations, and (3) the availability of Lisp. He adds, "It is fair to say that the subsequent interpreters and compilers developed by Warren played a major role in the acceptance of Prolog." Warren [1980] describes how Prolog itself can be used for compiler writing.

More information on Prolog programming techniques can be found in textbooks such as Sterling and Shapiro [1986] and Clocksin and Mellish [1987]. Example 8.5 and Exercise 8.7 are motivated by examples in Sterling and Shapiro [1986]. Cohen [1988] cites difference lists as Colmerauer's valuable contribution to Roussel's original Prolog interpreter; Clark and Tärnlund [1977] is a published reference for difference lists.

Cuts were introduced by Colmerauer to conserve memory space. See Clark [1978] for a treatment of negation-as-failure.

For a discussion of logic programming in general, see Kowalski [1979a] or Hogger [1984].

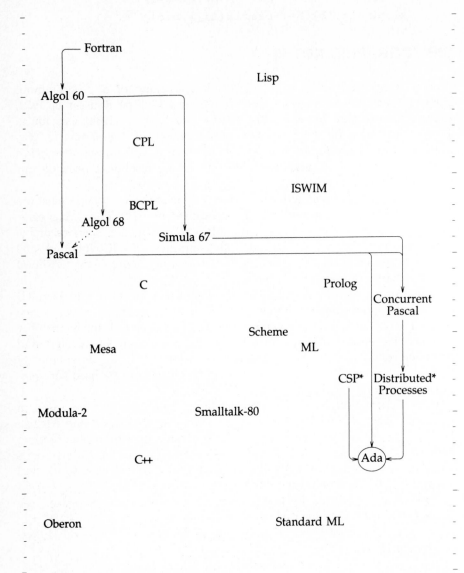

Fortran

Lisp

Algol 60

CPL

ISWIM

BCPL

Algol 68

Simula 67

Pascal

C

Prolog

Concurrent
Pascal

Scheme

ML

Mesa

CSP* Distributed*
Processes

Modula-2

Smalltalk-80

C++

Ada

Oberon

Standard ML

Ada is the result of language-design competition run by the U. S. Department of Defense. A series of increasingly detailed specifications—Strawman, Woodenman, Tinman, Ironman, Steelman—laid the basis for the winning design, named in honor of Augusta Ada, Babbage's programmer.

Concurrency in Ada was influenced by the communication primitives in a skeletal language CSP and by the language Distributed Processes.

Nine

An Introduction to Concurrent Programming

Concurrency in a programming language and parallelism in the underlying hardware are independent concepts. Hardware operations occur in *parallel* if they overlap in time. Operations in the source text are *concurrent* if they could be, but need not be, executed in parallel. Operations that occur one after the other, ordered in time, are said to be *sequential*. We can have concurrency in a language without parallel hardware, and we can have parallel execution without concurrency in the language. In short, concurrency refers to the potential for parallelism.

The fundamental concept of concurrent programming is the notion of a process. In this chapter, a *process* corresponds to a sequential computation, with its own thread of control. As discussed in Section 3.2, the thread of a sequential computation is the sequence of program points that are reached as control flows through the source text of the program. Sequential processes have traditionally been used to study concurrency. Ada, the working language of this chapter, deals with sequential processes.

Interactions between processes take two forms:

1. *Communication* involves the exchange of data between processes, either by an explicit message or through the values of shared variables. A variable is *shared* between processes if it is visible to the code for the processes.

2. *Synchronization* relates the thread of one process with that of another. If p is a point in the thread of a process P, and q is a point in the thread of a process Q, then synchronization can be used to constrain the order in which P reaches p and Q reaches q. In other words, synchronization involves the exchange of control information between processes.

The need for communication and synchronization can be visualized in terms of competition and cooperation between processes. Competition occurs when processes require exclusive use of a resource, such as when two processes compete to use the same printer, or to reserve a seat on a flight. Here, synchronization is needed to grant a process exclusive use of a resource. Cooperation occurs when two processes work on parts of the same problem, and typically involves both communication and synchronization.

9.1   PARALLELISM IN HARDWARE

Since hardware developments have long provided the impetus for studying and controlling concurrency, this section takes a brief look at machine organization.

Input/Output in Parallel with Execution

Parallelism in hardware dates back to the late 1950s, when the speed disparities between instruction execution and input/output led to the introduction of special-purpose processors called *data channels* for controlling input/output devices. A hundred thousand instructions could be executed in the time it took to read a single card or print a single line. By attending to input/output, channels allowed the central processor to concentrate on instruction execution.

Conceptually, the hardware organization changed from that in Fig. 9.1(a), with a single processor and a single memory, to that in Fig. 9.1(b), with several processors accessing a shared memory. The IBM 709, circa 1958, could have seven processors: a central general-purpose processor and up to six data channels. The machine could therefore simultaneously perform arithmetic operations and read from tapes or cards and write to tapes or printers.

The casual programmer was insulated from this complexity in the hardware by precursors of operating systems. Mock and Swift [1959] describe an elaborate buffering system for managing input/output so "programmers need not be particularly aware of the fact that parallel operations are occurring."

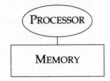

(a) Single processor.

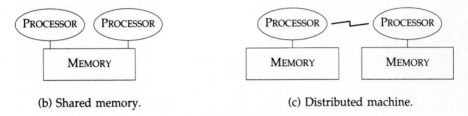

(b) Shared memory.   (c) Distributed machine.

Fig. 9.1. Three machine organizations.

Parallelism raised the problem of synchronized access to shared resources such as memory locations and input/output devices. How could a data channel be prevented from obliterating a precious value in a shared memory location, just before an instruction used it? Or, how could two data channels be prevented from writing to the same printer and mixing up its output?

An unattractive solution, called *busy waiting* or *polling*, consisted of having a processor continually check a condition, such as the completion of input/output by a data channel. The following pseudo-code for busy waiting emphasizes that no useful work is done until the condition becomes true:

    repeat (* nothing *) **until** ⟨*condition*⟩;

Interrupts and Time Sharing

Hardware signals called *interrupts* allowed the activities of a central processor to be synchronized with those of the data channels. If a program P needed to read a card, the processor could initiate the read action on a data channel and start executing another program Q. Once the card had been read, the channel sent an interrupt to the central processor, which could then resume execution of P.

Interrupts, together with a hardware clock, also made it possible to do *time sharing* or *time slicing*, whereby a processor divides its time between several programs. Every so often, the clock sends an interrupt to the processor, which then suspends one program and restarts another. Programs can of course be suspended for input/output as well.

A time-sharing system makes it appear as if several programs are running in parallel, although only one of them is making progress at a time. The rate at which the programs run is unpredictable because it depends on outside factors such as the number of programs that happen to be sharing the machine.

Time slicing can be used as an implementation technique for a concurrent language running on sequential hardware because it allows multiple processes to share a processor.

Multiprocessor Organization

True multiprocessors, with multiple central processors, were developed soon after channels. The Burroughs B5000, circa 1960, allowed two central processors and four channels to access a shared memory. A shared memory facilitates communication through shared variables that are visible to the communicating processes. Communication can then be *synchronous*; that is, a value is sent and received simultaneously, without communication delays.

The third organization in Fig. 9.1(c) is a distributed machine in which each processor has its own exclusive memory. Distributed processors communicate by message passing. If the processors are geographically separated, then communication delays cannot be ignored. With *asynchronous* communication, an unspecified amount of time can elapse between the time a message is sent and the time it is received.

Variants of the organizations in Fig. 9.1 can be created by using combinations of exclusive and shared memory or by imposing constraints on the processors. For example, SIMD (single-instruction multiple-data) machines have arrays of processors that all execute the same instruction at the same time on data local to each processor.

Reactive Systems

On a different scale, the potential for parallelism occurs in systems that interact with their environment. Examples of such *reactive systems* are user interfaces, process controllers, communication networks, and games.

Consider a user interface with a keyboard, a mouse, and a display supporting multiple windows. The keyboard and mouse are independent input devices, so the user interface must deal concurrently with characters typed at the keyboard and with the movements of the mouse. At the same time, it must display information in one or more windows. In a language that supports concurrency, separate processes can be used to manage the keyboard, the mouse, each window, and the display as a whole.

9.2   IMPLICIT SYNCHRONIZATION

Each process in this section is a traditional sequential program, in a language like C. Communication between processes is through their inputs and outputs, with the output of one process becoming the input of another.

Synchronization is conspicuous by its absence. If we measure the complexity of a concurrent program by the amount of explicit synchronization, then this section considers one of the simplest settings for concurrency— the individual processes are written in isolation, without thinking of how they will be put together to form a concurrent program. A process waits for its input to arrive, as a C program waits when it calls the standard function

```
getchar()
```

to get a character. Such waiting is the only form of synchronization between processes.

The Pipe Construct

The *pipe* construct of the UNIX operating system, written as "|," allows traditional sequential programs to be combined into a concurrent program. A UNIX command of the form

$$P_1 \mid P_2 \mid \cdots \mid P_k$$

specifies concurrent execution of the processes $P_1, P_2, \ldots, P_k$, with the the output of process P_i becoming the input of process P_{i+1}, for $1 \le i < k$. Such commands are referred to as *pipelines*. Each process in a pipeline is typically a program in a sequential language such as C. The sequence of values that flow from one process to another is called a *stream*.

A *process network* is a generalization of a pipeline. It consists of a set of processes together with edges of the form $P \to Q$, representing a stream flowing from process P to process Q. Each process runs concurrently with the others, at its own pace, as long as it has input. An edge $P \to Q$ therefore represents an unbounded buffer into which P puts values and from which Q gets values. Thus, P and Q are a producer-consumer pair.

A process in a process network is called a *coroutine*. It has zero or more input streams and zero or more output streams.

Examples of Pipelines

The pipeline

  bc | number

is illustrated in Fig. 9.2. Process **bc** transforms a stream of expressions into a stream of integers, which process **number** transforms into a stream of English words for the integers. A variant of this pipeline

  bc | number | speak

where **speak** converts English words into sounds, was used by blind programmers around Bell Laboratories.

 The power of pipes as a programming construct is based on

- a standard input/output interface, consisting of a stream of characters, and

- a suitable collection of primitive processes.

Each primitive process does a simple job, perhaps even a trivial job, but short pipelines of processes can do what would otherwise be done by substantial programs. Time and again, combinations of tools have been used for applications that their authors had not anticipated.

 Since UNIX tools transform character streams into character streams, a number of tools deal with character manipulation. Each tool treats a character stream as a sequence of lines.

Example 9.1. How frequently do names like **i** and **n** appear in a collection of programs? Do they appear more or less frequently than keywords like **while** and **if**? A name is any sequence of letters and digits beginning with a letter. Such information is helpful in designing the lexical analyzer in a compiler to ensure that it recognizes frequently occurring words quickly.

 One possible solution to this word-frequency problem is given by the following pseudo-code:

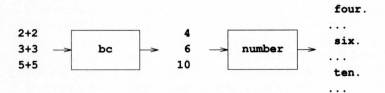

Fig. 9.2. Processes as stream transformers.

extract each string of letters and digits and place it on a separate line
| keep only the strings that begin with a letter
| sort lines so that all occurrences of a name are adjacent
| count occurrences and attach the count to each name
| sort the lines by order of decreasing count

Each line in this solution corresponds to a coroutine.[1] Figure 9.3 illustrates the effect of these coroutines on a small C program:

```
#include <stdio.h>
main(void) {
    char c;
    while( (c=getchar()) != EOF )
        putchar(c);
    return 0;
}
```

The output of the first coroutine consists of the strings of letters and digits extracted from this program, with each string appearing on a separate line. Names must begin with a letter, so the string **0** is eliminated

EXTRACT strings	KEEP names	SORT	COUNT	SORT
include				
stdio	include	EOF		
h	stdio	c		
main	h	c	1 EOF	3 c
void	main	c	3 c	1 while
char	void	char	1 char	1 void
c	char	getchar	1 getchar	1 stdio
while	c	h	1 h	1 return
c	while	include	1 include	1 putchar
getchar	c	main	1 main	1 main
EOF	getchar	putchar	1 putchar	1 include
putchar	EOF	return	1 return	1 h
c	putchar	stdio	1 stdio	1 getchar
return	c	void	1 void	1 char
0	return	while	1 while	1 EOF

Fig. 9.3. Finding the frequently occurring words in a program.

[1] For readers familiar with UNIX, the solution is based on the following program:
```
tr -cs A-Za-z0-9 '\012'|grep "^[A-Za-z]"|sort|uniq -c|sort -rn
```
The symbol **\012** is the ASCII code for a newline.

by the second coroutine. After the lines are sorted, all occurrences of a word appear on adjacent lines, with **EOF** as the first line. The number of occurrences of each word is then counted and attached at the beginning of the line. The final output is obtained by sorting the lines a second time, this time to put them in order of decreasing frequency of occurrence. Lines with the same count appear in reverse dictionary order in Fig. 9.3.   □

9.3   CONCURRENCY AS INTERLEAVING

Concurrent computations will be described in terms of events, where an *event* is an uninterruptible action. An event might be the execution of an assignment statement, a procedure call, the evaluation of an expression—in short, anything the language in question chooses to treat as atomic. The thread of a process corresponds to a sequence of events.

Interleaving of Threads

Interleaving of threads is a convenient technical device for studying the con- current execution of processes. An interleaving of two sequences s and t is any sequence u formed from the events of s and t, subject to the following constraint: The events of s retain their order in u and so do the events of t.

Interleaving is based on the assumption that concurrent programs can be characterized by the relative order of events. If a and z are concurrent events, then we consider the case in which a occurs before z and the case in which z occurs before a, but ignore the case in which a and z occur at the same time. As the number of events on a thread increases, the number of possible interleavings grows rapidly.

If an execution of a process A consists of two events $a\,b$ and an execution of a process Z consists of three events $x\,y\,z$, then concurrent execution of A and Z can be studied by considering the possible interleavings:

$$a \quad b \quad x \quad y \quad z$$
$$a \quad x \quad b \quad y \quad z$$
$$\cdots$$
$$x \quad y \quad z \quad a \quad b$$

Interleaving preserves the relative order of events in a thread, so a must occur before b, but x, y, and z, being on a separate concurrent thread, can occur in any order relative to a and b. Similarly, x must occur before y and y must occur before z, but a and b, being on a separate thread, can occur in any order relative to x, y, and z.

The 10 possible interleavings of the threads of A and Z are illustrated geometrically by the 10 diagrams in Fig. 9.4. The solid lines in each diagram have a horizontal step for an event in the thread of A and a verti-

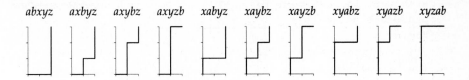

$abxyz$ $axbyz$ $axybz$ $axyzb$ $xabyz$ $xaybz$ $xayzb$ $xyabz$ $xyazb$ $xyzab$

Fig. 9.4. Interleavings of the threads $a\,b$ and $x\,y\,z$.

cal step for a thread in the event of B. Thus, the interleaving $a\,b\,x\,y\,z$ is represented by two horizontal steps followed by three vertical steps. Although interleaving generalizes to any number of tasks, two-dimensional diagrams can be drawn only for interleavings of two processes.

Concurrent Tasks in Ada

The rest of this section illustrates interleaving by considering processes in Ada.

The sequential aspects of Ada are similar enough to Modula-2 that they will be mentioned as needed. We concentrate on programs consisting of a single procedure, with the following structure:

```
procedure ⟨name⟩ is
    ⟨declarations⟩
begin
    ⟨statements⟩
end ⟨name⟩;
```

The complete sequential program in Fig. 9.5 prints the string

```
hello world
```

The first line of the program,

```
with text_io; use text_io;
```

imports procedure **put_line** from a module **text_io**.

Modules are called *packages* in Ada. Except in strings, Ada does not distinguish between uppercase and lowercase letters. Comments begin with -- and continue to the end of the line.

Processes, called *tasks* in Ada, correspond to modules with their own thread of control. A task is declared in two parts, called a *specification* and a *body*. A self-contained task that does not synchronize or communicate with other processes is specified simply by

```
task ⟨name⟩;
```

```
with text_io; use text_io;    -- import character input/output procedures
procedure hello is
begin
    put_line("hello world");
end hello;
```

Fig. 9.5. A complete Ada program.

The body of a task consists of optional declarations and a sequence of statements between **begin** and **end**. The body can be thought of as the implementation of a task.

Procedure **identify** in Fig. 9.6 contains the specifications and bodies of two tasks **p** and **q**. When a procedure is activated, the tasks declared within it are activated as well. The procedure activation is called the *parent* of the tasks activated within it. The tasks execute concurrently with their parent, so **p, q,** and the procedure body execute concurrently.

The calls to **put_line** in the procedure body and the two tasks can be interleaved in six possible ways, leading to the outcomes in the following columns:

p	p	q	q	r	r
q	r	p	r	p	q
r	q	r	p	q	p

```
with text_io; use text_io;
procedure identify is

    task p;                    -- task specification for p
    task body p is
    begin
        put_line("p");
    end p;

    task q;                    -- task specification for q
    task body q is
    begin
        put_line("q");
    end q;

begin                          -- procedure body sets up parent of p and q
    put_line("r");
end identify;
```

Fig. 9.6. A procedure with two tasks declared within it.

9.4   LIVENESS PROPERTIES

The concurrent execution of processes raises two kinds of correctness issues: safety and liveness. *Safety* deals with getting the "right" answer. *Liveness* deals with the rate of progress of a process; that is, with the rate at which its computation proceeds.

This section examines liveness issues by considering a problem in which processes called philosophers compete for resources called forks.

Competition for resources imposes constraints on the interleaving of threads. Consider two processes A and Z that compete for a resource. Suppose that the thread of process A is the sequence of events

$$a \quad lock_A(R) \quad b \quad c \quad unlock_A(R) \quad d$$

and the thread of process Z is

$$w \quad lock_Z(R) \quad x \quad y \quad unlock_Z(R) \quad z$$

Between events $lock_A(R)$ and $unlock_A(R)$, the resource R is unavailable to process Z; that is, event $lock_Z(R)$ cannot occur while process A maintains a lock on R. Similarly, $lock_A(R)$ cannot occur between $lock_Z(R)$ and $unlock_Z(R)$. Competition for the resource therefore constrains the possible interleavings of the threads for A and Z.

The competition between A and Z for resource R is illustrated geometrically in Fig. 9.7. The line stepping to the right and up from the origin corresponds to the interleaving

$$a \quad w \quad lock_A(R) \quad b \quad c \quad unlock_A(R) \quad lock_Z(R) \quad x \quad d \quad y \quad unlock_Z(R) \quad z$$

The region marked "infeasible" corresponds to situations that cannot occur because both processes cannot simultaneously hold the same resource.

The Dining Philosophers

Five philosophers sit at a table, alternating between eating spaghetti and thinking. In order to eat, a philosopher must have two forks (or chopsticks as in Fig. 9.8). The problem is that there is a single fork between each pair of philosophers, so if one of them is eating, a neighboring one cannot be eating. A philosopher puts down both forks in their place before thinking.

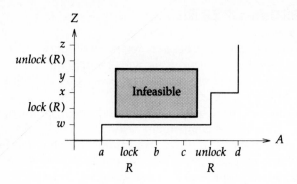

Fig. 9.7. Competition for a resource constrains interleaving.

Deadlock

A concurrent program is in *deadlock* if all processes are waiting, unable to proceed. For an example of deadlock, suppose that each philosopher executes the following pseudo-code:

loop
        pick up the fork to the left;
        pick up the fork to the right;
        eat;
        release the forks;
        think;
end;

The concurrent system consisting of two or more such philosophers deadlocks if each philosopher picks up the fork to the left and then waits for the fork to the right.

   Forks correspond to resources, and picking up a fork corresponds to locking the resource. Deadlock often involves a chain of dependencies in which one process depends on a resource held by the next. With the sys-

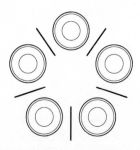

Fig. 9.8. Place settings for the dining philosophers.

tem of five philosophers, the first philosopher's left fork is the fifth philosopher's right fork.

Livelock

Another situation illustrated by the dining-philosophers problem is *livelock*, in which the system is not in deadlock, but no process makes any progress. Suppose that a philosopher's program is changed so that the left fork is released if the right fork is not available. Livelock occurs if all philosophers go into the infinite loop:

    pick up left fork;
    release left fork;
    pick up left fork
    release left fork;
        . . .

Fairness

This chapter makes the *finite-progress* assumption; that is, any process that wants to run will be able to do so within a finite amount of time. In other words, a process that wants to run cannot be blocked indefinitely.

The fairness assumption implies that any philosopher who wants to will eventually be able to eat. An unfair solution is to let just one philosopher eat all the time, with the other processes perpetually waiting. Fairness is a delicate issue, because processes may run at different rates. Thus, strict alternation between processes P and Q

$$P, Q, P, Q, P, Q, \cdots$$

may be unfair if P is 10 times as fast as Q and is needlessly delayed until Q takes its turn.

Deadlock Prevention

The deadlocked philosophers can be illustrated geometrically when the system consists of only two philosophers A and Z seated facing each other. Let R and S be the forks between them. Deadlock can occur if one philosopher picks up the forks in the order RS and the other picks up the forks in the opposite order SR. This ordering can leave both philosophers holding one fork and waiting for the other.

The geometric diagrams in Fig. 9.9 show the order in which philosophers A and Z pick up and release forks. In (a), the region marked "deadlock" corresponds to the case in which A holds fork R and Z holds fork S. Neither can now proceed. The infeasible region corresponds to situations that cannot occur because both philosophers cannot simultaneously hold the same fork.

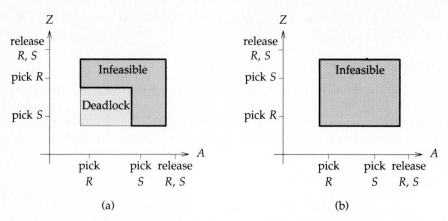

Fig. 9.9. Geometric interpretation of resource locking.

Deadlock can be prevented by *ordered resource usage*, whereby all processes request resources in the same order. When philosophers A and Z both pick up forks in the same order RS, then deadlock cannot occur. If R is unavailable, then S is left untouched, so the philosopher who gets R will be able to pick up S as well. The corresponding diagram in Fig. 9.9(b) has an infeasible region, but no region marked deadlock. Ordered resource usage works for any number of resources.

9.5   SAFE ACCESS TO SHARED DATA

This section explores a notion of safety for concurrent programs with shared variables.

"Nondeterministic" Processes

A program is *deterministic* if every execution of the program on the same data sets up the same computation. Programs that are not deterministic are said to be *nondeterministic*.[2]

With concurrent programs, it seems natural to allow arbitrary choices to be made during a computation, thereby giving up determinism. An element of choice enters into both of the following examples. Suppose that two processes P and Q send their output to a printer. As long as their output is not interleaved, it usually does not matter whether P's output appears first or Q's output appears first. As another example, suppose that two travel agents P and Q concurrently attempt to reserve the sole remain-

---

[2] The use of the term "nondeterministic" for "not deterministic" conflicts with the technical use of "nondeterministic" in automata theory. Since mathematical studies of concurrency use automata theory as a point of departure, care is needed in using the term "nondeterministic."

ing seat on a flight. Only one of them can get the seat, and from the point of view of the reservation system, it does not matter which one gets it.

Critical Sections and Mutual Exclusion

We now formulate a notion of safety that imposes constraints on interleaving without insisting on a unique deterministic result.

A *critical section* in a process is a portion or section of code that must be treated as an atomic event. Two critical sections are said to be *mutually exclusive* because their executions must not overlap.

A concurrent program with critical sections is *safe* if it executes the critical sections contiguously, without interleaving. The two cyclic processes in Fig 9.10 are allowed to execute their critical sections in any order, even if P executes more often than Q.

Example 9.2. For a technical example of the need for critical sections, consider the following two assignments:

$$x := x + 1; \quad x := x + 2;$$

In a sequential language, these assignments increment the value of x by 3. This behavior remains the same if the order of the assignments is reversed:

$$x := x + 2; \quad x := x + 1;$$

A concurrent language, however, might not treat an assignment as an atomic event. Suppose that these assignments are split and implemented as two concurrent processes P and Q:

PROCESS P	PROCESS Q
$t := x;$	$u := x;$
$x := t + 1;$	$x := u + 2;$

If the assignments of Q are interleaved between those of P,

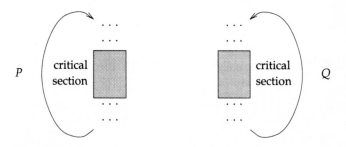

Fig. 9.10. Two cyclic processes with critical sections.

$$t := x;$$
$$\quad u := x;$$
$$\quad x := u + 2;$$
$$x := t + 1;$$

then x is incremented by 1 instead of 3. Such interleaving can be prevented by treating the assignments as critical sections.   □

More realistic examples of the use of critical sections arise in connection with objects that support operations on private data. Interleaved execution of the operations can produce undesirable results. Using the concept of data invariant from Chapter 5, sequential execution of the operations is expected to preserve the data invariants for the object, but interleaved execution could leave the private data in a state that does not satisfy the data invariants.

Serializability of Database Updates

In database systems, a set of processes is said to execute *serially* if one process executes completely before another process begins. Under the *serializability criterion*, any serial execution is said to produce a safe result. Furthermore, any interleaved execution of P and Q is said to be safe if it is equivalent to a serial execution. In other words, safety is taken to be synonymous with serializability.

Serializability generalizes the requirement that critical sections be uninterruptible because it allows critical sections to be interleaved as long as the result of the interleaving is the same as that produced by some serial execution.

Example 9.3. As a technical example, consider two processes P and Q:

Process P	Process Q
$t := x;$	$u := x;$
$x := t + 1;$	$y := u * 2;$

The serial order $P\,Q$ corresponds to the following computation:

$t := x;$	x is initially 0
$x := t + 1;$	x is now 1
$\quad u := x;$	
$\quad y := u * 2;$	$x = 1$ and $y = 2$

The opposite order $Q\,P$ corresponds to

$$u := x ; \qquad\qquad x \text{ is initially } 0$$
$$y := u * 2; \qquad\quad y \text{ is now } 0$$
$$t := x ;$$
$$x := t + 1; \qquad\quad x = 1 \text{ and } y = 0$$

The following interleaved execution is safe because it is equivalent to the serial order $Q\,P$:

$$u := x ; \qquad\qquad x \text{ is initially } 0$$
$$t := x ;$$
$$y := u * 2; \qquad\quad y \text{ is now } 0$$
$$x := t + 1; \qquad\quad x = 1 \text{ and } y = 0$$

As a quick exercise, explain why the interleaving in Example 9.2 is not serializable.   □

9.6 CONCURRENCY IN ADA

This section uses a sequence of small complete programs to introduce the concurrency constructs of Ada. The aim is to develop a reading knowledge of the language. The programs set up processes that simply identify themselves; more realistic applications appear in Section 9.7.

Synchronization by Rendezvous

Synchronization in Ada is achieved by a form of procedure call known as a *rendezvous*. We refer to the caller in the rendezvous as a *client* and to the callee as the *server*. A rendezvous combines two events (see Fig. 9.11):

1. a call within a client process P and
2. acceptance of the call by the server process Q.

Conceptually, the threads of the two processes come together during the rendezvous and then separate to let the two processes run independently. Alternatively, we can think of the client as being suspended during the rendezvous.

Since the client and the server have their own threads, they must both reach corresponding program points before a rendezvous can take place. The program point in the client is a call of the following form:

⟨*server-name*⟩ . ⟨*entry-name*⟩

In Fig. 9.11, the server name is Q, the entry name is *synch*, and the call is $Q.synch$.

The corresponding program point within the server is an **accept** statement for that entry name, of the following form:

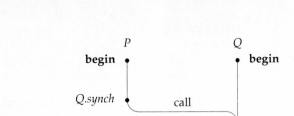

Fig. 9.11. A rendezvous.

accept ⟨*entry-name*⟩ **do**
   . . .
end ⟨*entry-name*⟩

We do not care about the order in which the client and server reach
these corresponding program points. For the moment, suppose that there
is a single client and a single server.

- If the client calls before the server is ready to accept, then the client
  waits until the rendezvous can occur.

- If the server reaches an **accept** statement before the client calls, then
  the server waits until the rendezvous can occur.

In general, a single server can have several clients. This asymmetric
relationship arises because a client explicitly names a server. Since several
clients can name the same server, there can be several waiting clients when
control reaches an **accept** statement. The server accepts the call from one
of these clients, executes the statements between the keyword **accept** and
the corresponding **end**, and continues with the rest of the body. The
remaining clients wait until the server is ready to accept again.

Synchronized Communication

Ada combines synchronization and communication during a rendezvous.
As with a procedure call, a call from the client can carry actual parameters
along with it, and the server can return a result to its caller.

For an example of communication from caller to callee, we shall redo the
earlier example in which three tasks printed out an identifying character.
Specifically, we want to set up two similar tasks **p** and **q** that accept a
character as a parameter and print it.

Task Types

Similar tasks can be declared by specifying a *task type*. The program in Fig. 9.12 specifies a task type **emitter** and then declares **p** and **q** as follows:

    p, q : emitter;

If there is only one task of a given task type, then the task can be declared directly. The following declaration of an independent task **p**

    task p;

is an abbreviation of

    task type p_type;
    p : p_type;

The threads of the three processes in the program of Fig. 9.12 are shown in Fig. 9.13; we treat the procedure body as a process, with a thread separate from that of the two tasks **p** and **q**. For clarity, the thread for the procedure body is drawn between the threads for **p** and **q**.

```
with text_io; use text_io;
procedure task_init is

    task type emitter is
        entry init(c : character);
    end emitter;

    p, q : emitter;

    task body emitter is
        me : character;
    begin
        accept init(c : character) do
            me := c;
        end init;
        put(me); new_line;
    end emitter;

begin
    p.init('p');
    q.init('q');
    put('r'); new_line;
end task_init;
```

Fig. 9.12. Rendezvous **init** initializes tasks of type **emitter**.

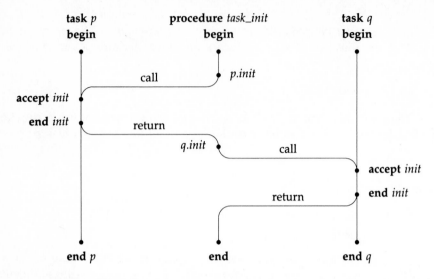

Fig. 9.13. Threads for the tasks set up by the program in Fig. 9.12.

The procedure body begins with a call **p.init('p')**. The corresponding accept statement is

```
accept init(c : character) do
    me := c;
end init;
```

When the rendezvous occurs, the actual parameter **'p'** corresponds to the formal **c** in the accept statement. This character is assigned to variable **me** and the rendezvous ends.

A similar rendezvous occurs when the procedure body executes the call **q.init('q')**.

The output from the three processes in Fig. 9.12 is not synchronized because

```
put(me); new_line;
```

in the body of task type **emitter** occur after the accept statement, and the statements in the procedure body

```
put('r'); new_line;
```

occur after the calls. Hence, these statements can be interleaved in any order.

Concurrency is maximized by putting as little as possible between an **accept** and its **end**. Often, such intervening statements are used just to pass parameters. For example, consider the effect of changing the body of task **emitter** to produce output during the rendezvous:

```
task body emitter is
    me : character;
begin
    accept init (c : character) do
        me := c ;
        put (me); new_line ;
    end init ;
end emitter ;
```

Now the only possible output of the program is

```
p
q
r
```

From Fig. 9.13, **'p'** is printed during the first rendezvous with task **p**, **'q'** is printed during the second rendezvous with task **q**, and then **'r'** is printed by the procedure body.

Task Initialization

Any communication between tasks in Ada must occur through a rendezvous. Upon activation, if a task needs any values to initialize itself, then an initial rendezvous is needed to pass these values. In this chapter, *init* will be the entry name for such an initial rendezvous. The first thing the parent of a task will do is to call *init*.

Dynamically Created Tasks

A pointer type is known as an *access type* in Ada. Tasks can be created dynamically through access types to tasks.

The program in Fig. 9.14 was formed by modifying the program in Fig. 9.12 to dynamically create tasks that print **'p'** and **'q'**. A bold font highlights the differences between the two programs.

The type **emitter_ptr** is declared to be a pointer to a task type **emitter** by

```
type emitter_ptr is access emitter;
```

Two tasks of type **emitter** are created dynamically when the following statements are executed:

```
p := new emitter;
q := new emitter;
```

```
with text_io; use text_io;
procedure pointers is

    task type emitter is
        entry init(c : character);
    end emitter;

    type emitter_ptr is access emitter;
    p, q : emitter_ptr;

    task body emitter is
        me : character;
    begin
        accept init(c : character) do
            me := c;
        end init;
        put(me); new_line;
    end emitter;

begin
    p := new emitter;
    q := new emitter;
    p.init('p');
    q.init('q');
    put('r'); new_line;
end pointers;
```

Fig. 9.14. Dynamic creation of tasks through access types.

Pointers to the newly created tasks are assigned to **p** and **q**. Pointers are dereferenced automatically in entry calls, so **p.init('p')** is a call to entry **init** of the task accessed through **p**.

Selective Acceptance

Until now, tasks have had at most one entry, so the question of choosing between entries has not arisen. The **select** construct in Ada allows a server to offer a selection of services to its clients. For example, a buffer process might offer two services, corresponding to information entering and leaving the buffer.

The code for a vending machine might use a select statement like the following to offer a choice between delivering milk and juice:

```
select
     accept deliver_milk do
         . . .
     end deliver_milk ;
or
     accept deliver_juice do
         . . .
     end deliver_juice ;
end select;
```

A more general form of the **select** construct allows the alternatives to be "guarded." A construct is *guarded* by a boolean expression if the boolean expression is tested to determine whether control should flow to the construct. The boolean expression is called a *guard*.

The accept statements in the following pseudo-code are guarded by *notfull* and *notempty*:

```
select
     when notfull  ⇒  accept enter (c : in character) do
         . . .
     end enter ;
or
     when notempty  ⇒  accept leave (c : out character) do
         . . .
     end leave ;
end select;
```

This pseudo-code is for a buffer process—guard *notfull* must be true for information to enter the buffer, and guard *notempty* must be true for information to leave the buffer.

The guards in a **select** statement in Ada are evaluated once when control reaches the select statement. An exception is raised if all guards are false.

9.7 SYNCHRONIZED ACCESS TO SHARED VARIABLES

Techniques for providing synchronized access to shared variables are illustrated in this section by considering the producer-consumer problem.

Again, a producer process and a consumer process communicate through a bounded buffer. The producer puts values into the buffer at some rate, and the consumer gets values out of the buffer at some possibly different rate. The problem is to synchronize the processes so that the buffer acts as a first-in-first-out queue. In particular, correctness can be compromised if the producer attempts to put values into a full buffer or if the consumer attempts to get values out of an empty buffer.

The diagrams in Fig. 9.15 illustrate the historical progression of constructs for synchronization. In (a), both processes have unsynchronized access to a circular buffer. Semaphores, introduced in this section, can be used to synchronize the processes so that the data invariants for the buffer are preserved. This section also briefly considers monitors, which encapsulate all the code for the buffer in one place. The final diagram (d) treats the buffer as a separate process, an approach that can be implemented directly in Ada.

Direct Access to the Buffer

If the producer and the consumer manipulate the buffer without synchronization, then a proof of correctness must take into account all possible interleavings of their actions.

The pseudo-code in Fig. 9.16 illustrates potential problems and is not recommended for programming.[3] It contains the bodies of two tasks *producer* and *consumer*, which manipulate the buffer. As in earlier chapters, the buffer consists of an array *buf*, an index *rear* telling the producer where to put the next value, and an index *front* telling the consumer from where to get the next value. We can see from the highlighted code that the producer and the consumer manipulate the buffer directly.

An array index is enclosed between parentheses in Ada, so the ith element of array a is written as $a (i)$. The procedures *get* and *put* are library procedures for character input and output, respectively.

Since the two tasks are not synchronized, their buffer-manipulation code can be interleaved. One possible interleaving is as follows:

producer	*consumer*
notfull returns **true**;	
get (*c*);	
buf (*rear*) := *c* ;	
	notempty returns **true**;
	c := *buf* (*front*);
	front := (*front* +1) **mod** *size* ;
rear := (*rear* +1) **mod** *size* ;	
	put (*c*);

Note that the consumer touches the buffer between the time the producer assigns a value to *buf* (*rear*) and the time it updates the index *rear*.

---

[3] The pseudo-code in Fig. 9.16 happens to work because of the guards *notfull* and *notempty*. In general, however, direct access can lead to incorrect results. Errors can occur if there is more than one producer, or if there is more than one consumer.

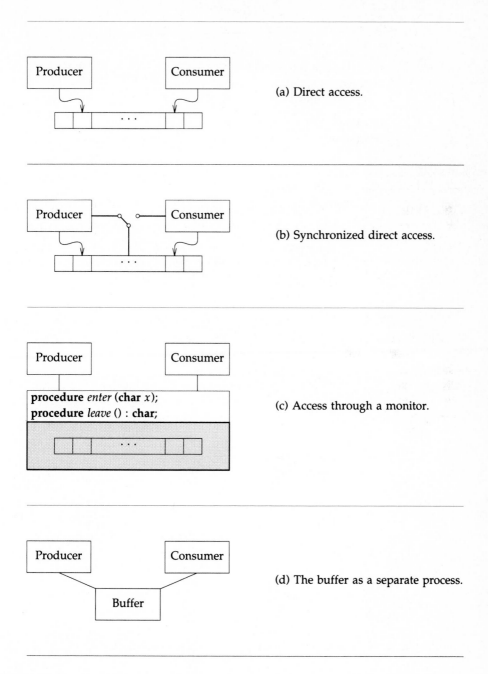

Fig. 9.15. Solutions to the producer-consumer problem.

```
with text_io ; use text_io ;
procedure direct is

    size : constant integer := 5;
    buf : array(0..size-1) of character;
    front, rear : integer := 0;

    function notfull return boolean is  · · ·  end notfull ;
    function notempty return boolean is · · · end notempty ;

    task producer ;
    task body producer is
        c : character;
    begin
        while not end_of _file loop
            if notfull then
                get (c);
                buf (rear) := c ;
                rear := (rear +1) mod size;
            end if;
        end loop;
    end producer ;

    task consumer ;
    task body consumer is
        c : character;
    begin
        loop
            if notempty then
                c := buf (front);
                front := (front +1) mod size;
                put (c);
            end if;
        end loop;
    end consumer ;

begin
    null;
end direct ;
```

Fig. 9.16. Pseudo-code for unsynchronized access to the buffer.

Semaphores: Mutual Exclusion

A *semaphore* is a construct that has an integer variable *value* and supports two operations:

1. If *value* ≥ 1, then a process can perform a p operation to decrement the value by 1. Otherwise, a process attempting a p operation waits until the value becomes greater than or equal to 1.

2. A process can perform a v operation to increment variable *value* by 1.[4]

A *binary semaphore* is a semaphore whose value is constrained to be either 0 or 1. If the value of a binary semaphore is 1, then a process attempting a v operation on it is suspended until its value becomes 0. In other words, the p and v operations on a semaphore must be performed alternately.

Ada does not provide semaphores directly; however, they can be implemented using tasks. Binary semaphores can be implemented by

```
task type binary_semaphore is
    entry p ;
    entry v ;
end binary_semaphore ;

task body binary_semaphore is
begin
    loop
        accept p ;
        accept v ;
    end loop;
end binary_semaphore ;
```

A binary-semaphore task has two entries p and v that are accepted one after the other. Since the accept statements are used purely for synchronization, the syntax

```
accept ⟨entry-name⟩;
```

can be used instead of the verbose

```
accept ⟨entry-name⟩ do
    null;
end ⟨entry-name⟩;
```

---

[4] Semaphores were introduced by Dijkstra [1968b]. Andrews and Schneider [1983] note that Dijkstra named the p operation after the Dutch word *passeren*, meaning "to pass," and the v operation after *vrygeven*, the Dutch word for "to release."

Mutual exclusion can be implemented by enclosing each critical section between the operations $s.p$ and $s.v$, where s is a binary semaphore:

Process Q Process R

$\quad \cdots$ $\quad \cdots$

$s.p$; $s.p$;
critical section for Q;   critical section for R;
$s.v$ $s.v$

$\quad \cdots$ $\quad \cdots$

Mutual exclusion of the critical sections is guaranteed by the constraint that the p and v operations on a semaphore must be performed alternately. If process Q is the first to execute $s.p$, then it enters its critical section immediately. Process R must wait to execute $s.p$ until after Q executes $s.v$.

Busy Waiting

Although the producer and consumer can indeed be synchronized by treating the highlighted code segments in Fig. 9.17 as critical sections, the code in the figure has another failing; namely, busy waiting. If the buffer is full, the producer busily loops and tests until the buffer is not full. Similarly, if the buffer is empty, the consumer busily loops and tests until the buffer is not empty.[5] Busy waiting will be avoided in the solutions discussed next.

Semaphores and a Bounded Buffer

Generalized semaphores can take on integer values greater than 0 and 1. After a brief look at how semaphores might be implemented in Ada, we return to the producer-consumer problem.

The body of task *semaphore* in Fig. 9.18 has three entries: *init*, *p*, and *v*. When a task of type *semaphore* is created, its parent should immediately call *init* to initialize variable *value* in the semaphore. After initialization, the task enters a loop around a select statement with alternatives for *p* and *v*. The *p* alternative has a guard *value* ≥ 1, so any task attempting a rendezvous when *value* $= 0$ will wait until some other task calls *v* to increment the value. The *v* alternative is unguarded, so the task is always ready to accept a rendezvous for *v*.

The solution of the producer-consumer problem in Fig. 9.19 uses three semaphores. The bodies of tasks *producer* and *consumer* appear side by side in Fig. 9.19 for ease of comparison. Calls to a binary semaphore *critical*

---

[5] Busy waiting also occurs in the program in Fig. 9.16, where the producer and consumer access the buffer directly. In one execution of the program, the guards *notfull* and *notempty* were false over 99% of the time; in other words, less than 1% of the loop iterations led to characters moving in or out of the buffer.

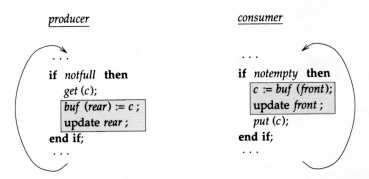

Fig. 9.17. The producer and consumer as cyclic processes with critical sections.

enclose their critical sections. A process waits to perform *critical.p* before it enters its critical section. On exit from the section it performs *critical.v* to release the semaphore. This semaphore ensures mutual exclusion of the critical sections.

Suitable initial values for the semaphores *filling* and *emptying* prevent the producer from entering a value into a full buffer and also prevent the consumer from taking a value from an empty buffer. If the buffer can hold *n* elements, then the initial values are given by

$$filling.value := n ; \quad emptying.value := 0;$$

```
task body semaphore is
     value : integer;
begin
     accept init (n : integer) do                    -- initialization
          value := n ;
     end init ;
     loop
          select
               when value ≥ 1 ⇒                      -- p operation
                    accept p do
                         value := value − 1;
                    end p ;
          or  accept v do                            -- v operation
                    value := value + 1;
               end v ;
          end select;
     end loop;
end semaphore ;
```

Fig. 9.18. A semaphore as a task in Ada.

```
task body producer is                    task body consumer is
  c : character;                            c : character;
begin                                    begin
  while not end_of_file loop               loop
    get (c);                                 emptying.p ;
    filling.p ;                              critical.p ;
      critical.p ;                             c := buf (front);
        buf (rear) := c ;                      front := (front +1) mod size ;
        rear := (rear +1) mod size ;         critical.v ;
      critical.v ;                           filling.v ;
    emptying.v ;                             put (c);
  end loop;                                 end loop;
end producer ;                           end consumer ;
```

Fig. 9.19. Use of semaphores *filling, emptying,* and *critical.*

The initial value *n* allows the producer to immediately execute *filling.p,* enter its critical section, and then execute *emptying.v.* On each pass through its critical section, the producer decrements semaphore *filling* and increments semaphore *emptying.*

The initial value 0 forces the consumer to initially wait at its *emptying.p* operation until the producer has passed through its critical section. A little thought shows that the semaphores correctly implement a bounded buffer of size *n.*

With its symmetric use of semaphores, the solution of Fig. 9.19 has a certain elegance, but it is also delicate because its correctness relies on the cooperation of the producer and the consumer. One misplaced *p* or *v* operation brings the solution to its knees. Furthermore, these operations appear in the code for the cooperating processes, so the correctness of the solution depends on calls dispersed in different places in the code.

A Brief Look at Monitors

Critical sections and semaphores represent an early approach to providing exclusive access to shared data. Another approach is to encapsulate the shared data in a construct called a monitor, which is a generalization of the class construct of Chapter 5. A *monitor object* is a collection of shared variables and procedures with the constraint that only one process is allowed to execute a monitor procedure at a time. In other words, the thread of at most one process can be within a monitor at a time.

The pseudo-code for a monitor, *buffer,* in Fig. 9.20 shows two procedures, *enter* and *leave,* for entering and extracting characters from the buffer, respectively. The pseudo-code does not show the private data and any private operations of the monitor.

```
monitor buffer is
    buf : ...;

    procedure enter(c :  in  character);
    begin
        if buffer full then wait( filling);          -- block producer
        enter c into buffer;
            . . .
        signal(emptying);                            -- unblock consumer
    end enter;

    procedure leave(c :  out  character);
    begin
        if buffer empty then wait(emptying);        -- block consumer
        c := next character;
            . . .
        signal( filling);                            -- unblock producer
    end leave;

begin
    initialize private data;
end buffer;
```

Fig. 9.20. A monitor for a bounded buffer.

If the producer process is executing procedure *enter*, then the consumer process is not allowed to execute procedure *leave*, and vice versa. Monitors allow a language to check and enforce synchronized access to shared data.

The main problem with monitors is that a process may block within a monitor. For example, suppose that a producer grabs a buffer monitor and starts to execute the *enter* procedure. What if the buffer is full? We face a problem because the producer has exclusive use of the monitor and finds it cannot complete execution of the procedure it has started.

Processes that block inside a monitor can be handled by maintaining queues of blocked processes. Execution by a process P of

    wait(q);

blocks P on the queue q. Subsequently, if a process R executes

    signal(q);

then a blocked process, if any, is taken off the queue q and restarted.

Procedure *enter* uses a queue *filling* to hold a producer that blocks when the buffer is full. Symmetrically, procedure *leave* uses a queue *emptying* to hold a consumer that blocks when the buffer is empty.

To see how queues are used, suppose that the buffer is not empty, and that a producer executes *enter*. After character *c* is entered into the buffer, the procedure body executes

  signal (*emptying*)

This signal has no effect if there is no blocked process in queue *emptying*; otherwise, a blocked process is taken off the queue and restarted.

Similarly, just before control exits from procedure *leave*,

  signal (*filling*)

allows a blocked producer, if any, to resume execution.

The advantage of monitors is that all the code for the buffer appears together. Queues of blocked processes have to be handled with care, however.

The Buffer as a Process

We conclude this section with a solution to the producer-consumer problem that is appropriate for a language like Ada, where processes can be used to synchronize access to shared data.

The time to test for a full buffer is before a producer starts to enter an element into the buffer and the time to test for an empty buffer is before a consumer starts to take an element out. In Ada these tests can be implemented as guards on an **accept** statement. An outline of a task *buffer* is as follows:

```
task body buffer is
    ⟨data-declarations⟩
begin
    loop
        select
            when notfull ⇒
                accept enter (x : in integer) do
                    . . .

                end  enter ;
        or    when notempty ⇒
                accept leave (x : out integer) do
                    . . .

                end  leave ;
        end select;
    end loop;
end buffer;
```

EXERCISES

9.1 Give geometric interpretations of all possible interleavings of
a) the threads *a b* and *y z*.
b) the threads *a b c* and *x y z*.

9.2 In each of the following cases, give a geometric interpretation of the interactions between the two processes. Plot the thread of one process along the horizontal axis, and the thread of the other process along the vertical axis. Clearly mark the infeasible regions.
a) A system of two philosophers executing the following pseudo-code:

> pick up left fork;
> pick up right fork;
> eat;
> release right fork;
> release left fork;

b) Two philosophers as in (c), but with the forks released in the opposite order.
c) A rendezvous between two tasks in Ada.
d) Two cyclic processes with critical sections.

9.3 Show how process networks can be implemented in Ada by inserting a buffer between two processes connected by an edge $P \rightarrow Q$. What are the interactions between the processes in your answer?

9.4 Consider a data type *stream* consisting of a possibly infinite sequence of values with three operations:

> *head* (*s*)   Return the first element of a stream *s*.
> *tail* (*s*)   Return the rest of *s* after the first element.
> *qcons* (*a, s*) Return a new stream with head *a* and tail *s*.

The difference between the operation *qcons* and **cons** in Scheme is that *qcons* performs *lazy evaluation*, where arguments are evaluated only as they are needed. Thus,

> *head* (*qcons* (*a, s*))

evaluates to *a* without attempting to evaluate *s*. For example, the following function *integers* returns a stream of integers starting with *n*:

> **fun** *integers* (*n*) = *qcons* (*n, integers* (*n* +1))

a) Define a function *nonmultiples* (*n, s*) to return a stream consisting of the elements of *s* that are not multiples of *n*. An integer *m* is a multiple of *n* if *m* **mod** *n* is 0.

  b) Define a function *sieve* to compute a stream of prime numbers. The sieve method for computing primes is discussed in Section 6.7.

  c) Scheme provides an operator **delay** to defer evaluation of an expression, and an operator **force** to evaluate a delayed expression. Implement function *sieve* from (b) in Scheme.

9.5 Consider the stream, *hamming*, consisting of integers of the form $2^i3^j5^k$, for $i \geq 0$, $j \geq 0$, $k \geq 0$, in increasing order. A variant *ham23* of *hamming*, consisting of integers of the form 2^i3^j is characterized by

$$ham23 \ = \ qcons \ (1, \ merge \ (times \ (2, ham23), \ times \ (3, ham23)))$$

where *qcons* is as in Exercise 9.4, *times* (n, s) returns the stream formed by multiplying each element of s by n, and *merge* (s, t) throws away duplicates as it merges the streams s and t of integers in increasing order.

  a) Define a function to compute the stream *hamming*.

  b) What are the first dozen elements of *hamming*? Explain how you computed these elements.

9.6 Show that the pseudo-code in Fig. 9.16, page 368, for unsynchronized access to a buffer, becomes unsafe if

  a) there is more than one producer.

  b) there is more than one consumer.

9.7 Write an Ada program to compute prime numbers using the sieve method described in Section 6.7. The program must create processes corresponding to the components for computing primes in Fig. 6.17, page 240.

9.8 Given $n > 0$ processes with critical sections, use semaphores to allow any k of them, $0 < k \leq n$, to simultaneously execute their critical sections.

  a) Use generalized semaphores.

  b) Use binary semaphores.

*9.9 Show that generalized semaphores can be simulated by binary semaphores; that is, any program using generalized semaphores can be transformed to use binary semaphores instead.

9.10 The readers-and-writers problem deals with readers, several of whom can simultaneously read a resource, and writers, who must have exclusive access to a resource.

  a) Give a solution in Ada for the readers-and-writers problem.

  b) Use semaphores to solve the problem.

9.11 Dijkstra's [1975] *guarded commands* are sequential statements of the form

$$\langle guard \rangle \rightarrow \langle statement\text{-}list \rangle$$

where $\langle guard \rangle$ is a boolean expression. The statement list in a guarded command is said to be *open* if its guard is true.

A *guarded alternative construct* has the form:

> **if** $\langle guard \rangle_1 \rightarrow \langle statement\text{-}list \rangle_1$
> [] $\langle guard \rangle_2 \rightarrow \langle statement\text{-}list \rangle_2$
> [] $\cdots$
> [] $\langle guard \rangle_k \rightarrow \langle statement\text{-}list \rangle_k$
> **fi**

An alternative construct is executed by choosing any one of the open statement lists and executing it. This choice makes programs using guarded commands nondeterministic. An error occurs if none of the guards is true.

A *guarded repetitive construct* has the form:

> **do** $\langle guard \rangle_1 \rightarrow \langle statement\text{-}list \rangle_1$
> [] $\langle guard \rangle_2 \rightarrow \langle statement\text{-}list \rangle_2$
> [] $\cdots$
> [] $\langle guard \rangle_k \rightarrow \langle statement\text{-}list \rangle_k$
> **od**

A repetitive construct is executed by repeatedly evaluating guards and executing one of the open statement lists. Control leaves a repetitive construct only when all the guards are false.

a) Use guarded commands to compute the minimum of x and y. Treat x and y symmetrically.

b) What are the possible threads through the following program fragment:

> initialize x, y, and z;
> $max := 0$;
> **do** $max < x \rightarrow max := x$
> [] $max < y \rightarrow max := y$
> [] $max < z \rightarrow max := z$
> **od**

9.12 Compare and contrast the rules for the guarded alternative construct in Exercise 9.11 with the rules for select statements in Ada.

BIBLIOGRAPHIC NOTES

The groundwork for the concepts in this chapter was laid by Dijkstra [1968b]. Written in 1965, this paper discusses mutual exclusion, a producer and consumer interacting through a bounded buffer, semaphores, and generalized semaphores. The dining-philosophers problem is from Dijkstra [1971]. Monitors, developed by Hoare [1974] and Brinch Hansen [1975] were influenced by classes in Simula.

Brinch Hansen [1975, 1978, 1981] has introduced a succession of languages for concurrent programming, including Concurrent Pascal, Distributed Processes, and Edison, The concepts of classes, monitors, and processes in Concurrent Pascal are subsumed into processes in Distributed Pascal. Holt et al. [1978] desribe a system CSP/k that uses monitors.

Among the books and surveys that explore concepts from concurrent programming are the survey by Andrews and Schneider [1983] and the book by Ben-Ari [1982]. A detailed review of the literature appears in Filman and Friedman [1984].

Ichbiah et al. [1979] note that the design of Ada was influenced by the communication primitives in CSP (Hoare [1978]) and by Distributed Processes (Brinch Hansen [1978]). CSP stands for communicating sequential processes. The books by Burns [1985] and Gehani [1984] discuss concurrent programming in Ada. Concurrency in Ada is compared with other proposals by Wegner and Smolka [1983] and Welsh and Lister [1981].

The historical surveys by Rosin [1969] and Rosen [1969] describe early hardware and operating systems.

Conway [1963] introduced the term coroutine, and applied the concept to organize a compiler. Simula 67 had a "resume" statement, which could be used to send control explicitly from one coroutine to another (Dahl and Hoare [1972]). The novelty of pipes, discussed in Section 9.2, is that independently written programs can be combined into a linear network. Ritchie [1984] notes, "Pipes appeared in UNIX in 1972 ... at the suggestion (or perhaps insistence) of M. D. McIlroy." Pipes have encouraged the development of collections of programs that can be used as primitives in a pipeline. Kernighan and Plauger [1976, 1981] describe such collections. The word frequency problem of Example 9.1 is explored by Bentley, Knuth, and McIlroy [1986]—Bentley posed the problem, Knuth solved it, and then McIlroy reviewed the solution. The pipeline in Fig. 9.3 is based on McIlroy's review. Hanson [1987] begins with the same problem.

The sieve method for computing prime numbers, discussed in Section 6.7, appeared in an unpublished yet influential manuscript by McIlroy [1968]. Kahn and MacQueen [1977] use the sieve method and the sequence *hamming* of Exercise 9.5 to illustrate process networks; the exercise is based on their work. Dijkstra [1976] attributes the sequence of Exercise 9.5 to R. W. Hamming, and gives a sequential solution using guarded commands.

Landin [1965] describes streams in connection with functional programming. Several examples of the use of the stream operations in Exercise 9.4 can be found in Burge [1975]. The concept of lazy evaluation appears in the work of Vuillemin [1974] and Wadsworth [1971], and was applied to Lisp-like programs by Henderson and Morris [1976] and Friedman and Wise [1976].

The observation that ordered resource usage prevents deadlock appears in Coffman, Elphick, and Shoshani [1971]. The book by Francez [1986] is a comprehensive treatment of fairness. The concept of serializability is due to Eswaran et al. [1976]; see also Papadimitriou [1986].

Theoretical studies of concurrency often build on Milner's [1980] CCS, Calculus of Communicating Systems. The theoretical version of CSP in Hoare [1985] is influenced by CCS.

Exercise 9.9 is based on Kessels and Martin [1979]. The readers-and-writers problem in Exercise 9.10 was introduced by Courtois, Heymans, and Parnas [1971].

Part III

Language Description

Language descriptions are organized around the syntactic structure of a language. Chapter 10 separates the notions of abstract and concrete syntax, and introduces the idea of attaching attributes to syntactic constructs.

An operational semantics for a language specifies the computations set up by a program in the language. Chapter 11 considers two ways of specifying operational semantics: as a set of logical rules, and as a syntax-directed interpreter.

Chapter 12 examines increasingly general notions of types.

Ten

Syntactic Structure

Syntax plays two roles in descriptions of programming languages:

1. The *abstract syntax* of a language identifies the meaningful components of each construct. Language descriptions and implementations are organized around the abstract syntax.

2. The *concrete syntax* of a language describes its written representation, including details such as the placement of keywords and punctuation marks.

The same abstract syntax underlies the Modula-2 program fragment

```
WHILE x <> A[i] DO
    i := i-1
END
```

and the C program fragment

```
while( x != A[i] )
    i = i-1;
```

Each of these fragments consists of a while-loop with an expression that tests whether **x** differs from **A[i]**. If so, the body of the while-loop decrements **i** by one.

Backus [1960] originally introduced grammars as a notation for specifying concrete syntax, to give a "precise description of the sequences of symbols which constitute legal [Algol] programs."

The Algol 60 report (Naur [1963a]) used grammars to do more than specify the concrete syntax. The nonterminals were chosen to correspond to meaningful constructs in the language. The report observes that nonterminal names "have been chosen to be words describing approximately the nature of the corresponding [nonterminal]." The "nature" or meaning of nonterminals is formalized in Section 10.2 by attaching "attributes" to nonterminals.

Abstract syntax is a convenient starting point for designing a grammar for a language. Once the meaningful constructs of a language are identified, corresponding nonterminals can be chosen.

The abstract syntax of a construct will be depicted by a tree showing the components and subcomponents of the construct. Such trees, called abstract syntax trees, were introduced in Section 2.2 to show the syntactic structure of expressions. The same tree

$$
\begin{array}{c}
+ \\
\diagup\; \diagdown \\
2 \qquad 3
\end{array}
$$

represents the structure of the prefix expression $+2\,3$, the infix expression $2+3$, and the postfix expression $2\,3+$.

Abstract syntax trees can be extended to other constructs besides expressions by defining special operators for each construct. Each node n in an abstract syntax tree is for an operator **op**, and the children of n are for the operands of **op**. For example, an abstract syntax tree for the above Modula-2 and C program fragments appears in Fig. 10.1. The operator **while** for a while-loop has two children, corresponding to the test expression and the body of the while-loop, respectively. The other operators in the tree are ≠ for testing inequality, **index** for array indexing, **assign** for assignment, and − for subtraction.

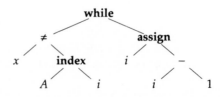

Fig. 10.1. An abstract syntax tree.

10.1   PARSE TREES DEPICT CONCRETE SYNTAX

This section examines how a grammar generates a string in a language. From the definition in Section 1.5, a context-free grammar has four parts:

1. A set of terminals.

2. A set of nonterminals.

3. A set of productions, where each production has a nonterminal as its left side, an ::=, and a string of terminals and nonterminals as its right side.

4. A nonterminal chosen as the starting nonterminal.

The following grammar serves as a running example for this chapter:

$$E \ ::= \ E + T \ | \ E - T \ | \ T$$
$$T \ ::= \ T * F \ | \ T \ \textbf{div} \ F \ | \ F$$
$$F \ ::= \ (\ E \ ) \ | \ \textbf{number}$$

(10.1)

Nonterminals begin with uppercase letters. Terminals consisting of symbols like + and − usually appear as is, but can be quoted for emphasis. Terminals in boldface like **number** appear as is. The nonterminals of this grammar are E, T, and F, and the terminals are

$+$ $-$ $*$ **div** $(\ )$ **number**

Lexical Syntax

Just as words in English are written using letters, the terminals or tokens in a grammar are written using characters. The actual character sequence used to write down an occurrence of a token is called the *spelling* of that occurrence.

A *lexical syntax* for a language specifies the correspondence between the written representation of the language and the tokens or terminals in a grammar for the language.

The spelling of a token will sometimes be shown as a subscript, to distinguish between occurrences of the token. Using **id** as the token for an identifier, a token stream for the character sequence

b * b − 4 * a * c

is

$\textbf{id}_b * \textbf{id}_b - \textbf{number}_4 * \textbf{id}_a * \textbf{id}_c$

Lexical syntax will not be formalized because informal descriptions usually suffice for white space, comments, and the correspondence between tokens and their spellings. Real numbers are a possible exception. The most complex rules in a lexical syntax are typically the ones describing the syntax of real numbers. The following are some of the ways of writing the same number in Modula-2:

314.E-2   3.14   0.314E+1   0.314E1

The leading **0** can be dropped in C, making **.314E1** an additional possibility.

A Parse Tree for a String

The productions in a grammar are rules for building strings of tokens. A parse tree shows how a string can be built.

A *parse tree* with respect to a grammar is a tree satisfying the following:

- Each leaf is labeled with a terminal or [], representing the empty string.

- Each nonleaf node is labeled with a nonterminal.

- The label of a nonleaf node must be the left side of some production and the labels of the children of the node, from left to right, must form the right side of that production.

- The root is labeled with the starting nonterminal.

A parse tree *generates* the string formed by reading the terminals at its leaves from left to right. The construction of a parse tree is called *parsing*.

For example, a nonleaf node labeled E with three children E, $-$, and T,

can appear in a parse tree with respect to a grammar containing the production

$$E ::= E - T$$

Such a node appears as the root of the parse tree in Fig. 10.2. The string generated by the parse tree is

number$_7$ * number$_7$ − number$_4$ * number$_2$ * number$_3$

Parse trees for realistic programs are large enough that the job of constructing them is best done by a computer.

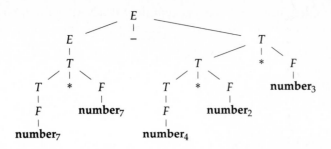

Fig. 10.2. A parse tree with respect to the expression grammar (10.1).

Syntactic Ambiguity

A grammar for a language is *syntactically ambiguous*, or simply *ambiguous*, if some string in its language has more than one parse tree. Programming languages can usually be described by unambiguous grammars. If ambiguities exist, they are *resolved* by establishing conventions that rule out all but one parse tree for each string.

A well known example of syntactic ambiguity is the *dangling-else* ambiguity, which arises if a grammar has two productions

S ::= **if** E **then** S
S ::= **if** E **then** S **else** S

where S represents statements and E represents expressions.

Neither production by itself leads to an ambiguity. When both appear in a grammar, however, it is not clear to which **if** an **else** belongs. The example in Fig. 10.3 shows only the relevant parts of two parse trees because it omits the subtrees below some of the nodes. The subscripts in the figure on nonterminals S and E simply distinguish between the occurrences of these nonterminals.

From left to right, the leaves of each tree are as follows:

if E_1 **then if** E_2 **then** S_1 **else** S_2

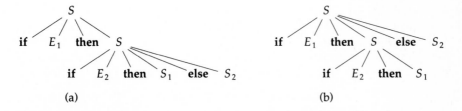

Fig. 10.3. In (a) the **else** is matched with the nearest unmatched **if**.

The dangling-else ambiguity is typically resolved by matching an **else** with the nearest unmatched **if**. Thus, the alternative in Fig. 10.3(a) is chosen.

Abstract syntax trees are unaffected by syntactic ambiguities. The two conditional constructs

$$S \; ::= \; \textbf{if } E \textbf{ then } S$$
$$S \; ::= \; \textbf{if } E \textbf{ then } S \textbf{ else } S$$

can be represented using the two different operators **if-then** and **if-then-else**, leading to nodes of the following form:

The use of the operators **if-then** and **if-then-else** leads to the two different abstract syntax trees in Fig. 10.4 for the string:

if E_1 **then if** E_2 **then** S_1 **else** S_2

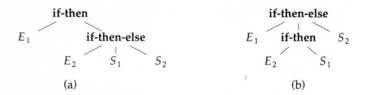

Fig. 10.4. Abstract syntax trees for the parse trees in Fig. 10.3.

10.2   SYNTHESIZED ATTRIBUTES

Syntactic structure can be used as follows to specify the semantics of a language:

1. Determine what constitutes the semantics of each construct. If we want to develop an expression evaluator, then the semantics of an expression 2+3 can be its value. Otherwise, if we want to develop an infix-to-postfix translator, then the semantics of 2+3 can be +23. In general, the semantics of a construct can be any quantity or set of quantities associated with the construct. A quantity associated with a construct is called an *attribute*. Examples of attributes are a set of strings, a value, a type, a snapshot of the memory of a computer.

2. Define the attributes of a construct in terms of the attributes of its components. That is, if construct A is defined in terms of components X, Y, and Z, then each attribute of A is defined in terms of the attri-

butes of X, Y, and Z. Attributes defined in this way are said to be *synthesized*.

This approach to defining semantics is said to be *syntax directed*. Rules defining the attributes of a construct are called *semantic rules*. Together, a syntax specification and its associated semantic rules are referred to as a *syntax-directed definition*.

Although syntax-directed definitions can be based on either concrete or abstract syntax, it is more natural to base them on abstract syntax.

Decorated Parse Trees

The syntax-directed definition in Fig. 10.5 attaches semantic rules to productions in the concrete syntax. We write $X.a$ to refer to attribute a of X, where X is either a nonterminal or a terminal. A semantic rule associated with a production $A ::= XYZ$ has the form

$A.a :=$ ⟨an expression involving attributes of X, Y, and Z⟩

The examples in this section deal with expressions in the language Little Quilt of Section 2.1. The two basic quilts are squares represented by tokens **a** and **b**:

a ◻   b ◻

Operator **sew** attaches a quilt to the right of another of equal height, and operator **turn** turns a quilt by 90°.

In Fig. 10.5, an expression E has two integer-valued attributes—*ht* for the height and *wid* for the width—written $E.ht$ and $E.wid$. If E is one of the tokens **a** and **b** for the basic square pieces, then $E.ht := 1$ and $E.wid := 1$. Turning a quilt 90° interchanges its height and width, so the rules associ-

PRODUCTION	SEMANTIC RULES
$E ::= \mathbf{a}$	$E.ht := 1$ $E.wid := 1$
$E ::= \mathbf{b}$	$E.ht := 1$ $E.wid := 1$
$E ::= \mathbf{turn}\ (\ E_1\ )$	$E.ht := E_1.wid$ $E.wid := E_1.ht$
$E ::= \mathbf{sew}\ (\ E_1\ ,\ E_2\ )$	$E.ht := \mathbf{if}\ E_1.ht = E_2.ht\ \mathbf{then}\ E_1.ht\ \mathbf{else\ error}$ $E.wid := E_1.wid + E_2.wid$

Fig. 10.5. Syntax-directed determination of the height and width of a quilt.

ated with $E ::= \textbf{turn}(E_1)$ say that $E.ht$ equals $E_1.wid$ and $E.wid$ equals $E_1.ht$. Two quilts must be of equal height if they are sewn together. Therefore, associated with the production

$$E ::= \textbf{sew} (E_1 , E_2)$$

is the semantic rule

$$E.ht := \textbf{if } E_1.ht = E_2.ht \textbf{ then } E_1.ht \textbf{ else error}$$

We assume that **error** is a special value; adding anything to **error** yields **error**.

Values of attributes ht and wid are shown just below each occurrence of nonterminal E in the parse tree in Fig. 10.6. Trees showing attribute values are said to be *decorated*.

Working from the leaves toward the root, consider the nodes created by the productions $E ::= \textbf{a}$ and $E ::= \textbf{b}$. From the semantic rules in Fig. 10.5, $E.ht := 1$ and $E.wid := 1$ at each such node.

The node created by the production

$$E ::= \textbf{sew} (E_1 , E_2)$$

has two children labeled E, corresponding to E_1 and E_2 in the production. Since the ht attribute at both children equals 1, the value of $E.ht$ at their parent also equals 1. $E.wid$ at their parent equals 2, the sum of the wid attributes at the children.

Finally, the root, created by

$$E ::= \textbf{turn} (E_1)$$

has one child labeled E. The ht and wid attributes at the root equal the wid and ht attributes, respectively, at this child.

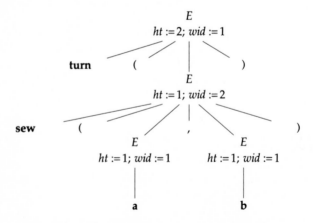

Fig. 10.6. Parse tree decorated with attribute values.

Decorated Abstract Syntax Trees

The abstract syntax trees in Fig. 10.7 show the structure of the expression generated by the parse tree in Fig. 10.6. The tree in Fig. 10.7(a) is decorated with the quilts represented by the nodes in the tree, and the tree in (b) is decorated with the values for attributes *ht* and *wid*.

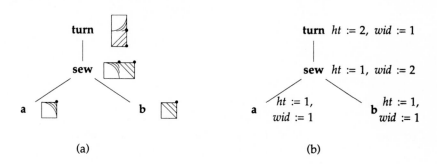

(a)   (b)

Fig. 10.7. Decorated abstract syntax trees.

10.3 GRAMMARS FOR EXPRESSIONS

Grammars can play a dual role in descriptions of programming languages. First, they specify the concrete syntax by characterizing the strings that belong to the language. Second, a well designed grammar can make it easy to pick out the meaningful components of a construct. In other words, with a well designed grammar, parse trees are similar enough to abstract syntax trees that the grammar can be used to organize a language description.

The abstract syntax

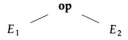

describes an expression built up by applying a binary operator **op** to two subexpressions E_1 and E_2. If **op** is +, then the value of E is the sum of the values of E_1 and E_2. Otherwise, if **op** is *, then the value of E is the product of the values of E_1 and E_2, and so on.

When expressions are written in infix notation, we need a grammar that makes it easy to identify the subexpressions of an expression.

Example 10.1. Consider infix expressions formed by applying the addition and subtraction operators to numbers. Some examples are

$$4 - 2 - 1$$
$$9 + 7 - 5 - 3$$

Since + and − are left associative, the following is a suitable grammar for such sequences of numbers separated by + or − signs:

$L ::= L +$ **number**
   $|$ $L −$ **number**
   $|$ **number**

A less desirable grammar is

$R ::=$ **number** $+ R$
   $|$ **number** $− R$
   $|$ **number**

Parse trees for $4−2−1$ with respect to these two grammars appear in Fig. 10.8.

Although both grammars are unambiguous, the grammar with starting nonterminal L is more suitable for specifying the values of expressions because its parse trees are closer to the abstract syntax of expressions. An abstract syntax tree for $4−2−1$ is

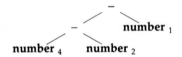

Since − is left associative, the subexpressions of

$$4 - 2 - 1$$

are $4−2$ and 1. These subexpressions can easily be identified when $4−2−1$ is generated by the production $L ::= L_1 −$ **number** because L_1 corresponds to $4−2$ and **number** corresponds to 1.   □

The productions for nonterminal E in the standard grammar for arithmetic expressions (see Fig. 10.9) correspond to those for L in Example 10.1.

Fig. 10.8. Parse trees with respect to two grammars.

Production	Semantic Rules
$E ::= E_1 + T$	$E.val := E_1.val + T.val$
$E ::= E_1 - T$	$E.val := E_1.val - T.val$
$E ::= T$	$E.val := T.val$
$T ::= T_1 * F$	$T.val := T_1.val * F.val$
$T ::= T_1 \text{ div } F$	$T.val := T_1.val \text{ \textbf{div} } F.val$
$T ::= F$	$T.val := F.val$
$F ::= (E)$	$F.val := E.val$
$F ::= \textbf{number}$	$F.val := \textbf{number}.val$

Fig. 10.9. Rules for evaluating arithmetic expressions.

The roles of nonterminal E for expression, T for term, and F for factor are given by:

- An expression is a sequence of terms separated by + or −.

- A term is a sequence of factors separated by * or **div**.

- A factor is a parenthesized expression or a number.

This stratification of expressions into terms and factors is motivated by the higher precedence of the multiplicative operators compared with the additive operators.

In the syntax-directed definition in Fig. 10.9, each grammar symbol has an attribute *val*. We illustrate the rules by considering the decorated parse tree in Fig. 10.10. Working bottom-up from the left, the rule $F.val := \textbf{number}.val$ defines attribute *val* of the leftmost node for F to be 7. The rule $T.val := F.val$ associated with $T ::= F$ copies this value, so $T.val$ is also 7. The value at a node generated by $T ::= T_1 * F$ is the product of the values of T_1 and F. Hence, the left child of the root has value 49. The production at the root is $E ::= E_1 - T$; the associated semantic rule defines the value of E to be the difference of the values at its children.

10.4 CONCRETE SYNTAX DOES MATTER

Although they are semantically irrelevant, details such as the placement of keywords and semicolons do matter. Compared with Pascal, Wirth [1983] writes, Modula-2 has "a more systematic syntax which facilitates the learning process." This section examines some of the syntactic differences between Pascal and Modula-2. The use of uppercase letters to spell keywords in Modula-2 is a matter of taste and will be ignored.

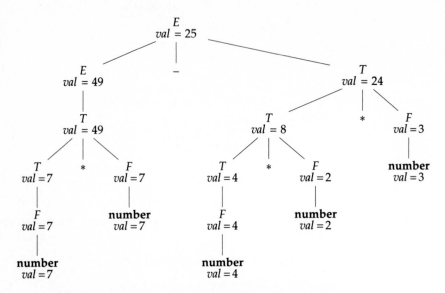

Fig. 10.10. Parse tree decorated with the values of subexpressions.

Sequences: Separators versus Terminators

Sequences—of statements, declarations, parameters—can be classified by asking the following questions:

- Can the sequence be empty? That is, can it have zero elements?
- Does a delimiter, if any, separate elements or terminate them? A delimiter *separates* elements if it appears between them. A delimiter *terminates* elements if it appears after each element.

There is evidence to indicate that fewer programming errors are made if semicolons terminate rather than separate statements.

Pascal uses semicolons primarily to separate statements, as in

> **begin** stmt$_1$; stmt$_2$; stmt$_3$ **end**

A parse tree for this string appears in Fig. 10.11. The grammar itself, in Fig. 10.12, has productions for a fragment of Pascal. Token **expr** represents an expression and token **stmt** represents the remaining statement constructs.

At first glance, it seems that the grammar in Fig. 10.12 allows statements to be terminated by semicolons as well, because the parse tree in Fig. 10.13 generates

> **begin** stmt$_1$; stmt$_2$; stmt$_3$; **end**

This string is obtained from

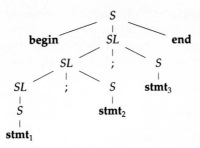

Fig. 10.11. Parse tree for **begin stmt ; stmt ; stmt end**.

$$S ::= [\,]$$
$$\quad | \ \textbf{stmt}$$
$$\quad | \ \textbf{begin } SL \textbf{ end}$$
$$\quad | \ \textbf{if expr then } S$$
$$\quad | \ \textbf{if expr then } S \textbf{ else } S$$
$$\quad | \ \textbf{while expr do } S$$

$$SL ::= SL \textbf{ ; } S$$
$$\quad | \ S$$

Fig. 10.12. A grammar for a fragment of Pascal.

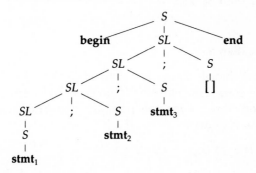

Fig. 10.13. Use of an empty statement to get a semicolon after **stmt₃**.

begin $S_1 ; S_2 ; S_3 ; S_4$ **end**

where S_4 generates the empty string. By allowing occurrences of S to "disappear," the production

$$S ::= [\,]$$

allows semicolons to be inserted before or after statements, as in

begin ; stmt ; ; stmt ; ; ; end

Empty statements make the placement of semicolons significant; insertion of a semicolon can change the meaning of a program in Pascal. Insertion of a semicolon after the keyword **then** has the presumably unintended effect of inserting an empty statement after **then**. Thus,

> **if expr then ; stmt**

is a sequence of two statements, semantically equivalent to

> **if expr then begin end ; stmt**

Here, **begin end** makes it explicit that no action is taken if **expr** represents **true**.

Why does insertion of a semicolon after S_1 in

> **if expr then** S_1 **else** S_2

lead to a syntactic error?

We now look at how Modula-2 deals with semicolons.

Opening and Closing Delimiters

Modula-2 avoids confusion due to misplaced semicolons by attaching a closing keyword **end**. The grammar in Fig. 10.14 has the production

> S ::= **if expr then** SL **end**

instead of

> S ::= **if expr then** S

in Fig. 10.12. This change allows a statement list to appear between **then** and **end,** so extraneous semicolons between these keywords are harmless.

The closing **end** also avoids the dangling-else ambiguity because the troublesome Pascal statement

> **if expr then if expr then** S **else** S

is forced to be rewritten unambiguously as either of the following:

$$S ::= [\,]$$
$$| \quad \textbf{stmt}$$
$$| \quad \textbf{if expr then } SL \textbf{ end}$$
$$| \quad \textbf{if expr then } SL \textbf{ else } SL \textbf{ end}$$
$$| \quad \textbf{while expr do } SL \textbf{ end}$$
$$SL ::= SL ; S$$
$$| \quad S$$

Fig. 10.14. A grammar for a fragment of Modula-2.

if expr then ⌐if expr then *SL* else *SL* end⌐ end

if expr then ⌐if expr then *SL* end⌐ else *SL* end

Closing delimiters can lead to a proliferation of keywords. If the Pascal-like string

if expr$_1$ then stmt$_1$
else if expr$_2$ then stmt$_2$
else if expr$_3$ then stmt$_3$
else
    stmt$_4$

is rewritten with closing keywords, we get

if expr$_1$ then stmt$_1$
else if expr$_2$ then stmt$_2$
    else if expr$_3$ then stmt$_3$
        else
            stmt$_4$
        end
    end
end

Modula-2 avoids a proliferation of **end** keywords in conditionals by using the following general form (in EBNF notation):

if expr then *SL* { elsif expr then *SL* } [else *SL*] end

Thus, there can be zero or more repetitions of

elsif expr then *SL*

and

else *SL*

is optional. The above example can therefore be rewritten as:

if expr$_1$ then stmt$_1$
elsif expr$_2$ then stmt$_2$
elsif expr$_3$ then stmt$_3$
else
    stmt$_4$
end

EXERCISES

10.1 For each of the following strings, draw a parse tree with respect to the expression grammar (10.1):
   a) 2 + 3
   b) (2 + 3)
   c) 2 + 3 * 5
   d) (2 + 3) * 5
   e) 2 + (3 * 5)

10.2 Draw abstract syntax trees for the expressions in Exercise 10.1.

10.3 Give a syntax-directed definition for building abstract syntax trees for expressions generated by the grammar (10.1). Implement nodes as variant records and use pointers to nodes as the attributes for the token **number** and the nonterminals *E*, *T*, and *F*.

10.4 Give a syntax-directed definition for translating expressions from infix into postfix notation.

10.5 Abstract syntax trees correspond directly to expressions in prefix notation, as we saw in Section 2.2.
   a) Devise a notation for describing abstract syntax trees that is similar to grammars. A "production" in the notation describes the relationship between a node and its children.
   b) Use your notation from (a) to specify the quilt grammar in Fig. 10.5 and the expression grammar in Fig. 10.9.
   c) Extend your notation from (a) to specify syntax-directed definitions based on abstract syntax trees.
   d) Use your notation from (c) to specify syntax-directed definitions corresponding to those in Fig. 10.5 and 10.9.

10.6 The following grammar is motivated by declarations in C:

$$
\begin{aligned}
\textit{Declaration} \quad &::= \quad \textit{Type} \;\; \textit{Declarator} \;\; ; \\
\textit{Type} \quad &::= \quad \textbf{int} \\
&\;\;| \quad \textbf{char} \\
\textit{Declarator} \quad &::= \quad * \;\; \textit{Declarator} \\
&\;\;| \quad \textit{Declarator} \;\; '[' \;\; \textbf{number} \;\; ']' \\
&\;\;| \quad \textit{Declarator} \;\; '(' \;\; \textit{Type} \;\; ')' \\
&\;\;| \quad '(' \;\; \textit{Declarator} \;\; ')' \\
&\;\;| \quad \textbf{name}
\end{aligned}
$$

   a) Prove the syntactic ambiguity of this grammar by finding a string that has more than one parse tree. Draw the parse trees.
   b) The constructs '[' **number** ']' and '(' *Type* ')' can be thought of as being postfix operators with a declarator as an operand. Sup-

pose that * has lower precedence than these operators. Write an unambiguous grammar that generates the same strings as this grammar, and makes it easy to identify the components of a declarator.

c) Suppose that the first production for *Declarator* is changed to make * a postfix operator. Why does the grammar then become unambiguous?

BIBLIOGRAPHIC NOTES

Grammars were introduced independently by Chomsky [1956] and Backus [1960]. Backus's notation was immediately adopted for describing Algol 60, and has come to be called Backus-Naur Form (BNF); Naur [1963a] edited the Algol 60 report. It was later learnt that a notation similar to BNF was used by Panini between 400 B.C. and 200 B.C. to describe the complex rules of Sanskrit grammar (Ingerman [1967]).

McCarthy [1963] introduced a specific form of abstract syntax with predicates to recognize a construct and functions to extract its components. He argued that an abstract syntax was all that was needed to translate a language or define its semantics. "That is why we do not care whether sums are represented by $a+b$, or $+ab$, or **(PLUS A B)**, or even by Gödel numbers $7^a 11^b$."

A syntax-directed compiler by Irons [1961] was one of the earliest explicit uses of synthesized attributes.

Syntax and syntax-directed definitions have been studied extensively; more information can be found in books on compilers, such as Aho, Sethi, and Ullman [1986].

Experiments by Gannon and Horning [1975] suggest that semicolons are less likely to be misplaced if statements are terminated rather than separated by semicolons. Exercise 10.6 is based on Sethi [1981].

Eleven

Definitional Interpreters

One way to define a language is to write an interpreter for it. Questions about the language can then be resolved by running the interpreter and seeing what it does. If an interpreter is readable enough, then it can serve as a language definition even if the interpreter exists only on paper.

This chapter illustrates *definitional interpreters*, so called because they are used primarily to define the interpreted language. They are meant to be readable; efficiency is not a concern. A definitional interpreter deals with two languages: a *defined* language that is interpreted and a *defining* language, in which the interpreter itself is written.

The goal of this chapter is to develop an interpreter for a small subset of Scheme. The interpreter is itself written in Scheme, making Scheme both the defined and the defining language.

11.1 NATURAL SEMANTICS

A syntax-directed interpreter can be characterized by a set of rules that associate a value with each expression in the defined language. This section introduces *natural semantics*, which is based on a logical notation. Natural semantics sidesteps issues of parsing and evaluation order, so it allows the semantics of a language to be captured in a small set of rules.

The rules transliterate directly into Prolog; Scheme implementations based on such rules appear in subsequent sections.

The defined languages in this section are fragments of Scheme. The defining language uses standard notations like $v_1 + v_2$ and will not be formalized.

A Calculator

We begin with a preliminary version of natural semantics that can be thought of as associating synthesized attributes with constructs in a language. In order to keep the semantics self-contained, we use the abstract syntax **num**(*val*) for numbers, where **num** is a token, and *val* is its associated value. Expressions therefore have the form

$$E ::= \textbf{num}(val)$$
$$\mid \ (\ \textbf{plus}\ E_1\ E_2\ )$$
$$\mid \ (\ \textbf{times}\ E_1\ E_2\ )$$

The preliminary version of natural semantics can handle these expressions, but it needs to be extended to handle variables, whose values depend on the context.

The value of **(plus** E_1 E_2**)** is the sum of the values of E_1 and E_2. This rule can be written as

$$\frac{E_1\ :\ v_1 \qquad E_2\ :\ v_2}{(\textbf{plus}\ E_1\ E_2)\ :\ v_1 + v_2} \qquad\qquad\qquad (\text{sum})$$

In words, if E_1 has value v_1 and E_2 has value v_2, then **(plus** E_1 E_2**)** has value $v_1 + v_2$. To the left of the colon in the formula

$$E : v$$

is an expression E. Its value v appears to the right of the colon. Thus, in the formula

$$(\textbf{plus}\ E_1\ E_2)\ :\ v_1 + v_2$$

the expression **(plus** E_1 E_2**)** belongs to the defined language, and $v_1 + v_2$ belongs to the defining language.

The rules for numbers, sums, and products are collected in Fig. 11.1. Each rule has a name, in parentheses to its right. As usual in logical rules, conditions appear above a line and the conclusion appears below the line. If there are no conditions, as in the rule for numbers, then the conclusion appears by itself, without a line. Rules without conditions are called *axioms*. The axiom for numbers says that the value of a number **num**(*val*) is simply its associated attribute, *val*.

$$\textbf{num}(val) \; : \; val \qquad \text{(number)}$$

$$\frac{E_1 \; : \; v_1 \qquad E_2 \; : \; v_2}{\textbf{(plus } E_1 \, E_2) \; : \; v_1 + v_2} \qquad \text{(sum)}$$

$$\frac{E_1 \; : \; v_1 \qquad E_2 \; : \; v_2}{\textbf{(times } E_1 \, E_2) \; : \; v_1 * v_2} \qquad \text{(product)}$$

Fig. 11.1. A preliminary example of natural semantics.

Environments Bind Names to Values

The value of an expression **(+ a b)** depends on the values of the variables **a** and **b**. To handle variables, we introduce environments, which bind a variable to a value.

Environments will be treated as objects with two operations:

1. *bind* (x, v, env) is a new environment that binds variable x to value v; the bindings of all other variables are as in the environment *env*.

2. *lookup* (x, env) is the value bound to variable x in environment *env*.

The empty environment *nil* binds no variables.

Environments are shown explicitly in natural semantics by writing formulas called *sequents*, of the form

$$env \; \vdash \; E \; : \; v$$

This formula says, "In environment *env*, expression E has value v." The rule for sums is now written as

$$\frac{env \; \vdash \; E_1 \; : \; v_1 \qquad env \; \vdash \; E_2 \; : \; v_2}{env \; \vdash \; \textbf{(plus } E_1 \, E_2) \; : \; v_1 + v_2} \qquad \text{(sum)}$$

Let Bindings

The defined language in Fig. 11.2 contains numbers, variables, sums, products, and let expressions. The rules for numbers, sums, and products are obtained by adding environments to the rules in Fig. 11.1.

The following axiom specifies that the value of a variable is looked up in the environment:

$$env \; \vdash \; x \; : \; lookup \, (x, env) \qquad \text{(variable)}$$

An application of this rule is

$$env \vdash \textbf{num}(val) \; : \; val \hspace{4cm} \text{(number)}$$

$$\frac{env \vdash E_1 \; : \; v_1 \qquad env \vdash E_2 \; : \; v_2}{env \vdash \textbf{(plus } E_1 \; E_2) \; : \; v_1 + v_2} \hspace{2cm} \text{(sum)}$$

$$\frac{env \vdash E_1 \; : \; v_1 \qquad env \vdash E_2 \; : \; v_2}{env \vdash \textbf{(times } E_1 \; E_2) \; : \; v_1 * v_2} \hspace{2cm} \text{(product)}$$

$$env \vdash x \; : \; lookup\,(x, env) \hspace{3.5cm} \text{(variable)}$$

$$\frac{env \vdash E_1 \; : \; v_1 \qquad bind\,(x, v_1, env) \vdash E_2 \; : \; v_2}{env \vdash \textbf{(let ((}x \; E_1\textbf{)) } E_2) \; : \; v_2} \hspace{1.5cm} \text{(let)}$$

Fig. 11.2. Environments are used in the rules (variable) and (let).

$$bind\,(\textbf{y}, 2, nil) \quad \vdash \quad \textbf{y} \; : \; 2$$

The environment $bind\,(\textbf{y}, 2, nil)$ binds $\textbf{y}$ to 2 and has no bindings for other variables. This value 2 is extracted by function $lookup$:

$$lookup\,(\textbf{y}, \; bind\,(\textbf{y}, 2, nil)) \; = \; 2$$

Let us read the following rule for let expressions backwards, from the conclusion to the conditions:

$$\frac{env \vdash E_1 \; : \; v_1 \qquad bind\,(x, v_1, env) \vdash E_2 \; : \; v_2}{env \vdash \textbf{(let ((}x \; E_1\textbf{)) } E_2) \; : \; v_2} \hspace{1.5cm} \text{(let)}$$

The value of the expression $\textbf{(let ((}x \; E_1\textbf{)) } E_2)$ is v_2, if

1. E_1 evaluates to v_1, and
2. E_2 evaluates to v_2 in an environment with x bound to v_1.

The value 2 for the expression $\textbf{(let ((y num}(2)\textbf{)) y)}$ is determined by the following application of the rule:

$$\frac{nil \vdash \textbf{num}(2) \; : \; 2 \qquad bind\,(\textbf{y}, 2, nil) \vdash \textbf{y} \; : \; 2}{nil \vdash \textbf{(let ((y num}(2)\textbf{)) y)} \; : \; 2}$$

As another example, the value of $\textbf{(let ((y num}(2)\textbf{)) (plus y y))}$ is 4:

$$\frac{nil \vdash \textbf{num}(2) \; : \; 2 \qquad bind\,(\textbf{y}, 2, nil) \vdash \textbf{(plus y y)} \; : \; 4}{nil \vdash \textbf{(let ((y num}(2)\textbf{)) (plus y y))} \; : \; 4}$$

A Prolog Implementation

The rules in the natural semantics of a language can be encoded directly in Prolog. Expressions in the defined language are encoded as terms, axioms are encoded as facts, and semantic rules are encoded as Prolog rules. The semantics in Fig. 11.2 leads to the Prolog rules in Fig. 11.3.

The defined language in Fig. 11.3 consists of terms of the form

$$E ::= \textbf{num(} \; val \; \textbf{)}$$
$$| \quad \textbf{var(} \; atom \; \textbf{)}$$
$$| \quad \textbf{plus(} \; E_1 \; , \; E_2 \; \textbf{)}$$
$$| \quad \textbf{times(} \; E_1 \; , \; E_2 \; \textbf{)}$$
$$| \quad \textbf{let(} \; \textbf{var(} \; atom \; \textbf{)} \; , \; E_1 \; , \; E_2 \; \textbf{)}$$

A little "syntactic sugar"—a minor change in syntax—converts these terms into expressions in the defined language of Fig. 11.2.

A sequent

$$env \vdash E \; : \; v$$

is encoded as

```
seq(Env, E, V)
```

Variables in Prolog begin with uppercase letters, so *env* is encoded as **Env** and *v* is encoded as **V**.

```
seq(Env, num(Val), Val).                              (number)

seq(Env, plus(E1, E2), V) :-                          (sum)
    seq(Env, E1, V1), seq(Env, E2, V2), V is V1 + V2.

seq(Env, times(E1, E2), V) :-                         (product)
    seq(Env, E1, V1), seq(Env, E2, V2), V is V1 * V2.

seq(Env, var(X), V) :-                                (variable)
    lookup(X, Env, V).

seq(Env, let(var(X), E1, E2), V2) :-                  (let)
    seq(Env, E1, V1), seq(bind(X, V1, Env), E2, V2).

lookup(X, bind(X, V, _), V).

lookup(X, bind(Y, _, Env), V) :-
    lookup(X, Env, V).
```

Fig. 11.3. A Prolog version of the natural semantics in Fig. 11.2.

The axiom

$$env \;\vdash\; \textbf{num}(val) \;:\; val \qquad\qquad\qquad\qquad\text{(number)}$$

in Fig. 11.2 leads to the following fact in Fig. 11.3:

```
seq(Env, num(Val), Val).
```

The following rule in the natural semantics

$$\frac{env \;\vdash\; E_1 \;:\; v_1 \qquad\qquad env \;\vdash\; E_2 \;:\; v_2}{env \;\vdash\; (\textbf{plus}\; E_1\; E_2) \;:\; v_1 + v_2} \qquad\qquad \text{(sum)}$$

leads to the rule

```
seq(Env, plus(E1, E2), V) :-
     seq(Env, E1, V1), seq(Env, E2, V2), V is V1 + V2.
```

The conclusion appears before the conditions in Prolog, with `:-` appearing between them. The goal

```
V is V1 + V2
```

evaluates the expression **V1 + V2** and associates its value with **V**.

Environments are represented simply as terms in Fig. 11.3. The environment

```
bind(y, 2, nil)
```

binds variable **var(y)** to the value 2.

The following query uses the rules in Fig. 11.3:

```
?- E = let(var(y), num(2), var(y)),   seq(nil, E, V).
     E = let(var(y),num(2),var(y))
     V = 2
```

For convenience, this query uses variable **E** to refer to the expression to be evaluated; the actual evaluation is done in response to the query **seq(nil, E, V)**. The result, 2, is the value computed by Prolog for **V**.

Another example is

```
?- Y = var(y), E = let(Y, num(2), plus(Y, Y)),
     seq(nil, E, V).
     Y = var(y)
     E = let(var(y),num(2),plus(var(y),var(y)))
     V = 4
```

11.2   LEXICALLY SCOPED LAMBDA EXPRESSIONS

With all functions, including those denoted by lambda expressions, there is a distinction between the environment in which the function is defined and the environment in which the function is applied. Call these the *definition* and *activation* environments, respectively.

For the highlighted lambda expression in

```
. . .
    (let ((f (lambda (y) (* y z)))) ; definition environment
       . . .
        (f 2) )))                   ; activation environment
```

the definition environment is the one in which it is bound to **f**, and the activation environment is the one in which the function is applied during the evaluation of **(f 2)**.

A difficulty arises if a lambda expression contains free variables, as in

```
(lambda (y) (* y z))
```

where **z** is free. The value of the formal parameter **y** will become available when this lambda expression is applied, but what is the value of the free variable **z**?

Under the *lexical scope* rules of Scheme, the value of a free variable is taken from the definition environment. Under the *dynamic scope* rules of other Lisp dialects, the value of a free variable is taken from the activation environment. The following example explores the distinction between these scope rules.

Example 11.1. Most expressions have the same values under both the lexical and dynamic scope rules. This example develops an expression that has different values under the two scope rules.

The essential building block is a lambda expression containing a free variable **z**:

```
(lambda (y) (* y z))
```

The following fragment binds **f** to this function and later applies it to the actual parameter **2**:

```
...
    (let ((f (lambda (y) (* y z))))   ; definition environment
      ...
        (f 2) )))                      ; activation environment
```

The two pieces missing from this fragment are bindings for **z**. We will choose them to ensure that the value of **z** in the definition environment is different from its value in the activation environment.

The definition environment binds **z** to **0**:

```
(let ((z 0))
    (let ((f (lambda (y) (* y z))))
      ...
        (f 2) )))
```

Already, we can say that Scheme will evaluate **(f 2)** to **0** in Scheme, independent of the missing piece. The complete expression is

```
(let ((z 0))
    (let ((f (lambda (y) (* y z))))
      (let ((z 1))
        (f 2) )))
      0
```

Lisp dialects that use dynamic scope evaluate this expression to **2** instead of to **0**.   □

Natural Semantics of Lambda Expressions

In the natural semantics in Fig. 11.4, the definition and activation environments are denoted by the variables *def-env* and *act-env*.

Before studying the rules, let us reexamine the example

```
...
    (let ((f (lambda (y) (* y z))))   ; definition environment
      ...
        (f 2) )))                      ; activation environment
```

The treatment of the lambda expression in this example can be explained as follows:

1. When the lambda expression is bound to **f**, the value of the free variable **z** is frozen.

Rule (lambda)

$$def\text{-}env \vdash \textbf{(lambda } (x) \ E\textbf{)} \ : \ \textbf{closure}(\textbf{(lambda } (x) \ E\textbf{)}, \ def\text{-}env)$$

Rule (apply-lambda)

$$\frac{\begin{array}{l} act\text{-}env \ \vdash \ F \ : \ \textbf{closure}(\textbf{(lambda } (x) \ B\textbf{)}, \ def\text{-}env) \\ act\text{-}env \ \vdash \ A \ : \ a \\ bind \ (x, \ a, \ def\text{-}env) \ \vdash \ B \ : \ v \end{array}}{act\text{-}env \ \vdash \ \textbf{(}F \ A\textbf{)} \ : \ v}$$

Fig. 11.4. Call-by-value evaluation of lexically scoped lambda expressions.

2. The body **(* y z)** is evaluated when the value of the formal parameter **y** becomes known. That is, a multiplication occurs during the evaluation of **(f 2)**.

The two rules in Fig. 11.4 correspond to these two steps. Rule (lambda) simply saves a lambda expression and its definition environment into a data structure called a *closure*. A closure formalizes the notion of freezing the values of the free variables in the lambda expression; whenever the value of a free variable is needed, it will be taken from the saved environment.

An explanation of rule (apply-lambda) is as follows. (Evaluation takes place in the activation environment, unless specified otherwise.) The expression *(F A)*, the application of *F* to *A*, has value *v* if three conditions hold:

1. *F* evaluates to a closure. The lambda expression in the closure has formal parameter *x* and body *B*. The environment saved in the closure is *def-env*.

2. *A* evaluates to *a*.

3. The body *B* of the lambda expression evaluates to *v* in an environment *bind* (*x*, *a*, *def-env*). In this environment, the formal parameter *x* is bound to the value *a* of the actual parameter. The definition environment *def-env*, saved in the closure, is used for the free variables in *B*.

An application of the rule (apply-lambda) yields the value 0 for the subexpression **(f 2)** in the running example:

```
(let ((z 0))
  (let ((f (lambda (y) (* y z))))
    (let ((z 1))
      (f 2) )))
```

Suppose that evaluation starts in the empty environment *nil*. The definition environment for the lambda expression is therefore *bind* (**z**, 0, *nil*). The details of the activation environment *act-env* are not shown. All we need to know is that *act-env* binds **f** to the closure shown in the following:[1]

$$act\text{-}env \ \vdash \ \textbf{f} \ : \ \textbf{closure((lambda (y) (* y z))}, \ bind\,(\textbf{z}, 0, nil))$$

$$act\text{-}env \ \vdash \ \textbf{2} \ : \ 2$$

$$\underline{bind\,(\textbf{y}, \, 2, \, bind\,(\textbf{z}, 0, nil)) \ \vdash \ \textbf{(* y z)} \ : \ 0}$$

$$act\text{-}env \ \vdash \ \textbf{(f 2)} \ : \ 0$$

11.3   A CALCULATOR IN SCHEME

Expressions consisting of numbers, sums, and products are simple enough that their interpreter can be shown in its entirety in Fig. 11.5. Its main routine **calc** uses predicates **constant?**, **sum?**, and **product?** to analyze the syntax of expression **E**. If a predicate returns true, then a corresponding function is called to evaluate **E**.

Constants in the defined language are numbers. Predicate **constant?** is therefore implemented by **number?**:

```
(define constant? number?)
```

Scheme interprets a number by returning its value, so **calc-constant** simply returns its argument:

```
(define (calc-constant E) E)
```

Scheme has a built-in lexical analyzer that converts the character representation of a number into an internal form, so we can think of numbers as numbers, not as tokens with associated values.

A sum has the form

$$\textbf{(plus} \ E_1 \ E_2 \ \cdots \ E_k\textbf{)}$$

Predicate **sum?** returns true if it is applied to a list, and the head of the list is the symbol **plus**:

---

[1] Technically, we should use the abstract syntax **num**(2) instead of **2** in the rules.

```
(define (calc E)                   ; the main routine
   (cond ((constant? E) (calc-constant E))
         ((sum? E)       (calc-sum E))
         ((product? E)   (calc-product E))
         (else (error "calc: cannot parse" E)) ))


(define constant? number?)         ; constants are numbers

(define (calc-constant E) E)       ; evaluating to themselves


(define (sum? E)                   ; a sum is a list with head plus
   (and (pair? E) (equal? 'plus (car E))) )

(define (calc-sum E)               ; evaluate subexpressions and apply +
   (apply + (map calc (cdr E))))


(define (product? E)               ; a product is a list with head times
   (and (pair? E) (equal? 'times (car E))) )

(define (calc-product E)           ; evaluate subexpressions and apply *
   (apply * (map calc (cdr E))))
```

Fig. 11.5. An interpreter for numbers, sums, and products.

```
(define (sum? E)
   (and (pair? E) (equal? 'plus (car E))) )
```

The interpreter evaluates a sum by evaluating each of the subexpressions and then using the Scheme function **+** to compute their sum. The subexpressions of **E** are given by **(cdr E)**. A list consisting of their values is computed by

```
(map calc (cdr E))
```

which applies **calc** to each element of the list of subexpressions **(cdr E)**. The function **apply** in Scheme satisfies the equality

$$\texttt{(apply + (list } E_1\ E_2\ \cdots\ E_k\texttt{))}\ =\ \texttt{(+ } E_1\ E_2\ \cdots\ E_k\texttt{)}$$

Function **apply** is used by **calc-sum** to add the values of the subexpressions of **E**:

```
(define (calc-sum E)
  (apply + (map calc (cdr E))) )
```

Since **calc-sum** is called only on sums, it does not check whether its argument **E** is indeed a sum.

Products are handled similarly.

11.4   AN IMPLEMENTATION OF ENVIRONMENTS

Association lists or simply *a-lists* are a traditional implementation of environments. Each element of an a-list is an association or binding, consisting of a variable and its value. The association list

```
((a 1) (b 2) (c 3)  ···  )
```

implements an environment that binds **a** to **1**, binds **b** to **2**, and so on.

It is convenient to have three operations on environments:

1. **bind** returns an environment with a new binding for a variable.
2. **bind-all** binds variables in a list **vars** to values in a corresponding list **values**.
3. **assoc** returns the most recent binding for a variable.

As in Fig. 11.6, **bind** places a binding at the head of an association list.

```
(define (bind var value env)
  (cons (list var value) env))
```

The code for **bind-all** is illustrated in Fig. 11.7.

```
(define (bind-all vars values env)
  (append (map list vars values) env) )
```

In words, **map** applies **list** to corresponding elements of the two lists **vars** and **values**. If **vars** is (a b c) and **values** is (1 2 3), then

```
(map list vars values)
```

yields

Fig. 11.6. Function **bind** adds a single binding to an association list.

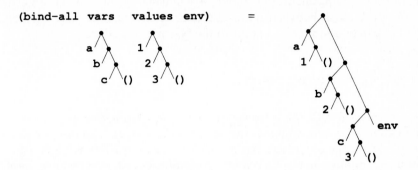

Fig. 11.7. Function **bind-all** extends an association list.

```
((a 1)  (b 2)  (c 3))
```

This list is then appended onto **env**.

Operation **assoc** is supported directly by Scheme; it extracts the first binding for a variable from an a-list, as in

```
(assoc 'a '((a 1)  (b 2)  (a 3)))
    (a 1)
(assoc 'b '((a 1)  (b 2)  (a 3)))
    (b 2)
```

If no binding is found, **assoc** returns false.

An Initial Environment

In Section 11.3, the desk calculator **calc** evaluated expressions of the form

```
(plus 2 3)
```

by using the addition procedure of Scheme to add the values of subexpressions **2** and **3**.

Interpreter **val** in Section 11.5 also allows Scheme's built-in procedures to be used, indirectly, through an initial environment. The following program fragment shows some of the bindings in **initial-env**:

```
(define initial-env
   (list (list '+ +)
         (list 'please-add +)
         (list 'null? null?)
         (list 'cons cons)
         ... ))
```

Within this environment, the symbol **+** evaluates to the Scheme procedure
+. To distinguish between these two uses of **+**, **initial-env** includes a
symbol **please-add**, also bound to the Scheme procedure **+**.

11.5   AN INTERPRETER

This section develops an interpreter **val** that takes two parameters: an
expression **E** to be evaluated and an environment **env** holding values for
the variables. Function **val** has a case for each of the following constructs:
numbers, quoted items, variables, conditionals, let expressions, lambda
expressions, and function applications. Function applications are kept to
the end because any list that does not match one of the earlier forms is by
default a function application.

```
(define (val E env)
   (cond ((constant? E)     (val-constant E env))
         ((quote? E)        (val-quote E env))
         ((variable? E)     (val-variable E env))
         ((if? E)           (val-if E env))
         ((let? E)          (val-let E env))
         ((lambda? E)       (val-lambda E env))
         ((application? E)  (val-application E env))
         (else (error "val: cannot parse" E)) ))
```

Now we examine the constructs one by one. The representation of a
construct is examined only by its predicate, its evaluation function, and
any supporting functions. For example, the representation of a let expression is examined only by the predicate **let?** and the evaluation function
val-let. Supporting functions will be defined only for lambda expressions.

Constants

Constants are numbers.

```
(define constant? number?)
```

Constants evaluate to themselves:

```
(define (val-constant E env) E)
```

Quoted Items

The syntax of a quoted item is

>   (**quote** *Item*)

Hence, **quote?** checks whether its argument is a pair with **quote** as its first element:

```
(define (quote? E) (starts-with? E 'quote))
(define (starts-with? E symbol)
  (and (pair? E) (equal? symbol (car E))) )
```

A quoted item is evaluated by stripping the quote and returning the item:

```
(define (val-quote E env) (cadr E))
```

Variables

A variable is represented as a symbol:

```
(define variable? symbol?)
```

A variable is looked up in the environment. If operation **assoc** finds a binding, the value from it is returned; otherwise, an error is reported.

```
(define (val-variable E env)
  (let ((found (assoc E env)))
    (if found (cadr found) (error "val: unbound" E)) ))
```

Conditionals

A conditional has the form

>   (**if** E_1 E_2 E_3)

For simplicity, predicate **if?** simply tests whether its argument is a list with **if** as its head. Further checking and error messages are left as an exercise.

```
(define (if? E) (starts-with? E 'if))
```

Function **val-if** uses **cadr**, **caddr**, and **cadddr** to pick out the subexpressions E_1, E_2, and E_3 in a conditional (see Fig. 11.8):

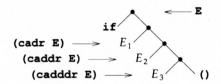

Fig. 11.8. A conditional expression (**if** E_1 E_2 E_3).

```
(define (val-if E env)
  (if (val (cadr E) env)
      (val (caddr E) env)
      (val (cadddr E) env) ))
```

Let Expressions

A let expression has the following form (see Fig. 11.9):

   (**let** ((x_1 E_1) (x_2 E_2) $\cdots$ (x_k E_k)) F)

Predicate **let?** returns true if its argument starts with keyword **let**:

   (define (let? E) (starts-with? E 'let))

Function **val-let** extracts a list **vars** of variables (x_1 x_2 $\cdots$ x_k). A corresponding list **exprs** consists of expressions (E_1 E_2 $\cdots$ E_k). The values of these expressions are collected in list **values**, and **bind-all** is called to bind the variables to the values. Expression F is evaluated in the new environment after the variables are bound.

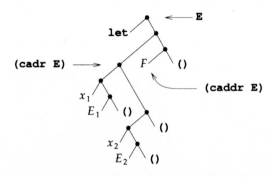

Fig. 11.9. The structure of (**let** ((x_1 E_1) (x_2 E_2)) F).

```
(define (val-let E env)
  (let* ((vars (map car (cadr E)))
         (exprs (map cadr (cadr E)))
         (values (map (lambda (x) (val x env)) exprs))
         (new-env (bind-all vars values env)) )
    (val (caddr E) new-env) ))
```

Lambda Expressions

A lambda expression has the form

(lambda (*Formals* **)** *E* **)**

Predicate **lambda?** returns true if its argument starts with symbol **lambda**:

```
(define (lambda? E) (starts-with? E 'lambda))
```

Lambda expressions are interpreted in two parts, corresponding to the two rules in the natural semantics of lambda expressions in Section 11.2. Function **val-lambda** builds a closure consisting of a lambda expression and its definition environment. The environment in the closure holds bindings for any free variables in the lambda expression. A closure will be represented as a list starting with symbol **closure**:

```
(define (val-lambda E env) (list 'closure E env) )
```

A supporting predicate **closure?** will be needed later:

```
(define (closure? x) (starts-with? x 'closure))
```

Function **apply-lambda** has two parameters: **clos**, a closure containing the lambda expression to be applied, and **actuals**, a list of values for the formal parameters of the lambda expression.

```
(define (apply-lambda clos actuals)
  (let* ((lam (cadr clos))
         (def-env (caddr clos))
         (formals (cadr lam))
         (body (caddr lam))
         (new-env (bind-all formals actuals def-env)))
    (val body new-env) ))
```

Variable **lam** represents the lambda expression, **def-env** its definition-time environment, **formals** its list of formal parameters, **body** its body, and **new-env** the environment formed after binding the formals to the actuals. Function **apply-lambda** returns the result of interpreting **body** with respect to **new-env**; that is, it returns the value of

```
(val body new-env)
```

Function Applications

If an expression **E** is not recognized as one of the earlier constructs, the interpreter **val** uses predicate **application?** to check whether **E** has the form

$$(E_1 \ E_2 \ \cdots \ E_k)$$

If so, E_1 evaluates to a function to be applied to the values of $E_2, \ldots, E_k$. Since E_1 can be any expression, predicate **application?** returns true if **E** is a list:

```
(define (application? E) (pair? E))
```

In the following code for **val-application**, variable **op** represents the value of E_1 in

$$(E_1 \ E_2 \ \cdots \ E_k)$$

and **actuals** represents the list of values of $E_2, \ldots, E_k$. If **op** denotes a Scheme procedure, then the procedure is applied directly to the list of values. Otherwise, if **op** denotes a closure formed from a lambda expression, then **apply-lambda** is called:

```
(define (val-application E env)
  (let ((op (val (car E) env))
        (actuals (map (lambda (x) (val x env))
                      (cdr E) )))
    (cond ((procedure? op) (apply op actuals))
          ((closure? op) (apply-lambda op actuals))
          (else (error "val-application: on" E)) )))
```

Examples

Finally, here are some examples of the use of the interpreter. A number evaluates to itself in any environment, even the empty environment **nil**:

```
(val 3.14 nil)
     3.14
```

The expression in

```
(val '(please-add 2 3) initial-env)
    5
```

is recognized as a function application. Symbol **please-add** evaluates to the Scheme addition procedure and **2** and **3** evaluate to themselves. The response *5* is the result of applying the addition procedure to the list of values of **2** and **3**.

A lambda expression by itself evaluates to a closure:

```
(val '(lambda (x) x) nil)
    (closure (lambda (x) x) ())
```

The closure is a list consisting of the symbol **closure**, the original lambda expression, and its empty definition-time environment. A similar example involving nested lambda expressions is

```
(val '(lambda (x) (lambda (y) x)) nil)
    (closure (lambda (x) (lambda (y) x)) ())
```

The response remains the same if we give name **K** to this lambda expression and ask for **K**.

```
(val '(let ((K (lambda (x) (lambda (y) x))))
         K )
     nil)
    (closure (lambda (x) (lambda (y) x)) ())
```

Now, we apply **K** to **5**:

```
(val '(let ((K (lambda (x) (lambda (y) x))))
         (K 5) )                              ; changed line
     nil)
    (closure (lambda (y) x) ((x 5)))
```

This time, the closure contains a lambda expression with a free variable **x**, and an environment binding **x** to **5**.

Finally, we get the desired response *0* for the running example of Section 11.2:

```
(val '(let ((z 0))
        (let ((f (lambda (y) (* y z))))
          (let ((z 1))
            (f 2) )))
      initial-env )
    0
```

EXERCISES

11.1 The natural semantics in Fig. 11.2, page 404, allows an expression in the defined language to be a number, a variable, a sum, a product, or a let expression.

    a) Extend the defined language to allow subtraction and division operations within expressions.

    b) Extend the defined language to allow a list of expressions to appear wherever a single expression is now allowed. The value of an expression list is the value of the last expression. A special variable **previous** refers to the value of the previous expression in a list.

11.2 Implement the semantic rules from Exercise 11.1 in Prolog.

11.3 Write an evaluator in Scheme corresponding to the Prolog rules in Fig. 11.3. Use syntactic sugar, as needed, to make the defined language easier to manipulate in Scheme.

11.4 Under dynamic scope rules, the value of a free variable is taken from the activation environment. Give semantic rules similar to those of Fig. 11.4 for call-by-value evaluation of dynamically scoped lambda expressions.

11.5 Suppose that a list **built-ins** consists alternately of symbols and their associated procedures, as follows:

    ('+ + 'please-add + '* * 'car car ···)

Using the Scheme predicates **procedure?** and **symbol?** define a function to build the initial environment **initial-env** of Section 11.4, from **built-ins**.

11.6 Add the following constructs to the defined language of the interpreter **val** in Section 11.5:

    a) the **cond** construct of Scheme.

    b) the construct

        $(F \text{ where } (x_1 \ E_1) \ (x_2 \ E_2) \ \cdots \ (x_k \ E_k))$

    with the same value as

        $(\text{let } ((x_1 \ E_1) \ (x_2 \ E_2) \ \cdots \ (x_k \ E_k)) \ F)$

11.7 How would you extend the interpreter **val** in Section 11.5 to allow
it to interpret itself?

BIBLIOGRAPHIC NOTES

McCarthy's original paper on Lisp contains a description of a Lisp function
eval [*e*, *a*] that computes the value of a Lisp expression *e* in an environment
a. McCarthy [1981] recalls, "S. R. Russell noticed that *eval* could serve as
in interpreter for LISP, promptly hand coded it, and we now had a programming language with an interpreter." The interpreter used dynamic
scope, which McCarthy [1981] viewed "as just a bug."

Interpreters for Lisp and Scheme are closely related to interpreters for
the λ-calculus, which is discussed in Chapter 12. Landin [1964] describes
an evaluator, called the SECD machine, for the λ-calculus. A definitional
interpreter is easier to write if constructs in the defined language can be
interpreted directly by constructs in the defining language. Reynolds
[1972] presents several interpreters, including one in which a language
with higher-order functions and call-by-name evaluation is defined using
first-order functions and call-by-value evaluation; call-by-name evaluation
is considered in Section 12.3.

Natural semantics grows out of the work of Plotkin [1981], and has been
vigorously pursued by Kahn [1987] and Clément et al. [1985], who have
automated the translation of natural semantics into Prolog.

Twelve

Static Types and the Lambda Calculus

Static or compile-time type checking anticipates run-time behavior, so it is reasonable to study types at the end, after the dynamic semantics of expressions is understood. Only then can we hope to make sense out of claims like "strong typing prevents run-time errors." It is easier to study error prevention if we know what an error is.

Claims about error prevention have to be worded carefully because static types prevent only certain kinds of run-time errors. At compile time, we can detect an attempt to add procedures instead of numbers or an attempt to use a pointer instead of a record, but we cannot always detect an attempt to divide by zero or an attempt to use an out-of-bounds array index.

The notion of the dynamic state of a computation, central to imperative programming, has little to do with static types, which are a property of the program text. Type checking of an assignment

$$i := i + 1$$

deals only with the types of the left and right sides and not with the values of variables. Types can therefore be studied by concentrating on expressions and functional languages. Statements can be checked by giving them a special type **void**. For example, the type-checking rule for conditional statements

$$S ::= \text{if } E \text{ then } S_1 \text{ else } S_2$$

can be expressed as follows:

> The **if-then-else** construct is built up of an expression E of type **bool** for boolean, and statements S_1 and S_2 of type **void**; the result S has type **void**.

This rule treats the **if-then-else** constructor as if it were an operator in an expression.

Functional languages can themselves be reduced to smaller core languages that are more convenient for the study of types.

Lambda Calculi

The small syntax of the lambda calculus makes it a convenient vehicle for studying types in programming languages. The pure lambda calculus has just three constructs: variables, function application, and function creation. Nevertheless, it has had a profound influence on the design and analysis of programming languages. Its surprising richness comes from the freedom to create and apply functions, especially higher-order functions of functions.

The lambda calculus gets its name from the Greek letter lambda, λ. The notation $\lambda x. M$ is used for a function with parameter x and body M. Thus, $\lambda x. x * x$ is a function that maps 5 to $5 * 5$. Functions are written next to their arguments, so $f a$ is the application of function f to argument a, as in $\sin \theta$ or $\log n$. In

$$(\lambda x.\ x * x) 5$$

function $\lambda x. x * x$ is applied to 5. Formulas like $(\lambda x. x * x) 5$ are called terms.

Church [1941] introduced the pure lambda calculus in the 1930s to study computation with functions. He was interested in the general properties of functions, independently of any particular problem area. The integer 5 and the multiplication operator $*$ belong to arithmetic and are not part of the pure calculus.

A grammar for *terms* in the *pure lambda calculus* is:

$$M ::= x \mid (M_1\ M_2) \mid (\lambda x. M)$$

We use letters f, x, y, z for variables and M, N, P, Q for terms. A term is either a *variable* x, an *application* $(M N)$ of function M to N, or an *abstraction* $(\lambda x. M)$. A constant c can represent values like integers and operations on data structures like lists. That is, c can stand for basic constants like **true** and **nil** as well as constant functions like + and *head*.

The lambda calculi are therefore a family of languages for computation with functions. Members of the family are obtained by choosing a set of constants. In informal usage, "the lambda calculus" refers to any member of this family.

The progression in this chapter is as follows:

- The pure lambda calculus is untyped. Functions can be applied freely; it even makes sense to write $(x\,x)$, where x is applied to itself. In formulating a notion of computation for the pure calculus, we look at scope, parameter passing, and evaluation strategies.

- A functional programming language is essentially a lambda calculus with appropriate constants. This view will be supported by relating a fragment of ML to a lambda calculus.

- The typed lambda calculus associates a type with each term.

- Finally, we consider a lambda calculus with polymorphic types that has been used to study types in ML.

12.1 EQUALITY OF PURE LAMBDA TERMS

This chapter opened with an informal description of the pure lambda calculus: x is a variable, $(M\,N)$ represents the application of function M to N, and the abstraction $(\lambda x.\,M)$ represents a function with parameter x and body M. Now it is time to be more precise about the roles of abstraction and application.

This section develops an equality relation on terms, called *beta-equality* for historical reasons. We write $M =_\beta N$ if M and N are beta-equal. Informally, if $M =_\beta N$, then M and N must have the "same value."

Beta-equality deals with the result of applying an abstraction $(\lambda x.\,M)$ to an argument N. In other words, beta-equality deals with the notions of function call and parameter passing in programming languages. An abstraction corresponds to a function definition, and an application to a function call. Suppose that function *square* is defined by

    fun *square* $(x) = x * x;$

The function call *square* (5) is evaluated by substituting 5 for x in the body $x*x$. In the terminology of this section, *square* (5) $=_\beta 5 * 5$.

Syntactic Conventions

The following abbreviations make terms more readable:

- Parentheses may be dropped from $(M\,N)$ and $(\lambda x.\,M)$. In the absence of parentheses, function application groups from left to right. Thus, $x\,y\,z$ abbreviates $((x\,y)\,z)$, and the parentheses in $x\,(y\,z)$ are necessary to ensure that x is applied to $(y\,z)$. Function application has higher precedence than abstraction, so $\lambda x.\,x\,z$ abbreviates $(\lambda x.\,(x\,z))$.

- A sequence of consecutive abstractions, as in $\lambda x.\,\lambda y.\,\lambda z.\,M$, can be written with a single lambda, as in $\lambda xyz.\,M$. Thus, $\lambda xy.\,x$ abbreviates $\lambda x.\,\lambda y.\,x$.

The following terms will be used within the examples in this chapter:

$I = \lambda x.\,x$

$K = \lambda xy.\,x$

$S = \lambda xyz.\,(x\,z)\,(y\,z)$

Here, S could have been written with fewer parentheses as $\lambda xyz.\,x\,z\,(y\,z)$. Its full form is

$$S = (\lambda x.\,(\lambda y.\,(\lambda z.\,((x\,z)\,(y\,z)))))$$

A pure lambda term without free variables is called a *closed term*, or *combinator*.

Free and Bound Variables

Abstractions of the form $\lambda x.\,M$ are also referred to as bindings because they constrain the role of x in $\lambda x.\,M$. Variable x is said to be *bound* in $\lambda x.\,M$. The set *free* (M) of *free variables* of M, the variables that appear unbound in M, is given by the following syntax-directed rules:

$free\,(x) = \{x\}$

$free\,(M\,N) = free\,(M) \cup free\,(N)$

$free\,(\lambda x.\,M) = free\,(M) - \{x\}$

In words, variable x is free in the term x. A variable is free in $M\,N$ if it is either free in M or free in N. With the exception of x, all other free variables of M are free in $\lambda x.\,M$.

Free variables have been a trouble spot in both programming languages and the lambda calculus, so we take a closer look at them. For example, z is a free variable of the following term because it is free in the subterm $\lambda y.\,z$:

$(\lambda y.\,z)\,(\lambda z.\,z)$

We now introduce a way of distinguishing between this first occurrence of z and the other ones in the subterm $(\lambda z.\,z)$.

The occurrence of x to the right of the λ in $\lambda x.\,M$ is called a *binding occurrence* or simply *binding* of x. All occurrences of x in $\lambda x.\,M$ are *bound* within the *scope* of this binding. All unbound occurrences of a variable in a term are *free*. Each occurrence of a variable is either free or bound; it cannot be both.

The only occurrence of x in $\lambda x.\,y$ is bound within its own scope. The lines in the following diagram go from a binding to a bound occurrence of y, and from a binding to bound occurrences of z.

$$\lambda\ y.\ \lambda\ z.\ x\ z\ (\ y\ z\ )$$

In this diagram, the occurrence of x is free because it is not within the scope of any binding within the term.

Substitution

The result of applying an abstraction $(\lambda x.\,M)$ to an argument N will be formalized by "substituting" N for x in M. Informally, N replaces all free occurrences of x in M. A definition of substitution is rather tricky, as evidenced by a long history of inadequate definitions. The following definition first tackles the easy case, which suffices for most examples. A more precise syntax-directed definition appears in Section 12.2.

The *substitution* of a term N for a variable x in M is written as $\{N/x\}\,M$, and is defined as follows:

1. Suppose that the free variables of N have no bound occurrences in M. Then, the term $\{N/x\}\,M$ is formed by replacing all free occurrences of x in M by N.

2. Otherwise, suppose that variable y is free in N and bound in M. Consistently replace the binding and corresponding bound occurrences of y in M by some fresh variable z.[1] Repeat the renaming of bound variables in M until case 1 applies. Then, proceed as in case 1.

Example 12.1. In each of the following cases, M has no bound occurrences, so N replaces all occurrences of x in M to form $\{N/x\}\,M$:

$$\{u/x\}\,x = u$$
$$\{u/x\}\,(x\,x) = (u\,u)$$
$$\{u/x\}\,(x\,y) = (u\,y)$$
$$\{u/x\}\,(x\,u)\,{}^{\cdot}= (u\,u)$$
$$\{(\lambda x.\,x)/x\}\,x = (\lambda x.\,x)$$

In the following cases, M has no free occurrences of x, so $\{N/x\}\,M$ is M itself:

---

[1] The syntax of λ-terms can be made independent of the spellings of variables by using positional indexes, as in de Bruijn [1972]. Positional indexes eliminate the need for renaming.

$$\{u/x\}y = y$$

$$\{u/x\}(y\,z) = (y\,z)$$

$$\{u/x\}(\lambda y.\,y) = (\lambda y.\,y)$$

$$\{u/x\}(\lambda x.\,x) = (\lambda x.\,x)$$

$$\{(\lambda x.\,x)/x\}y = y$$

In the following cases, free variable u in N has bound occurrences in M, so $\{N/x\}M$ is formed by first renaming the bound occurrences of u in M:

$$\{u/x\}(\lambda u.\,x) = \{u/x\}(\lambda z.\,x) = (\lambda z.\,u)$$

$$\{u/x\}(\lambda u.\,u) = \{u/x\}(\lambda z.\,z) = (\lambda z.\,z) \qquad\qquad\qquad \square$$

Beta-Equality

The key axiom of beta-equality is as follows:

$$(\lambda x.\,M)N \ =_\beta \ \{N/x\}M \qquad\qquad\qquad\qquad\qquad \text{(β axiom)}$$

Thus, $(\lambda x.\,x)u =_\beta u$ and $(\lambda x.\,y)u =_\beta y$.

The following axiom allows bound variables to be systematically renamed:

$$(\lambda x.\,M) \ =_\beta \ \lambda z.\,\{z/x\}M \quad \text{provided that } z \text{ is not free in } M \qquad \text{(α axiom)}$$

Thus, $\lambda x.\,x =_\beta \lambda y.\,y$ and $\lambda xy.\,x =_\beta \lambda uv.\,u$.

The remaining rules for beta-equality formalize general properties of equalities (see Fig. 12.1). Each of the following must be true with any notion of equality on terms:

Idempotence. A term M equals itself.

Commutativity. If M equals N, then, conversely, N must equal M.

Transitivity. If M equals N and N equals P, then M equals P.[2]

The replacement of equals for equals is formalized by the two *congruence* rules in Fig. 12.1. The first rule can be read as follows:

If $M =_\beta M'$ and $N =_\beta N'$, then $M\,N =_\beta M'\,N'$.

Furthermore,

If $M =_\beta M'$, then $\lambda x.\,M =_\beta \lambda x.\,M'$.

---

[2] An *equivalence* relation on a set S is any binary relation that has the idempotence, commutativity, and transitivity properties.

$$(\lambda x.\, M) \; =_\beta \; \lambda z.\, \{z/x\}\, M \quad \text{provided that } z \text{ is not free in } M \qquad (\alpha \text{ axiom})$$

$$(\lambda x.\, M)\, N \; =_\beta \; \{N/x\}\, M \qquad (\beta \text{ axiom})$$

$$M =_\beta M \qquad \text{(idempotence axiom)}$$

$$\frac{M =_\beta N}{N =_\beta M} \qquad \text{(commutativity rule)}$$

$$\frac{M =_\beta N \qquad N =_\beta P}{M =_\beta P} \qquad \text{(transitivity rule)}$$

$$\frac{M =_\beta M' \qquad N =_\beta N'}{M\, N =_\beta M'\, N'} \qquad \text{(congruence rule)}$$

$$\frac{M =_\beta M'}{\lambda x.\, M =_\beta \lambda x.\, M'} \qquad \text{(congruence rule)}$$

Fig. 12.1. Axioms and rules for beta-equality.

Example 12.2. The axioms and rules for beta-equality will be applied to show that

$$SII \; =_\beta \; \lambda z.\, z\, z$$

Application groups from left to right, so SII is written for $(SI)I$. S is reserved for $\lambda xyz.\, xz\, (yz)$ and I is reserved for $\lambda x.\, x$, so SII is

$$(\lambda xyz.\, xz\, (yz))\, (\lambda x.\, x)\, (\lambda x.\, x)$$

This example concentrates on the α and β axioms; subterms to which these axioms apply will be highlighted by underlining them. We begin by using the α axiom to rename bound variables, for clarity.

$$(\lambda xyz.\, xz\, (yz))\, \underline{(\lambda x.\, x)}\, (\lambda x.\, x) \; =_\beta \; (\lambda xyz.\, xz\, (yz))\, (\lambda u.\, u)\, (\lambda x.\, x)$$

The second copy of $\lambda x.\, x$ is now renamed into $\lambda v.\, v$:

$$(\lambda xyz.\, xz\, (yz))\, (\lambda u.\, u)\, \underline{(\lambda x.\, x)} \; =_\beta \; (\lambda xyz.\, xz\, (yz))\, (\lambda u.\, u)\, (\lambda v.\, v)$$

The resulting term on the right side of this equality has only one binding for each variable.

The first change in the structure of the term is due to the β axiom:

$$(\lambda xyz.\, xz\,(yz))\,(\lambda u.\, u)\,(\lambda v.\, v) \quad =_\beta \quad (\lambda yz.\,(\lambda u.\, u)\,z\,(yz))\,(\lambda v.\, v)$$

The right side is formed by substituting $(\lambda u.\, u)$ for x in $(\lambda yz.\, xz\,(yz))$. Three more applications of the β axiom are needed to complete the proof of $SII =_\beta \lambda z.\, zz$:

$$
\begin{aligned}
SII \quad &=_\beta \quad (\lambda yz.\,(\lambda u.\, u)\,z\,(yz))\,(\lambda v.\, v) \\[2mm]
&=_\beta \quad (\lambda yz.\, z\,(yz))\,(\lambda v.\, v) \\[2mm]
&=_\beta \quad \lambda z.\, z\,(\,(\lambda v.\, v)\,z\,) \\[2mm]
&=_\beta \quad \lambda z.\, zz \qquad\qquad\qquad \square
\end{aligned}
$$

12.2   SUBSTITUTION REVISITED

The description of substitution on page 427 can be summarized as follows. If the free variables of N have no bound occurrences in M, then $\{N/x\}M$ is formed by replacing all free occurrences of x in M by N; otherwise, bound variables in M are renamed until this rule applies. This section contains a syntax-directed definition of substitution.

The next example motivates the renaming of bound variables during substitution.

Example 12.3. Consider the term $\lambda xy.\, minus\, x\, y$. Formally, $minus$ is just a variable; intuitively, $minus\, x\, y$ stands for the subtraction $x - y$. This example studies the term

$$(\lambda uv.\, minus\, u\, v)\, v\, u$$

Since bound variables can be renamed, we can rewrite this term as

$$(\lambda xy.\, minus\, x\, y)\, v\, u$$

Two applications of the β axiom from Fig. 12.1 yield

$$
\begin{aligned}
(\lambda xy.\, minus\, x\, y)\, v\, u \quad &=_\beta \quad (\lambda y.\, minus\, v\, y)\, u \\[2mm]
&=_\beta \quad minus\, v\, u
\end{aligned}
$$

The original term therefore satisfies the equality

$$(\lambda uv.\, minus\, u\, v)\, v\, u \quad =_\beta \quad minus\, v\, u$$

The naive approach of implementing $\{N/x\}M$ by putting N in place of the free occurrences of x in M incorrectly suggests the following equality:

$$\{v/u\}(\lambda v.\, minus\, u\, v) \quad ?= \quad \lambda v.\, minus\, v\, v$$

The correct result is obtained if the bound variable v is renamed:

$\{v/u\}(\lambda z.\ minus\ u\ z)\ =\ \lambda z.\ minus\ v\ z$ $\square$

The *substitution* of N for x in M, written $\{N/x\}M$, is defined by the following syntax-directed rules. We use P and Q to refer to subterms of M.

$\{N/x\}x = N$

$\{N/x\}y = y$ $y \neq x$

$\{N/x\}(P\,Q) = \{N/x\}P\ \{N/x\}Q$

$\{N/x\}(\lambda x.\,P) = \lambda x.\,P$

$\{N/x\}(\lambda y.\,P) = \lambda y.\,\{N/x\}P$ $y \neq x, y \notin free\,(N)$

$\{N/x\}(\lambda y.\,P) = \lambda z.\,\{N/x\}\{z/y\}P$ $y \neq x, z \notin free\,(N), z \notin free\,(P)$

In words, the substitution of N for x in x yields N. If y is a variable different from x, then y is left unchanged by the substitution of N for x in y.

The substitution of N for x distributes across an application $(P\,Q)$; that is, we substitute N for x in both P and Q.

The tricky case occurs when N is substituted for x in an abstraction:

1. Since x is not free in $\lambda x.\,P$, the term $\lambda x.\,P$ itself is the result of substituting N for the free occurrences of x in it.

2. Consider the substitution of N for x in $\lambda y.\,P$, with y different from x. If y is not free in N, then the result is $\lambda y.\,\{N/x\}P$.

3. Finally, suppose that y is free in N. Bound variables can be renamed, so we rename y in $\lambda y.\,P$ by a fresh variable z. Of course, z must be a variable that is not free in N and not free in P. The renaming of y in $\lambda y.\,P$ yields $\lambda z.\,\{z/y\}P$. The substitution of N for x in $\lambda z.\,\{z/y\}P$ yields $\lambda z.\,\{N/x\}\{z/y\}\,P$.

Example 12.4. The reader is urged to verify the following equalities:

$\{u/x\}(\lambda u.\,x) = (\lambda z.\,u)$

$\{u/x\}(\lambda u.\,u) = (\lambda z.\,z)$

$\{u/x\}(\lambda y.\,x) = (\lambda y.\,u)$

$\{u/x\}(\lambda y.\,u) = (\lambda y.\,u)$

The first equality deals with the substitution of u for x in $(\lambda u.\,x)$. Blind substitution of u for x leads to the wrong answer $(\lambda u.\,u)$. $\square$

12.3   COMPUTATION WITH PURE LAMBDA TERMS

Computation in the lambda calculus is symbolic. A term is "reduced" into as simple a form as possible. Among the two beta-equal terms

$$(\lambda x.\, M)\, N \ =_\beta \ \{N/x\}\, M$$

the right side $\{N/x\}\, M$ is considered to be simpler than $(\lambda x.\, M)\, N$. Among

$$(\lambda xy.\, x)\, u\, v \ =_\beta \ (\lambda y.\, u)\, v \ =_\beta \ u$$

u is simpler than $(\lambda y.\, u)\, v$, which in turn is simpler than $(\lambda xy.\, x)\, u\, v$.

These observations motivate a rewriting rule called β-*reduction*. An additional rule, called α-*conversion*, renames bound variables.

$$(\lambda x.\, M)\, N \ \underset{\beta}{\Rightarrow} \ \{N/x\}\, M \qquad\qquad\qquad \text{(β-reduction)}$$

$$\lambda x.\, M \ \underset{\alpha}{\Rightarrow} \ \lambda y.\, \{y/x\}\, M \quad y \text{ not free in } M \qquad \text{(α-conversion)}$$

Now $(\lambda xy.\, x)\, u \underset{\beta}{\Rightarrow} (\lambda y.\, u)$ and $(\lambda y.\, u)\, v \underset{\beta}{\Rightarrow} u$.

This section examines β-reduction. A fundamental result of the lambda calculus implies that the result of a computation is independent of the order in which β-reductions are applied.

Reductions

We write $P \underset{\beta}{\Rightarrow} Q$ if a subterm of P is β-reduced to create Q. A subterm of the form $(\lambda x.\, M)\, N$ is called a *redex*, for "reduction expression." Thus, if $P \underset{\beta}{\Rightarrow} Q$ then P has a redex $(\lambda x.\, M)\, N$ that is replaced by $\{N/x\}\, M$ to create Q. Similarly, we write $P \underset{\alpha}{\Rightarrow} Q$ if α-conversion of a subterm of P yields Q.

A *reduction* is any sequence of β-reductions and α-conversions. A term that cannot be β-reduced is said to be in β-*normal form*, or simply in *normal form*. The term $\lambda z.\, zz$ is in normal form because none of its subterms is a redex of the form $(\lambda x.\, M)\, N$.

The following example considers alternative reductions that start with *SII* and end with the normal form $\lambda z.\, zz$.

Example 12.5. In Fig. 12.2, redexes are underlined and arrows represent β-reductions. Some of the lines are dashed for clarity.

The starting term at the top of the figure is *SII*. Again, *S* is $\lambda xyz.\, xz\,(yz)$ and *I* is $\lambda x.\, x$, so the starting term is

$$(\lambda xyz.\, xz\,(yz))\ (\lambda x.\, x)\ (\lambda x.\, x)$$

Upon β-reduction of the only redex in this term, we get

$$(\lambda yz.\, (\lambda x.\, x)\, z\,(yz))\ (\lambda x.\, x)$$

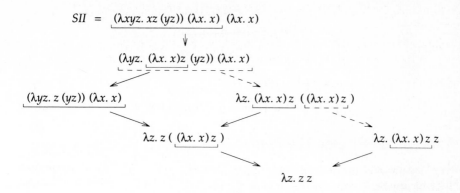

Fig. 12.2. Alternative reductions from SII to $\lambda z.\, zz$.

This term has two redexes. The entire term is a redex, and so is the sub-term $(\lambda x.\, x)\,z$. The following reduction begins by reducing the inner redex:

$$(\lambda yz.\, \underline{(\lambda x.\, x)\,z}\ (yz))\ (\lambda x.\, x) \underset{\beta}{\Rightarrow} \underline{(\lambda yz.\, z\ (yz))\ (\lambda x.\, x)}$$

$$\underset{\beta}{\Rightarrow} \lambda z.\, z\,(\underline{(\lambda x.\, x)\,z}\,)$$

$$\underset{\beta}{\Rightarrow} \lambda z.\, z\,z$$

Each path in Fig. 12.2 represents a reduction from SII to $\lambda z.\, zz$.　　　　□

Nonterminating Reductions

It is possible for a reduction to continue forever, without reaching a normal form. Reductions starting with

$$(\lambda x.\, xx)(\lambda x.\, xx)$$

do not terminate. For clarity, let us α-convert the first $(\lambda x.\, xx)$ into $(\lambda y.\, yy)$. Then

$$(\lambda y.\, yy)(\lambda x.\, xx) \underset{\beta}{\Rightarrow} (\lambda x.\, xx)(\lambda x.\, xx)$$

and we are back where we started.

The first few steps of a more "useful" nonterminating computation appear in Fig. 12.3. The computation begins with Yf, where Y is a special term such that Yf reduces to $f\,(Yf)$. Y is an example of a "fixed-point combinator."

A combinator is a pure lambda term without free variables. A combinator M is called a *fixed-point combinator* if $Mf =_\beta f\,(Mf)$. The significance of fixed-point combinators is explored in Section 12.4, where fixed-point combinators will be used to set up recursions.

$$Yf \;=\; (\lambda f.\,(\lambda x.\, f\,(xx))\,(\lambda x.\, f\,(xx)))\, f$$

$$\underset{\beta}{\Rightarrow}\; (\lambda x.\, f\,(xx))\,(\lambda x.\, f\,(xx))$$

$$\underset{\beta}{\Rightarrow}\; f\,((\lambda x.\, f\,(xx))\,(\lambda x.\, f\,(xx)))$$

$$=\; f\,(Yf)$$

Fig. 12.3. The term Yf β-reduces to $f\,(Yf)$.

The Church-Rosser Theorem

The result "normal forms are unique, if they exist," applies to reductions that terminate in normal forms. A stronger result, called the *Church-Rosser* theorem, applies to all reductions, even nonterminating ones. One form of this theorem is illustrated in Fig. 12.4. For all starting terms M, suppose that one sequence of reductions takes M to P and that another sequence takes M to Q. Then we can always find some common term R, such that P can reduce to R and Q can also reduce to R. The filled circles next to M, P, and Q emphasize that the result holds for all such M, P, and Q. The open circle at R emphasizes that only some terms R are reachable from both P and Q.

The following statement of the Church-Rosser theorem uses the notation $\overset{*}{\Rightarrow}$ for a sequence of zero or more α-conversions and β-reductions. We write $P \Rightarrow Q$ if $P \underset{\alpha}{\Rightarrow} Q$ or if $P \underset{\beta}{\Rightarrow} Q$. Then $P \overset{*}{\Rightarrow} Q$ if for some terms $P_0, P_1, \ldots, P_k$, where $k \geq 0$,

$$P = P_0 \Rightarrow P_1 \Rightarrow \cdots \Rightarrow P_k = Q$$

Note that $P \overset{*}{\Rightarrow} P$ holds; this case corresponds to $k = 0$.

Church-Rosser Theorem. For all pure λ-terms M, P, and Q, if $M \overset{*}{\Rightarrow} P$ and $M \overset{*}{\Rightarrow} Q$, then there must exist a term R such that $P \overset{*}{\Rightarrow} R$ and $Q \overset{*}{\Rightarrow} R$.   □

The Church-Rosser theorem says that the result of a computation does not depend on the order in which reductions are applied. All possible

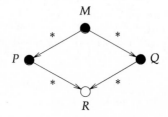

Fig. 12.4. If M reduces to P and to Q, then both can reach some common R.

reduction sequences progress toward the same end result. The end result is a normal form, if one exists.

The Church-Rosser theorem extends to any two beta-equal terms: If $P =_\beta Q$ then there must exist a term R such that $P \stackrel{*}{\Rightarrow} R$ and $Q \stackrel{*}{\Rightarrow} R$.

Computation Rules

Function applications $M N$ in programming languages are often implemented as follows: evaluate both M and N, then pass the value of the argument N to the function obtained from M. With this approach, functions are said to be called by value. A similar computation rule can be defined for the lambda calculus.

A *reduction strategy* for the lambda calculus is a rule for choosing redexes; formally, a reduction strategy maps each term P that is not in normal form into a term Q such that $P \underset{\beta}{\Rightarrow} Q$.

The *call-by-value* reduction strategy chooses the leftmost-innermost redex in a term. By contrast, the *call-by-name* reduction strategy chooses the leftmost-outermost redex. Here, inner and outer refer to nesting of terms. For example, the entire term is the outermost redex in

$$(\lambda yz.\ (\lambda x.\ x)z\ (yz))\ (\lambda x.\ x)$$

The innermost redex is the subterm $(\lambda x.\ x)z$:

$$(\lambda yz.\ \underline{(\lambda x.\ x)z}\ (yz))\ (\lambda x.\ x)$$

The call-by-name strategy is also referred to as *normal-order* reduction; it is guaranteed to reach a normal form, if one exists. Call-by-value, on the other hand, can get stuck, forever evaluating an argument that will never be used. An example can be constructed using $K = \lambda xy.\ x$:

$$(\lambda xy.\ x)z\,N \underset{\beta}{\Rightarrow} (\lambda y.\ z)N \underset{\beta}{\Rightarrow} z \qquad\qquad \text{(call-by-name)}$$

Call-by-value, however, will reduce the innermost redex in the subterm N rather than the entire term $(\lambda y.\ z)N$. If reductions starting from N do not terminate, then call-by-value will fail to reach the normal form z. Such an N is $(\lambda x.\ xx)(\lambda x.\ xx)$, which reduces to itself:

$$
\begin{aligned}
(\lambda y.\ z)((\lambda x.\ xx)(\lambda x.\ xx)) \underset{\beta}{\Rightarrow}\ & (\lambda y.\ z)((\lambda x.\ xx)(\lambda x.\ xx)) \\
\underset{\beta}{\Rightarrow}\ & (\lambda y.\ z)((\lambda x.\ xx)(\lambda x.\ xx)) \qquad \text{(call-by-value)} \\
\underset{\beta}{\Rightarrow}\ & \cdots
\end{aligned}
$$

Despite the possibility of an avoidable runaway evaluation, functional languages use call-by-value because it can be implemented efficiently and it reaches the normal form sufficiently often.

Example 12.6. Call-by-value can reach a normal form faster than call-by-name, where faster means using fewer β-reductions. The term in this example has the form $(\lambda x. xx) N$. Since the body xx of $\lambda x. xx$ has two copies of x, call-by-value will win by first reducing N to a normal form.

The call-by-value reduction takes three steps:

$$
\begin{aligned}
(\lambda x. xx)(\underline{(\lambda y. y)(\lambda z. z)}) \;&\Rightarrow_{\beta}\; (\lambda x. xx)(\lambda z. z) \\
&\Rightarrow_{\beta}\; (\lambda z. z)(\lambda z. z) \\
&\Rightarrow_{\beta}\; (\lambda z. z)
\end{aligned}
$$

The call-by-name reduction takes four steps:

$$
\begin{aligned}
\underline{(\lambda x. xx)((\lambda y. y)(\lambda z. z))} \;&\Rightarrow_{\beta}\; ((\lambda y. y)(\lambda z. z))((\lambda y. y)(\lambda z. z)) \\
&\Rightarrow_{\beta}\; (\lambda z. z)((\lambda y. y)(\lambda z. z)) \\
&\Rightarrow_{\beta}\; (\lambda y. y)(\lambda z. z) \\
&\Rightarrow_{\beta}\; (\lambda z. z) \qquad\qquad\qquad \square
\end{aligned}
$$

12.4   PROGRAMMING CONSTRUCTS AS λ-TERMS

Constants and a little syntactic sugar will be added to the pure lambda calculus in this section to build a tiny functional programming language, called ML0 . The purpose is not to build a real language but to support the claim that a functional language is essentially a lambda calculus. Certain properties of programming languages can therefore be studied in terms of the lambda calculus.

An Applied Lambda Calculus

Terms in an *applied lambda calculus* have the following syntax:

$$
M \;::=\; c \;\mid\; x \;\mid\; (M_1 \, M_2) \;\mid\; (\lambda x. M)
$$

Constants, represented by c, correspond to the built-in constants and operators in a programming language. Each applied lambda calculus has its own set of constants. The constants in this section are

> **true, false**
> **if**
> **0, iszero, pred, succ**
> **fix**

The definitions of free and bound variables, substitution, α-conversion, and β-reduction carry over from the pure calculus to an applied calculus. As usual, parentheses can be dropped, so

$$\textbf{if } x \; y \; \textbf{false}$$

is a way of writing

$$(((\textbf{if } x) \; y) \; \textbf{false})$$

Currying

Functions of several variables are simulated in the lambda calculus by using a technique called "currying," after the logician Haskell B. Curry, who used it extensively.

Function g is said to be a *curried* version of a function f if f and g satisfy the equality

$$f \, (x_1, x_2, \ldots, x_k) \; = \; g \, x_1 x_2 \cdots x_k$$

Function f has $k \geq 0$ arguments, which g takes one at a time. A curried form of the binary operator $*$ is

$$\lambda xy. \; x * y$$

The arithmetic expression $2 * 3$ corresponds to $(\lambda xy. \; x * y) \, 2 \, 3$:

$$(\lambda xy. \; x * y) \, 2 \, 3 \quad \underset{\beta}{\Rightarrow} \quad (\lambda y. \; 2 * y) \, 3 \quad \underset{\beta}{\Rightarrow} \quad 2 * 3$$

Currying is useful for partial evaluation, where the arguments of a function are not all available at once. With only the first argument 2 available,

$$(\lambda xy. \; x * y) \, 2 \quad \underset{\beta}{\Rightarrow} \quad \lambda y. \; 2 * y$$

is a function that multiplies its argument y by 2.

Reduction Rules for Constants

The intended use of a constant is formalized by defining reduction rules called δ-rules. The following are two of the δ-rules from Fig. 12.5:

$$\textbf{if true } M \; N \quad \underset{\delta}{\Rightarrow} \quad M$$
$$\textbf{if false } M \; N \quad \underset{\delta}{\Rightarrow} \quad N$$

The constant **if** is a curried conditional. These δ-rules capture the property that a conditional with first argument **true** reduces to its second argument and a conditional with first argument **false** reduces to its third argument.

For an example of the use of these rules, consider a combinator *or*, defined by

$$or \; = \; \lambda xy. \; \textbf{if } x \; \textbf{true } y$$

Now *or* x y reduces to **true** if x is **true** and to y if x is **false**. Only the first argument x is supplied in the following reductions:

$$(\lambda xy.\ \textbf{if}\ x\ \textbf{true}\ y)\ \textbf{true}\ \underset{\beta}{\Rightarrow}\ \lambda y.\ \textbf{if}\ \textbf{true}\ \textbf{true}\ y$$
$$\underset{\delta}{\Rightarrow}\ \lambda y.\ \textbf{true}$$

$$(\lambda xy.\ \textbf{if}\ x\ \textbf{true}\ y)\ \textbf{false}\ \underset{\beta}{\Rightarrow}\ \lambda y.\ \textbf{if}\ \textbf{false}\ \textbf{true}\ y$$
$$\underset{\delta}{\Rightarrow}\ \lambda y.\ y$$

The δ-rule for the constant **fix** is

$$\textbf{fix}\ M\ \underset{\delta}{\Rightarrow}\ M(\textbf{fix}\ M)$$

Technically, **fix** is not needed in an untyped lambda calculus because the fixed point combinator Y plays a similar role:

$$Y\ M\ =_{\beta}\ M\ (Y\ M)$$

The need for **fix** will become evident when types are added. Also, there are alternative fixed-point combinators, such as ZZ defined as follows:

$$ZZ\quad \text{where}\quad Z = \lambda z.\ \lambda x.\ x(z\ z\ x)$$

By using **fix** we avoid commitment to any particular choice of fixed-point combinator.

The notation $M^k\ N$, for $k \geq 0$, stands for k successive applications of M to N. More precisely, $M^0\ N = N$ and $M^k\ N = M^{k-1}\ (M\ N)$, for $k > 0$.

The remaining δ-rules in Fig. 12.5 simulate integer arithmetic. The constants **succ** and **pred** correspond to the successor and predecessor functions, respectively. Thus, $\textbf{succ}^k\ 0$ corresponds to the integer k and $\textbf{pred}^k\ 0$

$$\textbf{if}\ \textbf{true}\ M\ N\ \underset{\delta}{\Rightarrow}\ M$$
$$\textbf{if}\ \textbf{false}\ M\ N\ \underset{\delta}{\Rightarrow}\ N$$
$$\textbf{fix}\ M\ \underset{\delta}{\Rightarrow}\ M(\textbf{fix}\ M)$$
$$\textbf{iszero}\ 0\ \underset{\delta}{\Rightarrow}\ \textbf{true}$$
$$\textbf{iszero}\ (\textbf{succ}^k\ 0)\ \underset{\delta}{\Rightarrow}\ \textbf{false}\qquad \text{where}\ k \geq 1$$
$$\textbf{iszero}\ (\textbf{pred}^k\ 0)\ \underset{\delta}{\Rightarrow}\ \textbf{false}\qquad \text{where}\ k \geq 1$$
$$\textbf{succ}\ (\textbf{pred}\ M)\ \underset{\delta}{\Rightarrow}\ M$$
$$\textbf{pred}\ (\textbf{succ}\ M)\ \underset{\delta}{\Rightarrow}\ M$$

Fig. 12.5. Reduction rules for some constants.

corresponds to the integer $-k$. We return to integer arithmetic after introducing some syntactic sugar.

The Language ML0

ML0 is a syntactically sugared version of an applied lambda calculus. Its constructs appear in Fig. 12.6. Variables, constants, and functional application have the same syntax in the two languages. Following the Standard ML programming language, $\lambda x. M$ is written as **fn** $x \Rightarrow M$ in ML0. As mentioned earlier, **succ**^{k} 0 is written as k, so **succ**^{1} 0 is written as 1 and **succ**^{2} 0 as 2. Similarly, **pred**^{1} 0 is written as -1 and **pred**^{2} 0 as -2.

The keywords **then** and **else** make conditionals more readable. Thus, **if** P M N is written as

> **if** P **then** M **else** N

The relationship between x, N, and M in the redex $(\lambda x. M) N$ motivates the notation

> **let val** $x = N$ **in** M **end**

This **let-val** construct can be written for $(\lambda x. M) N$. For example,

> **let val** $x =$ **false**
> **in**   **if** x **then true**
>   **else** y
> **end**

Construct	Lambda-Calculus	ML0
variable	x	x
constant	c	c
application	$M\,N$	$M\,N$
abstraction	$\lambda x. M$	**fn** $x \Rightarrow M$
integer	**succ**^{k} 0, for $k > 0$	k
integer	**pred**^{k} 0, for $k > 0$	$-k$
conditional	**if** P M N	**if** P **then** M **else** N
let	$(\lambda x. M) N$	**let val** $x = N$ **in** M **end**
recursive function	$(\lambda f. M)(\mathbf{fix}\,(\lambda f. \lambda x. N))$	**let fun** $f\,(x) = N$ **in** M **end**

Fig. 12.6. Syntactic sugar for an applied lambda calculus.

is a sugared form of the term

$(\lambda x.\ \textbf{if}\ x\ \textbf{true}\ y)\ \textbf{false}$

The Fixed-Point Operator

How does the constant **fix** give us the ability to define recursive functions? The relevant δ-rule is

$$\textbf{fix}\ M\ \underset{\delta}{\Rightarrow}\ M\ (\textbf{fix}\ M)$$

In dealing with **fix** it is convenient to have a notion of equality that takes δ-rules into account. The relation $=_{\beta\delta}$ is an extension of beta-equality that treats terms P and Q as equal if $P \underset{\delta}{\Rightarrow} Q$. A formal definition of $=_{\beta\delta}$ can be given by adding a δ axiom to the axioms and rules for beta-equality in Section 12.1.

We explore the relationship between **fix** and recursive functions by developing a term *plus* motivated by the arithmetic operator $+$. Just as $+$ satisfies the equality

$$x + y\ =\ \begin{cases} y & \text{if } x = 0 \\ (x-1) + (y+1) & \text{otherwise} \end{cases}$$

plus satisfies the equality

$$plus\ x\ y\ =_{\beta\delta}\ \begin{cases} y & \text{if } \textbf{iszero}\ x \\ plus\ (\textbf{pred}\ x)\ (\textbf{succ}\ y) & \text{otherwise} \end{cases}$$

The term *plus* must therefore satisfy the following equality:

$$plus\ =_{\beta\delta}\ \lambda xy.\ \textbf{if}\ (\textbf{iszero}\ x)\ y\ (plus\ (\textbf{pred}\ x)\ (\textbf{succ}\ y)) \qquad (12.1)$$

We claim that a suitable term for *plus* is **fix** M, where M is

$$M\ =\ \lambda f.\ \lambda xy.\ \textbf{if}\ (\textbf{iszero}\ x)\ y\ (f\ (\textbf{pred}\ x)\ (\textbf{succ}\ y))$$

The claim that *plus* = **fix** M satisfies the equality (12.1) can be verified as follows. Begin with the following equality based on the δ-rule for **fix**:

$$\textbf{fix}\ M\ =_{\beta\delta}\ M\ (\textbf{fix}\ M)$$

Since *plus* is **fix** M, the term $M\ (\textbf{fix}\ M)$ is simply $M\ (plus)$. From the definition of M,

$$plus\ =_{\beta\delta}\ M\ (plus)\ =\ (\lambda f.\ \lambda xy.\ \textbf{if}\ (\textbf{iszero}\ x)\ y\ (f\ (\textbf{pred}\ x)\ (\textbf{succ}\ y)))\ plus$$

Beta-reduction of the term on the right yields

$$plus =_{\beta\delta} \lambda xy.\ \textbf{if}\ (\textbf{iszero}\ x)\ y\ (plus\ (\textbf{pred}\ x)\ (\textbf{succ}\ y))$$

and we have verified the equation (12.1).

Another example of the use of **fix** is

$$times\ =\ \textbf{fix}\ \lambda f.\ \lambda xy.\ \textbf{if iszero}\ x\ \textbf{then}\ 0$$
$$\textbf{else}\ plus\ y\ (f\ (\textbf{pred}\ x)\ y)$$

The right side is based on the equality $x*y = y + (x-1)*y$.

Finally, the ubiquitous factorial function can be defined as

$$factorial\ =\ \textbf{fix}\ \lambda f.\ \lambda x.\ \textbf{if iszero}\ x\ \textbf{then}\ (\textbf{succ}\ 0)$$
$$\textbf{else}\ times\ x\ (f\ (\textbf{pred}\ x))$$

12.5   THE TYPED LAMBDA CALCULUS

Constants brings the lambda calculus closer to programming languages because constants can play the role of built-in data values and operations. Constants can represent values like 0 and operations like +.

Constants raise a problem, however, because they permit "erroneous" terms like $(0\,x)$, where 0 is applied to x, and **if** $(\lambda x.x)\ y\ z$, where a function $\lambda x.x$ appears instead of **true** or **false**.[3]

Restrictions on the use of constants will be studied in this section by introducing types into the lambda calculus. Consider type expressions with the following syntax:

$$\tau\ ::=\ b\ \ |\ \ \tau \to \tau$$

Letters a and b will be used for basic types like **int**, and the Greek letters σ and τ will be used for type expressions. As usual, the type expression $\sigma \to \tau$ represents a function from type σ to type τ. Examples of type expressions are

> **int**
> **int** $\to$ (**int** $\to$ **bool**)
> $(a \to b) \to (a \to b)$

---

[3] Errors can be formalized by partitioning terms in normal form into those that are in error and those that are not. For example, normal forms include undesirable terms like $(0\,x)$ and desirable terms like $\textbf{succ}\,0$, which corresponds to 1. This approach is predicated on the existence of unique normal forms. As the following contrived example shows, ill-chosen δ-rules need not lead to unique normal forms. The example consists of three constants **a**, **b** and **c** and the rules $\textbf{a} \underset{\delta}{\Rightarrow} \textbf{b}$ and $\textbf{a} \underset{\delta}{\Rightarrow} \textbf{c}$. The term **a** can lead to two different normal forms **b** and **c**.

The $\rightarrow$ type constructor associates to the right, so $(a \rightarrow b) \rightarrow (a \rightarrow b)$ can be written equivalently as $(a \rightarrow b) \rightarrow a \rightarrow b$. This type is not the same as $a \rightarrow b \rightarrow a \rightarrow b$, which is equivalent to $a \rightarrow (b \rightarrow (a \rightarrow b))$.

Since types are motivated by constants, it may seem surprising that the following syntax for the *typed lambda calculus* does not include constants:

$$M ::= x \quad | \quad (M\ N) \quad | \quad (\lambda x : \tau.\ M)$$

According to this syntax, a term is either a variable x, an application $(M N)$, or a typed abstraction $(\lambda x : \tau.\ M)$, where the bound variable x is declared to have type τ. The typed calculus inherits from the pure calculus the conventions for dropping parentheses, the definition of substitution, and the notion of reductions.

An identity function from integers to integers is written as

$$\lambda\ x : \mathbf{int}.\ x$$

The type of a term in the typed lambda calculus can be deduced from the types of its free variables. It is this provision for free variables that allows us to drop constants from the syntax, because the type checking rules for constants are similar to those for free variables. In a term

$$\mathbf{if}\ x\ y\ z$$

if, x, y, and z are all treated as free variables, whose type is given by an environment. There is no need to single out the "constant" **if** for special treatment.

Another reason for dropping constants is that "nonsensical" expressions can now be constructed using variables alone. Since the bound variable x is declared to have type **int**, the subterm $x\ y$ makes as much, or as little, sense as $(0\ y)$:

$$\lambda\ x : \mathbf{int}.\ x\ y$$

Natural Semantics for Type Deduction

A term in the typed lambda calculus will be said to be *type correct* if the natural semantics in Fig. 12.7 associates a type with the term; otherwise, the term is *type incorrect*. (See Section 11.1 for an introduction to natural semantics.)

The rules in Fig. 12.7 are written in terms of sequents of the form

$$env \vdash M : \tau$$

where *env* is an environment mapping variables to types, M is a term, and τ is a type. The axiom for variables says that the type of a variable is looked up in the environment:

$$env \vdash x : lookup\ (x, env) \hspace{4cm} \text{(variable)}$$

$$env \vdash x \: : \: lookup\,(x,\,env) \qquad\qquad\qquad\qquad\text{(variable)}$$

$$\frac{env \vdash M \: : \: \sigma \to \tau \qquad env \vdash N \: : \: \sigma}{env \vdash (M\,N) \: : \: \tau} \qquad\qquad\text{(application)}$$

$$\frac{bind\,(x,\,\sigma,\,env) \vdash M \: : \: \tau}{env \vdash (\lambda x\!:\!\sigma.\,M) \: : \: \sigma \to \tau} \qquad\qquad\text{(abstraction)}$$

Fig. 12.7. Type-deduction rules for the typed lambda calculus.

The rule for function application ensures that the type of an argument is the same as the type expected by a function. In the following rule, the argument N has type σ, the function M has type $\sigma \to \tau$, and the type of $(M\,N)$ is τ:

$$\frac{env \vdash M \: : \: \sigma \to \tau \qquad env \vdash N \: : \: \sigma}{env \vdash (M\,N) \: : \: \tau} \qquad\qquad\text{(application)}$$

The rule for abstractions deduces a result type from the type of the bound variable. If with x bound to type σ, the type of M is τ, then $\lambda x : \sigma.\,M$, where x is declared to have type σ, must be a term of type $\sigma \to \tau$:

$$\frac{bind\,(x,\,\sigma,\,env) \vdash M \: : \: \tau}{env \vdash (\lambda x\!:\!\sigma.\,M) \: : \: \sigma \to \tau} \qquad\qquad\text{(abstraction)}$$

Example 12.7. This example applies the rules in Fig. 12.7 to deduce the type $a \to (b \to a)$ for $\lambda x : a.\lambda y : b.\,x$ in the empty environment *nil*.
    With x bound to a and y bound to b, the type of the variable x is a:

$$bind\,(y,\,b,\,bind\,(x,\,a,\,nil)) \vdash x \: : \: a$$

The rule for abstractions now yields

$$bind\,(x,\,a,\,nil) \vdash (\lambda y\!:\!b.\,x) \: : \: b \to a$$

A second application of rule (abstraction) yields the desired type:

$$nil \vdash (\lambda x\!:\!a.\,\lambda y\!:\!b.\,x) \: : \: a \to (b \to a) \qquad\qquad\qquad \square$$

The type-checking rules in Fig. 12.7 are similar to those for languages like Modula-2 and C, in which each name has a unique type that can be determined at compile time.

12.6   POLYMORPHIC TYPES

The Standard ML programming language motivates the study in this section of a lambda calculus with polymorphic types. Before introducing the lambda calculus, we consider some ML examples.

Examples from Standard ML

The ML function **hd** determines the head or first element of a list, and the function **tl** determines the tail or rest of the list. This description of **hd** and **tl** is independent of the types of the elements of a list; that is, **hd** and **tl** can be applied to integer lists, string lists, lists of integer lists, or any other type of list.

The notion of polymorphic types in this section formalizes the types of functions like **hd** and **tl**. Meanwhile a polymorphic type can be thought of as a parameterized type.

ML was one of the earliest programming languages to allow user-defined polymorphic functions. Realistic examples of polymorphic functions deal with lists, a prototypical example being *map*, which takes as arguments a function f and a list x, and applies f to each element of list x. The only constraint on the types of f and x is that f be applicable to the elements of x. If x is a list of elements of type s, then f must have type $s \to t$, for some t. Here s and t are type variables.

The running example in this section is a toy function *twice* based on the untyped lambda term

$$\lambda f. \; \lambda x. \; f(fx)$$

The name *twice* comes from the two applications of f to x in $f(fx)$.

We will use an ML version of *twice* to compute 2 by applying an integer successor function twice to 0. The successor function **succ** is defined by

```
fun succ(n) = n+1;
    val succ = fn : int -> int
```

The response says that **succ** is a function value of type integer to integer.

The ML syntax

fn f **=>** M

corresponds to $\lambda f. M$. The following let expression therefore defines **twice** as the ML counterpart of $\lambda f. \lambda x. f(fx)$ and applies it to the function **succ** and the constant **0**:

```
let val twice =
    fn f => fn x => f(f x)
in
    twice succ 0
end;
    val it = 2 : int
```

The subterm **twice succ 0** is equivalent to

```
succ(succ(0));
    val it = 2 : int
```

The polymorphic nature of **twice** will become evident when we examine the subexpression

```
twice twice succ 0
```

in the following program fragment:

```
let val twice =
    fn f => fn x => f(f x)
in
    twice twice succ 0
end;
    val it = 4 : int
```

The result **4** seems deceptively reasonable. The reader is encouraged to reduce

```
twice twice succ 0
```

to a β-normal form to see how **twice** is used in this subexpression.
    How does ML determine a type for the following application?

```
twice twice
```

Answers to such questions require a more general notion of types than in the typed lambda calculus of Section 12.5, which does not permit self-applications of the form $x\,x$.

Explicit Polymorphism

The name *Core-XML* for the language in this section stands for "core of an explicitly typed variant of ML." Core-XML allows types to be supplied as parameters. A variant of *twice* in Core-XML is based on the following idea:

Given a type t,
   a function f of type $t \rightarrow t$,
      and a term x of type t,
         the result is $f\ (f\ x)$.

Type t is an explicit parameter. It must be bound just as f and x are bound. For clarity, we use an uppercase lambda, Λ, to denote a type binding. Lowercase lambda, λ, will continue to be used for variable bindings. The variant of *twice* is written as

$$\Lambda t.\ \lambda f : t \rightarrow t.\ \lambda x : t.\ f\ (f\ x)$$

A term that is a Λ-abstraction will be called an *explicitly polymorphic* function, abbreviated for convenience to *polymorphic* function. A polymorphic function expects to be applied to a type.

The polymorphic variant of *twice* expects to be applied to a type t and then to a function f of type $t \rightarrow t$. In the following term, it is applied to **int** and then to **succ**:

$$(\Lambda t.\ \lambda f : t \rightarrow t.\ \lambda x : t.\ f\ (f\ x))\ \textbf{int}\ \textbf{succ}$$

Monotypes and Polytypes

The typed lambda calculus of Section 12.5 deals with terms that have a *monotype* or single type. This section introduces *polytypes*, which are quantified types of the form

for all types t, $\langle$some expression involving $t\rangle$

Their syntax is as follows:

$$
\begin{aligned}
Polytype &\ ::=\ \tau\ \mid\ \forall\, t\, .\ Polytype \\
\tau &\ ::=\ b\ \mid\ t\ \mid\ \tau \rightarrow \tau
\end{aligned}
$$

As in Section 12.5, the letters a and b represent basic types, and the Greek letters σ and τ represent type expressions. The letters s and t will be used for type variables.

A monotype suffices for the term

$$\lambda f : \textbf{int} \rightarrow \textbf{int}.\ \lambda x : \textbf{int}.\ f\ (f\ x)$$

which has type $(\textbf{int} \rightarrow \textbf{int}) \rightarrow \textbf{int} \rightarrow \textbf{int}$. A polytype is needed, however, for the polymorphic function

$$\Lambda t.\ \lambda f : t \rightarrow t.\ \lambda x : t.\ f\ (f\ x)$$

This term has type $\forall t. (t \to t) \to (t \to t)$, or, dropping parentheses, $\forall t. (t \to t) \to t \to t$.

Another example is the polymorphic identity function

$$\Lambda t.\ \lambda x : t.\ x$$

which has polytype $\forall t.\ t \to t$.

The syntax of Core-XML is given by

$M ::= x$		variable
$\mid (M\ M)$		application
$\mid (\lambda\ x : \tau\ .\ M\ )$		abstraction
$\mid (M\ \tau)$		type application
$\mid (\Lambda\ t\ .\ M\ )$		type abstraction
$\mid$ **let** $x : Polytype = M$ **in** M		let expression

The key difference between a lambda binding in an abstraction and a let-binding in a let expression is that a lambda-bound variable has a mono-type, but a let-bound variable can have a polytype. This distinction is motivated by a similar distinction in ML.

The following Core-XML program computes 2 by applying **succ** twice to the constant 0:

> **let** $twice : \forall t. (t \to t) \to t \to t\ =$
> $\Lambda t.\ \lambda f : t \to t.\ \lambda x : t.\ f\ (f\ x)$
> **in**
> $twice$ **int succ** 0

Note the two uses of $twice$ in the following program for computing 4:

> **let** $twice : \forall t. (t \to t) \to t \to t\ =$
> $\Lambda t.\ \lambda f : t \to t.\ \lambda x : t.\ f\ (f\ x)$
> **in**
> $twice$ (**int** $\to$ **int**) ($twice$ **int**) **succ** 0

This program makes the polymorphic nature of $twice$ explicit because $twice$ is applied to the type **int** $\to$ **int** and separately to the type **int**.

Type Rules for Core-XML

The rules for variables, application, and abstraction in Fig. 12.8 are essentially the same as the corresponding rules for the typed lambda calculus. The only difference is that a type expression τ in Core-XML can be a type variable.

The rule for let expressions is in terms of the polytype $poly_M$ of M and $poly_N$ of N:

$$env \;\vdash\; x \;:\; lookup\,(x,\,env) \qquad\qquad\qquad\qquad \text{(variable)}$$

$$\frac{env \;\vdash\; M \;:\; \sigma \to \tau \qquad env \;\vdash\; N \;:\; \sigma}{env \;\vdash\; (M\ N) \;:\; \tau} \qquad\qquad \text{(application)}$$

$$\frac{bind\,(x,\,\sigma,\,env) \;\vdash\; M \;:\; \tau}{env \;\vdash\; (\lambda x\!:\!\sigma.\ M) \;:\; \sigma \to \tau} \qquad\qquad \text{(abstraction)}$$

$$\frac{env \;\vdash\; M \;:\; poly_M \qquad bind\,(x,\,poly_M,\,env) \;\vdash\; N \;:\; poly_N}{env \;\vdash\; \mathbf{let}\ x\!:\!poly_M = M\ \mathbf{in}\ N \;:\; poly_N} \qquad \text{(let)}$$

$$\frac{env \;\vdash\; M \;:\; \forall t.\ poly}{env \;\vdash\; (M\ \tau) \;:\; \{\tau/t\}poly} \qquad\qquad \text{(type application)}$$

$$\frac{env \;\vdash\; M \;:\; poly}{env \;\vdash\; (\Lambda t.\ M) \;:\; \forall t.\ poly} \qquad t \text{ not free in } env \qquad \text{(type abstraction)}$$

Fig. 12.8. Type rules for Core-XML.

$$\frac{env \;\vdash\; M \;:\; poly_M \qquad bind\,(x,\,poly_M,\,env) \;\vdash\; N \;:\; poly_N}{env \;\vdash\; \mathbf{let}\ x\!:\!poly_M = M\ \mathbf{in}\ N \;:\; poly_N} \qquad \text{(let)}$$

If with x bound to polytype $poly_M$, the type of N is $poly_N$, then the type of the let expression is $poly_N$.

The rule for type application is a form of β-reduction for types. If M has a polytype $\forall t.\ poly$, then the type of term $M\ \tau$ is obtained by substituting τ for the free occurrences of t in $poly$:

$$\frac{env \;\vdash\; M \;:\; \forall t.\ poly}{env \;\vdash\; (M\ \tau) \;:\; \{\tau/t\}poly} \qquad\qquad \text{(type application)}$$

The notion of free occurrences of t is with respect to the binder $\forall$. Note also that the type substituted for t is a monotype.

The final rule is for type abstraction. When a Λ binds type t in a term M, a corresponding $\forall$ binds t in the type $poly$ of M:

$$\frac{env \;\vdash\; M \;:\; poly}{env \;\vdash\; (\Lambda t.\ M) \;:\; \forall t.\ poly} \qquad t \text{ not free in } env \qquad \text{(type abstraction)}$$

The caveat that t not be free in env prevents the newly introduced variable t from clashing with any free variables in the type expressions in env.

The derivation in Fig. 12.9 determines the polytype

$$\forall t.\ (t \to t) \to t \to t$$

for the expression

$$x:t, \; f:t{\to}t, \; env \; \vdash \; x \; : \; t \qquad\qquad\qquad\qquad\qquad \text{variable}$$

$$x:t, \; f:t{\to}t, \; env \; \vdash \; f \; : \; t{\to}t \qquad\qquad\qquad\qquad \text{variable}$$

$$x:t, \; f:t{\to}t, \; env \; \vdash \; fx \; : \; t \qquad\qquad\qquad\qquad\; \text{application}$$

$$x:t, \; f:t{\to}t, \; env \; \vdash \; f(fx) \; : \; t \qquad\qquad\qquad\; \text{application}$$

$$f:t{\to}t, \; env \; \vdash \; \lambda x:t. \; f(fx) \; : \; t{\to}t \qquad\qquad\quad\; \text{abstraction}$$

$$env \; \vdash \; \lambda f:t{\to}t. \; \lambda x:t. \; f(fx) \; : \; (t{\to}t){\to}t{\to}t \qquad\quad \text{abstraction}$$

$$env \; \vdash \; \Lambda t. \; \lambda f:t{\to}t. \; \lambda x:t. \; f(fx) \; : \; \forall t. \; (t{\to}t){\to}t{\to}t \qquad \text{type abstr.}$$

Fig. 12.9. Derivation of a polytype for a Core-XML term.

$$\Lambda t. \; \lambda f:t{\to}t. \; \lambda x:t. \; f(fx)$$

To fit sequents on a line, the environment

$$bind\,(x, \; t, \; bind\,(f, \; t{\to}t, \; env))$$

is written as

$$x:t, \; f:t{\to}t, \; env$$

Similarly, *bind* $(f, \; t{\to}t, \; env)$ is written as $f:t{\to}t, \; env$.
The last line of the derivation

$$env \; \vdash \; \Lambda t. \; \lambda f:t{\to}t. \; \lambda x:t. \; f(fx) \; : \; \forall t. \; (t{\to}t){\to}t{\to}t$$

is obtained by the rule for type abstraction. We assume that t is not free in
the environment *env*. Note how t is simultaneously bound by Λ in the
term and by $\forall$ in the type.

The usage of *twice* in

$$twice \; (\mathbf{int}{\to}\mathbf{int}) \; (twice \; \mathbf{int}) \; \mathbf{succ} \; 0$$

can be explored by starting with

$$twice:\forall t. \; (t{\to}t){\to}t{\to}t, \; env \; \vdash \; twice \; : \; \forall t. \; (t{\to}t){\to}t{\to}t$$

Let $\sigma = \mathbf{int}{\to}\mathbf{int}$. The mnemonic significance of σ is that it is the type of
the successor function. The type application *twice* σ yields

$$twice:\forall t. \; (t{\to}t){\to}t{\to}t, \; env \; \vdash \; twice \; \sigma \; : \; (\sigma{\to}\sigma){\to}\sigma{\to}\sigma$$

Similar reasoning yields the type $\sigma \to \sigma$ for *twice* **int**:

$$twice:\forall t. \; (t{\to}t){\to}t{\to}t, \; env \; \vdash \; twice \; \mathbf{int} \; : \; \sigma \to \sigma$$

The rule for applications now yields

$$\cdots \quad \vdash \; (twice \; \sigma) \; (twice \; \mathbf{int}) \; : \; \sigma \to \sigma$$

This function is now ready to be applied to **succ**.

It follows from the discussion of explicit types that the ML subexpression

```
twice twice succ 0
```

does not apply **twice** to itself. Instead, the two occurrences of **twice** represent functions of different monotypes, obtained from the same polymorphic function.

EXERCISES

12.1 Use the syntax-directed definition of substitution in Section 12.2 to verify the following equalities:

    a) $\{u/x\} \, (\lambda u. \; x) = (\lambda z. \; u)$

    b) $\{u/x\} \, (\lambda u. \; u) = (\lambda z. \; z)$

    c) $\{u/x\} \, (\lambda y. \; x) = (\lambda y. \; u)$

    d) $\{u/x\} \, (\lambda y. \; u) = (\lambda y. \; u)$

12.2 Verify the following equalities:

    a) $SIII =_\beta I$, where S is $\lambda xyz. \; (xz)(yz)$ and I is $\lambda x. \; x$.

    b) $twice(twice) f \; x =_\beta f(f(f(f \; x)))$, where $twice$ is $\lambda f \; x. \; f(f \; x)$.

12.3 Draw a diagram showing all possible reductions from $twice(twice) f \; x$ to the normal form $f(f(f(f \; x)))$.

12.4 The term ZZ, where Z is $\lambda z. \; \lambda x. \; x(z \; z \; x)$, satisfies the requirement of fixed-point combinators that $ZZM =_\beta M(ZZM)$. Show that it satisfies the stronger requirement $ZZM \overset{*}{\Rightarrow} M(ZZM)$.

12.5 Using the applied lambda calculus of Section 12.4, define a function to compute elements of the Fibonacci sequence.

12.6 Construct terms in the typed lambda calculus of Section 12.5 by adding types to each of the following pure λ-terms:
    a) $\lambda x. \; x$
    b) $\lambda xy. \; x$
    c) $\lambda xyz. \; (x \; z) \; (y \; z)$
    d) $(\lambda x. \; x) \; (\lambda x. \; x)$
    e) $(\lambda xyz. \; (x \; z) \; (y \; z)) \; (\lambda x. \; x) \; (\lambda x. \; x)$

12.7 Consider the term

> **let** $I = \lambda x.\, x$ **in** $I\,(I)$

a) Add types to this term to obtain a program in the language Core-XML of Section 12.6.

b) Use the type rules for Core-XML to verify that your answer to (a) is well typed.

12.8 Instead of the type rule (let) in Fig. 12.8,

$$\frac{env \;\vdash\; M \;:\; poly_M \qquad bind\,(x,\, poly_M,\, env) \;\vdash\; N \;:\; poly_N}{env \;\vdash\; \textbf{let}\; x : poly_M = M \;\textbf{in}\; N \;:\; poly_N}$$

Mitchell and Harper [1988] use the rule

$$\frac{env \;\vdash\; M \;:\; poly_M \qquad bind\,(x,\, poly_M,\, env) \;\vdash\; N \;:\; \tau_N}{env \;\vdash\; \textbf{let}\; x : poly_M = M \;\textbf{in}\; N \;:\; \tau_N}$$

Note that the type of N is restricted to be a monotype in their rule. Does the replacement of rule (let) by this restricted rule change the types that can be derived using the type rules in Fig. 12.8? Justify your answer.

BIBLIOGRAPHIC NOTES

Rosser [1984] is a brief history of the lambda calculus of Church [1941]. Combinators predate the lambda calculus, despite the definition of combinators as closed lambda terms in Section 12.1. Combinatory logic, the use of combinators to study functions, complements the lambda calculus. Combinators were introduced independently by Schönfinkel [1924] and by Curry in the 1930s; see Curry and Feys [1958]. The two fundamental combinators are K and S, characterized by the following equations:

> $Kxy = x$
> $Sxyz = xz\,(yz)$

All pure lambda terms without free variables correspond to terms built up entirely out of K and S.

It was not until 1969 that a mathematical semantics was given for the lambda calculus by Scott; see Scott [1977] for a retrospective view.

Hindley and Seldin [1986] give an introductory treatment of the lambda calculus and combinators. Barendregt [1984] is a comprehensive account. The essays collected by Hindley and Seldin [1980] are representative of research topics that were being pursued at the time the collection appeared.

Applied lambda calculi, or functional languages, have long been used as defining languages for specifying the semantics of programming languages. The definitional interpreters in Chapter 11 have a functional defining language. Landin [1965] used a modified lambda calculus to define Algol 60. The denotational semantics approach of Scott and Strachey [1971] uses an applied lambda calculus, without modifications. For more on denotational semantics, see the books by Gordon [1979], Schmidt [1986], and Stoy [1977].

The survey by Cardelli and Wegner [1985] is a good starting point for studying static types. The papers in Kahn, MacQueen, and Plotkin [1984] are a more advanced starting point.

Lambda calculi with polymorphic types were introduced independently by Girard [1972] and Reynolds [1974]. The language Core-XML is from Mitchell and Harper [1988].

Types do not have to be declared explicitly in the ML programming language because the implementation uses a clever algorithm based on unification to infer types. Extending Curry's work on type inference (see Curry and Feys [1958]), Hindley [1969] observed that unification could be used for type inference. A similar independent observation by Milner led to the type checking algorithm for ML (Milner [1978]). Type rules for ML are given by Damas and Milner [1982]; see also Clément et al. [1986]. The interaction between types and modules in ML can be seen from MacQueen's description of the module facility in the composite report by Harper, MacQueen, and Milner [1986].

Bibliography

Abelson, H., and Sussman, G. J. [1985]. *Structure and Interpretation of Computer Programs.* MIT Press, Cambridge, Mass. With J. Sussman.

Aho, A. V., Kernighan, B. W., and Weinberger, P. J. [1988]. *The AWK Programming Language.* Addison-Wesley, Reading, Mass.

Aho, A. V., Sethi, R., and Ullman, J. D. [1986]. *Compilers: Principles, Techniques, and Tools.* Addison-Wesley, Reading, Mass.

Andrews, G. R., and Schneider, F. B. [1983]. Concepts and notations for concurrent programming. *ACM Computing Surveys* **15:1**, 3-43.

Apt, K. R. [1981]. Ten years of Hoare's logic: a survey—Part I. *ACM TOPLAS* **3:4**, 431-483.

Backus, J. W. [1960]. The syntax and semantics of the proposed international algebraic language of the Zurich ACM-GAMM Conference. *International Conference on Information Processing, June 1959.* Unesco, Paris, 125-132.

Backus, J. W. [1978]. Can programming be liberated from the von Neumann style? A functional style and its algebra of programs. *Comm. ACM* **21:8**, 613-641.

Backus, J. W. [1981]. The history of Fortran I, II, and III. In Wexelblat [1981], 25-74.

Backus, J. W., Beeber, R. J., Best, S., Goldberg, R., Haibt, L. M., Herrick, H. L., Nelson, R. A., Sayre, D., Sheridan, P. B., Stern, H., Ziller, I., Hughes, R. A., and Nutt, R. [1957]. The Fortran automatic coding system. *Western Joint Computer Conference*, 188-198.

Baker, B. S., and Kosaraju, S. R. [1979]. A comparison of multilevel **break** and **next** statements. *J. ACM* **26:3**, 555-566.

Barendregt, H. P. [1984]. *The Lambda Calculus: Its Syntax and Semantics,* 2nd Ed. North-Holland, Amsterdam.

Ben-Ari, M. [1982]. *Principles of Concurrent Programming.* Prentice-Hall International, Englewood Cliffs, N. J.

Bentley, J. L. [1986]. *Programming Pearls.* Addison-Wesley, Reading, Mass.

Bentley, J. L., Knuth, D. E., and McIlroy, M. D. [1986]. Programming pearls: a literate program. *Comm. ACM* **29:6**, 471-483.

Birtwistle, G. M., Dahl, O. J., Myhrhaug, B., and Nygaard, K. [1979]. *Simula Begin.* Studentlitteratur, Box 1717, S-221 01 Lund, Sweden.

Böhm, C., and Jacopini, G. [1966]. Flow diagrams, Turing machines and languages with only two formation rules. *Comm. ACM* **9:5**, 366-371.

Borning, A., and Ingalls, D. [1982]. Multiple inheritance in Smalltalk-80. *AAAI-82, The National Conference on Artificial Intelligence,* American Association for Artificial Intelligence, 234-237.

Brinch Hansen, P. [1975]. The programming language Concurrent Pascal. *IEEE Trans. Software Engineering* **SE-1:2**, 199-207.

Brinch Hansen, P. [1978]. Distributed processes: a concurrent programming concept. *Comm. ACM* **21:11**, 934-941.

Brinch Hansen, P. [1981]. The design of Edison. *Software—Practice and Experience* **11**, 363-396.

Brooks, F. P. Jr. [1975]. *The Mythical Man-Month.* Addison-Wesley, Reading, Mass.

Bruno, J., and Steiglitz, K. [1972]. The expression of algorithms by charts. *J. ACM* **19:3**, 517-525.

Burge, W. H. [1975]. *Recursive Programming Techniques.* Addison-Wesley, Reading, Mass.

Burks, A. W., Goldstine, H. H., and von Neumann, J. [1947]. Preliminary discussion of the logical design of an electronic computing instrument. In *John von Neumann: Collected Works,* Vol. V, Macmillan, New York, (1963), 34-79.

Burns, A. [1985]. *Concurrent Programming in Ada.* Cambridge Univ. Press.

Cardelli, L., and Wegner, P. [1985]. On understanding types, data abstraction, and polymorphism. *ACM Computing Surveys* **17:4**, 471-522.

Chomsky, N. [1956]. Three models for the description of language. *IRE Trans. on Information Theory* **IT-2:3**, 113-124.

Church, A. [1941]. *The Calculi of Lambda Conversion*. Annals of Math. Studies, No. 6, Princeton University Press, Princeton, N. J.

Clark, K. L. [1978]. Negation as failure. In H. Gallaire and J. Minker (Eds.), *Logic and Databases*. Plenum Press, New York, 293-322.

Clark, K. L., and Tärnlund, S. A. [1977]. A first order theory of data and programs. *Information Processing 77*. North-Holland, Amsterdam, 939-944.

Clarke, L. A., Wileden, J. C., and Wolf, L. [1980]. Nesting in Ada is for the birds. *ACM SIGPLAN Notices* **15:11** (November), 139-145.

Clément, D., Despeyroux, J., Despeyroux, T., Hascoet, L., and Kahn, G. [1985]. Natural semantics on the computer. Rapport de Recherche No. 416, INRIA, Sophia-Antipolis, France.

Clément, D., Despeyroux, J., Despeyroux, T., and Kahn, G. [1986]. A simple applicative language: Mini-ML. *1986 ACM Conference on Lisp and Functional Programming*, 13-27.

Clocksin, W. F., and Mellish, C. S. [1987]. *Programming in Prolog*, 3rd Ed. Springer-Verlag, New York.

Coffman, E. G. Jr., Elphick, M. J., and Shoshani, A. [1971]. System deadlocks. *ACM Computing Surveys* **3:2**, 67-78.

Cohen, J. [1988]. A view of the origins and development of Prolog. *Comm. ACM* **31:1**, 26-36.

Conway, M. E. [1963]. Design of a separable transition-diagram compiler. *Comm. ACM* **6:7**, 396-408.

Cook, S. A., and Reckhow, R. A. [1972]. Time-bounded random access machines. *Fourth ACM Symposium on Theory of Computing*, 73-80.

Cooper, D. C. [1967]. Böhm and Jacopini's reduction of flow charts. *Comm. ACM* **10:8**, 463,473.

Courtois, P. J., Heymans, F., and Parnas, D. L. [1971]. Concurrent control with readers and writers. *Comm. ACM* **14:10**, 667-668.

Curry, H. B., and Feys, R. [1958]. *Combinatory Logic*, Vol. 1. North-Holland, Amsterdam.

Dahl, O. J., Dijkstra, E. W., and Hoare, C. A. R. [1972]. *Structured Programming*. Academic Press, London.

Dahl, O. J., and Hoare, C. A. R. [1972]. Hierarchical program structures. In Dahl, Dijkstra, and Hoare [1972], 175-220.

Damas, L., and Milner, R. [1982]. Principal type-schemes for functional programs. *Ninth ACM Symposium on Principles of Programming Languages*, 207-212.

Darlington, J., Henderson, P., and Turner, D. A. (Eds.). [1982]. *Functional Programming and its Applications: An Advanced Course.* Cambridge Univ. Press.

de Bruijn, N. G. [1972]. Lambda calculus notation with nameless dummies, a tool for automatic formula manipulation. *Indag. Math.* **34**, 381-392. See Appendix C of Barendregt [1984].

Deutsch, L. P. [1984]. Efficient implementation of the Smalltalk-80 system. *Eleventh ACM Symposium on Principles of Programming Languages*, 9-16.

Dijkstra, E. W. [1960]. Recursive programming. *Numerische Math.* **2**, 312-318. Reprinted in Rosen [1967], 221-228.

Dijkstra, E. W. [1968a]. Go to statement considered harmful. *Comm. ACM* **11:3**, 147-148.

Dijkstra, E. W. [1968b]. Co-operating sequential processes. In F. Genuys (Ed.), *Programming Languages: NATO Advanced Study Institute.* Academic Press, London, 43-112.

Dijkstra, E. W. [1971]. Hierarchical ordering of sequential processes. *Acta Informatica* **1**, 115-138.

Dijkstra, E. W. [1972]. Notes on structured programming. In Dahl, Dijkstra, and Hoare [1972], 1-82.

Dijkstra, E. W. [1975]. Guarded commands. *Comm. ACM* **18:8**, 453-457.

Dijkstra, E. W. [1976]. *A Discipline of Programming.* Prentice-Hall, Englewood Cliffs, N. J.

Eswaran, K. P., Gray, J. N., Lorie, R. A., and Traiger, I. L. [1976]. The notions of consistency and predicate locks in a database system. *Comm. ACM* **19:11**, 624-633.

Filman, R. E., and Friedman, D. P. [1984]. *Coordinated Computing.* McGraw-Hill, New York.

Fleck, A. C. [1976]. The impossibility of content exchange through the by-name parameter transmission technique. *ACM SIGPLAN Notices* **11:11** (November), 38-41.

Floyd, R. W. [1967]. Assigning meanings to programs. In J. T. Schwartz (Ed.), *Mathematical Aspects of Computer Science*. Symposium on Applied Math. **19**, American Math. Society, Providence, Rhode Island, 19-32.

Francez, N. [1986]. *Fairness*. Springer-Verlag, New York.

Friedman, D. P., and Wise, D. S. [1976]. Cons should not evaluate its arguments. In S. Michaelson and R. Milner (Eds.), *Automata, Languages and Programming*. Edinburgh Univ. Press, 257-284.

Gannon, J. D., and Horning, J. J. [1975]. Language design for programming reliability. *IEEE Trans. Software Engineering* **SE-1:2**, 179-191.

Gehani, N. H. [1984]. *Ada: Concurrent Programming*. Prentice-Hall, Englewood Cliffs, N. J.

Geschke, C. M., Morris, J. H. Jr., and Satterthwaite, E. H. [1977]. Early experience with Mesa. *Comm. ACM* **20:8**, 540-553.

Girard, J. Y. [1972]. *Interpretation fonctionelle et elimination des coupres de l'arithmetique d'ordre superieur*. These D'Etat, Universite Paris VII.

Goguen, J. A., Thatcher, J. W., and Wagner, E. G. [1978]. An initial algebra approach to the specification, correctness, and implementation of abstract data types. In R. T. Yeh (Ed.), *Current Trends in Programming Methodology: Vol. IV Data Structuring*. Prentice-Hall, Englewood Cliffs, N. J., 80-149.

Goldberg, A., and Robson, D. [1983]. *Smalltalk-80: The Language and its Implementation*. Addison-Wesley, Reading, Mass.

Goldstine, H. H. [1972]. *The Computer: from Pascal to von Neumann*. Princeton Univ. Press, Princeton, N. J.

Gordon, M. J. C. [1979]. *The Denotational Description of Programming Languages*. Springer-Verlag, New York.

Gordon, M., Milner, R., Morris, L., Newey, M., and Wadsworth, C. [1978]. A metalanguage for interactive proof in LCF. *Fifth ACM Symposium on Principles of Programming Languages*, 119-130.

Gries, D. [1981]. *The Science of Programming*. Springer-Verlag, New York.

Hamming, R. W. [1969]. One man's view of computer science. *J. ACM* **16:1**, 3-12.

Hanson, D. R. [1981]. Is block structure necessary? *Software—Practice and Experience* **11**, 853-866.

Hanson, D. R. [1987]. Literate programming: printing common words. *Comm. ACM* **30:7**, 594-599. Moderated by C. J. Van Wyk and reviewed by J. R. Gilbert.

Harper, R., MacQueen, D. B., and Milner, R. [1986]. Standard ML. ECS-LFCS-86-2, Laboratory for Foundations of Computer Science, Univ. of Edinburgh.

Harper, R., Milner, R., and Tofte, M. [1988]. The definition of Standard ML, Version 2. ECS-LFCS-88-62, Laboratory for Foundations of Computer Science, Univ. of Edinburgh.

Henderson, P., and Morris, J. H. Jr. [1976]. A lazy evaluator. *Third ACM Symposium on Principles of Programming Languages*, 95-103.

Hindley, J. R. [1969]. The principal type-scheme of an object in combinatory logic. *Trans. AMS* **146**, 29-60.

Hindley, J. R., and Seldin, J. P. (Eds.). [1980]. *To H. B. Curry: Essays on Combinatory Logic, Lambda Calculus and Formalism.* Academic Press. New York.

Hindley, J. R., and Seldin, J. P. [1986]. *Introduction to Combinators and λ-Calculus.* Cambridge Univ. Press, New York.

Hoare, C. A. R. [1962]. Quicksort. *Computer J.* **5:1**, 10-15.

Hoare, C. A. R. [1969]. An axiomatic basis for computer programming. *Comm. ACM* **12:10**, 576-580,583.

Hoare, C. A. R. [1972]. Notes on data structuring. In Dahl, Dijkstra, and Hoare [1972], 83-174.

Hoare, C. A. R. [1972]. Proof of correctness of data representations. *Acta Informatica* **1**, 271-281.

Hoare, C. A. R. [1973]. Hints on programming language design. CS-73-403, Computer Science Dept., Stanford Univ. Reprinted in Horowitz [1987], 31-40, and in Wasserman [1980], 43-52.

Hoare, C. A. R. [1974]. Monitors: an operating system structuring concept. *Comm. ACM* **17:10**, 549-557.

Hoare, C. A. R. [1978]. Communicating sequential processes. *Comm. ACM* **21:8**, 666-677.

Hoare, C. A. R. [1981]. The emperor's old clothes. *Comm. ACM* **24:2**, 75-83.

Hoare, C. A. R. [1985]. *Communicating Sequential Processes.* Prentice-Hall International, Englewood Cliffs, N.J.

Hogger, C. J. [1984]. *Introduction to Logic Programming.* Academic Press, Orlando, Fl.

Holt, R. C., Graham, G. S., Lazowska, E. D., and Scott, M. A. [1978]. *Structured Concurrent Programming with Operating Systems Applications.* Addison-Wesley, Reading, Mass.

Horn, A. [1951]. On sentences which are true of direct unions of algebras. *J. Symbolic Logic* **16**, 14-21. Referenced in Kowalski [1979a].

Horowitz, E. (Ed.). [1987]. *Programming Languages: A Grand Tour.* Computer Science Press. Rockville, Maryland.

Ichbiah, J. D., Barnes, J. G. P., Heliard, J. C., Krieg-Brueckner, B., Roubine, O., and Wichmann, B. A. [1979]. Rationale for the design of the Ada programming language. *ACM SIGPLAN Notices* **14:6B** (June).

Ingalls, D. H. H. [1978]. The Smalltalk-76 programming system: design and implementation. *Fifth ACM Symposium on Principles of Programming Languages,* 9-16.

Ingerman, P. Z. [1967]. Panini-Backus form suggested. *Comm. ACM* **10:3**, 137.

Irons, E. T. [1961]. A syntax directed compiler for Algol 60. *Comm. ACM* **4:1**, 51-55.

Jackson, M. [1975]. *Principles of Program Design.* Academic Press, New York.

Jensen, K., and Wirth, N. [1974]. *Pascal User Manual and Report.* Springer-Verlag, New York. 3rd Ed. (1985) prepared by A. B. Mickel and J. F. Miner.

Johnson, S. C. [1975]. Yacc—yet another compiler compiler. Computing Science Technical Report No. 32, AT&T Bell Laboratories, Murray Hill, N. J.

Johnson, S. C., and Ritchie, D. M. [1978]. Portability of C programs and the UNIX system. *Bell System Technical J.* **57:6.2**, 2021-2048.

Johnson, S. C., and Ritchie, D. M. [1981]. The C language calling sequence. Computing Science Technical Report No. 102, AT&T Bell Laboratories, Murray Hill, N. J.

Kahn, G. [1987]. Natural semantics. Rapport de Recherche No. 601, INRIA, Sophia-Antipolis, France.

Kahn, G., and MacQueen, D. B. [1977]. Coroutines and networks of parallel processes. *Information Processing 77.* North-Holland, Amsterdam, 993-998.

Kahn, G., MacQueen, D. B., and Plotkin, G. (Eds.). [1984]. *Semantics of Data Types*. Lecture Notes in Computer Science **173**, Springer-Verlag. Berlin.

Kernighan, B. W. [1982]. PIC – a language for typesetting graphics. *Software—Practice and Experience* **12:1**, 1-21.

Kernighan, B. W., and Plauger, P. J. [1976]. *Software Tools*. Addison-Wesley, Reading, Mass.

Kernighan, B. W., and Plauger, P. J. [1978]. *The Elements of Programming Style*, 2nd Ed. McGraw-Hill, New York.

Kernighan, B. W., and Plauger, P. J. [1981]. *Software Tools in Pascal*. Addison-Wesley, Reading, Mass.

Kernighan, B. W., and Ritchie, D. M. [1988]. *The C Programming Language*, 2nd Ed. Prentice-Hall, Englewood Cliffs, N. J.

Kessels, J. L. W., and Martin, A. J. [1979]. Two implementations of the conditional critical region using a split binary semaphore. *Information Processing Letters* **8:2**, 67-71.

King, K. N. [1988]. *Modula-2: A Complete Guide*. D. C. Heath, Lexington, Mass.

Knuth, D. E. [1971]. An empirical study of Fortran programs. *Software—Practice and Experience* **1**, 105-133.

Knuth, D. E. [1974]. Structured programming with go to statements. *ACM Computing Surveys* **6:4**, 261-301.

Knuth, D. E. [1986]. *Computers and Typesetting*, Vol. 1: TEX. Addison-Wesley, Reading, Mass.

Knuth, D. E., and Trabb Pardo, L. [1977]. Early development of programming languages. *Encyclopedia of Computer Science and Technology* **7**, 419-493.

Koenig, A. [1988]. An example of dynamic binding in C++. *J. Object-Oriented Programming* **1:3** (August/September), 60-62.

Kosaraju, S. R. [1974]. Analysis of structured programs. *J. Computer and System Sciences* **9**, 232-255.

Kowalski, R. A. [1979a]. *Logic for Problem Solving*. Elsevier North Holland, New York.

Kowalski, R. A. [1979b]. Algorithm = Logic + Control. *Comm. ACM* **22:7**, 424-436.

Kowalski, R. A. [1988]. The early years of logic programming. *Comm. ACM* **31:1**, 38-43.

Landin, P. J. [1964]. The mechanical evaluation of expressions. *Computer J.* **6:4**, 308-320.

Landin, P. J. [1965]. A correspondence between Algol 60 and Church's lambda-notation. *Comm. ACM* **8:2,3**, 89-101,158-165.

Landin, P. J. [1966]. The next 700 programming languages. *Comm. ACM* **9:3**, 157-166.

Liskov, B., and Guttag, J. [1986]. *Abstraction and Specification in Program Development*. MIT Press, Cambridge, Mass.

Liskov, B., and Zilles, S. [1974]. Programming with abstract data types. *ACM SIGPLAN Notices* **9:4** (April), 50-59.

McCarthy, J. [1960]. Recursive functions of symbolic expressions and their computation by machine, Part I. *Comm. ACM* **3:4**, 184-195.

McCarthy, J. [1963]. Towards a mathematical science of computation. *Information Processing 1962*. North-Holland, Amsterdam, 21-28.

McCarthy, J. [1981]. History of Lisp. In Wexelblat [1981], 173-185.

McCarthy, J., Abrahams, P. W., Edwards, D. J., Hart, T. P., and Levin, M. I. [1965]. *Lisp 1.5 Programmer's Manual*, 2nd Ed. MIT Press, Cambridge, Mass.

McIlroy, M. D. [1968]. Coroutines. manuscript, AT&T Bell Laboratories, Murray Hill, N. J.

Metropolis, N., Howlett, J., and Rota, G. C. (Eds.). [1980]. *A History of Computing in the Twentieth Century*. Academic Press. New York.

Miller, G. A. [1967]. *The Psychology of Communication*. Basic Books, New York.

Milner, R. [1978]. A theory of type polymorphism in programming. *J. Computer and System Sciences* **17:3**, 348-375.

Milner, R. [1980]. *A Calculus of Communicating Systems*. Lecture Notes in Computer Science **92**, Springer-Verlag, New York.

Minker, J., and Minker, R. G. [1980]. Optimization of boolean expressions – historical developments. *Annals of the History of Computing* **2:3**, 227-238.

Mitchell, J. C., and Harper, R. [1988]. The essence of ML. *Fifteenth ACM Symposium on Principles of Programming Languages*, 28-46.

Mock, O., and Swift, C. J. [1959]. The Share 709 system: programmed input-output buffering. *J. ACM* **6**, 145-151.

Moon, D. [1986]. Object-oriented programming with Flavors. *ACM SIG-PLAN Notices* **21:11** (November), 1-16.

Morris, J. H. Jr., Schmidt, E., and Wadler, P. [1980]. Experience with an applicative string processing language. *Seventh ACM Symposium on Principles of Programming Languages*, 32-46.

Morrison, P., and Morrison, E. (Eds.). [1961]. *Charles Babbage and his Calculating Engines*. Dover. New York.

Naur, P. [1963a]. Revised report on the algorithmic language Algol 60. *Comm. ACM* **6:1**, 1-17.

Naur, P. [1963b]. Go to statements and good Algol style. *BIT* **3:3**, 204-208.

Naur, P. [1981]. The European side of the last phase of the development of Algol 60. In Wexelblat [1981], 92-172.

Nygaard, K., and Dahl, O. J. [1981]. The development of the Simula languages. In Wexelblat [1981], 439-493.

Papadimitriou, C. [1986]. *The Theory of Database Concurrency Control.* Computer Science Press, Rockville, Maryland.

Parnas, D. L. [1972]. On the criteria to be used in decomposing systems into modules. *Comm. ACM* **15:12**, 1053-1058.

Plotkin, G. D. [1981]. A structural approach to operational semantics. DAIMI FN-19, Computer Science Dept., Aarhus Univ., Aarhus, Denmark.

Randell, B., and Russell, L. J. [1964]. *Algol 60 Implementation.* Academic Press, New York.

Rees, J., and Clinger, W. [1986]. Revised[3] report on the algorithmic language Scheme. *ACM SIGPLAN Notices* **21:12** (December), 37-79.

Reynolds, J. C. [1972]. Definitional interpreters for higher-order programming languages. *25th ACM Annual Conference*, 717-740.

Reynolds, J. C. [1974]. Towards a theory of type structure. *Colloque sur la Programmation.* Lecture Notes in Computer Science **19**, Springer-Verlag, New York, 408-425.

Richards, M. [1969]. BCPL: a tool for compiler writing and systems programming. *AFIPS Conference Proceedings*, 34, 557-566.

Ritchie, D. M. [1978]. UNIX time-sharing system: a retrospective. *Bell System Technical J.* **57:6.2**, 1947-1969.

Ritchie, D. M. [1984]. The evolution of the UNIX time-sharing system. *AT&T Bell Laboratories Technical J.* **63:8.2**, 1577-1593.

Robinson, J. A. [1965]. A machine-oriented logic based on the resolution principle. *J. ACM* **12:1**, 23-41.

Rosen, S. [1967]. *Programming Systems and Languages.* McGraw-Hill, New York.

Rosen, S. [1969]. Electronic computers: a historical survey. *ACM Computing Surveys* **1:1**, 7-36.

Rosin, R. [1969]. Supervisory and monitor systems. *ACM Computing Surveys* **1:1**, 37-54.

Ross, D. T., and Rodriguez, J. E. [1963]. Theoretical foundations for the computer-aided design system. *AFIPS Spring Joint Computer Conference*, 305-322.

Rosser, J. B. [1984]. Highlights of the history of the lambda-calculus. *Annals of the History of Computing* **6:4**, 337-349.

Schmidt, D. A. [1986]. *Denotational Semantics: A Methodology for Language Development.* Allyn and Bacon, Boston, Mass.

Schönfinkel, M. [1924]. Uber die Bausteine der mathematischen Logik. *Mathematische Annalen* **92**, 305-316. English translation, "On the building blocks of mathematical logic," in van Heijenoort [1967], 355-366.

Scott, D. S. [1977]. Logic and programming languages. *Comm. ACM* **20:9**, 634-640.

Scott, D. S., and Strachey, C. [1971]. Towards a mathematical semantics for computer languages. *Symposium on Computers and Automata.* Polytechnic Press, Brooklyn, N. Y., 19-46.

Sedgewick, R. [1978]. Implementing Quicksort programs. *Comm. ACM* **21**, 847-857.

Sethi, R. [1981]. Uniform syntax for type expressions and declarators. *Software—Practice and Experience* **11:6**, 623-628.

Shepherdson, J. C., and Sturgis, H. E. [1963]. Computability of recursive functions. *J. ACM* **10:2**, 217-255.

Shriver, B., and Wegner, P. [1987]. *Research Directions in Object-Oriented Programming.* MIT Press, Cambridge, Mass. Preliminary versions of several of the papers in this collection appear in *ACM SIGPLAN Notices*, **21:10** (October 1986).

Snyder, A. [1986]. Encapsulation and inheritance in object-oriented languages. *ACM SIGPLAN Notices* **21:11** (November), 38-45.

Steele, G. L. Jr. [1984]. *Common LISP*. Digital Press, Burlington, Mass.

Steele, G. L. Jr., and Sussman, G. J. [1975]. Scheme: an interpreter for the extended lambda calculus. Memo 349, MIT Artificial Intelligence Lab., Cambridge, Mass.

Sterling, L., and Shapiro, E. [1986]. *The Art of Prolog*. MIT Press, Cambridge, Mass.

Stoy, J. E. [1977]. *Denotational Semantics*. MIT Press, Cambridge, Mass.

Strachey, C. (Ed.). [1966]. *CPL working papers*. Univ. Mathematical Laboratory, Cambridge and Univ. of London Institute for Computer Science.

Stroustrup, B. [1986]. *The C++ Programming Language*. Addison-Wesley, Reading, Mass.

Stroustrup, B. [1987a]. Multiple inheritance in C++. *European UNIX system User Group Conference*, EUUG Secretariat, Owles Hall, Buntingford, Herts, SG9 9PL, United Kingdom, 189-208.

Stroustrup, B. [1987b]. The evolution of C++: 1985 to 1987. *USENIX Association C++ Workshop*, P. O. Box 2299, Berkeley, Calif., 1-22.

van Heijenoort, J. (Ed.). [1967]. *From Frege to Gödel*. Harvard University Press. Cambridge, Mass.

van Wijngaarden, A., Mailloux, B. J., Peck, J. E. L., Koster, C. H. A., Sintzoff, M., Lindsey, C. H., Meertens, L. G. L. T., and Fisker, R. G. [1975]. Revised report on the algorithmic language Algol 68. *Acta Informatica* **5**, 1-236.

Vuillemin, J. [1974]. Correct and optimal implementations of recursion in a simple programming language. *J. Computer and System Sciences* **9:3**, 332-354.

Wadsworth, C. [1971]. *Semantics and Pragmatics of the Lambda Calculus*. Ph. D. Thesis, Oxford Univ.

Warren, D. H. D. [1980]. Logic programming and compiler writing. *Software—Practice and Experience* **10:2**, 97-125.

Wasserman, A. I. (Ed.). [1980]. *Tutorial: Programming Language Design*. IEEE Computer Society Press.

Wegner, P. [1976]. Programming languages—the first 25 years. *IEEE Trans. Computers* **C-25:12**, 1207-1225.

Wegner, P., and Smolka, S. A. [1983]. Processes, tasks, and monitors: a comparative study of concurrent programming primitives. *IEEE Trans. Software Engineering* **SE-9:4**, 446-462.

Weizenbaum, J. [1966]. Eliza—a computer program for the study of natural language communication between man and machine. *Comm. ACM* **9:1**, 36-45.

Weizenbaum, J. [1976]. *Computer Power and Human Reasoning.* W. H. Freeman, San Francisco, Calif.

Welsh, J., and Lister, A. [1981]. A comparative study of task communication in Ada. *Software—Practice and Experience* **11**, 257-290.

Wexelblat, R. L. (Ed.). [1981]. *History of Programming Languages.* Academic Press. New York.

Wilkes, M. V., Wheeler, D. J., and Gill, S. [1951]. *Preparation of Programs for an Electronic Digital Computer.* Addison-Wesley, Reading, Mass. Reprinted by Tomash Publishers, Los Angeles, 1982.

Wirth, N. [1971]. The programming language Pascal. *Acta Informatica* **1:1**, 35-63.

Wirth, N. [1976]. *Algorithms + Data Structures = Programs.* Prentice-Hall, Englewood Cliffs, N. J.

Wirth, N. [1979]. The module: a system structuring facility in high-level programming languages. *Language Design and Programming Methodology.* Lecture Notes in Computer Science **79**, Springer-Verlag, New York, 1-24.

Wirth, N. [1983]. *Programming in Modula-2,* 2nd, corrected Ed. Springer-Verlag, New York. 3rd, corrected Ed. (1985).

Wirth, N. [1988]. From Modula to Oberon. *Software—Practice and Experience* **18:7**, 661-670.

Wirth, N., and Hoare, C. A. R. [1966]. A contribution to the development of Algol. *Comm. ACM* **9:6**, 413-431.

Wulf, W. A., and Shaw, M. [1973]. Global variables considered harmful. *ACM SIGPLAN Notices* **8:2** (February), 80-86.

Zuse, K. [1980]. Some remarks on the history of computing in Germany. In Metropolis, Howlett, and Rota [1980], 611-627.

Index